MILDLY HANDICAPPED CHILDREN AND ADULTS

MILDLY HANDICAPPED CHILDREN AND ADULTS

TOM E.C. SMITH
University of Arkansas

BARRIE JO PRICE
University of Arkansas

GEORGE E. MARSH, II
University of Arkansas

WEST PUBLISHING COMPANY
St. Paul • New York • Los Angeles • San Francisco

Cover Art: *Copyright © 1983 by Lance Hidy, Newburyport, MA*
Composition: *Boyer and Brass*
Copyediting: *Mary Hough*
Interior Art: *Boyer and Brass*
Interior Design: *The Quarasan Group, Inc.*
Photography: *Arleen Casto Lewis*

COPYRIGHT © 1986 By WEST PUBLISHING COMPANY
50 West Kellogg Boulevard
P.O. Box 64526
St. Paul, MN 55164-1003

All rights reserved
Printed in the United States of America

Library of Congress Cataloging-in-Publication Date

Smith, Tom E. C.
   Mildly handicapped children and adults.

   Includes index.
    1. Handicapped—United States. 2. Handicapped
children—Education—United States. 3. Handicapped—
Functional assessment. 4. Handicapped—Educations—
United States.   I. Price, Barrie Jo, 1947–
II. Marsh, George E.   III. Title
HV1553.S6   1986   305.9′08   85-20331
ISBN 0-314-85301-4

TO OUR PARENTS:
  PETE AND MATTIE FERN SMITH
  BART AND ALMA PRICE
  GEORGE AND ABBIE MARSH

CONTENTS

Preface xv

Chapter One
INTRODUCTION xviii

HISTORICAL PERIODS OF TREATMENT AND SERVICES 3
    Pre-Twentieth Century 4
    Twentieth Century 4
    Traditional Systems of Service Delivery 8
HIGHLIGHT: *Plight of Disabled Children Told* 10
    Litigation 12
    Legislation and the Handicapped 16
HIGHLIGHT: *How L.D.'s Are Handled in New York's Schools* 18
GENERIC/NONCATEGORICAL SPECIAL EDUCATION AND THE MILDLY
    HANDICAPPED 23
HIGHLIGHT: *'Mainstreaming' Still a Problem in Special Education* 24
SUMMARY 26

Chapter Two
THE MILDLY HANDICAPPED: A CONCEPTUAL FRAMEWORK 30

INTRODUCTION 32
SOCIOLOGICAL ASPECTS UNDERLYING LABELS 32
LABELING AND SPECIAL EDUCATION 33
    Advantages and Disadvantages of Labeling 34
TRADITIONAL CATEGORICAL GROUPINGS IN SPECIAL EDUCATION 36
    Mental Retardation 36

      Learning Disabilities   37
      Emotional Disturbance/Behavioral Disorders   39
      Hearing Impaired   41
      Visually Impaired   42
      Physical and Health Impairments   43
      Speech and Language Disorders   43
TRENDS IN CATEGORIES FOR THE HANDICAPPED   44
THE MILDLY HANDICAPPED   45
      Reasons for the Mild Category   45
      Definition of the Mildly Handicapped   50
      Prevalence of the Mildly Handicapped   51
      Obstacles to the Mildly Handicapped Category   51
SUMMARY   52

Chapter Three
ETIOLOGY OF THE MILDLY HANDICAPPED   56
INTRODUCTION   58
ORGANIZATION OF ETIOLOGICAL SYSTEMS   58
TRADITIONAL CLASSIFICATION SYSTEMS FOR THE ETIOLOGY OF SPECIFIC
   CATEGORIES OF HANDICAPPED CHILDREN   59
      Etiology of Mental Retardation   60
      Etiology of Learning Disabilities   63
      Etiology of Emotional Disturbance   64
HIGHLIGHT: *Brain Studies Shed Light on Disorders*   **65**
ETIOLOGICAL SYSTEM FOR THE MILDLY HANDICAPPED   68
      Organic and Biological Factors and Mild Disabilities   68
HIGHLIGHT: *Study Released on Baby Brain Disorders*   **71**
      Environmental Factors and Mild Disabilities   74
SUMMARY   83

Chapter Four
ASSESSMENT OF THE MILDLY HANDICAPPED   86
INTRODUCTION   88
PURPOSES OF ASSESSMENT   89
      Screening   90
      Identification   90
      Determination and Evaluation of Teaching Programs and Strategies   90
      Determination of Current Performance Level and Educational Need   91
      Decisions about Classification and Program Placement   91
      Development of Individual Educational Programs   93
CRITICISMS OF TESTING   94
LEGAL CONSIDERATIONS IN ASSESSMENT   94
      Nondiscriminatory Assessment   97
THE ASSESSMENT PROCESS   98
REQUIREMENTS FOR ADEQUATE ASSESSMENT   99
      Qualified Personnel   99
      Proper Selection and Use of Assessment Tools   99
CONSIDERATIONS IN ASSESSMENT   101
      Group versus Individual Tests   101
      Norm-Referenced and Criterion-Referenced Tests   102

Test Environment   103
ASSESSMENT DOMAINS   103
PERSONNEL INVOLVED IN ASSESSMENT   104
INSTRUMENTS USED IN ASSESSMENT   106
   Intelligence Tests   107
   Achievement Tests   109
   Perceptual-Motor Tests   109
   Adaptive Behavior   110
   A Listing of Common Instruments   111
ROLE OF TEACHERS   111
SUMMARY   116

Chapter Five
EDUCATING MILDLY HANDICAPPED STUDENTS: THE IEP PROCESS   120

INTRODUCTION   122
UNDERSTANDING THE IEP PROCESS   123
   Child Find   124
   Referral   124
   Evaluation   132
HIGHLIGHT: *State Programs Are Many and Varied*   **134**
LEAST RESTRICTIVE SETTING   136
   Service Models   137
   Placement Selection   143
WRITING THE IEP   144
   IEP Form   144
   Required Conference   145
   Relationship of the IEP to Daily Instruction   145
EVALUATION AND MONITORING   145
DUE PROCESS AND PARENTAL INVOLVEMENT   148
MAINSTREAMING   150
   Shared Responsibility: A Philosophy   151
   Shared Responsibility: The Reality   152
SUMMARY   153

Chapter Six
PRESCHOOL MILDLY HANDICAPPED CHILDREN   156

INTRODUCTION   158
EARLY IDENTIFICATION   158
   Problems in Early Identification   159
HIGHLIGHT: *Spotting Problem and Setting a Course*   **162**
THE IDENTIFICATION PROCESS   165
   Child-Find   166
   Screening   166
   Diagnosis   168
   Assessment   168
PROFESSIONALS INVOLVED WITH IDENTIFICATION   169
   Medical Personnel   170
   Public School Personnel   172
   Other Professionals Involved with Identification   172

SERVICE DELIVERY: MODEL PROGRAMS   173
   Home-Based Models   174
   Home and Center-Based Model   175
   Center-Based Models   176
CURRICULAR APPROACHES   177
   Normal Development Model   177
   Behavioral Model   177
   Cognitive Developmental Model   178
BARRIERS TO PRESCHOOL SERVICES   178
   Legislation   178
   Funding   179
   Socioeconomic Structure   179
SUMMARY   179

Chapter Seven
ELEMENTARY-AGED MILDLY HANDICAPPED CHILDREN   182
INTRODUCTION   184
CHARACTERISTICS AND NEEDS   184
   Academic Characteristics and Needs   184
HIGHLIGHT: *Showcasing Talent Among Disabled*   *186*
   Social/Emotional Characteristics and Needs   188
THE ELEMENTARY SCHOOL   188
   Elementary School Administration   189
   Organizational Arrangements   190
   School Policies   190
   Curriculum   192
   The Regular Classroom   192
EDUCATING MILDLY HANDICAPPED CHILDREN IN REGULAR ELEMENTARY
   SCHOOLS   196
HIGHLIGHT: *Day Camps Proving Boon to Handicapped*   *197*
   Accommodative Strategies   199
   Teaching Strategies for Specific Subjects   199
SUMMARY   206

Chapter Eight
MILDLY HANDICAPPED ADOLESCENTS   210
INTRODUCTION   212
THEORIES OF ADOLESCENCE   212
   Developmental Theory   215
   Psychoanalytic Theory   216
   Evolutionary View   217
   Biological Explanation   217
THE ADOLESCENT SUBCULTURE   218
   Influences of the Peer Culture   219
   Peer Membership and the Handicapped   220
SPECIAL PROBLEMS OF ADOLESCENCE   223
   Drug Abuse   223
   Alcoholism   224
   Running Away   224
   Stealing   224

Pregnancy 225
Suicide 226
HIGHLIGHT: *Case Study of One Teen-Ager's Victory* **227**
EDUCATIONAL NEEDS OF HANDICAPPED ADOLESCENTS 229
  Service Models 231
CAREER DECISIONS 232
HIGHLIGHT: *Many Colleges Now Offer L.D. Programs* **233**
SUMMARY 235

Chapter Nine
MILDLY HANDICAPPED ADULTS 238
INTRODUCTION 240
NEEDS AND CHARACTERISTICS OF MILDLY HANDICAPPED ADULTS 241
  Social Adjustment 241
  Vocational Opportunity and Adjustment 242
  Community Acceptance 248
  Other Problems 250
SERVICES FOR MILDLY HANDICAPPED ADULTS 250
  Education 251
  Vocational 255
  Housing Services 257
HIGHLIGHT: *'Life Styles': A Place Where People Are Learning To Live* **260**
  Recreation and Leisure Time Opportunities 262
  Self-Help Groups 263
THE ELDERLY MILDLY HANDICAPPED 264
  Characteristics of the Aged Disabled 265
  Needs of the Elderly Disabled 266
SUMMARY 266

Chapter Ten
ATTITUDES AND THE MILDLY HANDICAPPED 274
INTRODUCTION 276
DEFINITION OF ATTITUDES 277
VARIABLES AFFECTING ATTITUDES 277
  Contact 277
HIGHLIGHT: *Church Sets Quota on Retarded* **278**
  Knowledge 278
  Other Variables 279
  Labeling and Behavior 279
ROLE OF ATTITUDES IN THE EDUCATION AND TREATMENT OF MILDLY
  HANDICAPPED PERSONS 280
HIGHLIGHT: *Court to Decide Rights of Retarded in Texas Case* **282**
ATTITUDES OF KEY PERSONS 284
  Attitudes of Physicians 285
  Attitudes of Teachers 285
  Attitudes of School Administrators 286
  Attitudes of Parents 288
  Attitudes of Peers 291
  Attitudes of Employers 291
  Mildly Handicapped Self-Attitudes 292

CHANGING ATTITUDES 293
    Assessment of Attitudes 294
    Techniques to Change Attitudes 295
SUMMARY 299

Chapter Eleven
THE FAMILY AND THE MILDLY HANDICAPPED STUDENT 304

INTRODUCTION 306
ORGANIZATIONAL PATTERNS OF FAMILIES 307
    Nuclear Family 308
    Extended Family 308
    Blended Family 309
    Common Law Family 309
    Single-Parent Family 310
    Commune Family 310
    Serial Family 310
    Composite Family 310
    Cohabitation 311
    Formation of Family: Its Life Cycle 311
PURPOSES OF THE FAMILY 313
    The Possible Effects of a Handicapped Child on Family Purposes 314
FAMILY REACTIONS 318
    Typical Reactions 318
SIBLINGS 319
RELATIONSHIP BETWEEN FAMILIES AND SCHOOL PERSONNEL 321
    Collaboration between Parents and School 321
    Primary Procedural Safeguards 323
    Role of School Personnel 323
SUMMARY 325

Chapter Twelve
CAREER AND VOCATIONAL EDUCATION 328

INTRODUCTION 330
CAREER EDUCATION 330
    Objectives of Career Education 332
    Components of a Career Education Program 332
    Need for Career Education in Special Education 334
    Objectives of Career Education for Handicapped Students 334
    Developing Career Education Programs 336
    Career Education for Elementary Handicapped Students 336
    Career Education in Secondary Schools 338
    Role of Special Education Teacher 340
VOCATIONAL EDUCATION 340
    Developing Vocational Education Programs 342
    Goals and Objectives for Programs 343
    Problems in Delivering Vocational Education to the Handicapped 343
    Vocational Evaluation 345
    Service Delivery 346
    Role of Personnel in Vocational Education 349
SUMMARY 352

Chapter Thirteen
THE FUTURE   356
INTRODUCTION   358
CURRENT AND FUTURE TRENDS   360
   Reduced Federal Role   360
   Parent Advocacy   361
   Special Education and Professional Standards   361
   Technology and Special Education   363
HIGHLIGHT: *Blind Boy Learning to 'See' with Help of Sonic Glasses*   365
HIGHLIGHT: *Alternative to Amniocentisis?*   368
   Deinstitutionalization   368
   The Reform Movement   369
CONCLUSIONS   372
SUMMARY   373

GLOSSARY   375

RESOURCES   381

PREFACE

The objective of this textbook is to provide students preparing to be teachers with a general overview of mildly handicapped children and adults. The text is designed to be appropriate for special education majors and students majoring in elementary or secondary education. For special education majors, the book is intended for use in an introductory course, either an introduction to special education, or as a follow-up to a survey course. The book will clarify many issues concerning mildly handicapped children and adults that will not be included in many survey textbooks. We have also designed the book so it will be an excellent introduction to special education for regular education majors who will undoubtedly have many mildly handicapped students in their classrooms.

The book provides information related to the generic category of mildly handicapped children and adults. As a result of many states serving children in noncategorical settings, teachers must teach many children with varying categorical labels, primarily mildly mentally retarded, learning disabled, and behaviorally disordered, but also possibly children with physical disabilities. The book does not venture into the area of the severely handicapped since most special education teachers and regular classroom teachers will not serve this population.

Although the text presents information related to the mildly handicapped, many of the citations are from studies conducted on categorical populations. It was necessary to include this information because there has been very little research completed using the generic category, mildly handicapped, as subjects. Therefore, citations documenting studies related to categorical groups of children and adults have been interpreted to apply to the mildly handicapped category since a great deal of research has shown the overlap of characteristics, needs, and etiologies of these groups.

The text is organized into five sections. Section one, overview of the mildly handicapped, includes content on the purpose of special education, as well as legislation and litigation that focus on special education. Discussions are also included as to why some categories of handicapped children are collapsed into a generic, mildly handicapped category. Justifications for a generic approach are provided, as well as a definition of the mildly handicapped. Section two, etiology, assessment, and services, describes the causes of mildly handicapping conditions, how to identify mildly handicapped individuals, and how services are provided to this population.

Section three of the text focuses on specific populations of the mildly handicapped category. Chapters include preschool children, elementary aged children, adolescents, and adults. The adult chapter is included for two reasons: first, few textbooks in special education provide information on the adult disabled population, and secondly if teachers understand the needs of the mildly handicapped adult, they will better understand the programs needed by these individuals during their school years.

Section four, special concerns, deals with attitudes, the family, and vocational and career education. These topics are included because of their importance in the education and training of mildly handicapped persons. For example, we feel that attitudes play a vital role in the services provided these individuals. The chapter on attitudes will better enable students to understand this role and be able to deal with their own attitudes, as well as the attitudes of others.

The final section of the text predicts the future of services for the mildly handicapped population. In a very rapidly changing world, mildly handicapped persons are subjected to changes that have a major impact on their lives. For example, technology is exploding in our country. As technological advances are made, services for the mildly handicapped population will definitely change.

We have presented information that future teachers, both regular classroom teachers and special education teachers, should know in order to provide appropriate educational and other services to the mildly handicapped. An understanding of the population of handicapped children served in public school programs will enable teachers to be better prepared to carry out their roles as team members, and will enable them to be more aware of the needs of this special population.

In addition to the 13 chapters, we have included highlights focusing on current articles in newspapers and magazines to describe current information being written about mildly handicapped persons; a glossary of terms; and a list of organizations and agencies where students may write for additional information.

ACKNOWLEDGMENTS

We would like to gratefully acknowledge the contribution of the following individuals who greatly contributed to the development of this textbook: Ms. Marilyn Smith, whose expertise at the typewriter saved many errors; Drs. Max and Arleen Lewis, whose critiques and encouragement kept us on track; and all our spouses, families, and friends who supported our many hours. We would also like to thank individuals who formally reviewed the manuscript and offered a great deal of advice along the way.

Dave Naylor, *University of Central Arkansas*
Pat Coonley, *Central Missouri State University*
Don Shane, *Central State University*
Howard Drucker, *Cal Poly Tech, San Luiso*
Larry Wheeler, *SW Texas State*

Dave Hill, *Ohio State University*
Joan Sagotsky-Rich, *University of Minnesota*
Colleen Mandell, *Bowling Green*
Daniel Reschley, *Iowa State University*

And finally, we would like to acknowledge the staff of West Publishing Company, especially Clark Baxter, who had faith from beginning to end.

Tom E.C. Smith
Barrie Jo Price
George E. Marsh, II

Chapter One

INTRODUCTION

CHAPTER OUTLINE

HISTORICAL PERIODS OF TREATMENT AND SERVICES
    Pre–Twentieth Century
    Twentieth Century
    Traditional Systems of Service Delivery
    Litigation
    Legislation and the Handicapped
GENERIC/NONCATEGORICAL SPECIAL EDUCATION AND THE MILDLY
    HANDICAPPED
SUMMARY

CHAPTER OBJECTIVES

After reading this chapter, you should be able to:
- Trace and discuss the historical treatment of handicapped children and adults;
- Describe the role of the federal government with handicapped children and adults;
- Discuss landmark court cases that have shaped special education and other services for mildly handicapped children and adults;
- Discuss traditional service delivery models for mildly handicapped children.

Handicapped children and adults are currently receiving more positive attention than ever before. As a result of legislation, litigation, advocacy, and professional involvement, members of the disabled population are finally receiving some of the basic rights and services that have been guaranteed to the nondisabled community for many years. The focus is less on the disabilities, and more on the abilities of handicapped people. During the past several years, their educational, social, and personal integration has increased significantly. Although problems still exist for handicapped children and adults, major progress has been made (Turnbull and Barber 1984). One area of progress has been the reconceptualization of the categories of disabilities.

Consideration of a group of individuals who are called **mildly handicapped** represents a significant step in the history of special education. It primarily refers to a group that is most noticeably different from others during the school years in ability to learn efficiently, and during adulthood in ability to experience social and vocational success. Reasons for the increasing popularity of the noncategorical movement include a disenchantment with labeling and the revelation that categorical groups of children do not dictate similar instructional techniques (Hallahan and Kauffman 1978).

While considering such a group is viewed by many as a step forward, it is also considered a controversial move by others (Epstein and Cullinan 1983). *Categorical* versus noncategorical approaches to serving disabled persons is the issue. Should children with mild disabilities such as educable mental retardation, learning disabilities, and behavior disorders be lumped into a larger group called the mildly handicapped? Or do children in these traditional categories present such unique characteristics and needs that they must be served in categorical groups? Another question is who should be included in a group called the mildly handicapped? Does this new classification only include children from the larger categorical groups, or should children with visual and auditory problems, physical disorders, and other low incidence conditions be included? Many issues are involved in classifying children and adults as mildly handicapped.

Throughout history the handicapped have been treated in accordance with the prevailing philosophies, religious doctrines, values, customs, and beliefs of the time. Physical and mental characteristics of people are defined in each society as acceptable or unacceptable, competent or incompetent, and desirable or undesirable. The mental abilities and physical appearance or physical limitations of individuals dictate how they will be treated and what opportunities are open to them. For each individual in every age it is necessary to struggle for survival or acceptance by adapting to one's environment. As Kolstoe notes, "Those persons who do not seem able to achieve a reasonable level of adequacy in their adaptive behavior are given some special consideration" (Kolstoe 1976, 3). Inadequacy will never be ignored and will be dealt with by the society in some manner depending upon the complex cultural imperatives of values, religious doctrines, economic factors, and political philosophies.

The perceptions and treatment of handicapped individuals must always be interpreted within the context of a particular culture at any point in time. In the United States, the changes of the last two decades have prompted consideration of a new classification of persons who might be regarded as mildly handicapped or disabled. Much of special education has been based on the past failures of the schools, as noted by high drop-out rates and declining standardized test scores (Ysseldyke and Algozzine 1982). The demands for literacy, compulsory school attendance laws, and the civil rights movement have also created a demand for a new classification of the handicapped. Without these forces, such a distinction would have had little meaning and limited support. It would have been inconceivable in past centuries to designate a group of individuals as "mildly handicapped."

The unique political philosophy of the United States and its political system has been important in altering the fundamental practices of education in our society by permitting special programming for students who have difficulty learning in the classroom. Gains that have been made on behalf of these children in recent years are but the latest events in a long history of educational practices.

HISTORICAL PERIODS OF TREATMENT AND SERVICES

The history of the mildly handicapped is so new that its antecedents must be found in the more "severe" categories of handicapping conditions that have long been recognized in virtually all societies. A number of writers have referred to the history of handicapped people in terms of societal attitudes toward them. This is usually viewed as a continuum ranging from an era of harsh treatment to one of compassion and caring. Although this history may be accurate, harsh treatment, negative attitudes, and prejudice can exist in any society at any time, as they do today and certainly will in the future. For example, Hewett (1974), in a thorough coverage of the history of special education, indicates that treatment of the handicapped has a cyclical pattern. In every age there have been advances and retreats determined by such forces as a need for survival, superstition, advances of science, and societal patterns of service. Whereas the handicapped might be accorded a degree of respect and appropriate treatment in one period, later they might be ridiculed and feared, depending upon the unique circumstances of political, economic, and religious factors. As today, when the needs of special education are weighed against other needs in competition for scarce tax dollars, gains of the past few years can be swept away if the needs of gifted children, the elderly, or national defense are elevated in importance. Therefore, while significant gains have recently been made regarding the education and treatment of the handicapped, these advances could fade away rather quickly under certain circumstances.

Special education has a relatively short history. It was not until recent times that education for all children was considered to be important and necessary for all segments of society. Less than a century ago compulsory school attendance laws became widespread. Prior to the Common School movement in the nineteenth century, education was important for only a small segment of American society—the white, male children of upper class families. Other children—middle class, poor, female, or culturally diverse—were excluded from school, their roles being defined differently by the culture. Inadequacy in learning ability was therefore a problem for only a minority of the population. It was not until economic conditions and technological advances created a need for universal education that virtually all children were expected to attend school. Until then it was impossible to conceive of a group of mildly handicapped pupils, and because of the historical course education took, it was not until very recently that special education services became a major subject of concern for such children.

Special education is a relatively new concept. As Gearheart (1980) notes, blindness, deafness, mental retardation, and mental illness have been recognized for centuries, but serious educational programming for these children has a short history. Education for persons with exceptional ability was an early concern of Alexander the Great, who prompted a talent search throughout his kingdom to find young boys with keen

4 Mildly Handicapped Children and Adults

Table 1-1   Eras of Treatment of the Handicapped

Era	Description
Extermination	During this era, which occurred during the Greek city states of Sparta and Athens, persons with physical or mental deviations were killed. Individuals who could not contribute to their basic survival were simply eliminated. There are other examples of cultures where peculiar birth marks and other less obvious deviations were sufficient to assure a death sentence.
Ridicule	This is a period when the handicapped were tolerated, but were used for amusement and entertainment. There are documented instances of handicapped persons and insane people being displayed in "zoos" for public entertainment, serving as court jesters, and being ridiculed in other ways.
Asylum	The era of asylum marked a time when elements of society attempted to provide the basic necessities of life to disabled people. This was the beginning of institutions. Organizations, primarily churches, provided shelter and food to disabled persons in monasteries, charity houses, poor houses, and asylums. Although far from adequate services, these attempts demonstrated a change in attitude in some individuals.
Education	This period began with the attempts of Itard, a French physician, to educate Victor the wild boy found in the forests of France. Victor had no, or limited, previous contact with human beings. Although disappointed in the outcomes with Victor, Itard did show that some learning could take place in individuals devoid of learning experiences. Following Itard, Sequin worked with mentally retarded persons, while others developed materials and programs for other types of disabled individuals.

Source: Kolstoe, Teaching educable mentally retarded children *(2nd ed.).* New York: Holt, Rinehart and Winston, 1976.

minds and potential abilities to strengthen his nation's commerce, arts, and military strength. Otherwise, the record of education for persons who deviated markedly from others in physical or mental characteristics is short, and has its roots in segregation and persecution.

Pre-Twentieth Century

Kolstoe (1976) has discussed four major eras in the treatment and education of the handicapped. These periods were primarily characterized by the prevalent conditions of existence for the handicapped and the nature of attitudes that affected them. Except for the last era, they characterize the history of the handicapped prior to the twentieth century. Table 1-1 describes these eras of treatment.

Twentieth Century

The identification of mildly handicapping conditions grew out of the theories of several individuals who suggested differences in children. For example, Francis Galton (1822–1911) maintained that genius is an inheritable trait. This led others to realize that basic differences exist among children's abilities. The work of Alfred Binet (1857–1911) in France to measure intelligence, and the subsequent work of Lewis Terman (1877–1956) in America to use intelligence tests to identify gifted children, are significant. Lilly (1979) indicates that their work marked the beginning of the modern concept of mildly handicapped.

Prior to 1815 schools were primarily church related. As noted previously, the sons of only wealthy families attended school—a relatively small proportion of school-aged children. Even after schools were supported by local taxation, beginning in the first half of the nineteenth century, there was little concern about disabled children. In fact, many nondisabled children did not attend school, and children with mental or physical disabilities either did not attend or elected to drop out because they were unable to meet the demands of the curriculum. The curriculum was not altered in any way for them. If individuals were not capable of being successful, they were expected to drop out. Thus, most children in local communities had an opportunity to attend school, but there was no concern about adapting the curriculum and instructional techniques to suit a particular child. Nor was there concern about children who deviated significantly from the norm; they simply did not attend. It was not until the beginning of compulsory school attendance in the late nineteenth century and early twentieth century that some children were recognized as having problems. Although these problems were recognized at this time, major attempts to ameliorate them were still not implemented.

The curriculum of the school, designed to meet the needs of the elite society, was unsuitable for the children of immigrants and the poor. It became obvious that these children would not be able to achieve the same levels of educational success as other children. Intelligence tests were used to explain why many of these children failed. According to Lilly (1979), a new handicap was defined. These children, who had not been identified as handicapped prior to compulsory attendance laws and did not deviate markedly in society outside of school, were now singled out and identified by intelligence testing as different. Lilly maintains that this was a most "significant happening" in special education because it represented the first definition of mildly handicapping conditions—these children were said to be mildly retarded. The conditions for failure were recognized in the child and family rather than in the interaction between the child and the school environment. In other words, the school was not considered to have failed the child; the child came to the school different enough to experience difficulties and therefore be labeled atypical.

Although recognized as needing assistance, mildly handicapped children received limited services and often dropped out of school. Some were even denied admission to school because many states had laws excluding children from school unless they had "educable minds." Dunn (1973) indicated that for well over a century after some compulsory attendance laws were passed, school authorities looked for solutions to the problems presented by these children. Some "solutions" included: (1) the residential school movement, (2) public school exclusion and exemption laws, (3) the day school movement in special education, (4) sorting and tracking of pupils in the public schools, and (5) special services for deviant pupils without segregation.

As a result of these barriers to school admission, many parents of handicapped children created private day schools for children who were excluded from public schools but whose disabilities were not severe enough for residential placement. In some cases the general dissatisfaction of parents with a lack of access to public schools prompted some schools to operate publicly supported special classes. However, it was not until the formation of the National Association for Retarded Children, now known as the **National Association for Retarded Citizens** (NARC), that lobbying activities and litigation had a substantial impact on schools and legislatures. Much of the landmark litigation in special education, and the passage of *P.L. 94-142*, stem from the efforts of parents and parents' organizations.

In addition to the mentally retarded, other handicapped groups began to gain the attention of educators. Another mild condition that started receiving attention during the 1950s began with Strauss and his associates (Strauss and Lehtinen 1947), who dichotomized mental retardation into classifications that had different causes and required different teaching methods. Endogenous mental retardation has come to be equated with inherited mental retardation, while the exogenous mental retardation results from brain damage and trauma to the central nervous system. Although the early work of Strauss and Lehtinen was with moderately-severely mentally retarded individuals, their dichotomizing led to the recognition of another disability.

The writings of many authors who had previously been associated with the exogenous line of research, such as Kephart (1960), Cruickshank (1961), and Kirk (1963), ultimately led to the acceptance of a condition that is generally known today as learning disabilities. As was mild retardation, deficiencies associated with learning disabilities were of little concern prior to compulsory school attendance laws. Interest in reading disorders, in difficulty with language usage, and in other literate activities was confined to adults who had lost such abilities as a result of brain damage. But gradually it became apparent that certain children with adequate intelligence were unable to meet standards of achievement expected in the school. These children could not be regarded as mentally retarded, yet they were experiencing major academic difficulties.

The concepts of Strauss and his associates have been dramatically expanded and debated. Children with poor academic records, especially in reading, have been characterized as having minimal cerebral dysfunctions or dyslexia, or as having perceptual, perceptual-motor, and language impairments that interfered with their ability to achieve normally. There have been intensive debates about the importance of heredity, brain damage, and experience in the learning disabilities literature. But today this group of children exists in the schools as a recognized category of mildly handicapped students differentiated from the mildly retarded by their slightly higher intelligence quotient, as measured by a standardized IQ test. Although still a controversial category, learning disabilities has been accepted as a major category of mildly handicapped children found in the school.

Finally, children whose primary problems in school are regarded as emotional or behavioral have been identified as a new category of mildly handicapped children. Children with serious emotional problems such as schizophrenia and autism were institutionalized in much the same way as the mentally retarded during the 1800s and early 1900s. However, organized special education for students with emotional problems is primarily a recent development. Reasons for the recent expansion of services for this group of children include:

1. Growing interest in studying psychological development of children
2. Efforts to promote children's welfare
3. Development of the special education profession
4. Litigation and legislation
5. Development of psychological models for understanding and treatment (Cullinan, Epstein, and Lloyd 1983)

Emotionally disturbed children have not been served as extensively as other categories in special education because of the negative connotations of emotional disturbance. Children identified as having emotional problems were often served in self-contained programs or institutions. They were also likely to be labeled learning disabled because it is more acceptable than being labeled **emotionally disturbed** (Chandler and Jones 1983). Like the category of mental retardation, which was expanded to include a mild form, psychiatrically oriented classification systems of

Normalization assures equal opportunities for handicapped adults.

emotional disturbance gave way to behaviorally oriented systems in the 1970s. Today schools are much more likely to have classes for children with behavioral disorders because of the tendency to focus on classroom behaviors in diagnosis rather than on psychiatric interpretations of subjective test responses.

The philosophical foundations of serving handicapped children is **normalization.** This principle, which was begun in the Scandinavian countries (Nirje 1969), "simply implies that the handicapped ought to be able to live a life as equal as possible to a normal existence and with the same rights and obligations as other people" (Juul 1978, 326). Some obvious actions that have resulted from the normalization philosophy include (Juul 1978):

- Number of residents housed in residential facilties for the handicapped has been reduced
- The architecture for residential facilities for the handicapped has been restructured
- Education of the handicapped has been significantly altered, currently requiring education in the least restrictive environment
- Vocational training for the handicapped has become widespread
- Leisure time needs have been taken into consideration
- Attitudes concerning the interactions between sexes have changed

In the United States, two significant concepts that have resulted from normalization have been mainstreaming and deinstitutionalization.

Principles of normalization in this country were implemented with the assistance of litigation, legislation, and advocacy lobbying. As a result of these activities, handicapped children and adults are to be assured equal opportunity, equal access, and assimilation within the society at large. While these changes have their roots in the normalization movement begun in the Scandinavian countries, they are unique within the cultural contexts of the United States. Models may have been borrowed from other cultures, but the forces that have urged mainstreaming and deinstitutionalization have emerged independently on the North American continent.

One result of normalization has been mainstreaming. Many of the mild conditions, as described above, and the traditionally severe categories such as blindness, deafness, crippling conditions, and chronic health disorders, have been merged in the regular classroom. The lines that distinguish between these categorical handicapped groups have become fuzzy and difficult to defend. A new trend is coming to the forefront—noncategorical services and generic programming. The next sections will show the relationship between events of the last two decades and the generic trend that leads us to a period of significant change in the precepts and practices of special education. This will conclude the historical development of the field now recognized as the mildly handicapped.

Traditional Systems of Service Delivery

The historical record shows that compulsory attendance laws, the testing movement, the school's difficulty in dealing with learning and behavioral differences of children, and parental demands for equal access to public education on behalf of their children have combined to shape the trends of special education. In the recent past, the activities of parents, professionals, and advocates have had the greatest impact.

After parents organized in the middle 1950s, some schools yielded to demands that handicapped children be educated with public funds. The methods of providing services, which at first were satisfying to parents, eventually became unacceptable. This can be attributed in part to the administrative models used in education.

Categorical grouping. The delivery of special education services has been determined, until very recently, exclusively along **categorical** lines—that is, by category of handicapping condition. Mentally retarded children, learning disabled children, behaviorally disordered/emotionally disturbed children, and so forth, have been grouped by label for special education. The training of teachers, certification standards for teachers in the states, and funding patterns to support special education have been based on these categories. Many professionals are concerned that when categorical labels are applied they damage children by, among other things, lowering their self-esteem and changing the expectations teachers and peers have of them.

Self-contained Classes. For most of the history of special education, children were classified by category and segregated from nonhandicapped peers in **self-contained classrooms.** They would remain in the same room with the special education teacher for the entire instructional day. This has become a major point of contention in the field of special education. Johnson (1983) noted that self-contained services were attacked as a result of a combination of the civil rights movement and high national productivity and affluence. At any rate, the efficacy of such placement as well as the discriminatory nature of such programming for any class of student, no matter how defined, have been seriously questioned.

Special Schools. Another model used extensively in the past was to use public funds to operate a segregated facility for all the handicapped children in a school district. In essence, this is not different from the self-contained classroom except that it is much more blatant as a form of segregation. While special schools for handicapped children still exist, the number of children served in such settings has been greatly reduced.

Institutional Settings. Institutionalization was an early method of intervention for a significant number of handicapped individuals. A number of children were placed in private and public institutions that were unsatisfactory to a large number of parents. Currently, there are a number of private schools for the learning disabled and many private institutions for mentally retarded children. These private facilities, however, are available only to parents with substantial financial means. As a general rule, except for those parents with the most severely handicapped children or those with high incomes who have access to private residential programs, many parents have found institutions to be unsatisfactory. A current major trend is toward **deinstitutionalization.** This movement has resulted from inadequate treatment accorded some children and adults in institutions, and the emergence of civil rights principles in special education. The trend has obviously been popular to many legislators because it is less expensive to provide services in the community. Humanitarian and professional reasons may not always be a factor.

Efficacy Studies. In the late 1960s and early 1970s, professional criticism of categorical, segregated placement of mentally retarded children became strong and widespread. This criticism was based on emotionalism, a sense of equality, and some research. In the professional literature, the research became known as **efficacy studies,** comparisons of the performance of educable mentally retarded children in self-contained classrooms and regular classrooms (Yoshida 1984). The most famous and perhaps influential attack on traditional, segregated special education services came from Dunn (1968), who criticized the practice of special education for mentally retarded children and who called for a reexamination of the procedures employed in schools to educate handicapped children. Later, Dunn (1973) outlined a series of negative conclusions about the effectiveness of traditional special education classes:

1. As a group, mildly retarded pupils make as much or more progress in regular classes as their counterparts in special classes
2. Mentally retarded children do not work up to their mental age capacity whether they are in regular classrooms or special classes
3. Special class children do not achieve academically above randomly selected regular-class-placed mentally retarded children
4. Mentally retarded students with higher IQs develop a dislike for special class placement and have increased feelings of self-derogation about such placement
5. Low IQ children who make the best progress in the regular grades are those who come from ethnic minorities and who are adjusted and accepted in their communities

Dunn also noted some positive aspects of self-contained programs such as: lower IQ students tend to gain more in special class placement; mentally retarded children in special classes appear to be superior to regular class counterparts in terms of the ability to brainstorm and to engage in free thinking; special classes are more effective in districts that have supervisory personnel to work with special teachers; and special

HIGHLIGHT

Plight of Disabled Children Told

By Bobbie Rodriguez, *Times Staff Writer*

Stephen Brees, 32, knows what he's talking about when he familiarizes disabled elementary school children with non-disabled ones in the Fountain Valley School District.

It's his job. And Brees, who received his master's degree in psychology last summer from Cal State Fullerton, also has firsthand experience. He has cerebral palsy.

When he was 3, Brees was sent to a special education school. At 16, Brees entered a "regular" high school, where he was able to interact with non-disabled students. Although he will always require an assistant to help with the most basic needs, Brees hopes he will eventually be able to assume financial responsibility for himself.

"I am convinced that whatever social benefit I may be to my community is largely possible because of the relationships I have had and still have in educational and vocational settings," he said Friday.

Brees was one of several witnesses at the Hilton Towers hotel in Anaheim testifying before the Select Committee on Children, Youth and Families.

The committee was formed to examine the problems faced by families with disabled children. It will make recommendations to Congress later this year.

Committee members were told that financial support for disabled students should be redirected to families and communities and away from institutions.

Some parents of disabled children testified that they had to choose between caring for their children at home and trying to integrate them into the public school system or placing them in private care homes.

Beverly Bertaina, of Sebastopol, Calif., whose son Adam, 12, has cerebral palsy, profound retardation and seizures, said, "It took two years and a fair hearing to get Adam into an integrated program, but it is 15 miles and a one-hour bus ride away.

"Do we ruin ourselves financially or place our kids? It's a terrible quandary. It is an amazing paradox that institutional care for Adam would cost $35,000 to $65,000 per year but the federal and state government are willing to spend only $2,000 to $3,000 per year to help us keep Adam at home," Bertaina said.

According to the Disability Rights Education and Defense Fund, in-home care for a severely disabled child in 1984 cost $7,000 to $8,000 a year compared with $38,000 to $40,000 annually for institutionalizing that child.

Mary K. Short of Fountain Valley is the mother of a 5½-year-old severely handicapped daughter. While caring for her daughter at home, she has had to contend with non-support from her ex husband.

"I have been divorced since August 1981. (The father of her child) has been on probation for non-support since December, 1982, . . . He currently is $5,050 in arrears in the child support payments."

Short said her daughter is temporarily in a private care home until she can earn enough money to hire live-in help.

"For those of us who for whatever reason, do have our children placed (in a home), the system is beautifully efficient. The systems for in-home and out-of-home handicapped children need to be equalized."

Los Angeles Times 20 April 1985, Part II.

As a result of professional disenchantment with segregated classrooms, teachers have developed alternatives for educating handicapped children.

classes seem to be best suited for certain types of mentally retarded children, like those from unstable homes.

On the whole, Dunn was of the opinion that the effectiveness of special, segregated, or self-contained classes could not be demonstrated. He therefore recommended that such classes be eliminated. Other voices that joined Dunn included Blatt (1960), Johnson (1962), Fisher (1967), Johnson (1969), Christopolos and Renz (1969), Jansen, Ahm, Jensen, and Leerskov (1970). Still other professionals stood firm and defended special class placement for many mentally retarded children. Kolstoe, one of the leading defenders of special class placement, has criticized some of the efficacy studies that have been used to attack special classes. Some of these criticisms Kolstoe objects to include:

1. Mental retardation, noticeable during the school-age years, disappears when the children attain adult status
2. Special class placement has a negative effect on the children's self-concepts
3. Teachers expect children to have low academic achievement and thereby contribute to it
4. Special class, segregated programs are not effective (Kolstoe 1976, 46–49)

Other professionals have also voiced concerns about the shift to mainstreaming. Johnson suggested that "social philosophy has replaced appropriate educational objectives based upon knowledge of a child's characteristics and the application of accepted psychological principles of learning and adjustment" (Johnson 1983, 101) and has resulted in labeling all programs as bad if handicapped children do not spend most of their time in classes with nonhandicapped children.

Although such criticisms of mainstreaming were presented by respected authorities, the tide had turned. The efficacy studies, regardless of their empirical validity, fit neatly into a trend that has swept over education during the 1970s; they provided a basis for questioning accepted placement practices (Yoshida 1984). Kolstoe noted this when he said:

> It is most disturbing that catch words like normalization and mainstreaming lend themselves to being used to exploit special education programs for purposes that have little to do with what has been demonstrated to be helpful to children. . . . Both normalization and mainstreaming have been used to assure nondiscriminating programs for minorities, despite clear evidence that these programs are not very successful. (Kolstoe 1976, 53)

Normalization and mainstreaming have spread effectively throughout the school systems and are undeniably civil rights trends. Whether or not the efficacy studies were good research is of little consequence now because they played an important part in the professional deliberations. These discussions helped to usher in the normalization movement and to alter conceptualizations of handicapping conditions now referred to as mild conditions. Professionals and lay persons believed that the purposes of segregated programming could not be defended or justified. It was also thought that children would benefit from placement in nonsegregated environments and that the elimination of categorical labels would prevent harm to self-esteem and life opportunities. Another important factor in the development of current special education practices has been litigation.

Litigation

The **litigation** involving special education has been extensive since the early 1970s. Prior to the seventies, litigation affecting general education laid the groundwork for the subsequent lawsuits affecting handicapped children and special education. The first major court case that had a later impact on special education and that changed the role of the courts in education was *Brown v. Board of Education* in 1954. This case made it unlawful to discriminate against minorities in education. Prior to that case, the United States Supreme Court had expressed little interest in becoming a "super school board" (Fisher 1979, 109). The *Brown* case, however, forever changed the role of the federal courts. This role of increased involvement appears to have grown during the 1970s.

Federal and state courts now handle cases dealing with the following (McCarthy & Cambron 1981):

- rights to free expression by students
- compulsory attendance
- mandatory curriculum offerings
- school finance
- employment practices
- student discipline
- malpractice by educators
- sex discrimination
- collective bargaining
- desegregation
- rights of the handicapped

The courts have thus become heavily involved in educational issues. Special education issues now comprise a large portion of the education issues dealt with by the legal system.

Status of Special Education Litigation. Beginning in the 1970s, special education litigation became widespread. In a study conducted by Marvell, Galfo, and Rockwell (1981), it was determined that 769 of the 1,632 cases analyzed related to civil rights issues of students in special education. These cases included issues such as placement outside public schools, placement inside schools, least restrictive setting, extended school year, transportation, due process procedures, and discipline.

Major Litigation in Special Education. As previously stated, the number of special education lawsuits has increased greatly since the 1970s. Among the many cases dealing with all kinds of special education issues, a few have been given "landmark" status. A description of some of these cases follows.

Pennsylvania Association for Retarded Citizens (PARC) v. Pennsylvania. This case, filed in 1971 by the parents of thirteen mentally retarded children, on behalf of all mentally retarded children in Pennsylvania, contended that mentally retarded children were being denied a public education because they were considered "uneducable." This premise that some mentally retarded children were incapable of benefiting from public education was totally destroyed by expert witnesses. The result was a decree issued by three judges that emphasized the majority of mentally retarded children are capable of benefiting from education and should not be denied public education (Laski 1974). The decree further required that Pennsylvania school officials seek out mentally retarded school age children and provide services to them (Turnbull and Turnbull 1978). This case has been designated by many professionals as the "right to education" case.

Mills v. Board of Education, Washington, D.C. Another case dealing with the right to education occurred in Washington, D.C. in 1972. As with the PARC case, parents filed suit because handicapped children were being denied access to public education. Children represented by the plaintiffs included not only mentally retarded children, but also those classified as physically, emotionally, and socially handicapped (Meyen 1982). The decision in this case, in favor of the plaintiffs, underlined the right of all children to an appropriate education and "put the final nails in the coffin of the concept of uneducability, making its ruling applicable regardless of degree or type of exceptionality and regardless of the fiscal impact on the school system" (Laski 1974, 17). Removing the defense of financial inability has had significant long-range effects on schools and services to handicapped children.

Mattie T. v. Holladay. This suit, filed in Mississippi in 1975, challenged several practices dealing with handicapped children. These included (Postlewaite 1977):

- denial of special education services
- segregation of handicapped children
- discriminatory assessment practices
- lack of procedural due process
- limited efforts at child find

The resulting consent decree issued in 1979 required the state of Mississippi to develop appropriate procedures and services for handicapped children in the state.

Larry P. v. Riles. This 1979 case differed from right-to-treatment cases in that it focused not on services but on assessment procedures used in California to identify children as handicapped. The central focus of the suit was on tests used to identify black children as mentally retarded. Other issues included the use of IQ tests in placement and the disproportionate number of black children classified and served as mentally retarded (Martin 1980). The ruling in this case significantly affected assessment practices used to identify children as handicapped. It also enjoined the defendents from using standardized IQ tests for identification and placement of black children in special education classes for the mentally retarded without prior court approval (Education for the Handicapped Law Report, 551:296).

In ruling for the plaintiffs, the court determined that the use of standardized intelligence tests violated Title VI of the Civil Rights Act of 1964, the Rehabilitation Act of 1973, P.L. 94-142, the Education for All Handicapped Children Act, and the constitutional guarantee of equal protection laws (Cremins 1981).

Armstrong v. Kline. Do handicapped children have a right to an education beyond the normal nine months provided for nonhandicapped children? That was the central issue in this case. The plaintiffs, parents of three severely handicapped children, requested that the court strike down the Pennsylvania policy that handicapped children could not be provided an educational program beyond the normal 180 days provided for nonhandicapped children. Plaintiffs wanted local districts to have the option of developing programs for handicapped children without consideration of the 180-day limitation (Stotland and Mancuso 1981).

The ruling, in favor of the plaintiffs, suggested that some handicapped children may require educational programs in excess of the regular 180-day school year. These children, as a result of P.L. 94-142, have a right to such a program (Education for the Handicapped Law Report, 551:260). While indicating that some handicapped children require extended year school programs, the court in this case and subsequent cases has made it clear that it must be shown that an extended year program is required for each child. The rulings have not made such a requirement for all handicapped children (Podemski, Price, Smith, and Marsh 1984).

Wyatt v. Stickney. Other court cases have focused on rights other than those afforded children in public school programs. One such case, *Wyatt v. Stickney*, is considered the right-to-treatment case. In this case, filed in 1972, the court was asked to determine the rights of institutionalized mental patients who were not receiving treatment but were simply being maintained. The case, which was subsequently expanded to include mentally retarded persons, was decided in favor of the plaintiffs. The court held that the state had no right to remove individuals from society without reasonable justification, a plan of treatment, and regular reevaluations. Institutions were required to develop individual treatment plans for residents.

Board of Education v. Rowley. Although a large amount of litigation related to P.L. 94-142 occurred after the PARC case, it was not until 1982 that the United States Supreme Court made its first interpretation of the Education for All Handicapped Children Act. The central issue in the *Board of Education v. Rowley* was whether or not a local school district was required to provide a sign language interpreter for a *hearing impaired* child who was making adequate academic progress. The parents contended that such a support service was required to enable the child to achieve her maximum level. Lower courts had ruled in favor of the child. The Supreme Court, however, in reversing the lower courts' decisions, "ruled that since the child was receiving substantial specialized instruction and related services at public expense, she was receiving an appropriate education under P.L. 94-142 and was not entitled to a sign language interpreter" (McCarthy 1983, 520). In writing the decision, Justice Rehnquist indicated that Congress had not intended P.L. 94-142 to impose a standard of quality for the education of handicapped children (Heaney 1984).

This ruling is considered a landmark decision because it is the first interpretation by the Supreme Court concerning the services required under P.L. 94-142. The decision was not received positively by many advocacy groups. While the decision in the *Rowley* case was viewed by some advocates as inappropriate, the major concern resulting from the decision is the precedence the case may set. Some professionals and advocates are concerned that the decision may lead to a general reduction in services to handicapped children, and that states and local education agencies may eliminate needed services as well as extraordinary ones (McCarthy 1983).

Many other cases could be discussed, and the body of case law related to handicapped children and adults is still growing. While it is not the intent of this chapter to present all cases dealing with special education, it should be remembered that litigation, as a function and result of parent activism, and professional attitudes created a formidable force for change. The ultimate impact was the passage of one of the most significant pieces of legislation in the history of American education, P.L. 94-142. Prior to the passage of this law, however, other important legislation was passed that related to the education and treatment of handicapped persons.

Handicapped children have a right to an appropriate education at public expense.

Table 1-2 Federal Legislation

Legislation	Date	Major Provisions
PL 19-8	1823	Provided a land grant to establish an asylum for the deaf in Kentucky
PL 45-186	1879	Granted $10,000 to American Printing House for the Blind to develop materials
PL 66-236	1920	Made civilians eligible for vocational rehabilitation benefits
PL 80-617	1948	Eliminated discrimination in hiring physically handicapped persons in the civil service system
PL 83-531	1954	Provided federal funds for research in the area of mental retardation
PL 85-926	1958	Provided funds to train college instructors who would train teachers for the mentally retarded
PL 88-164	1963	Expanded teacher training to include disabilities in addition to mental retardation; provided funding for research and demonstration projects
PL 89-10	1964	Provided significant money for educational programs for the disadvantaged. Handicapped children indirectly benefited
PL 89-313	1965	Provided funds to support children in hospitals and institutions
PL 89-750	1966	Created the Bureau of Education for the Handicapped; provided money for preschool programs; established an advisory committee
PL 90-480	1968	Eliminated barriers for the physically handicapped
PL 90-538	1968	Established experimental demonstration centers
PL 91-230	1969	Consolidated existing federal programs for handicapped children; recognized learning disabilities and required actions dealing with gifted children; made provisions for research, model programs, and teacher preparation
PL 92-424	1972	Mandated that 10 percent of Head Start programs serve handicapped children
PL 93-112	1973	The Vocational Rehabilitation Act Amendments of 1973. Included Section 504, basic civil rights legislation
PL 93-380	1973	Forerunner to PL 94-142; required actions by schools to remain eligible for federal funds

Source: Boston 1977; Gearheart 1980

Legislation and the Handicapped

Legislation at both the federal and state levels has had a major impact on the education and treatment of handicapped persons. Since state legislation differs from state to state, the information presented will focus on federal legislation. Although P.L. 94-142 has had the most significant impact, other federal legislation prior to it actually laid the groundwork for current services. The first federal legislation that affected the handicapped was passed in 1823. This act, P.L. 19-8, provided a federal grant for establishing an asylum for the deaf in Kentucky. Since this legislation, a great deal of additional legislation has been passed. See table 1-2.

P.L. 94-142, Education for All Handicapped Children Act. This law was passed in 1975 and became effective in 1978. The proponents of this legislation contend that it is the most significant education legislation ever passed by Congress; its opponents claim it is too costly, unrealistic, and requires too much paperwork (Podemski et al. 1984).

P.L. 94-142 has revolutionized educational services to handicapped children. A major intent of the legislation was to ensure that every school-aged handicapped child be provided a *free appropriate public education*. Securing the passage of such a massive piece of federal legislation was not an easy task. Some of the factors leading to its passage included:

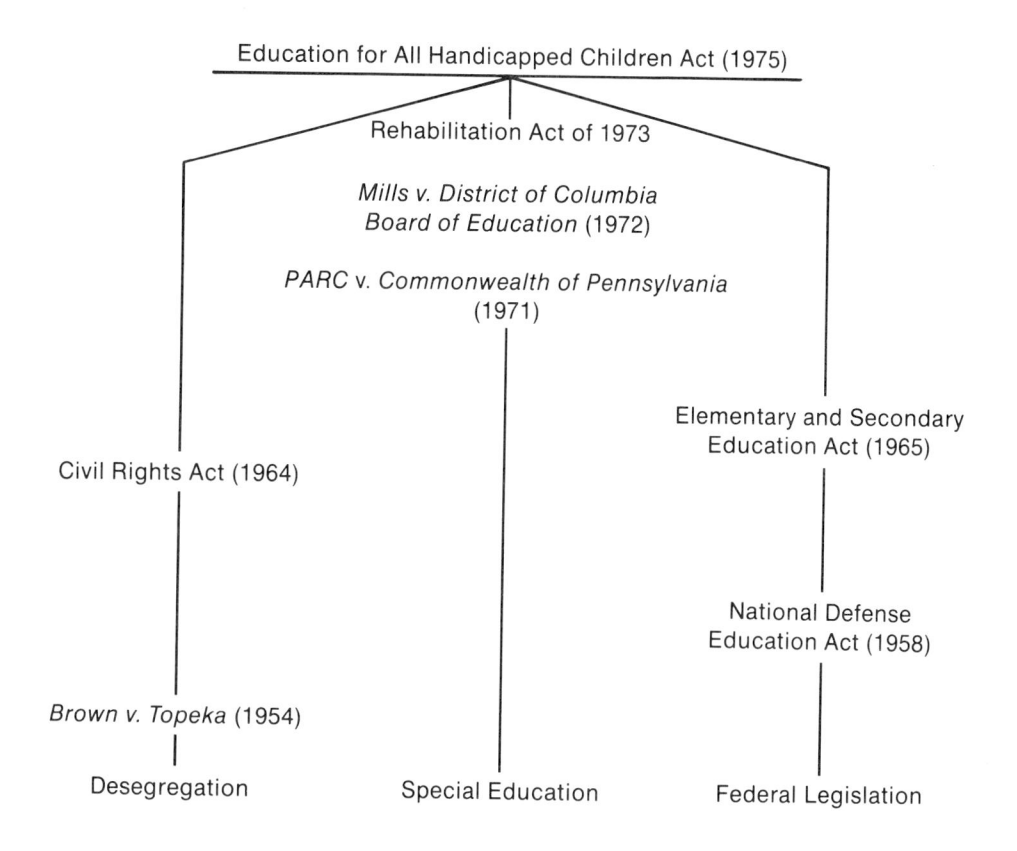

```
                    Education for All Handicapped Children Act (1975)
                    ────────────────────────┬────────────────────────
                                            │
                              Rehabilitation Act of 1973
                              ┌─────────────┴─────────────┐
                              │  Mills v. District of Columbia  │
                              │    Board of Education (1972)   │
                              │                                │
                              │  PARC v. Commonwealth of Pennsylvania │
                              │              (1971)            │
                              │                                │
                              │                    Elementary and Secondary
                              │                      Education Act (1965)
     Civil Rights Act (1964)  │                                │
                              │                                │
                              │                                │
                              │                         National Defense
                              │                        Education Act (1958)
     Brown v. Topeka (1954)   │                                │
              │               │                                │
         Desegregation     Special Education             Federal Legislation
```

Fig. 1-1. Paths leading to Public Law 94-142. Reprinted, by permission from L. L. Schwartz, *Exceptional Students in the Mainstream* (Belmont, Calif.: Wadsworth Publishing Co. 1984), 7.

- the civil rights movement
- activism by parents' groups
- activism by professional groups
- litigation dealing with special education and handicapped children
- federal and state legislation

Two basic tracts actually led to the passage of the act. One, focusing on civil rights, had its beginning with the *Brown v. Topeka* case in 1954. The other used federal legislation related to education. These two tracts merged with the early litigation in special education. Schwartz (1984) depicts this model in figure 1-1.

P.L. 94-142 has several major components. These include (1) *least restrictive environment,* (2) *individual educational program,* (3) *nondiscriminatory assessment,* (4) *due process* safeguards, and (5) *related services.*

Least Restrictive Environment. The word **mainstreaming** has created a great deal of controversy in public schools. The word, while not found in P.L. 94-142 or the regulations implementing this law, means "least restrictive environment." **Least restrictive environment** means that handicapped children should be educated with nonhandicapped children as much as possible. In order to accomplish this, schools

HIGHLIGHT

How L.D.'s Are Handled In New York's Schools

By Nicole Simmons

Children diagnosed as learning disabled in the New York City school system fall under the jurisdiction of the division of special education, which is also concerned with the mentally retarded, and the physically and emotionally handicapped. Almost every school in the city has a variety of classes designed for L.D. youngsters.

When classroom teachers notice that their students are having problems in learning, they refer them to the school district's Committee on the Handicapped. By testing and interviewing the children, the committee decides what the students' specific handicaps are and which classes they will attend.

Under state regulations still in effect in most city's schools, the committee places children in classes based only on the type and severity of their disabilities. The city is phasing in some revised rules, which require children to be grouped in classes not because they have the same disability but because they learn at the same rate and need to learn the same things. Under this system, a child who is mildly retarded might be taught in the same classroom as one who is dyslexic, if the two are considered to be at the same educational level. Schools in Queens and some in Brooklyn now place children according to the revised regulations, and the rest of the city's schools are required to do so within two years.

The basic types of classes, however, remain unchanged. A child with only mild reading problems, for instance, might go to a "resource room" for reading instruction one hour out of the day. Children who are two or three years behind their grade level are placed in a special-education class all day long, with one teacher to each 12 students. For severely hyperactive children, the school provides three adults for each ten students.

At Public School 156 in Springfield Gardens, Queens, Roz Goldsmith teaches the second type of class. All ten children in her classroom have some type of learning disability.

At the beginning of the school year, 9-year-old Bobby had trouble with writing. "When I tried to write," he said, "My hands hurt. I didn't like it. I used to cry." Bobby was so discouraged, said his teacher, that he didn't even try to learn. But now, Bobby gestures proudly to a poem pinned prominently to the classroom wall. "I try to work by myself," it says, in a shaky hand. "Test me. I like it. I will not cry."

For each student, the committee draws up an individual program, which sets learning goals for the year. To meet the disparate goals for the children in her class, Mrs. Goldsmith has divided the 10 into three reading groups, and some have "learning contracts" that assign them to do additional work independently.

When giving all the children the same assignment—a blackboardful of multiplication problems, for example—she allows each special tools that suit a stu-

(continued)

Education Fall Survey *New York Times*, 11 November 1984, sec. 12.

dent's needs. Bobby, for instance, at first received a carbon copy of another child's math problems, because the difficulty of copying them on his paper hindered his learning the math.

By paying attention to each child's problems individually, and telling children accustomed to failure that they can succeed in school, they will learn, Mrs. Goldsmith said. When they first come to her class, she added, "these kids are afraid to answer because they've been put down so often. I say to them trust your brain, trust your feelings."

Her coworkers say Mrs. Goldsmith, whose mere presence seems to calm a roomful of noisy children, has made her students think of schoolwork as more a privilege than a burden.

"I'm a workaholic," said Bobby, pointing to a cluster of writing assignments posted on the wall. "I got more stuff up there than anybody else."

"I work my head off in here," concurred 11-year-old Jim, the most advanced student in the class, and the only one whom Mrs. Goldsmith is trying to "mainstream," or put back in the regular classroom.

Jim was identified as learning-disabled at the end of first grade. For two years, he attended class in a "resource room," one period each day, but the class didn't seem to help him much; his math and reading skills were well below the norm. So last year, he was placed in Mrs. Goldsmith's class full time.

"Jim couldn't attend to tasks," Mrs. Goldsmith said. "He would hold his pencil and he would daydream." But when tutored privately, she said, he was able to read.

Many youngsters with learning disorders, Mrs. Goldsmith said, have problems organizing their time and remembering what to do next. Mrs. Goldsmith uses memory aids to help those children—index cards taped to their desks, for instance, that list all the assignments due that day. When asking a child to run an errand, she often has him repeat her instructions. "For many of these children," she said, "you have to break down tasks into the most simple terms."

By the beginning of this school year, she said, Jim's reading skills were two years above grade level, and he began to attend regular classes for part of the day. "I check his notebook to see what he's doing," Mrs. Goldsmith said, "and sometimes he needs another lesson."

Could Jim explain his sudden progress? "My brain just clicked into a different gear," he said.

---

should have available a **continuum of services** ranging from total regular classroom placement to institutionalization. Handicapped children are placed in the appropriate setting, with the intent of placing them in the least restrictive setting. Obviously, regular classroom placement is less restrictive than special education classrooms. Special education classrooms are less restrictive than institutions. The least restrictive setting must be determined on an individual basis, taking into consideration each child's individual strengths, weaknesses, and needs.

Least restrictive environment involves more than simply physically placing a child in a particular setting. The concept includes social integration as well as physical integration (Podemski et al. 1984). Simply securing a desk for a handicapped child in a regular classroom does not implement the intent of the least-restrictive-environment concept. In fact, placing children in certain settings without regard for their social integration might be more restrictive than placing them in a physically more restrictive setting.

Curriculum materials must respond to diversity in ability and experience.

Individual Education Program (IEP). One of the requirments of P.L. 94-142 that has had an impact on many instructional-level individuals is the **individual education program** (IEP). P.L. 94-142 requires that every handicapped child served in special education have an IEP. Furthermore, each IEP must contain:

- current level of functioning
- annual goals
- services to be provided
- dates for the services
- criteria for annual evaluation

IEPs must be for a single child, include only elements related to educational programming, and be an actual program to be followed (Weintraub 1977). If the IEP requirement of P.L. 94-142 is implemented as intended by Congress, it will actualize the individualization of instruction, something educators have proposed for many years.

One problem, however, is that schools can comply with the IEP requirement on paper, but never meet the intent of the legislation. For example, some schools have very similar IEPs for children classified in the same disability group. While many people may think all mildly handicapped or to be more specific, mildly mentally retarded children, have similar needs, each child must be treated individually. Every child is different, including those in the mildly handicapped category. IEPs for handicapped children must reflect these differences.

Several people should be involved in the development of IEPs. Regulations that implemented P.L. 94-142 require that the following be involved:

1. A representative of the public agency, other than the child's teacher, who is qualified to provide or supervise the provision of special education
2. The child's teacher
3. One or both of the child's parents
4. The child, where appropriate
5. Other individuals at the discretion of the parent or agency
6. Someone familiar with the evaluation of the child when the child has been evaluated for the first time (34 C.F.R. §300.344)

As a result of so many different individuals having to be involved in the development and implementation of IEPs, it is no wonder that this requirement has affected many professionals in education.

Nondiscriminatory Assessment. In order for children to be determined eligible for special education, a comprehensive evaluation must take place. Unfortunately, many of the instruments used in most evaluations can be discriminatory toward certain groups of children, namely those from minority cultural groups and low socioeconomic groups. The developers of P.L. 94-142 recognized this and as a result placed in the regulations provisions to prohibit discrimination during the assessment process. Requirements and suggestions for implementing nondiscriminatory assessment can be found in chapter 3.

Due Process Procedures. Still another very important part of P.L. 94-142 focuses on the due process rights of handicapped children and their parents. The right to due process is guaranteed by the Fifth and Fourteenth Amendments to the U.S. Constitution and is basically the right to protest (Turnbull and Turnbull 1978). Minimum due process guarantees required by P.L. 94-142 include:

- access to records
- right to an independent evaluation
- right to have surrogate parents in case the child's parents are unknown, unavailable, or the child is a ward of the state
- advance notification for change of placement or evaluation
- complaints and due process hearings

These are not intended to be exhaustive of the due process rights of parents and their children, only minimal safeguards. See table 1-3.

While parents have utilized all due process rights, the right to present their complaints in a formal, due process hearing has possibly been their major avenue to express dissatisfaction with school programs for handicapped children. A study by Smith (1981) reported that three years after the implementation of P.L. 94-142, hearings had been conducted in thirty-eight of the forty-two states responding to the survey. The conclusion drawn was that parents and school officials are using due process hearings to settle disputes.

Related Services. In addition to special education, P.L. 94-142 requires that handicapped children be provided **related services,** which include

> transportation and such developmental, corrective, and other supportive services as are required to assist a handicapped child to benefit from special education, and includes speech

Table 1-3 Due Process Requirements of Public Law 94-142

Requirement	Explanation	Reference
Opportunity to examine records	Parents have a right to inspect and review all educational records.	Sec. 121a.502
Independent evaluation	Parents have a right to obtain an independent evaluation of their child at their expense or the school's expense. The school pays only if it agrees to the evaluation or is required by a hearing officer.	Sec. 121a.503
Prior notice; parental consent	Schools must provide written notice to parents before the school initiates or changes the identification, evaluation, or placement of a child. Consent must be obtained before conducting the evaluation and before initial placement.	Sec. 121a.504
Contents of notice	Parental notice must provide a description of the proposed actions in the written native language of the home. If the communication is not written, oral notification must be given. The notice must be understandable to the parents.	Sec. 121a.505
Impartial due process hearing	A parent or school may initiate a due process hearing if there is a dispute over the identification, evaluation, or placement of the child.	Sec. 121a.506

Source: Final regulations, P.L. 94-142

pathology and audiology, psychological services, physical and occupational therapy, recreation, early identification and assessment of disabilities in children, counseling services, and medical services for diagnostic or evaluation purposes. The term also includes school health services, social work services in schools, and parent counseling and training. (20 U.S.C. §1401 (16))

While the need for certain related services should be obvious, the decision as to who receives which services and when has created conflicts. For example, the regulations state that the list of related services included are not meant to be exhaustive. This leaves schools and parents significant flexibility to determine what is a legitimate "related service." While such flexibility can be used to the advantage of all parties, it can also create conflicts when one party wants a service and the other states that such a service is not a requirement under the law. These conflicts frequently result in due process hearings.

P.L. 94-142 has placed many requirements on public schools. Other legislation, namely, Section 504 of the Rehabilitation Act of 1973, has similarly placed requirements on other segments of our society. While P.L. 94-142 is legislation for children, Section 504 affects all handicapped persons, regardless of age.

Section 504 of the Rehabilitation Act of 1973. This particular section of the Rehabilitation Act is a basic civil rights act for the handicapped. It states that "no otherwise qualified handicapped individual in the United States, . . . shall, solely by reason of handicap, be excluded from the participation in, be denied the benefits of, or be subjected to discrimination under any program or activity receiving Federal financial assistance." Areas specifically mentioned in the regulations implementing Section 504 include employment, education, and accessibility. As a result of this legislation, employers cannot refuse to hire someone simply because that person has a handicap.

Also, public buildings and educational programs must be physically accessible to handicapped persons.

GENERIC/NONCATEGORICAL SPECIAL EDUCATION AND THE MILDLY HANDICAPPED

Some writers have indicated that categorical special education has little practical usefulness (Smith and Neisworth 1975; Lilly 1979; Hallahan and Kauffman 1978; Marsh, Price, and Smith 1983). Specific criticisms of categorical services include:

1. The categories are educationally irrelevant
2. Categorical groupings overlap
3. Categories label children as "defective," implying that the cause of the educational or developmental deficiency lies only within the child
4. Special educational instructional materials and strategies are not category-specific
5. Preparation of teachers along traditional categorical lines results in redundancy of course work and barriers within the profession
6. Patterns of funding for special education have perpetuated the categorical approach (Smith & Neisworth 1975, 8–9)

There are many reasons to move toward the **noncategorical** or generic approach to serving handicapped children. The primary one appears to be that categorical descriptions of mildly handicapped children are meaningless in a system that is gravitating rapidly toward the inclusion of new services for handicapped persons. The "mild" conditions that emerged in the field during the past several years, namely, the mildly or educable mentally retarded, the learning disabled, and the mildly emotionally disturbed/behaviorally disordered, comprise the largest number of children who are regarded as handicapped. Hallahan and Kauffman (1978) note that these categories overlap in all dimensions—psychologically, educationally, and behaviorally. Lilly (1979) totally abandons the categories and refers simply to **exceptional children** as those who require special services of a substantive nature and degree in order to assure optimum learning and educational development.

All of this rationale will be opposed by most traditional special educators who continue to hold onto the strict categorical approach to special education. However valid some of the arguments presented by this group, the trend appears to be a clear movement toward the noncategorical approach. One major reason for this trend is the current emphasis on delivering services to handicapped children in public schools using the resource room model. Handicapped children are less likely to be segregated into groups with similar categorical labels; they are more likely to be served in small, heterogeneous groups in **resource rooms.** A majority of their school day may be spent in the regular classroom. In traditional, self-contained programs, the label determined everything. Currently, the labels may not relate to services. For example, resource rooms frequently serve children with many different categorical labels, primarily mild mental retardation, learning disabled, and emotionally disturbed/behaviorally disturbed. Other, lower incidence categories such as visually impaired, hearing impaired, and physically disabled may also be served by the resource teacher. Placement is dictated by need rather than label (Cremins 1981). In any event, the instruction of these children is shared by the special education staff and regular education staff. The concept of "shared responsibility" is a reality in the resource/mainstreaming model.

HIGHLIGHT

'Mainstreaming' Still a Problem in Special Education

By Susan G. Foster

Washington—Many of the tensions that have arisen for students, teachers, and parents as a result of "mainstreaming" and other changes brought about by the Education for All Handicapped Children Act of 1975 remain to be addressed, according to participants at a recent conference here on the subject.

Despite the widening acceptance by educators of the terms of the complex law, P.L. 94-142, the problems of students classified as handicapped—particularly the "learning disabled"—and of both the regular and special-education teachers who work with them are not yet clearly understood, said speakers at the annual meeting of the Association for Children and Adults with Learning Disabilities.

Children with learning disabilities account for most of the dramatic growth in the number of special-education students in regular classrooms that has occurred since the passage of P.L. 94-142, according to a recent Education Department report to the Congress. Of the more than four million school-age children receiving special-education services, over 35 percent have been identified as "learning disabled."

Unlike children with physical handicaps, children with learning disabilities usually show no obvious signs of their handicap and when mainstreamed are able to blend in with their peers in regular classrooms, speakers at the conference pointed out. This, they said, places strains on regular teachers who do not know how to adapt instruction to such students particular needs.

Research studies have found, for example, that some children with learning disabilities also have weaker social skills than other children and do not relate well to their peers, according to Gaye McNutt, professor of education at the University of Oklahoma. But regular teachers may not be aware of this phenomenon, she suggested.

"It's a frustrating problem [for many teachers] to look at a student who seems normal and can grasp a problem one day and then not understand it the next day," Ms. McNutt said.

"Regular-education teachers think that special-education children are 'fixed' when they return to the regular classroom," said Eileen Stan Spence, a special-education consultant. But, she added, that is not the case.

Ms. Spence said that because regular teachers are not trained to modify curricula for their learning-disabled students, they often resent being asked to accept them.

"It is the misperceptions that cause fear" among regular teachers, she said. Such misperceptions can be corrected if teachers become aware of the problems associated with teaching handicapped children.

The onus of dealing with these misperceptions and of building closer relationships with regular teachers usually falls

(continued)

Education Week 2 March 1983

on the special-education teachers, according to several speakers at the conference.

"It's always been the burden of the special-education teacher to do something nice, to stroke regular-education teachers in some way, so that they will see that the children are nice." Elinore Ehrlich, principal of P.S. 226 in Brooklyn, N.Y., told a group of parents and teachers.

In the past, according to Ms. McNutt, special-education teachers neglected to develop close working relationships with their counterparts in the regular classrooms.

"Mainstreaming was a new concept and perhaps special-education teachers thought they knew it all," she said. "It's taken us a while," she added, but education schools are now providing teacher candidates with "consultative" skills so that they can work with children as well as adults.

J. Lee Wiederholt, professor of special education at the University of Texas, agreed that strained relationships between special-education teachers and regular teachers are a problem in some districts. But that problem should be viewed in a larger context, he argued.

Society, he added, had demanded too much of teachers—first with the integration of minorities into the schools and the problems that has created and now with the mainstreaming of the handicapped.

"I don't think teachers are opposed to having handicapped students in their classrooms," Mr. Wiederholt said. "They are reacting negatively [because they think] they can't do all they are being asked to do."

Mr. Wiederholt said he believed that the teachers focused their anger on the handicapped students, when in fact they are angry about the overall lack of parental support of education in general. Ms. Ehrlich said that in her school, regular teachers and their classes are paired with special-education teachers and their students so that they will learn to work together.

She recommended that school administrators promote a positive climate so that teachers and students will agree that "everyone belongs in the school."

More teachers need exposure to handicapped students, according to Ms. Ehrlich. "We have to show that children are more alike than they are different," she added.

Ms. Spence agreed, noting that stereotypical images of handicapped students are promoted when special-education classrooms are located in the basement of a school building in "a former boiler room." Ms. Spence, reflecting on an earlier period in her career as a special-education teacher, told of special-education classes in Vermont that were conducted in an old ski lodge. "When it snowed they had to move to another room," she said.

Reynolds and Birch (1977) assert that the only important characteristics of children are those that relate to or interact with instruction. Obviously, many characteristics that are used to determine in which traditional category a child should be placed are not relevant to instruction. They are simply characteristics and traits that determine categorization based on a medical model, not an educational or instructional model.

In the final analysis, the similarities among handicapped children and adults are larger than the differences; instructional approaches do not differ significantly across categories; and methods of instruction that have been based on categories have not been very successful. Etiologies, psychological characteristics, and physical characteristics are not very helpful in the development and implementation of educational programs. The remainder of the text will approach several traditional categories of handicapped children as one general group of individuals. The group will be called "mildly handicapped." In order to facilitate the understanding of this group, the remainder of the text will focus on the mildly handicapped as a general category of handicapped individuals.

SUMMARY

In this chapter, we have traced the history of the treatment and services accorded to handicapped individuals. It was noted that such treatment was marked by various periods or eras. From ancient times, the treatment has gradually improved. In the earliest periods, treatment was characterized by persecution and abuse, which led to death and ridicule. Following such periods of negative treatment, institutionalization became predominant. Institutions enabled handicapped persons to receive the basic necessities of food and shelter.

Since the early 1950s, however, treatment of handicapped individuals has changed dramatically. These changes resulted from litigation, legislation, and advocacy pressure. Several landmark court cases, including *PARC v. Pennsylvania, Mills v. District of Columbia Board of Education, Wyatt v. Stickney, Larry P. v. Riles,* and *Kline v. Pennsylvania,* to name a few, have had a significant impact on the education and treatment of handicapped persons. Legislation has been the final major force that has shaped services to the handicapped. Beginning in the early 1800s, legislation favoring handicapped individuals culminated in the passage of P.L. 94-142 in 1975 and Section 504 of the Rehabilitation Act of 1973. These two legislative acts have mandated major changes in the education of handicapped children in schools, as well as the civil rights afforded to handicapped children and adults.

Finally, as a result of legislation, litigation, and parent power, services to handicapped children in public schools have changed. No longer are most handicapped children served in self-contained, segregated settings. The major service delivery approach currently used is the resource room. In this model, handicapped children receive a portion of their educational program in regular classrooms, and a portion in the special education resource room. Such a delivery model, coupled with research that has revealed the limited benefits gained from categorical groupings of handicapped children, has led the way to the noncategorical/generic approach to identifying and serving handicapped children.

REFERENCES

Blatt, B. Some persistently recurring assumptions concerning the mentally subnormal. *Training School Bulletin* 57 (1960):48–59.

Board of Education of the Hendrick Hudson Central School District, Westchester County v. Rowley ex rel. Rowley, 458 U.S. 176 (1982).

Boston, B. O. *Education policy and the Education for All Handicapped Children Act (PL 94-142).* Washington, D.C.: Institute for Educational Leadership, The George Washington University, 1977.

Chandler, H. N., and K. Jones. Learning disabled or emotionally disturbed: Does it make any difference? *Journal of Learning Disabilities* 16, no. 7 (1983): 432–34.

Christoplos, F., and P. Renz. A critical examination of special education programs. *Journal of Special Education* 3 (1969):371–79.

Cremins, J. J. Larry P. and the EMR child. *Education and Training of the Mentally Retarded* 16, no. 2 (1981):158–61.

Cruickshank, W. *A training method for brain injured and hyperactive children.* Syracuse: Syracuse University Press, 1961.

Cullinan, D., M. H. Epstein, J. W. Lloyd. *Behavior disorders of children and adolescents.* Englewood Cliffs, N.J.: Prentice-Hall, 1983.

Dunn, L. M. Special education for the mildly retarded: Is much of it justified? *Exceptional Children*, 35 (1968):5–22.

―――. *Exceptional children in the schools: Special education in transition.* New York: Holt, Rinehart, and Winston, 1973.

Epstein, M. H., and D. Cullinan. Academic performance of behaviorally disordered and learning-disabled pupils. *Journal of Special Education* 17, no. 3 (1983):303–307.

Fisher, H. K. What is special education? *Special Education in Canada* 41 (1967):9–16.

Fischer, L. Law and educational policy. *Educational Forum* 44, no. 1 (1979):109–114.

Gearheart, B. R. *Special education for the 80s.* St. Louis: C. V. Mosby, 1980.

Hallahan, D. B., and J. W. Kauffman. *Exceptional children.* Englewood Cliffs, N.J.: Prentice-Hall, 1978.

Hewett, F. M. *Teaching children with behavior disorders: Personal perspectives.* Edited by J. Kauffman and C. Lewis. Columbus, Ohio: Charles E. Merrill, 1974.

Jansen, M., J. Ahm, P. E. Jensen, and A. Leerskov. Is special education necessary? Can this program possibly be reduced? *Journal of Learning Disabilities* 3, no. 9 (1970):11–16.

Johnson, G. O. Special education for the mentally retarded—A paradox. *Exceptional Children* 29 (1962):62–69.

―――. Inconsistencies in programming. *Education and Training of the Mentally Retarded* 18, no. 2 (1983):101–102.

Johnson, J. L. Special education in the inner city: A challenge for the future or another means of cooling the markout? *Journal of Special Education* 3 (1969):241–51.

Juul, K. D. European approaches and innovations in serving the handicapped. *Exceptional Children* 44, no. 5 (1978):322–30.

Kephart, N. C. *The slow learner in the classroom.* Columbus, Ohio: Charles E. Merrill, 1960.

Kirk, S. A. Behavior diagnosis and remediation of learning disabilities. *Proceedings of the First Annual Meeting of the Conference on the Exploration into the Problems of the Perceptually Handicapped Child, First Annual Meeting,* Vol. 1, 16 April 1963.

Kolstoe, O.P. *Teaching educable mentally retarded children.* New York: Holt, Rinehart, and Winston, 1976.

Laski, F. Civil rights victories for the handicapped—I. *The Record* 1, no. 5 (1974):15–20.

Lilly S. *Children with exceptional needs: A survey of special education.* New York: Holt, Rinehart and Winston, 1979.

McCarthy, M. M. The Pennhurst and Rowley decisions: Issues and implications. *Exceptional Children* 49, no. 6 (1983):517–22.

McCarthy, M. M., and N. H. Cambron. *Public school law: Teachers' and students' rights.* Boston: Allyn and Bacon, 1981.

Martin, R. *Workshop materials: The impact of current legal action on educating handicapped children.* Champaign, Ill.: Research Press Company, 1980.

Marvell, T., A. Galfo, and J. Rockwell. *Student litigation: A compilation and analysis of civil cases involving students 1977–1981.* Williamsburg, Va.: National Center for State Courts, 1981.

Meyen, E. L. *Exceptional children and youth: An introduction.* Denver: Love Publishing Company, 1982.

Podemski, R. S., B. J. Price, T. E. C. Smith, and G. E. Marsh. *Comprehensive special education administration.* Rockville, Md.: Aspen Systems, 1984.

Postlewaite, J. *Mattie T. v. Holladay:* Denial of equal education. *Amicus* 2, no. 3 (1977):38–44.

Reynolds, M. C., and J. W. Birch. *Teaching exceptional children in all America's schools.* Reston, Va.: The Council for Exceptional Children, 1977.

Schwartz, L. L. *Exceptional students in the mainstream.* Belmont, Calif.: Wadsworth, 1984.

Smith, T. E. C. Status of due process hearings. *Exceptional Children* 48, no.3 (1981):232–36.

Stotland, J. F. and E. Mancuso. U.S. Court of Appeals decision regarding *Armstrong v. Kline:* The 180 day rule. *Exceptional Children* 47, no. 4 (1981):266–70.

Strauss, A. A., and L. E. Lehtinen. *Psychopathology and education of the brain-injured child.* New York: Grune and Stratton, 1947.

Turnbull, H. R., and P. Barber. Perspectives on public policy. *Mental retardation: Topics of today—Issues of tomorrow.* Edited by E. L. Meyen. Lancaster, Pa.: Lancaster Press, 1984.

Turnbull, H. R., and A. P. Turnbull. Procedural due process and the education of handicapped children. *Focus on Exceptional Children* 9, no. 9 (1978):1–12.

Weintraub, F. J. Understanding the individualized education program (IEP). *Amicus* 2, no. 3 (1977):26–31.

Yoshida, R. K. Perspectives on Research. *Mental retardation: Topics of today—Issues of tomorrow.* Edited by E. L. Meyen. Lancaster, Pa.: Lancaster Press, 1984.

Ysseldyke, J. E., and B. Algozzine. *Critical issues in special and remedial education.* Boston: Houghton Mifflin Co., 1982.

Chapter Two

THE MILDLY HANDICAPPED: A CONCEPTUAL FRAMEWORK

CHAPTER OUTLINE

INTRODUCTION
SOCIOLOGICAL ASPECTS UNDERLYING LABELS
LABELING AND SPECIAL EDUCATION
    Advantages and Disadvantages of Labeling
TRADITIONAL CATEGORICAL GROUPINGS IN SPECIAL EDUCATION
    Mental Retardation
    Learning Disabilities
    Emotional Disturbance/Behavioral Disorders
    Hearing Impaired
    Visually Impaired
    Physical and Health Impairments
    Speech and Language Disorders
TRENDS IN CATEGORIES FOR THE HANDICAPPED
THE MILDLY HANDICAPPED
    Reasons for the Mild Category
    Definition of the Mildly Handicapped
    Prevalence of the Mildly Handicapped
    Obstacles to the Mildly Handicapped Category
SUMMARY

CHAPTER OBJECTIVES

After reading this chapter, you should be able to:
- Describe the traditional categories of handicapped children and adults;
- Understand and discuss the sociological aspects underlying labeling;
- Know the advantages and disadvantages of labeling;
- Understand the rationale for the mildly handicapped category;
- Define mildly handicapped;
- Describe the characteristics of mildly handicapped children and adults; and
- State the prevalence of mildly handicapped children and adults.

INTRODUCTION

The purpose of this chapter is to consider the definitions, categories, classification systems, and characteristics of mildly handicapped children and adults. All special services to the handicapped, such as teacher training, teacher certification, funding, service delivery, and methodologies, relate to definitions and classification systems. The present and future of special education and other services to the handicapped will depend greatly on the methods used to label and categorize this population. But these methods are also central to much of the controversy in special education. If definitions and categories change, so will assessment procedures, placement practices, instructional methods, and rehabilitation services.

Labels and definitions used to identify individuals as different are a function of society. They are more likely based on the values of the majority culture than on scientific facts and principles. Therefore, in attempting to understand the labeling and categorization of the handicapped, the sociological aspects of the culture must be considered. For example, to consider special education only as a matter of education is too limited; the way children are identified, labeled, grouped, and served is a result of societal values, not simply the professional opinions of educators.

SOCIOLOGICAL ASPECTS UNDERLYING LABELS

Until recently, most labels assigned to handicapped children and adults have described various kinds of role failure; that is, individuals in our culture are expected to perform adequately in specific roles (e.g., student, citizen, parent). If they do not, they may be considered failures and then be officially labeled and denied certain rights. The institution (e.g., school, government, industry, military) likely performs the official act of labeling to designate incompetence or deviance, and therefore, an incapability of performing the tasks defined by society as important. The predominant American culture requires a high level of individual competence, so its standards and expectations are significant in defining roles and role failure.

Prior to compulsory education, mental retardation was only considered within the contexts of the family and the community. The category took on added importance as role failure when children deviated significantly from the school standards of conduct and achievement. These children may have been regarded as failures but at the same time were considered to be functioning well within the expectations of the family and the community. Before the mainstreaming movement, the mentally retarded label might have meant removal from other students and teachers in the school. It still may mean isolation, rejection, and barriers to participating in sports, clubs, and organizations. Many scholars and activists have attacked labeling for this reason: it may cause children to lose rights and privileges, and potentially affect the attitudes of peers and teachers toward those who have been labeled.

Labels such as **impairment,** disability, and handicap must be viewed within a particular culture and at a particular point in time in order to be fully understood. Stevens (1962) viewed an impairment as a physiological anomaly, such as the absence of limbs or damaged nerves. A **disability** is a functional failure or limitation associated with an impairment. Thus, some impairments may lead to disabilities while others may not. A handicap, according to Stevens, is an individual's personal conceptualization of, and reaction to, the impairment and the disability. This approach means that some

Conformity with social roles is important for acceptance by peers and others.

people can have impairments and disabilities and not be handicapped, while others with the same impairments and disabilities would be considered very handicapped. Each impairment or disability is defined within a social context. Thus, a scar or missing limb might be admirable in a warrior's society, convening status and prestige; in another society a person with the same scar might be regarded as a hideous freak. It all depends upon the prevailing values of the mainstream culture. Therefore, regardless of the nature of the impairment or disability, the handicap is not strictly a condition determined personally by the impaired/disabled person. Society has created an underlying value system that defines acceptance or rejection and the limits of the person's role.

LABELING AND SPECIAL EDUCATION

Most conditions in special education are regarded as role failures in the school. Whether or not special education students are classified as role failures outside school or beyond the school years depends upon different standards and social contexts. Some are, while others are not. Standards by which school-aged children are measured for role failure include the following abilities:

1. To obey and cooperate;
2. To acquire the standard language skills of the mainstream culture in reading and written expression;

3. To develop abstract reasoning ability and to use it for serious pursuit of knowledge, and to be motivated and aspire to success; and
4. To have adequate physical skills.

Most conditions in special education can be viewed in contrast with these four norms. Emotionally disturbed or behaviorally disordered children primarily violate the first norm; mentally retarded children violate the last three norms; learning disabled children violate the second; hearing impaired, speech impaired, and deaf children also violate the second. Although visually impaired, blind, health impaired, and physically impaired children violate none of these norms, they tax the system because most schools have been unable or unwilling to deal effectively with the unique needs of these groups.

Students who meet or exceed the norms will be regarded as successful and will reap rewards. Those rated as substandard may be labeled handicapped and then be served in special education programs. The actions taken by the schools to label children as deviant, incompetent, or handicapped result from the extent to which deviations occur from one or more of these standard norms. The social significance can be further clarified by the additional descriptors used in each of the categories of special education. Children with deficient cognitive development are labeled "mentally retarded," those with emotional problems are considered "emotionally disturbed" or "behaviorally disordered," and children with normal intelligence who cannot read or achieve in other areas commensurate with their ability are called "learning disabled."

The definitions and characteristics used to describe the mildly handicapped, as well as the instructional methodologies used with this group, have all been subject to social interpretation. In addition to the four norms listed above, mildly handicapped children and adults deviate from norms in other areas and this makes them unacceptable for certain roles or responsibilities such as getting married, serving in the military, and securing particular kinds of employment.

Advantages and Disadvantages of Labeling

Labeling individuals as different with terms such as deviant, incompetent, or more specific categorical labels, like mentally retarded, learning disabled, or emotionally disturbed, is a reality. Many argue that labeling children and adults is unnecessary and promotes stereotyping, while others view the process as vital and necessary to provide services.

Advantages of Labeling. The primary purpose for labeling children is to enable them to access special services (Ysseldyke and Algozzine 1982; Mandell and Fiscus 1981). By labeling and classifying children as "different," they become eligible for certain specialized services from the school. For school-aged children, this includes special education and related services. For adults, labels might permit eligibility for government assistance programs such as rent subsidy, vocational rehabilitation, and medical services. Other advantages of labeling include (1) identifying children with similar characteristics for the purposes of instruction (Gajar 1980), (2) providing a focal point for advocacy, (3) developing a target group for research (Keogh 1983), and (4) facilitating research into etiology, which could result in preventive measures (Mandell and Fiscus, 1981).

Disadvantages of Labeling. Just as there are those who support labeling for the reasons cited, many others claim that labeling has more disadvantages than advantages. Yssel-

The primary purpose of labeling is to make students eligible for special education services.

dyke and Algozzine (1982) suggest that labeling can have detrimental effects on two areas: self-perceptions and others' perceptions. For example, labels can have a negative effect on teacher expectations, teacher interactions, and student performance (Burdg and Graham 1984; Algozzine, Mercer, and Countermine 1977). Also, Aloia and MacMillan (1983) found that the label "educable mentally retarded" had a negative effect on teachers' initial expectations of a student's academic ability, of teacher ability, and of teachers' general overall impression of EMR students.

36 Mildly Handicapped Children and Adults

Burdg and Graham (1984) studied the effects of labels on individuals administering tests to children. In the study, examiners administered the Animal House and Block Design subtests of the Wechsler Preschool and Primary Scale of Intelligence to non-handicapped preschoolers aged four to six. Results indicated that children who had been assigned to groups supposedly for developmentally delayed students performed lower on the tasks than those assigned to groups for nondelayed children. Results suggest that the examiners "failed to elicit optimal performance from children who were assigned a bias-inducing label" (Wechsler 1967, 425).

In addition to affecting teacher expectations, labels:

- Focus on deficits rather than strengths of students (Cremins 1981);
- Are difficult to remove (Mandell and Fiscus 1981);
- Imply the problem is internal to the child rather than external (Mandell and Fiscus 1981); and
- May produce limits on behavior that is considered acceptable (Algozzine et al. 1977).

Evidence can be found on both sides of the labeling issue. Some investigators have revealed the negative effects of labeling, while others have noted limited or no negative effects (Aloia and MacMillan 1983). As a result, more efforts are needed to further investigate the effects of labeling and to develop alternative ways to identify children and establish their eligibility for special services.

TRADITIONAL CATEGORICAL GROUPINGS IN SPECIAL EDUCATION

Several traditional categories have been used to group handicapped individuals.

Mental Retardation

The widely accepted definition of **mental retardation** (MR) is provided by the American Association on Mental Deficiency (AAMD). This definition states that "mental retardation refers to significantly subaverage general intellectual functioning resulting in or associated with concurrent impairments in adaptive behavior and manifested during the developmental period" (Grossman 1983, 11).

The definition has three major parts. The first part, "significantly subaverage general intellectual functioning," is defined by the AAMD as an intelligence quotient of 70 or below obtained on an individually administered intelligence test. The IQ of 70 is provided as a guide; the score could actually go as high as 75 or above, depending on the reliability of the IQ test used (Grossman 1983). The second part of the definition, "impairments in adaptive behavior," means "significant limitations in an individual's effectiveness in meeting the standards of maturation, learning, personal independence, and/or social responsibility that are expected for his or her age level and cultural group" (Grossman 1983, 11). The AAMD defines the final part, "developmental period," as the period between conception and the eighteenth birthday.

While many different definitions of mental retardation exist, the AAMD definition is the one used by most states, as well as the federal government. Most other definitions of mental retardation utilize a similar criterion of IQ score. While an effort has been made

Table 2-1 IQ Criteria for AAMD Groups

Category	IQ Criteria
Mild Mental Retardation	50–55 to approximately 70
Moderate Mental Retardation	35–40 to 50–55
Severe Mental Retardation	20–25 to 35–40
Profound Mental Retardation	Below 20 or 25

Source: Grossman 1983.

to limit the importance placed on an IQ score, it still appears to be central in most definitions of mental retardation.

A variety of classification schemes have been employed with the mentally retarded. One method, popular in education, was developed by Kirk and Johnson (1951). This system used classifications of slow learner, educable mentally handicapped, trainable mentally handicapped, and totally dependent. The AAMD has another frequently used system that classifies persons as either mild, moderate, severe, or profound. Prior to 1973 the AAMD had a borderline category for individuals with IQs in the 70 to 85 range. This grouping was dropped, however, with the 1973 revision of the definition and classification system.

The AAMD system, as well as most other classification systems for mental retardation, relies on IQ scores as a major criterion for the various levels. Table 2-1 describes the IQ criteria for each AAMD group. It should be noted that the vast majority of mentally retarded individuals fall into the mild category. This means that the overwhelming majority of mentally retarded children are able to attend school and benefit from school programs, especially under the terms of Public Law 94-142. Likewise, most retarded adults are mildly retarded and are capable of independent or semi-independent living. The familiar stereotype that most mentally retarded people are severely handicapped and need institutionalization is just not true.

Learning Disabilities

Learning disabilities (LD) has captured a great deal of interest and has been highly controversial in its short history. Until 1960, no classes for learning disabled children were offered in public schools; however, since then learning disabilities has grown to become one of the largest single categories for special education. The growth of the category is illustrated by the following facts:

1. The strong parent group, Association for Children with Learning Disabilities, was not established until 1963 (Siegel and Gold 1982).
2. Publications focusing on the learning disabled were developed in 1965 *(Academic Therapy)* and in 1968 *(The Journal of Learning Disabilities)* (Siegel and Gold 1982).
3. In 1964, only four universities received federal grants to train teachers of the learning disabled (Kirk and Chalfant 1984). Currently hundreds of university training programs receive funding.
4. The Specific Learning Disabilities Act of 1969 (Public Law 91-230) was the first federal legislation dealing with learning disabled children (Kirk and Chalfant 1984).

5. Although only beginning in the late 1960s, every state had programs for learning disabled children by 1975 (Gillespie, Miller, and Fielder 1975).
6. Public Law 94-142 included the learning disabled as a part of the large group of handicapped children, thus applying all the aspects of the act to LD children.

This growth of the learning disabilities movement was primarily stimulated and sponsored by the middle class. Mental retardation and learning disabilities are both social phenomena, but mental retardation is frequently found in impoverished and environmentally poor homes. Learning disabilities, however, is a mild disorder and primarily occurs in middle class homes. Some of the definitions for learning disabilities actually include criteria that make it difficult for environmentally and economically disadvantaged children to be labeled and served as learning disabled.

From the many different definitions of learning disabilities, the one most accepted is provided by the federal government:

> Specific learning disability means a disorder in one or more of the basic psychological processes involved in understanding or in using language, spoken or written, which may manifest itself in an imperfect ability to listen, think, speak, read, write, spell, or to do mathematical calculations. The term includes such conditions as perceptual handicaps, brain injury, minimal brain dysfunction, dyslexia, and developmental aphasia. The term does not include children who have learning problems which are primarily the result of visual, hearing, or motor handicaps, or mental retardation, or of environmental, cultural, or economic disadvantage. *Federal Register* 42:163 (29 December 1977):65083.

The diagnosis of a learning disability presumably proceeds on the basis that a child with average or above average intelligence reveals a significant discrepancy between expected levels of achievement and actual achievement in school subjects. The discrepancy is presumably explained by a process disorder that may be described as a perceptual, perceptual-motor, or language deficit interfering with the child's academic ability.

While a major category in special education, learning disabilities remains very controversial. Coles (1978) asserts that there is no special knowledge about learning disabilities, the definition is vague, the conditions mentioned such as dyslexia are difficult to define, and by excluding certain economic groups the definition focuses on middle and upper middle class children. Similar criticisms about the definition of learning disabilities, as well as other aspects of the category, are frequently presented.

Parent organizations for the learning disabled are primarily middle class. They object to their children being referred to as "retarded" and prefer that they not be mixed with other categories of handicapped children. The use of noncategorical resource rooms for all children with mild handicaps has not been supported by many of these advocate groups. Learning disabilities, therefore, is somewhat of a class distinction. This, unfortunately, only adds to the controversy.

The characteristics associated with learning disabilities are numerous and vague. Hyperactivity, perceptual disorders, emotional instability, disorders of attention, impulsivity, disorders of speech and hearing, and neurological signs, in addition to problems of acquiring basic skills are commonly cited. Reynolds and Birch (1977) have indicated that much energy has gone into the attempt to find physiological, psychological, sociological, and educational correlates to tie these children together with common threads, but the results have been discouraging. Increasingly, many practitioners are taking the view that the only characteristic common to learning disabled children is that they do not perform well in school. Unless it becomes possible to identify specific neurological conditions that have common characteristics and treatment approaches, the current confusion about the definition and characteristics is likely to remain.

Emotional Disturbance/Behavioral Disorders

This area is plagued, like others in special education, with problems of definition and characteristics. The term *emotional disturbance* (ED) has had many forerunners—lunacy, psychosis, neurosis, schizophrenia, and others. The social stigma associated with a condition of mental aberration was "craziness," and historically, organized religion and superstition explained mental illness in terms of demonic possession and witchcraft. If mental retardation and lack of academic facility were tolerated by the schools, mental illness was not. Very few public school programs have existed for children who would be labeled in this general category.

The term *emotional disturbance* grew out of the influence of behaviorism in education and psychology and permitted schools to use a category that was devoid of the terminology and influences of psychiatry and psychoanalysis. Instead of dealing with psychiatric interpretations of etiologies, the school could simply focus on the observable behavior of the child. But regardless of the constructs used, psychiatric or behavioral, the premise has been that certain children deviate from social standards of conduct and behavior in some remarkable ways that warrant intervention. With this group of children, schools have been less concerned with academic performance and have concentrated instead on assisting children to exhibit normal behavior.

Of all the definitions in special education, the area of emotional and behavioral disorders poses the greatest problems for the labeler. As perplexing as learning disabilities has been, the label can be defended in terms of deviation from common school achievement criteria. Mental retardation can be measured, no matter how debatable, in terms of deviations in measured intelligence and adaptive behavior. Children who cannot see, hear, or walk may also be measured against a common standard related to those skills. Behavioral and emotional deviations, on the other hand, have no clear indices. In fact, many behaviors that might be considered as abnormal are normal for most children at certain stages of development or under certain conditions. Therefore, some definitions require that children exhibit certain deviant characteristics over a long period of time before being classified as disturbed. Furthermore, these behaviors must be considered excessive.

The major features of definitions in this area are behaviors that markedly deviate from "acceptable" modes of conduct, frequently, intensely, and over a long period of time. It is clear then that any condition of emotional disturbance or behavioral disorder is judged within the social context, as are other conditions of special education.

Kirk (1972) succintly defined a **behavior disorder** as a deviation from age-appropriate behavior that significantly affects growth and development of the child and/or the lives of others. Kauffman (1977, 23) suggested that children with behavior disorders are those who "chronically and markedly respond to their environment in socially unacceptable and/or personally unsatisfying ways." According to Quay (1975), emotional disturbance can be classified within three general categories: conduct, personality, and immaturity problems. **Conduct disorders** include striking other children, destroying objects, fighting, disobedience, and temper tantrums. The child with personality disorders might be shy, withdrawn, or have feelings of inferiority or self-

Table 2-2 Intervention Strategies for Emotionally Disturbed/Behaviorally Disordered

Strategy	Description
Behavioral	• Based on behaviorism theory • Assumes normal, healthy behaviors can be learned • Focuses on overt behavior problems • Is not concerned with etiology
Biophysical	• Assumes problems result from biological, genetic, or neurological variables • Requires teachers and medical professionals to work together • Intervention relies on psychopharmological actions
Sociological	• Intervention focuses on changing the concept of deviance • Requires changes in school structure
Ecological	• Problems result from interaction of child and environment • Adjustment is required by persons in child's ecosystem • Major method is consultation
Developmental	• Is based on hierarchial sequence of education goals • Difficulties are considered "lags" not abnormal
Academic	• Blends biophysical and remedial teaching • Assumes remediation of academic problems has a positive effect on behavior problems
Psychodynamic	• Goal focuses on unconscious conflicts within the child • Heavy emphasis placed on ancillary professionals; teachers are support • Aim is to develop insight within child
Psychoeducational	• Combines aspects of the psychodynamic approach with attention to overt behavior • Classroom application focuses on remediation of academic and affective areas
Countertheoretical	• Focuses on humanizing education • Deemphasizes labels • Attends to individualization

Source: Swanson and Reinert 1984.

consciousness. The immature child would be one characterized as having poor attention or short attention spans, passivity, or clumsiness. The problem with all these descriptions and characterizations is a lack of specificity about what is a standard of behavior and what is considered deviant.

Another major controversy in the area of emotional disturbance and behavior disorders focuses on intervention. How should these children be treated? Several major theoretical approaches have been used with these children. Table 2-2 describes these approaches. In addition to these traditional approaches are other intervention approaches for these children, including life-space interview technique (Redl 1959), crisis intervention (Morse 1971), play therapy (Axline 1947), and art therapy.

An approach very popular in the 1960s, and still frequently used, is drug therapy. Children considered aggressive, hyperactive, distractible, and inattentive have been administered medication to alter their behavior and, presumably, to improve school performance. Many writers have provided evidence to question the effectiveness of medication with children (Wolman, Egan, and Ross 1978; Fish 1971; Walden and Thompson 1981). Some of the findings include: (1) drugs do not create learning; (2) drugs are not necessarily effective in altering behavior; (3) drugs sometimes cause negative side effects; (4) drugs are often used as a first resort rather than a last resort;

and (5) a variety of other techniques exist that may be used to assist children without the risks of medication.

Environmental, ecological, and behavioral interventions have been much more popular in public schools than some of the more therapeutic approaches. Using these interventions, the schools can watch, observe, measure, and compare the behaviors of referred students in various settings; it can focus attention on the nature of interactions rather than on simply what is wrong with the child.

Of the currently used interventions, the behavioral view is the most useful to the school because it avoids the problems of dealing with identification through the clinical (subjective) approach, through etiological classification, and through classification systems that use mental illness constructs. Behavioral disorders and emotional conflicts are explained as learned behavior that may be directly treated through various types and schedules of reinforcement. The approach assumes that acceptable behavior can be learned.

The behavioral view is also acceptable because interventions can be made that do not deal with specific etiologies (Kauffman 1977). Thus, the behavioral approach, especially with regard to emotional problems or behavior disorders, enables the school to sidestep thorny issues surrounding mental illness and to focus on factors that the school can treat directly. Behaviorists do not ask what is the underlying cause of the inappropriate behavior, but simply how can the behavior be changed.

Hearing Impaired

Children with hearing impairments have been regarded as "severely" impaired by school authorities, while adults with this disorder have tended to be segregated into deaf communities and largely ignored by the general population. Elderly persons with hearing problems are recognized by their families as having deterioration of hearing ability as a natural part of the aging process. Few programs are warranted by the society for this group because their lives are considered short and their period of productivity is limited.

Children and young adults may be subdivided into degrees of hearing loss with educational and rehabilitation significance attached to such classifications. The school does not view the **hearing impaired** child as deviant; rather it maintains that its basic facilities and methodologies are simply inadequate to accommodate such children. The position is held that the qualifications of teachers, necessary support services, and additional expense simply require that these children be placed in separate facilities.

With less social and instructional consequences for the public school, and with greater clarity about what is meant by hearing impairment, the definition has been much less controversial than in the conditions discussed above. Essentially, the definition uses a standard of normal hearing acuity and measures hearing loss against the standard with electronic equipment.

Most schools have accepted the definition of hearing impairment for educational purposes that was adopted by the Conference of Executives of American Schools for the Deaf (Moores 1978). According to this definition, a **deaf** person is one whose hearing is disabled to an extent that precludes the understanding of speech through the ear alone, with or without the assistance of an amplification device. A **hard-of-hearing** person is one whose hearing is disabled to such an extent that it is difficult to understand speech through the ear alone, with or without a hearing aid.

Determination of a hearing loss is made by means of an **audiometer** using international standards: the International Standard Organization (ISO) or the American National Standards Institute (ANSI). Hearing acuity is measured with an audiometer in terms of decibels (dB) and frequencies or cycles per second indicated as Hertz (Hz) units. The normal range of hearing in conversational speech spans the frequency range from approximately 500 to 2,000 Hz at loudness ranging from 25 to 60 dB. Children and adults with hearing loss measured in decibels from 25 to about 90 are considered to be hard of hearing; those with losses greater than 90 are generally considered to be deaf. But classifying children is much more troublesome. Many terms are used such as slight, mild, moderate, severe, and profound hearing loss. The primary concern, however, should not be the precise hearing loss as measured by electronic devices, but what the child can do in acquisition of various skills despite the presumed severity of the impairment.

If one considers carefully the hearing impaired group, it is obvious that the majority of students are mildly affected. The deaf student gets most of the recognition because of the severity of the condition. Nonetheless, it has become apparent to many school authorities that mildly hearing impaired students and deaf students are able to attend regular classes. The descriptors "severe" or "profound" refer only to the decibel loss in measured hearing from accepted standards. This in no way indicates that such children should not be considered mildly handicapped even if they are able to benefit from placement and instructional programming in the regular classroom.

Visually Impaired

Like the hearing impaired, visually impaired individuals comprise a low-incidence group with less than one percent of the school-aged population in this category. Also, like the hearing impaired, the number of children who are virtually totally blind is small compared to others who have less severe visual losses. Two recognized groups, the **blind** and the **partially sighted** or low-vision group, make up the visually impaired category.

Visual impairment has both an educational and legal definition. The generally accepted legal definition uses **visual acuity,** or the distance at which a sighted person would be expected to see an object clearly, as the standard. **Legal blindness** is defined as a visual acuity of less than 20/200 in the better eye with best correction, or a field restriction of 20 degrees or less. It should always be remembered that different people with the same visual acuity will have different functional vision and be able to use their residual vision differently.

Definitions used by educators attempt to account for these differences in practical ways. The focus is on how well visually impaired children use their vision for instruction. Blind children are those who must rely on the use of Braille or other compensatory instructional systems; low-vision students, or those classified as partially sighted, can use printed materials such as large print books or regular print books with the assistance of technological devices. Functional abilities are the most important characteristics considered for classification. A child's visual acuity, while useful, does not help school personnel know what type of educational program is best suited for a particular child.

Regardless of the definition used, the majority of students with visual impairments have, by comparison, relatively minor visual impairments and may be expected to participate in regular public school programs. Many of these children attend regular classrooms and may or may not have the assistance of resource rooms or other support services. Also, many totally blind children attend regular classes. These children, obviously, need more support than those with some functional vision.

Physical and Health Impairments

Defining a group of children with physical and health impairments by limiting the definition to specific clusters of symptoms and common terminology is impossible. There can be as many separate definitions as categories under this rubric. By cutting across all of the conditions commonly placed in this group, it is possible to define the category as a variety of medical conditions, physical or health impairments, manifested by children that require the school to adjust teaching methodology and physical environment.

Numerous conditions might be considered in this category. Schools most often deal with cerebral palsy and other neurological impairments, epilepsy, muscular dystrophy, diseases or injury of the spinal cord, arthritis, sleep disturbances, bowel and bladder control problems, musculoskeletal disorders, diabetes, cystic fibrosis, asthma, allergies, congenital and surgical amputations, and other physical impairments due to disease or accidents. The list is limitless.

Many of these conditions, as well as others, will be seen by regular classroom and special education teachers. Some children will require little support from special personnel while others will need considerable support in the areas of therapy and medical intervention. But for most of these children, the classroom teacher will be the primary source of instruction. The problems presented by this group will usually not involve disorders of learning, but rather, physical management, accommodation in the classroom, and concern about socioemotional development. With proper support most of these children can perform adequately in the public school classroom, which makes it difficult to consider them as severely handicapped.

Speech and Language Disorders

The definitions of speech and language disorders have certainly caused problems and disputes. Three general categories of communication disorders are nonverbal children, language-disordered children, and speech-impaired children. Regular classroom teachers rarely have to deal with the first category; the other two types of disorders are frequently found in regular classrooms.

The widely accepted definition of communication disorders states that a person has a communication disorder if his or her speech differs from the speech of others to the extent that it calls attention to itself, interferes with the message that is intended, or causes distress to the speaker or listener (Van Riper 1978). Within this large group are obvious subgroups. Children who are classified as nonverbal constitute a small segment. These children, for a variety of reasons, do not have speech and language ability. This may be due to brain damage, emotional problems, or severe mental retardation. Another relatively small group of children has problems of dysfluency, usually characterized as stuttering or voice disorders, but the majority of children in this category have articulation problems. These include omission, substitution, or distortion of sounds. Most such conditions occur singly or in association with other impairments; they yield readily to remediation; and the majority occur during the preschool and elementary school years. Ordinarily the classroom teacher will have little difficulty managing and supporting such children in regular classrooms.

TRENDS IN CATEGORIES FOR THE HANDICAPPED

Along with the movements of mainstreaming and normalization in this society have come a tolerance of handicapping conditions and a changing view among school personnel about the severity of various conditions. As noted earlier, at one time when children were unable to meet the standards of the school, they were either excluded or elected on their own to stop attending school. Compulsory attendance laws changed that. Requiring children to attend school created major problems for the schools that they have been attempting to deal with for over a hundred years: primarily, how are these children best served? In the beginning, handicapped children in the school and handicapped adults in the community were excluded by institutionalization. Later, the exclusion was by segregation within the school in self-contained special education classrooms and tracking. In communities, segregation was implemented through limited housing and job opportunities. The civil rights movement, litigation, and state and federal legislation have changed these practices. Educational and vocational opportunities have been "equalized" by law. One result has been an altered view about the severity of handicapping conditions.

No longer are people considered severely handicapped simply because they are impaired visually, aurally, or physically. Only a relative minority of handicapped children are today considered to be severely handicapped—the retarded at the low end of the developmental continuum, the severely withdrawn and emotionally ill, and the ones dangerous to themselves and others. Otherwise, even the physically handicapped, health impaired, and vision and hearing impaired are often attending regular classrooms, at least for a portion of each school day. And this trend is increasing. For a majority of handicapped children, the many characteristics used to describe them have little to do with the expectations for them or for instructional plans. Increasingly the field is shifting from an emphasis on clinical observations and theoretical constructs to consideration of the instructional characteristics of the environment. Information concerning traditional classification labels, etiology, and prognosis is considered less important than immediate learning and teaching variables.

New classification systems are emerging for handicapped children and adults. Although many variations of the traditional categorical model exist, the new emphasis is on functional ability, not clinical label. Classification is more likely to be a dichotomy such as mildly handicapped and severely handicapped, with the mildly handicapped being those who can benefit from traditional public school programs. Massachusetts has moved to a system where the program is classified, not the child. In this approach, children are placed in programs along a continuum ranging from a regular classroom with modification to a hospital setting. Placement is based on the needs of the students, not their label (Cremins 1981). The system in Arkansas has five categories: mild, moderate-profound, hearing impaired, visually impaired, and seriously emotionally disturbed.

Even with a nontraditional, functional classification system, labels must be assigned. Despite the risk that these new, more functional labels will someday be as negative and suggestive as the traditional labels currently used, they are necessary. Labels can be developed, however, that at least temporarily do not convey the negative characteristics associated with such terms as mental retardation. One suggestion made by Mann, Davis, Boyer, Metz, and Wolford (1983) and supported by Keogh (1983) is to label all "mildly handicapped" children as learning disabled. Regardless of the labels attached to the new, more functional groupings, they are less important than the criteria established for group assignment. Hallahan and Kauffman (1977) suggest that chronological age, sex, and characteristic social behavior be used to group children for social experiences, but for purposes of grouping for academic instruction, the primary criterion that should be used is specific academic skill level. This trend to the more functional grouping is a movement toward phenotypic classification, what a person does, and away from genotypic classification, what a person is like (Neisworth and Greer 1975). Many states have made the transition from categorical services to noncategorical or generic services. Using a noncategorical delivery system enables children to be served based on their functional needs, not on labels.

THE MILDLY HANDICAPPED

The label that has emerged most often in newer classification schemes is the "mildly handicapped." This label is applied to children whose disabilities affect their educational performance, but not to such an extent that they cannot benefit from programs generally provided in public schools. Many states have begun to serve children using this generic classification rather than more traditional categorical labels.

Reasons for the Mild Category

Due to a long tradition of exclusion and differential treatment of students who were unable to meet expectations of the school, a condition we have referred to sociologically as role failure in our culture, the school has repeatedly created specialized programs for each category of student it defines as different. The mentally retarded, learning disabled, and emotionally disturbed have been managed categorically. Teacher training programs, state certification of teachers, funding patterns for services, and special education classes have been determined by categorical classifications. But since the beginning of professional concern about such practices in the late 1960s, followed by litigation, legislation, mainstreaming, and normalization, a trend has emerged to group students noncategorically because of concern about the damage of labeling.

More significant has been the practical consideration of schools to serve a greater number of students in noncategorical resource rooms and regular classrooms. At the same time there has been a renewed interest in the academic problems of students and less interest in noneducational therapies, such as perceptual-motor training. Major points presented by those who have favored the move to noncategorical classification include (1) confusing categorical definitions, (2) similar etiologies, (3) similar social and behavioral characteristics, and (4) virtually identical instructional methodologies.

Confusing definitions. One of the reasons for moving toward noncategorical services and grouping has been the confusion caused by categorical definitions. As stated by Hallahan and Kauffman (1977, 139), "the first sign that the three mildly handicapped areas should not be considered as distinct unique categories is the fact that each of their definitions reflects a great deal of confusion." The following points describe the problems in defining learning disabilities, emotional disturbance, and mental retardation (Hallahan and Kauffman 1977):

- The LD definition relies a great deal on excluding certain types of children.
- Prevalence rates estimated for LD children have been extremely varied.
- There are many varied definitions of ED, primarily based on theoretical models.

- Prevalence estimates for ED children also range from very low to extremely high.
- The 1973 change in the AAMD definition of mental retardation has caused confusion and will likely cause many children formerly labeled mentally retarded to be labeled learning disabled.

The failure of professionals to agree on definitions of children and adults traditionally grouped together suggests that there are not enough similarities within these groups to warrant separate labels. The identification of many emotionally disturbed children as learning disabled and their placement in LD resource rooms for services (Chandler and Jones 1983) reinforce the lack of distinction between some of the traditional categorical groups.

Similar etiologies. Many factors that cause mental retardation can also cause various disabilities such as learning disabilities and emotional disturbances. One such etiological factor is brain injury. If the injury is severe enough, mental retardation could result. If it is in various locations, cerebral palsy with or without mental retardation could result. If the injury affects other parts of the brain, emotional disabilities could occur. And brain injury is associated with learning disabilities, as well as various visual and hearing disabilities.

In addition to brain injury, environment can cause many different disabilities. Mental retardation, emotional disturbance, and even learning disabilities have been associated with certain types of environmental conditions. Therefore, etiological factors are not unique to certain disabilities. Since many conditions can result from the same factors, the uniqueness of traditional categories of disabilities is lessened.

Social and behavorial characteristics. One of the main reasons for labeling individuals—to group persons with similar characteristics—also supports continued categorical classifications of disabled children and adults. When the characteristics of traditional groups are compared, however, many similarities among the groups obviously exist.

Neisworth and Greer (1975, 20) state that "when educational objectives are pinpointed and derived from specific skills assessment, considerable overlap between educable retardation and learning disability problems can exist." They also note that these similarities include distractibility, discrimination difficulties, motivation, and retention.

Academic achievement has long been used as a characteristic for handicapped children. Mentally retarded children, as a result of their limited intellectual abilities, have below average academic achievement. By definition, learning disabled and emotionally disturbed children also have achievement problems. In a study by Epstein and Cullinan (1983), the achievement levels of behaviorally disordered and learning disabled children were compared using three standardized achievement tests. Results indicated significant differences between the two groups on several measures. While the authors contend that this is evidence to support the continuation of categorical labels, it should be noted that the achievement differences, while statistically significant, were not greatly different in any area except reading and spelling. There were no significant differences between the two groups on general information or one math measure. Since reading disorders are the major problems experienced by learning disabled children, it should be expected that this group would do poorly on standardized reading achievement measures. The similarities of the two groups on the other areas suggest that with the exception of reading, behaviorally disordered and learning disabled children have similar achievement levels.

While underachievement is a major characteristic with learning disabled children, it

Reading and writing skills are important determinants of school performance.

is also found in emotionally disturbed and mentally retarded children (Hallahan and Kauffman 1977). Gajar (1979) studied the characteristics of educable mentally retarded children, learning disabled children, and emotionally disturbed children. Results indicated that while the three groups showed significant differences in achievement, all three had below average achievement scores in reading, spelling, and arithmetic.

Intelligence levels have also been used to distinguish between various types of handicapped children and adults. Mentally retarded children and adults obviously have less than average IQ scores. Definitions of this condition, with few exceptions, use low IQ scores as a major criterion for mental retardation. But intelligence levels of emotionally disturbed children and learning disabled children are also below the mean. In the study conducted by Epstein and Cullinan (1983), the mean IQ was 92.9 for the behaviorally disordered group, and 89.9 for the learning disabled group. Gajar (1980) investigated the characteristics of educable mentally retarded (EMR), LD, and ED children and found that the mean IQ scores for the three groups were 63 for the EMR children, 93.3 for the LD group, and 91.0 for the ED children. Another study by Gajar (1979) revealed that the subjects from the EMR, LD, and ED groups had mean IQ scores of 70.14, 91.67, and 91.48, respectively. Although not as low as the IQs for mentally retarded children, evidence does suggest that the distribution of intelligence for emotionally disturbed and learning disabled students "reflects a skewness which places a majority of these children below the mean of the total population" (Hallahan and Kauffman 1977, 145).

Personality and adjustment problems are thought of as characteristics predominantly affecting emotionally disturbed/behaviorally disordered children and adults. Evidence suggests, however, that mentally retarded and learning disabled individuals may also experience difficulties in this area. Although not the primary characteristics of each group, personality and adjustment problems are found in the learning disabled and mentally retarded populations (Hallahan and Kauffman 1977). Gajar (1979) used a checklist to determine that the three traditional groups each scored highest on the immaturity-inadequacy factor, which again suggests similar problems in this area.

The characteristics of mildly handicapped children and adults, who have traditionally been labeled mentally retarded, learning disabled, and emotionally disturbed, appear to have many similarities. It should be noted that each group is primarily associated with one set of characteristics: mentally retarded persons with lowered intelligence levels; learning disabled students with academic achievement problems; and emotionally disturbed/behaviorally disordered children and adults with personality and adjustment problems. The key is to realize that individuals may manifest one set of characteristics more than the others, but this does not mean that they are void of the other negative traits or that these traits can be ignored. If they are present they must be dealt with by teachers and other instructional personnel. Behavior problems manifested by mentally retarded children must be considered. Visual-perception problems exhibited by mentally retarded children must be a focus of part of the instructional program. And lower than average intellectual levels, although not in the range of mental retardation, have to be remembered when developing and implementing individual education programs.

Although the traditional groupings of handicapped children and adults have similarities and differences, it must be remembered that as individuals approach the accepted ranges of normalcy, their characteristics increase in similarity (Neisworth and Greer 1975). The current discussion, therefore, is not intended to convince the reader that all traditional categories of handicapped children and adults should be collapsed into one general category because individuals are all alike. Instead, it is intended to point out that many of the children and adults served in the past under categorical labels may be more alike than different.

Instructional methodologies. In addition to etiology and characteristics, the major reason for grouping children using the traditional categorical system is to enable teachers to use the same instructional methods with similar children. The premise has been, therefore, that mentally retarded children would benefit from similar instruction, learning disabled children would benefit from similar instruction, and emotionally disturbed children would benefit from similar instruction. This premise is counter to Public Law 94-142, which requires an individualized educational program for each handicapped child. The contributers to the legislation apparently understood that every handicapped child, regardless of label, is unique and requires an individualized program. Labels, therefore, do not necessarily dictate programs. In fact, Chandler and Jones (1983, 433) stated that "in most cases the label will make little difference in the student's actual program."

Rather than classifying according to medical or psychological characteristics, educators should classify according to educational needs. For instructional purposes, Hallahan and Kauffman (1977) recommend grouping based on academic and social deficits. Therefore, children would be placed in classes because they would need a certain kind of instruction, not because of their traditional special education label. A system similar to

Similarities among handicapped children of various categories are greater than their differences.

the one used in Massachusetts appears to meet the needs of children better than systems used in other states. In Massachusetts, rather than classifying students, a continuum of services is classified (Cremins 1981).

The basic premise for advocating such a system is that children nearing normalcy are far more alike than different. And while various methods used with these children may have been called different things in the past when associated with categories of handicapped children, they all represent ways of manipulating stimulus input and consequences (Neisworth and Greer 1975). Related to labeling and instruction, the following should be noted (Marsh, Price, and Smith 1983, 9):

1. The similarities among handicapped students of various categories are greater than their differences. Characteristics associated with one condition or another overlap significantly, and materials useful for one diagnostic category are also appropriate for another. In the same vein it can be said that the differences among children labeled within one category are greater than their similarities. Characteristics are significant only as they are applied to a particular student.
2. Teaching should be based on what the student can and cannot do, on what the curricular sequence should be in response to specific individual objectives, and on what the teacher should or should not do to improve change and learning in the student.
3. Instructional methods and materials should be selected to meet the needs and characteristics of an individual learner rather than those that seem to be appropriate

for a label or certain type of group assignment deemed appropriate for children who share certain theoretical characteristics.

Definition of the Mildly Handicapped

When most professionals consider the mildly handicapped as a group, they are referring to the traditional categories that comprise the largest group of students in special education, the educable mentally retarded, learning disabled, and emotionally disturbed/behaviorally disordered. They are also referring to the borderline student, the dull normal, slow learner, dyslexic, and culturally disadvantaged. We would propose to extend the term *mildly handicapped* to encompass a broader group of students: children with visual and hearing impairments, health problems, and physical handicaps. The rationale for this is simply that any child who may be placed in and profit from instruction in a regular classroom, or a noncategorical resource room, has a mild disability. If children do not need to be excluded from the regular classroom, then they need not be considered severely handicapped. The emphasis of mildly handicapped is on the classroom environment and instructional processes that interact with the student, not on classification or prognostic characteristics.

In order to define the mildly handicapped, it is necessary to contrast this group with those classified as **severely handicapped.**

> Severely handicapped children are those who because of the intensity of their physical, mental, or emotional problems, need educational, social, psychological and medical services beyond those which are traditionally offered by regular and special education programs, in order to maximize participation in society and self-fulfillment. Such severely handicapped children may possess severe language or perceptual-cognitive deprivations and evidence a number of abnormal behaviors including failure to attend to even the most pronounced stimuli, self-mutilation, manifestations of durable and intense temper tantrums, and the absence of even the most rudimentary forms of verbal control. They may also have extremely fragile physiological conditions (U.S. Office of Education, 1975, Sec. 121.2)

Severely handicapped children, therefore, include those who are unable to benefit from traditional public school programs. Instead, they require more intensive intervention in order to achieve at their maximum levels. The majority of public school programs is not capable of meeting the needs of this group of children.

The term *mildly handicapped* refers to the large group of students who differ from nonhandicapped students in cognitive-academic, sensoriphysical, and socioemotional characteristics to such an extent that special education and related services are required, but not to the degree that segregated special class placement is necessary. These are children who violate the norms of the school in some way: behavior, academics, acquisition of standard English in spoken or written forms, motivation, and aspirations for achievement. Terms commonly used for individuals in this category include educable mentally retarded, learning disabled, emotionally disturbed/behaviorally disordered, visually impaired, hearing impaired, and physically handicapped.

Adults can also be classified as mildly handicapped. Adults appropriate for placement in this category would be those with disabilities that require special services such as rehabilitation, housing, recreation and leisure time, self-help skills, accommodation, and advocacy. Individuals in this category might only require minor accommodations, such as counseling services and reading assistance, or more extensive services, such as group home care and vocational rehabilitation. At any rate, adults with disabilities, but who can be successful in the community with some assistance, should be classified mildly handicapped. It should be noted that while many mildly handicapped adults are assimilated into society, communities, and jobs and do not require a great deal of assistance, others have problems that result in their needing specific kinds of services. Chapter 9 will discuss more of these needs and services.

Prevalence of the Mildly Handicapped

Estimating the prevalence of handicapped persons is difficult. While the numbers of these individuals are estimated by various professional and governmental groups (Ysseldyke, Algozzine and Richey 1982), it is often difficult to accurately estimate the prevalence. Reasons for this difficulty include:

- Disagreement with definitions,
- Problems with standardized assessment,
- Cultural diversity among regions, and
- Differing criteria used by different professional groups.

Since the mildly handicapped is a relatively new classification, little has been written concerning the combined prevalence of children in traditional categories of disabilities that could be reclassified as mildly handicapped. Therefore, in order to attempt to ascertain the numbers of mildly handicapped children, prevalence of traditional categories must be considered. The accepted prevalence rate of mental retardation is 3 percent. Of this group, the majority are mildly mentally retarded. Therefore, approximately 2.5 percent of the population can be estimated to be mildly mentally retarded. The United States Office of Education estimates that 3 percent of the population is learning disabled. The number of children emotionally disturbed/behaviorally disordered is more difficult to determine; however, 2 percent often appears in the literature. Therefore, approximately 7.5 percent of the school population could be classified as mildly handicapped based on the three large traditional categories. Another one percent could also be added to include those mildly disabled falling into the traditional visual, hearing, and physical disabilities groups.

This means that an estimated 8.5 percent of the school population is mildly handicapped. Miller and Davis (1982) suggest that the prevalence rate is between 4 percent and 15 percent. The United States Department of Education estimated that 9.5 percent of the school population was served in special education programs during the 1979–1980 school year (U.S. Department of Education 1980). Since mildly handicapped children should be served in public school programs, the majority of this 9.5 percent should be mildly handicapped. Therefore, the 8.5 prevalence figure appears to be a good estimate.

Obstacles to the Mildly Handicapped Category

As previously stated, collapsing some of the traditional special education categories into a large, mildly handicapped group is controversial. Many professionals, parents, and advocates are opposed to the change. They prefer to retain the traditional categories. Several obstacles threaten the trend to serve children in the mildly handicapped category. First is the issue of teacher training. If colleges and universities continue to train teachers to teach in categorical special education classrooms, these individuals may be unprepared to deal with multicategories of children. For example, teachers trained to teach emotionally disturbed children may have been taught how to use primarily behavior management techniques. While behavior management is important for all special education teachers, a knowledge of methods needed to teach children with various process deficits is also required. Teachers must be trained, therefore, to deal with more than one of the traditional categories of handicapped children.

Teacher training programs are not likely to change unless states issue noncategorical teaching certificates. Belch (1979) surveyed the fifty states and the District of Columbia and determined that eleven states had a comprehensive special education certificate and another twelve states were in the process of moving toward a noncategorical certificate. The remaining states reported no plans to issue noncategorical special education certificates.

Responding to the need for certified, noncategorical special education teachers, colleges and universities have developed noncategorical training programs. Lilly (1979) stated that noncategorical training programs are currently found in many states, and that teachers from these programs are trained to deal with academic and social problems. The implementation of a mildly handicapped teaching certificate by states, and the corresponding development of teacher training programs by colleges and universities, will solidify the trend toward classifying children and adults as mildly handicapped rather than toward using the traditional labels.

SUMMARY

In this chapter, we have presented a discussion of the definitions of traditional categories in special education. It was indicated that the reasons for special education have emerged for more social purposes than educational purposes. It was also noted that although society has gradually accorded handicapped persons more acceptance, schools have maintained a common set of standards and expectations for all students. Students are expected to abide by certain standards of conduct, to succeed academically, to develop self-motivation, and to develop facility in written and spoken English. Those who do not meet these expectations have generally been considered failures in the role expectations established by society.

Role failure has been officially labeled by the school in the form of special education categories. Although labeling has negative results, the primary purpose of the process is to establish eligibility for special services. The categories that primarily developed in special education were mental retardation, emotional disturbance, and physical disabilities, including visual and hearing disorders. Learning disabilities is the newest category, only emerging since the 1960s.

Each of the traditional categories related to mild handicaps was defined and discussed. All of the traditional categories have a large percentage of individuals who can rightly be classified as mildly handicapped. Unfortunately, the *severe* label has been routinely applied to many individuals who are now considered mildly disabled.

A great deal has been written concerning the efficacy of either maintaining the traditional labels and categories or moving toward noncategorical systems. Although many professionals continue to defend the categorical system, many of their arguments can be discounted. For example, problems with definitions, overlaps in etiologies, similarities in characteristics, and similarities in instructional methodologies all support the abandonment of the traditional, categorical system.

Finally, a definition of *mildly handicapped* was proposed. This definition focuses on the needs of students and adults for services, rather than on clinical characteristics that may not transfer into intervention programs. The new definition includes children and adults with disabilities that require services but who are not severe enough to require segregation in schools or in communities. Approximately 8.5 percent of the population is considered mildly handicapped.

Although the trend is toward classifying children and adults as mildly handicapped rather than mentally retarded, learning disabled, etc., certain barriers to this movement persist. Two primary barriers include teacher training and teacher certification. With approximately half of the fifty states currently certifying teachers in the area of the mildly handicapped, or considering such a practice, and with teacher training programs following suit by developing noncategorical training programs, these two barriers appear to have been circumvented.

REFERENCES

Algozzine, B., C. D. Mercer, and T. Countermine. The effects of labels and behavior on teacher expectations. *Exceptional Children* 44, no. 2 (1977): 131–32.

Aloia, G. F., and D. L. MacMillan. Influence of the EMR label on initial expectations of regular-classroom teachers. *American Journal of Mental Deficiency* 88, no. 3 (1983): 255–62.

Axline, V. *Play therapy.* Boston: Houghton Mifflin Co., 1947.

Belch, P. J. Toward noncategorical teacher certification in special education—Myth or reality? *Exceptional Children* 46, no. 2 (1979): 129–31.

Burdg, N. B., and S. Graham. Effects of sex and label on performance ratings, children's test scores, and examiners' verbal behavior. *American Journal of Mental Deficiency* 88, no. 4 (1984): 422–27.

Chandler, H. N., and K. Jones. Learning disabled or emotionally disturbed: Does it make any difference? *Journal of Learning Disabilities* 16, no. 7 (1983): 432–34.

Coles, G. S. The learning-disabilities test battery: Empirical and social issues. *Harvard Educational Review* 48, no. 3 (1978): 313–40.

Cremens, J. J. Larry P. and the EMR child. *Education and Training of the Mentally Retarded* 16, no. 2 (1981): 158–61.

Epstein, M. H., and D. Cullinan. Academic performance of behaviorally disordered and learning disabled pupils. *Journal of Special Education* 17, no. 3 (1983): 303–07.

Fish, B. The "one child, one drug" myth of stimulants in hyperkinesis. *Archives of General Psychiatry* 25 (1971): 193–203.

Gajar, A. Educable mentally retarded, learning disabled, emotionally disturbed: Similarities and differences. *Exceptional Children* 45, no. 6 (1979): 470–72.

Gajar, A. Characteristics across exceptional categories: EMR, LD, and ED. *Journal of Special Education* 14, no. 2 (1980): 165–73.

Gillespie, P., T. Miller, and V. Fielder. Legislative definitions: Roadblocks to effective service. *Journal of Learning Disabilities* 8 (1975): 660–66.

Grossman, H. J., ed. *Classification in mental retardation.* Washington, D.C.: American Association on Mental Deficiency, 1983.

Hallahan, D. P., and J. M. Kauffman. Labels, categories, behaviors: ED, LD, and EMR reconsidered. *Journal of Special Education* 11, no. 2 (1977): 139–48.

Kauffman, J. M. *Characteristics of children's behavior.* Columbus, Ohio: Charles E. Merrill Publishing Co., 1977.

Keogh, B. K. Classification, compliance, and confusion. *Journal of Learning Disabilities* 16, no. 1 (1983): 25.

Kirk, S. A. *Educating exceptional children.* Boston: Houghton Mifflin, 1972.
Kirk, S. A., and J. C. Chalfant. *Academic and developmental learning disabilities.* Denver: Love Publishing Company, 1984.
Kirk, S. A., and G. O. Johnson. *Educating the retarded child.* Boston: Houghton Mifflin, 1951.
Lilly, M. S., ed. *Children with exceptional needs: A survey of special education.* New York: Holt, Rinehart, and Winston, 1979.
Mandell, C. J., and E. Fiscus. *Understanding exceptional people.* St. Paul, Minn.: West Publishing Company, 1981.
Mann, L., C. Davis, C. Boyer, C. Metz, and B. Wolford. LD or not LD, that was the question. *Journal of Learning Disabilities* 16, no. 1 (1983): 14–17.
Marsh, G. E., II, B. J. Price, and T. E. C. Smith. *Teaching mildly handicapped children: Methods and materials.* St. Louis: The C. V. Mosby Co., 1983.
Miller, T. L., and E. E. Davis. The mildly handicapped: A Rationale. In *The mildly handicapped student,* edited by T. L. Miller and E. E. Davis. New York: Grune and Stratton, 1982.
Moores, D. F. *Educating the deaf: Psychology, principles, and practices.* Boston: Houghton Mifflin Co., 1978.
Morse, W. C. The crisis or helping teacher. In *Conflict in the classroom.* 2d ed., edited by N. J. Long, W. C. Morse, and R. G. Newman. Belmont, Calif.: Wadsworth, 1971.
Neisworth, J. T., and J. G. Greer. Functional similarities of learning disability and mild retardation. *Exceptional Children* 42, no. 1 (1975): 17–21.
Quay, H. C. Classifications in the treatment of delinquency and anti-social behavior. In *Issues in the classification of children,* edited by H. Hobbs. San Francisco: Jossey-Bass, 1975.
Redl, F. Strategy and techniques of the life space interview. *American Journal of Orthopsychiatry* 29 (1959): 1–18.
Reynolds, M. C., and J. W. Birch. *Teaching exceptional children in all America's schools.* Reston, Va.: The Council for Exceptional Children, 1977.
Siegel, E., and R. Gold. *Educating the learning disabled.* New York: Macmillan, 1982.
Stevens, G. D. *Taxonomy in special education for children with body disorders.* Pittsburgh: Department of Special Education and Rehabilitation, University of Pittsburgh, 1962.
Swanson, H. L., and H. R. Reinert. *Teaching strategies for children in conflict.* 2d ed. St. Louis: C. V. Mosby, 1984.
U.S. Department of Education. *To assure the free appropriate public education of all handicapped children.* Second annual report to Congress, 1980.
U.S. Office of Education. *Estimated number of handicapped children in the United States, 1974–75.* Washington, D.C.: Bureau of Education for the Handicapped, 1975.
Van Riper, C. *Speech correction: Principles and methods.* 6th ed. Englewood Cliffs, N.J.: Prentice-Hall, 1978.
Walden, E. L., and S. A. Thompson. A review of some alternative approaches to drug management of hyperactivity in children. *Journal of Learning Disabilities* 14 (1981): 213–17.
Wechsler, D. *Wechsler Preschool and Primary Scale of Intelligence.* New York: Psychological Corporation, 1967.
Wolman, B. B., J. Egan, and A. O. Ross, eds. *Handbook of treatment of mental disorders in childhood and adolescence.* Englewood Cliffs, N.J.: Prentice-Hall, 1978.
Ysseldyke, J. E., and B. Algozzine. *Critical issues in special and remedial education.* Boston: Houghton Mifflin Co., 1982.
Ysseldyke, J. E., B. Algozzine, and L. Richey. Judgment under uncertainty: How many children are handicapped? *Exceptional Children* 48, no. 6 (1982): 531–34.

Chapter Three

ETIOLOGY OF THE MILDLY HANDICAPPED

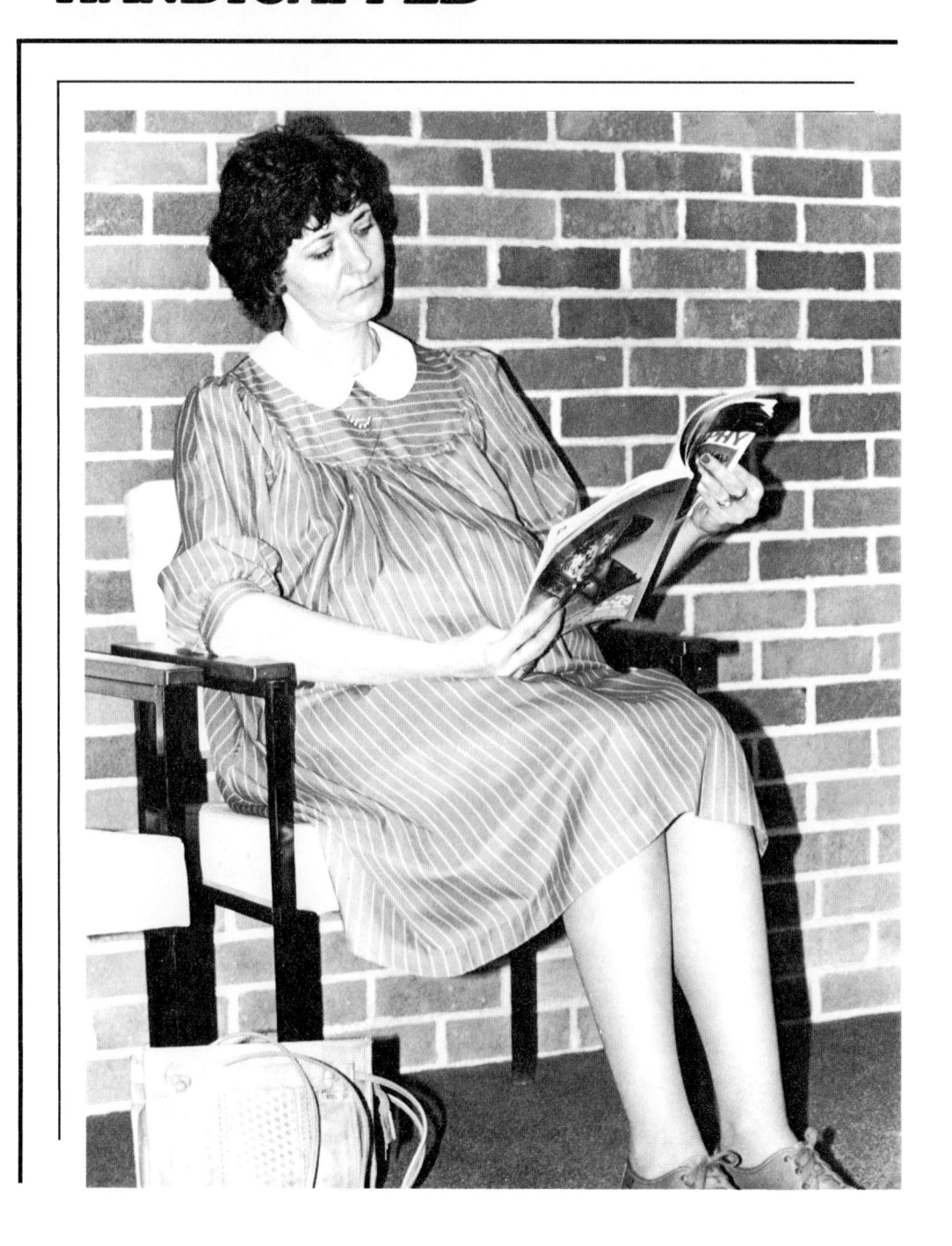

CHAPTER OUTLINE

INTRODUCTION
ORGANIZATION OF ETIOLOGICAL SYSTEMS
TRADITIONAL CLASSIFICATION SYSTEMS FOR THE ETIOLOGY OF SPECIFIC
   CATEGORIES OF HANDICAPPED CHILDREN
    Etiology of Mental Retardation
    Etiology of Learning Disabilities
    Etiology of Emotional Disturbance
ETIOLOGICAL SYSTEM FOR THE MILDLY HANDICAPPED
    Organic and Biological Factors and Mild Disabilities
    Environmental Factors and Mild Disabilities
SUMMARY

CHAPTER OBJECTIVES

After reading this chapter, you should be able to:
- Understand and describe the reasons for studying the etiology of the mildly handicapped;
- State the major causes of mental retardation;
- State the major causes of learning disabilities;
- State the major causes of emotional disturbance;
- Describe the etiological system presented for the mildly handicapped;
- Discuss the differences between organic causes of mild handicaps and environmental causes; and
- Describe the environmental causes of mild disabilities.

INTRODUCTION

The etiology of mildly handicapping conditions is studied by many professionals—medical personnel, psychologists, and educators. In some cases, accurately determining the **etiology,** or cause of a condition, is necessary for adequate educational intervention (Chaney and Eyman 1982). Determining the etiology can also:

- provide a better understanding of the child,
- enable better communication among various professionals,
- suggest a particular treatment approach,
- provide information that may facilitate referrals outside the educational system, and
- enable more accurate prognosis.

Knowing what causes a child's disability also enables teachers to more effectively counsel parents who may be experiencing a great deal of guilt because the child is disabled. By understanding the etiology, teachers may be able to lessen some of this guilt, which is often a major concern of parents (Affleck, Allen, McGrade, and McQueeney 1982), and therefore remove a barrier to effective communication between teachers and parents.

Still another reason for understanding etiology is prevention. Preventing disabilities is difficult if not impossible without an understanding of the cause. An example of the relationship between etiology and prevention is the description by Thoene, Higgins, Krieger, Schmickel, and Weiss (1981) of the Michigan Genetic Screening Program. Over a two-year period, 727 individuals were screened. The screening revealed 72 chromosomal abnormalities, 20 metabolic disorders, and 10 dysmorphic syndromes. Of these cases, 24 were found to be familial, which could cause additional disabilities in those families. Therefore, by understanding the etiology of the disabilities, several cases of disabilities may have been prevented as a result of parents opting not to have children due to the risk of disabilities.

These reasons justify the study of the etiology of the mildly handicapped by teachers and individuals training to be teachers. It must be noted, however, that a brief study of etiology does not make teachers experts in the diagnosis and determination of causes. The information should facilitate an understanding of various causes related to the mildly handicapped and therefore make teachers more knowledgeable in all aspects of the identification/intervention process. While teachers should not make etiological decisions on their own, an understanding of etiology should enable them to be more effective members of interdisciplinary teams.

ORGANIZATION OF ETIOLOGICAL SYSTEMS

Many different methods can classify and organize etiological systems for disabilities. Some authors prefer to organize the causes of a disability according to the point in the child's development when the disability occurs, such as prenatal, perinatal, and postnatal. Other authorities focus on the origin of the disability, such as organic and environmental. Still other etiological systems utilize specific causes as groupings; the American Association on Mental Deficiency (AAMD) uses this system to organize the causes of mental retardation (Grossman 1983). Table 3-1 describes some methods of classifying etiologies and the professionals who use them. No single method for organizing

Table 3-1 Organization of Etiological Systems

Handicapping Category	Major Approach	Authority
Mental Retardation	Type of Cause (10 major categories)	Grossman (1983)
Mental Retardation	Type of Cause • Genetic Disorders • Toxic agents and infectious diseases • Environmental factors	Kirk and Gallagher (1983)
Mental Retardation	Period of Development • Heredity • Development (prenatal) • Problems of birth • The growing child	Jordon (1976)
Mental Retardation	Major Type of Cause • Biology and MR • Environment and MR	Neisworth and Smith (1978)
Learning Disabilities	Period of Development • Prenatal factors • Perinatal factors • Postnatal factors	Siegel and Gold (1982)
Learning Disabilities	Major Type of Cause • Organically based • Environmentally based	Reid and Hresko (1983)
Learning Disabilities	Type of Cause • Physical conditions • Psychological conditions • Environmental factors	Kirk and Gallagher (1983)
Learning Disabilities	Type of Cause • Perinatal stress • Biochemical disturbances • Eye function	Meyen (1982)
Behavior Disorders	Major Type of Cause • Environmental factors • Biophysical factors	Kirk and Gallagher (1983)
Behavior Disorders	Major Type of Cause • Biological factors • Psychological factors • Interplay of biological and psychological	Cullinan, Epstein, and Lloyd (1983)

etiological agents has been accepted, but it is important that their presentation is organized and understandable.

TRADITIONAL CLASSIFICATION SYSTEMS FOR THE ETIOLOGY OF SPECIFIC CATEGORIES OF HANDICAPPED CHILDREN

The literature presents an extensive view of the etiology of various specific categories of handicapped persons. Since special education, rehabilitation, and psychology have been involved with these categorical groups for many years, some of the etiological classification systems are quite refined. But more newly identified groups of handicapped individuals, e.g., the learning disabled, do not have one accepted etiological system. In these less well-defined groups, the presentation of their etiology is more haphazard.

Etiology of Mental Retardation

Probably the one handicapped group with the greatest consensus of etiology is mental retardation. As the leading professional group in the field, the American Association on Mental Deficiency has publicized the etiological system that is generally accepted by most professionals. This etiological system for mental retardation is so refined because of the length of time researchers have investigated this condition. Unlike some of the newer categories of disabilities, mental retardation has been investigated for many years, giving professionals extensive opportunities to develop and refine etiological systems.

The AAMD etiological system breaks down the causes of mental retardation into ten major categories with specific causes appropriately located within each major grouping. Figure 3-1 depicts the ten categories and the major conditions under each. It should be noted that many of these causes lead to moderate to profound mental retardation.

Infections and Intoxications. This first category includes infections such as rubella and syphillis that affect fetal development, as well as postnatal infections such as encephalitis and meningitis. Conditions included in the intoxicant group include lead poisoning, prescribed and over-the-counter drugs, illegal drugs, and environmental pollutants. Intoxicants can affect the child prenatally or postnatally.

Trauma or Physical Agent. Included in this category are physical injuries to the fetus, physical injuries to the child during delivery, and physical postnatal injury. Anoxia, or lack of oxygen pre-, peri-, or postnatally, is also included.

Metabolism or Nutrition. Congenital disorders of metabolism, such as phenylketonuria, galactosemia, Tay Sach's disease, and hypoglycemia, are included as metabolic disorders that can lead to mental retardation. Nutrition, either prenatally or postnatally, is also included. Often intervention with specific diets can reduce or eliminate the effects of these conditions.

Gross Brain Disease. These conditions, which develop postnatally, include neurofibromatosis, tuberous sclerosis, tumors, and Huntington disease. The etiology of the conditions is either unknown or uncertain, and negative consequences are often progressive.

Unknown Prenatal Influence. These are conditions that exist prior to birth and have no known cause. Included are anencephaly, when the brain is totally or partially absent; microcephalus, when the cranial cavity is too small; macrocephalus, when the cranial cavity is too large; and hydrocephalus, when cerebrospinal fluid collects in the ventricles of the brain. In the case of hydrocephalus, a shunt procedure can minimize the resulting retardation.

Chromosomal Abnormalities. There are many chromosomal abnormalities. Every cell in the human body, with the exception of eggs and sperm, has twenty-three pairs of

INFECTIONS AND INTOXICATIONS
Prenatal infection
Postnatal cerebral infection
Intoxication

TRAUMA OR PHYSICAL AGENT
Prenatal injury
Mechanical injury at birth
Perinatal hypoxia
Postnatal hypoxia
Postnatal injury

METABOLISM OR NUTRITION
Neuronal lipid storage diseases
Carbohydrate disorders
Amino acid disorders
Other and unspecified disorders of metabolism
Mineral disorders
Endocrine disorders
Nutritional disorders
Other (unspecified)
Other (specified)

GROSS BRAIN DISEASE
Neurocutaneous dysplasia
Tumors
Cerebral white matter, degenerative
Specific fiber tracts of neural groups, degenerative
Cerebrovascular system
Other (unspecified)
Other (specified)

UNKNOWN PRENATAL INFLUENCE
Cerebral malformation
Craniofacial anomaly
Status dysraphicus
Hydrocephalus, congenital
Hydranencephaly
Multiple malformations (specified)
Single umbilical artery
Other (unspecified)
Other (specified)

CHROMOSOMAL ANOMALIES
Down Syndrome
Patau Syndrome
Edwards Syndrome
Autosomal deletion syndromes
Balanced autosomal translocation in normal individual
Other conditions due to autosomal anomalies
Gondal dysgenesis
Klinefelter Syndrome
Other conditions due to sex chromosome anomalies
Conditions due to anomaly of unspecified chromosome

OTHER CONDITIONS ORIGINATING IN THE PERINATAL PERIOD
Disorders relating to short gestation and unspecified low birthweight
Slow fetal growth and fetal malnutrition
Disorders relating to long gestation and high birthweight
Maternal nutritional disorders
Other (unspecified)
Other (specified)

FOLLOWING PSYCHIATRIC DISORDER
Psychosis
Other Psychiatric disorder

ENVIRONMENTAL INFLUENCES
Psychosocial disadvantage
Sensory deprivation
Other (unspecified)
Other (specified)

OTHER CONDITIONS
Defects of special senses (specified)

Figure 3-1. AAMD Classification of Etiology of Mental Retardation (Grossman 1983)

Perceptual-motor experiences are important in the development of young children and infants.

chromosomes or a total of forty-six chromosomes. Too few, too many, or **aberrations** to chromosomes can cause mental retardation and other disabilities. The abnormality that is frequently reported in the literature is Down's Syndrome, which results from an extra number 21 chromosome. Other conditions, although less prevalent, include Cri du Chat Syndrome, Klinefelter Syndrome, and Turner Syndrome.

Other Conditions Originating in the Prenatal Period. Included in this category are such conditions as prematurity, low birth weight, and postmaturity. Although they frequently do not lead to disabilities, these factors increase the risk of disabilities.

Table 3-2 **Etiology of Learning Disabilities**

Category	Conditions
I. Inadequate learning environments without organic problems	1. Poor teaching 2. Poor curricula 3. Poor physical conditions 4. Poor parental/professional attitudes 5. Family disorganization 6. Emotional disturbance/social maladjustment
II. Minor organic difficulties compounded by environment	1. Maturational lags 2. Vitamin deficiencies 3. Allergic reactions 4. Sugar or food additives
III. Major organic problems	1. Organic brain damage 2. Brain injury 3. Neurological handicaps 4. Central processing disorders

Source: Mandell and Fiscus 1981, 328–29.

Following Psychiatric Disorder. This category is related to individuals whose retardation follows a psychiatric disorder when any sign of cerebral damage is no longer present.

Environmental Influences. Individuals with mental retardation resulting from adverse environmental conditions are included in this group. Included are situations where other family members are mentally retarded or child-parent interactions are atypical.

Other Conditions. This category includes situations where the retardation results from sensory deficits and cases where the cause is unknown—no known physical or structural defects, no negative environmental conditions, and no psychosocial factors.

Etiology of Learning Disabilities

Unlike mental retardation, which has many known, specific etiological factors, learning disabilities does not offer such a well-defined set of causes. In fact, considerable disagreement exists over the causes of this condition. Mandell and Fiscus (1981) describe three general categories of causes of learning disabilities. These include (1) inadequate learning environments without organic problems, (2) minor organic problems that are compounded by poor environments, and (3) major organic problems that affect learning despite an adequate environment. Table 3-2 describes the various factors related to each of these major general categories.

The causes of learning disabilities are divided into two major classes by Reid and Hresko (1981). These include **organically based causes** reflecting inadequate neurological functions, and **environmentally based causes** resulting from poor or negative environmental factors.

Although professionals disagree on the causes of learning disabilities, the one cause most frequently hypothesized is **brain damage** or minimal brain damage (Kirk and Chalfant 1984). The relationship between brain damage and learning problems was emphasized by Strauss and Lehtinen in 1947 when learning disabilities was in the early stages of development as a recognized category of disabilities. Later, as a result of some negative reactions to this term, *minimal brain damage* was used to describe children with learning and behavior problems who did not fit the mental retardation diagnosis. This shift in terminology and a search for a cause occurred in the 1960s. It was promoted by Clements, the director of Task Force I—a federal effort to investigate learning disabilities (Mercer 1983). Professionals selected the LD label because they were identifying children with obvious learning problems but without apparent mental retardation and emotional disturbance. Therefore, while brain damage was suspect, evidence was too limited to use the term *brain damaged*. The phrase **minimal brain dysfunction** became popular because it suggested brain damage but emphasized the functional result of such damage (Smith 1983).

In attempting to determine the relationships between learning disabilities and brain injury, many researchers have investigated the presence of electroencephalogram (EEG) irregularities in learning disabled children. Despite many studies, the results have ranged from finding high relationships to very low relationships (Ohlson 1978). Still other studies have determined that EEG irregularities are present in children without learning problems as often as they are present in children with learning problems (Smith 1983). Efforts to link brain injury to learning disabilities still continue; however, "despite the interest in this etiological theory, actual physiological documentation of neurological damage is often not possible" (Houck 1984, 59). The evidence is still inconclusive (Hallahan and Kauffman 1982).

Another factor difficult to confirm as affecting learning disabilities is environment. While evidence supports that children from low socioeconomic environments have more learning problems than other children, the interaction between environment and biological factors makes it difficult to isolate which factor is more related to the learning difficulties. Also, the federal definition, as well as other definitions of learning disabilities, actually excludes children from being classified as learning disabled if their disability is primarily the result of poor environment. This exclusionary provision adds to the confusion of the role of environment in learning disabilities. Factors such as environment and the presence of neurological damage only create difficulties in establishing the etiology of learning disabilities.

While the roles played by neurological damage and environmental factors are equivocal, several variables have been identified as correlating with learning disabilities. These include maturational delay of the neurological system, genetic relationships, metabolic abnormalities, and nutritional deficiencies (Houck 1984). Still others have suggested that learning disabilities result from ecological factors, the interaction between children and their environment (Mercer 1983). Regardless of the many theories, determining exact etiological factors related to learning disabilities has proven to be a difficult task. One reason is that medical technology simply has not become sophisticated enough to detect minimal brain dysfunction.

Etiology of Emotional Disturbance

As with learning disabilities, the category of emotional disturbance has a confusing set of etiologies. This results from differing opinions concerning the definition of emotional disturbance, difficulty in defining adequate mental health, disagreement over the intervention method that should be used, and the complex nature of the relationship between emotional problems and other disabilities.

Many etiological factors are associated with emotional problems. These include (1) biological factors such as temperament, disease, malnutrition, and brain trauma; (2)

HIGHLIGHT

Brain Studies Shed Light on Disorders

By Sandra Blakeslee

Psychologists and parents have struggled for decades with questions of why Johnny can't read, speak clearly, sit still, stop fighting or listen. In recent years, however, scientists have for the first time begun to discover some of the biological mechanisms that underlie learning disorders. By slicing the brain tissue of deceased dyslexic adults, looking at the brain electrical activity of children who can't sit still, and studying the family trees of children who can't read, they are beginning to shed light on what's gone awry in the brains of people with learning disorders.

What has long impeded the study of the disorders, said Frank Duffy, a neurologist at Boston Children's Hospital, is the tendency of educators to lump these people together by their test scores. While children with certain disorders may look similar to a teacher, he said, their brains can look very different to a neurologist.

The emerging view is that hundreds of different agents—genetic factors, drugs, hormones, infection, injury and so forth—can cause changes in brain structure or function that can lead to learning disorders. Thus the main research strategy today is to identify anatomical, electrical and chemical differences in the brains of those afflicted and try, for the first time, to separate the disorders into biological subgroups.

The first breakthrough came in 1979 when Albert Galaburda and Thomas Kemper, also neurologists at Children's Hospital, obtained the brain of a dyslexic man who died in an accident. By cutting the tissue into nearly 3,000 slices, they were able to identify structural abnormalities. Cells were out of place or misaligned in several regions, particularly in structures of the brain's left side known to have language function.

Five dyslexic brains have been dissected so far, Dr. Galaburda said, and all show similar patterns of abnormality. Since the structures are formed during fetal development, it appears that some disorders stem from imperfections in prenatal "hardwiring."

This view is supported by Dr. Duffy, a pioneer in the method of mapping brain electrical activity. In experiments, Dr. Duffy placed up to 32 electrodes on the heads of children diagnosed to have a similar type of reading problem. Electrical activity around each electrode was measured and then mapped.

"Essentially, we found characteristic differences in the brains of dyslexics," Dr. Duffy said. Moreover, these differences showed up in parts of the brain "that fit very well with where a neurologist would say language abnormalities are found," he said.

But there was also a surprise. The midline, or medial frontal lobe, also looked different in the dyslexic children. Since that finding, researchers have turned their attention to this portion of the brain and found it to have an important role in language and speech.

More detective work is under way in

(continued)

Education Fall Survey, New York Times, 11 November, 1984, Sec. 12.

the laboratory of George Ojemann, a professor of neurosurgery at the University of Washington. Through a technique called electrical stimulation mapping, Dr. Ojemann has found that "verbally bright" and "verbally less bright" people rely on different areas of the brain to recall things.

The verbally unskillful people do not necessarily suffer from dyslexia, Dr. Ojemann said, but the experiments "raise additional evidence that difficulties in using language are to some degree associated with different biological patterns."

Elsewhere, scientists are studying families in which disorders seem to appear generation after generation. In well over half the families in which one person has a learning problem, another family member has similar problems.

A recent study at the Institute for Behavioral Genetics in Boulder, Colo., found more than 90 percent of identical twins shared similar learning problems.

To find out exactly what is being inherited and how it is passed through families, Dr. Shelley Smith, a geneticist at the Boy's Town National Institute for Communication Disorders in Children in Omaha, has carried out genetic-linkage studies. By identifying a marker gene—say one that determines blood type—and looking to see if a learning problem is inherited along with that same marker, Dr. Smith has found that human chromosome 15 may carry a gene, or genes, associated with one subgroup of reading disorder.

Many theoreticians have turned their attention to prenatal events that might affect how the brain is "wired." During the second trimester of pregnancy, a fetal brain sends primitive neurons out from its center, through surrounding white matter, to form the outer cortex where throught, language and other higher functions reside. It is a dynamic process that involves the migration and interconnection of billions of cells.

One view of disorders is that some nerve cells only get, say, nine-tenths of the way to their destination. They stop too soon. This is clearly the pattern shown by the dyslexic brains that Dr. Galaburda has dissected. Little globs of nerve cells in the cortex are out of place and have not established normal connectivity.

Another possibility is that some nerve cells don't die off the way they are supposed to. As the fetal brain grows, neurons compete fiercely for space and, in the process, many die off before the brain is complete. Again, Dr. Galaburda has found such an abnormality in dyslexic brains. There are neurons on one side of the dyslexic brains, he said, that aren't there in normal brains.

Such anatomical differences are indisputable but deciding what caused them to happen is open for debate. Certainly maternal stress, use of drugs or injury could cause the fetal brain to malform. Also, malnourished or congenitally underweight infants have a very high rate of learning disorders.

In the view of Norman Geschwind, a neurologist at Children's Hospital, the trouble may start with the fetus itself. Before coming to that conclusion, he looked at a number of factors. Boys are much more likely to develop learning disorders than girls, and the rate is 10 times as high in extreme left-handers than in extreme right-handers. Also, left-handers have an elevated rate of immune-system disorders. Finally, the left side of the rat brain develops more slowly than the right.

What could these factors have in common? Dr. Geschwind believes it is the male hormone, testosterone. When a fetus produces excessive testosterone, he said, it has the effect of slowing growth on the left side of the brain. In this view, more boys would have the disorders because only boys produce fetal testosterone. If testosterone slows growth in the left brain, the

(continued)

right brain would tend to have more surviving neurons. Right-brained people are usually left-handed. And they are talented in art, architecture and music.

Also, testosterone inhibits the development of major structures of the immune system, hence the association with allergies and learning disorders. Also, chromosome 15 plays an important role in testosterone production and in immunity. What could be inherited, Dr. Geschwind said, is the tendency for cells in the left brain to migrate improperly. Which disorder results is a matter of which cells are involved and where they happened to end up.

The model of there being errors in fetal brain development is powerful and may one day explain many brain disorders, including autism, stuttering, schizophrenia and epilepsy. It fits the experience of many people with learning disorders who discover they never outgrow the "hardwired" problem. They learn to cope with varying degrees of success. Some learn by using other sensory pathways—listening to information, for example, instead of reading it.

It is now possible to biologically recategorize learning disorders. What was recently considered to be one language impairment, Dr. Duffy said, has been separated into five different, recognizable, clinical subtypes that involve different areas of the temporal lobe.

"Eventually if our methods work," Dr. Duffy said, "we could develop a set of descriptors which would say you are normal or impaired. If impaired, we could tell if you are most likely to be dyslexic, dyscalculic (trouble with numbers) or hyperactive. If dyslexic, which subcategory are you in? It may be possible to have a decision tree like this." Such precision would help prevent people from being misdiagnosed, he said.

family factors such as poor parent-child relationships and negative interactions between the child and mother; and (3) school factors including teachers' insensitivity, too high or too low expectations, and inconsistent discipline (Hallahan and Kauffman 1982.)

Cullinan, Epstein, and Lloyd (1983) dichotomize the etiological factors of emotional disturbance into (1) biological factors, including heredity, physical development and deviance, brain disorders, and behavior disorders; and (2) psychological factors, which include socialization, self-concept, and stress.

An emerging view is that behavior and emotional problems result from an interaction between the child and the environment. Labeled the ecological model, proponents believe that an individual's behavior is a product of many factors including relationships with peers, siblings, parents, and teachers; the physical environment; and biological and hereditary factors. The behavior results from "the interchange of an individual's unique characteristics with the environment" (Mercer 1983, 59).

Regardless of the system used to describe the causes of emotional problems, the knowledge related to etiology and emotional problems is extremely limited at this time. This inability to be more precise in determining causes has led to the many improper reasons given for emotional problems "at our current level of knowledge, there is more error than accuracy in predicting children's disorders on the basis of any of the factors known to contribute to poor emotional development." The etiology of this disability area, therefore, remains unclear. While some factors obviously have the potential of leading to emotional problems, they do not always result in disability. Also, factors that may not affect the emotional stability of the majority of individuals may create severe emotional problems for others.

ETIOLOGICAL SYSTEM FOR THE MILDLY HANDICAPPED

The remaining section of this chapter presents a system for classifying the etiological factors related to the mildly handicapped. The focus is on specific etiological factors, not on categories or labels. The system actually takes the existing etiologies for mental retardation, learning disabilities, and emotional and behavior problems and groups them in a generic approach. When investigating the causes of mental retardation, learning disabilities, and emotional and behavior disorders, it is obvious that many of the same etiological factors can be involved in each of the three disabilities. For example, **anoxia,** or lack of oxygen, can result in damage to the central nervous system. The location and extensiveness of the damage will dictate which type of disability, if any, is manifested—mental, physical, emotional, or learning. Factors that cause anoxia, therefore, may be related to several disabilities.

The proposed etiological system for the mildly handicapped is divided into two major groups: (1) organic and biologically based causes and (2) environmentally based causes. In some instances these two categories overlap. For example, malnutrition would be considered an environmental cause; however, the effect of malnutrition on brain development is what causes the disability to occur. Malnutrition then is related to environmental causes because it is controlled by the environment, but it is also related to organic causes because it affects brain tissue.

Factors that cause mild handicaps can occur either prenatally, perinatally, or postnatally. In a study of the etiology of mental retardation, Chaney and Eyman (1982) determined that **prenatal factors** are the most numerous, followed by **perinatal** and **postnatal** in that order.

Regardless of the difficulties in developing an etiological system, the major factors that lead to mild disabilities are categorized into either the organic and biological group or environmental group. Table 3-3 provides an overview of the classification system. A discussion of the various factors within these categories follows.

Organic and Biological Factors and Mild Disabilities

Many factors classified as organic or biological in nature can lead to mild handicapping conditions. Basically, these are conditions that indicate suboptimal neurological functioning (Reid and Hresko 1981) or that are related to other biological functioning. The following section details some of the biological and organic conditions related to mild disabilities.

Infections. Several infections can cause mild handicaps. These may occur prenatally, perinatally, or postnatally. While most maternal infections do not cause harm to the fetus (Siegel and Gold 1982), some have the potential to cause problems. The prenatal infection that has probably received the greatest amount of attention is **rubella,** commonly referred to as German measles. While not always leading to fetal problems, if a pregnant woman contracts this infection during the first trimester of pregnancy, the risks of mental retardation, deafness, heart disease, visual problems, and growth irregularities are increased significantly (Siegel and Gold 1982). The first trimester

Table 3-3	Etiology of the Mildly Handicapped

1.0 Organic and Biological
  1.1 Infections
  1.2 Drugs and poisons
  1.3 Physical injury
  1.4 Reduced oxygen
  1.5 Biochemical disorders
  1.6 Chromosomal aberrations
  1.7 Hereditary
  1.8 Gestational
	2.0 Environmental
	  2.1 Nutrition
	  2.2 Poverty
	  2.3 Abuse and neglect
	  2.4 Diet
	  2.5 Psychological
	  2.6 Other environmental factors

appears to be the critical period, with later onset of the condition having less severe effects on fetal development.

Congenital syphilis has also been related to mild disabilities. This results from "transplacental infection of the fetus from syphilis in the mother" (Grossman 1983, 135). Prenatal syphilis can lead to miscarriages, stillbirths, mental retardation, visual and hearing problems, and bone inflammation. If the mother with syphilis is properly treated by the eighteenth week of pregnancy, the fetus will not be affected (Robinson and Robinson 1976). Two other prenatal infections include cytomegalic inclusion disease that results from maternal infection, and toxoplasmosis, a maternal infection caused by a protozoan (Grossman 1983).

Perinatally, herpes can be a factor. While the fetus is in the uterus, it is protected from the infection; however, if the herpes of the mother is active during delivery, the child is exposed to the infection during the normal birth process. For herpes-affected women, the key is to perform a cesarean section if the herpes if active. A cesarean section prevents the child's exposure to the herpes virus and therefore reduces the danger.

Infections can also cause mild handicaps if they occur postnatally. Encephalitis and meningitis, two infections that affect the brain cells and the covering of the brain, can lead to problems. In the majority of cases, however, children suffer no long-term problems if treatment is provided for these conditions.

Drugs and poisons. Included in this category of causes are prescribed medication, over-the-counter medication, illicit drugs, and alcohol. Various poisons such as lead have also been found to have a negative effect on the developing fetus. While research has found many drugs affecting animal fetuses, no more than twenty have been related to actual defects in humans (Siegel and Gold 1982). The problem is too little information concerning the effects of drugs on the developing fetus. To be on the safe side, some obstetricians encourage extremely limited intake of any drugs during pregnancy, including aspirins.

Children born from drug addicted mothers are often born with addiction and undergo withdrawal. While potentially harmful, the long-term effects of this prenatal addiction have not been confirmed (Siegel and Gold 1982). On the other hand, the effects of alcohol on the fetus are well known. Mental retardation is present in approximately 50 percent of babies born to mothers classified as severely and chronically alcoholic. The condition of these children, labeled *fetal alcohol syndrome,* is also characterized by prenatal and postnatal growth deficiency (Umbreit and Ostrow 1980). While fetal alcohol syndrome results from heavily drinking mothers, the amount of alcohol that can safely be consumed during pregnancy has not been determined. Some obstetricians recommend none, while others indicate that moderate amounts will not have a negative effect on the fetus.

Still another factor in fetal development that could be classified as a drug is smoking. A report of the United States Surgeon General indicates that smoking by pregnant women may affect physical growth, mental growth, and behavior (Siegel and Gold 1982). Two socially accepted practices, drinking and smoking, may therefore have negative effects on the developing fetus. The relationship between how much alcohol consumption or daily smoking is safe and what levels are dangerous has not been determined.

Another factor included as a poison is radiation. While the effects of low levels of radiation on the fetus are still unknown, the effects of large doses, such as those experienced by women during the atomic bombings in Japan, are well documented. Babies whose mothers were exposed to these high levels of radiation during pregnancy were often microcephalic with high rates of mental retardation. While the effects of low-level radiation are equivocal, it is best to avoid dental and chest x-rays and other minimal exposure during pregnancy unless medical reasons require such risks (Neisworth and Smith 1978).

Today our society is experiencing frequent chemical spills, identification of chemical dumps, and other forms of environmental pollution. Other toxins found in the environment that may cause problems for some individuals include coal, petroleum, natural gas derivatives (Mayron 1978), and lead. The effects of these poisons are not known. Additional research should show whether or not these elements are etiological factors in mild disabilities.

Physical injury. Any physical injury to the brain can lead to cognitive and behavior deficits. Physical injury could result from problems during delivery, such as labor difficulties resulting from malposition (Grossman 1983) or high forceps delivery. These factors, however, have been shown to be rare (Robinson and Robinson 1976). Head injuries that occur postnatally include falls, automobile accidents, sporting accidents, or physically abusive parents (Siegel and Gold 1982). Any of these occurrences that result in damage to brain tissue could lead to cognitive and learning problems.

Reduced oxygen supply. Anytime the brain is deprived of oxygen for an extended period of time, brain cells die. This can occur during fetal development, perinatally, or after birth. A prenatal cause of anoxia is umbilical strangulation, when the umbilical cord becomes wrapped around the neck of the fetus. Anoxia, however, is more likely to occur during delivery or postnatally. Perinatal causes of anoxia include premature placental separation and umbilical cord collapse. Postnatally, several factors could lead to a reduced oxygen supply to the brain, including drowning, strangulation, cardiac arrest, electrocution, and carbon monoxide poisoning. All conditions that reduce the oxygen supply to the brain do not lead to mild disabilities. The critical element in reduced oxygen supply is the length of deprivation (Neisworth and Smith 1978).

Biomedical disorders. Included in the category of biomedical disorders are metabolic disorders and other biochemical imbalances. Metabolic disorders are inborn errors of metabolism that result in faulty metabolism of certain substances and often in the collection of nonmetabolized substances on brain tissue.

Although biomedical disorders often lead to severe disabilities, they can affect children minimally. For example, **phenylketonuria,** more commonly referred to as

> **HIGHLIGHT**
>
> ## Study Released On Baby Brain Disorders
>
> By Warren E. Leary
> AP Science Writer
>
> Washington (AP)—It may be hard for parents to accept, but they cannot blame their doctor or themselves when their newborn child suffers brain disorders, says an expert panel.
>
> Most cases of babies born with neurological defects cannot be blamed on a specific cause or negligence by the parents or the doctors involved, a National Institutes of Health panel said Monday.
>
> In releasing a 450-page report on brain disorders in the newborn, the group said doctors rarely can isolate a specific event in the development of a fetus that is solely responsible for a brain defect.
>
> While a number of events can be factors, such as trauma or decreased oxygen supply during labor, most children who suffer these problems at birth end up being normal and healthy.
>
> Dr. John M. Freeman of Johns Hopkins Hospital, chairman of the panel, told a news briefing that people increasingly want to know the cause of defects in their newborns, sometimes in order to attach blame.
>
> "Our report indicates that for the vast majority of infants with these disorders, we cannot find a cause," Freeman said, "Therefore, we certainly cannot fix blame."
>
> The report is not a "whitewash" to exonerate obstetricians who are increasingly being sued by parents of youngsters with brain disorders, he said.
>
> "There is less tolerance for imperfection, but people have to understand that there is a lot we don't know," Freeman said in an interview. "As people limit the size of their families, they want the one or two children they have to be perfect babies.
>
> "That is not always possible, no matter how hard everyone tries," he continued.
>
> Northwest Arkansas Times Vol. 117 no. 297 10 April 1985

PKU, can result in severe mental retardation if not treated. The condition results from an inability to metabolize an amino acid, phenylaline. The phenylaline accumulates on the brain causing brain damage. A phenylaline-free diet can greatly minimize the effects of PKU.

Another biomedical disorder that can cause mild problems is hypoglycemia, or low blood sugar. A diet that eliminates sugar and caffein can usually control any problems that result from the condition (Siegel and Gold 1982). Other biomedical disorders such as Tay Sachs Disease, an inability to metabolize a fatty substance, ganglioside (Neisworth and Smith 1978), and mucopolysaccharidoses, which results from an accumulation and excretion of glycosaminoglycans (Horwitz 1979), lead to more severe disabilities.

Older mothers have a much greater chance of giving birth to a child with Down's Syndrome.

Chromosomal aberrations. While the normal human body contains cells with forty-six chromosomes (twenty-three pairs), several conditions can exist as a result of faulty chromosomal makeup. Many of these lead to severe disabilities but can result in only minor problems. The most common chromosomal aberration is Down's Syndrome, previously referred to as Mongolism. This condition results from an extra number 21 chromosome, and can be caused by **nondysjunction** of the number 21 chromsome pair during meiosis when sperm and eggs are formed; translocation, when a number 21 chromosome becomes attached to another chromosome pair before meiosis; and

Table 3-4 **Characteristics of Chromosomal Abnormalities**

Type	Chromosome Group Affected	Clinical Condition	Frequency
Too many	21 group	Down's syndrome—mental retardation; other anomalies, especially congenital heart disease	1 in 700
Too many	18 group	Mental retardation; many anomalies; early death (first year)	1 in 4,500
Too many	13–15 group	Severe involvement of all organ systems (especially the brain); early death (first three months)	1 in 14,500
Too many	Male sex chromosome (XYY)	Male appearance; may be tall; considerable controversy over possible social delinquency; fertile	1 in 250 to 1,000
	Female (XXY)	Male appearance; mental retardation; infertile	1 in 400 to 600
	Female (XXX)	Female appearance; termed "superfemale", usually retarded and infertile	1 in 670
Too few	Female (only one X)	Female appearance; termed "Turner's syndrome"; may be retarded; always infertile	1 in 3,500

Reprinted, by permission, from Neisworth and Smith, 1978, 123.

mosaicism, when nondysjunction occurs during mitosis following egg fertilization. Regardless of the type of Down's Syndrome, the result is an extra number 21 chromosome in most or all of the body's cells. Maternal age has been found to be associated with Down's Syndrome. While the majority of Down's Syndrome children living at home are in the moderate retardation range, some are only mildly retarded (Robinson and Robinson 1976).

Many other chromosomal aberrations can occur, including an extra number 18 chromosome, an extra chromosome in the number 13–15 pair, an extra male sex chromosome, and one too few female sex chromosomes. In addition, many chromosomal aberrations are unknown. Table 3-4 describes some of the known chromosomal abnormalities.

Heredity. The role of heredity as an etiological factor in mild handicaps is controversial. For many years, researchers have argued the "nature-nurture" controversy. Although it is obvious that the hereditary mechanism has the earliest effect on fetal development, the exact role it plays in the development of mild disabilities is unclear.

Regardless of the exact role of heredity on mild disabilities, studies have consistently found a relationship between heredity and disability. After Neisworth and Smith (1978) reviewed studies linking heredity and mental retardation, they concluded that the relationship between intelligence and heredity increases with family relatedness. In studying the effect of heredity on learning disabilities, Smith (1983) summarizes several studies that show heredity linked to learning problems. Table 3-5 summarizes these studies. Emotional problems have also been linked to heredity. Meyen (1982) acknowledges that the genetic correlation between heredity and emotional problems has long been recognized. For example, schizophrenia tends to occur more often in individuals who have relatives who manifest the condition than in individuals without such a hereditary link.

Table 3-5 **Studies Linking Learning Problems and Heredity**

Investigation	Nationality	Disorder	Shared Incidence
Hallgren (1950)	Swedish	general learning difficulty	88% shared with their family members
Critchley (1970)	European	reading	60% shared with relatives
Denckla (1973)	American	reading and spelling	88% shared with similar family histories or subtle language disorders
Ingram, Mason, & Blackburn (1970)	American	speech	more frequent in the family histories of poor readers than normal readers
Silver (1971b)	American	learning disabilities	39% shared with parents and siblings, even if the LD children's difficulties could possibly be attributed to brain trauma

From Corinne Roth Smith, Learning Disabilities: The Interaction of Learner, Task, and Setting. Copyright © 1983 by Corinne Roth Smith. Reprinted by permission of Little, Brown & Co.

Gestational Disorders. Also related to environment are gestational disorders—prematurity, postmaturity, and low birth weight or small-for-date. A problem in including these as etiological factors is that most of them are related to other problems such as twinning, poor prenatal nutrition, and maternal illnesses like toxemia, tobacco abuse, alcohol abuse, socioeconomic status, and poor prenatal health care (Seigel and Gold 1982). At any rate, gestational disorders have been linked to various learning and behavior disorders, including mental retardation (Grossman 1983), learning disabilities (Seigel and Gold 1982), and behavior problems (Cullinan et al. 1983). While most premature, postmature, and low birth weight babies grow up normally and do not develop disabling conditions, gestational disorders can increase the risk of disabilities.

Environmental Factors and Mild Disabilities

In addition to the multitude of organic and biological factors that cause mild disabilities, many environmental conditions can lead to these disorders. Mayron (1978) categorizes these environmental causes as (1) anxiety, (2) malnutrition, (3) toxicity, (4) allergy, and (5) electromagnetic radiation. Other major categories could include poverty, family dynamics, and other emotional problems.

Many of the organic factors cannot be prevented, but most causes of mild disabilities associated with the environment are preventable. And those not prevented can often be remediated once the ecological relationship to the disability has been identified (Mayron 1978). From the moment of conception, environment begins to affect the developing fetus. Maternal health and nutrition during pregnancy, intake of drugs, and the emotional state of the mother are examples of environment factors that can affect fetal development. The following describes some environmental factors related to mild handicaps.

Nutrition. Of the many environmental causes of mild handicaps, nutrition is probably the most investigated—but still the least understood (Reid and Hresko 1981). Because of the interrelationship of malnutrition and other environmental variables, such as socioeconomic status, educational levels of the home, and child-rearing practices, it is very difficult to separate these factors and determine which is the most critical to the child.

The role nutrition plays in cognitive development depends on (1) age of onset, (2) duration and intensity, and (3) sociocultural conditions (Reid and Hresko 1981). The fetus must depend on the mother for nutrition. When her diet is inadequate, the developing fetus could suffer. The size of the fetus may be smaller due to maternal malnutrition, but the effects on brain development may not be as damaging. In fact, it appears that the brain is usually spared during such critical periods (Batshaw and Perret 1981), resulting in limited, if any damage from maternal malnutrition. This is due to metabolic properties that "enable the fetus to obtain proteins at the mother's expense" (Reid and Hresko 1981, 11). But other authorities believe that the number of brain cells may be reduced up to 15 to 20 percent by maternal malnutrition (Perkins 1977). The effects of maternal malnutrition on fetal brain development, therefore, are unclear.

The negative effects of malnutrition after birth have been well documented, however. The brain, unlike most of the other organs of the human body, grows extremely rapidly during the early years. At birth, the brain weighs approximately 40 percent of its adult weight, 80 percent by age three, and 90 percent by age four. Children experiencing malnutrition during the latter stages of fetal development and during the first few years of life may lose as much as 40 percent of their expected brain weights (Perkins 1977). Nutritional intake after birth, therefore, may be related to mild disabilities. Because of the frequent occurrences of malnutrition and poverty, it is often difficult to establish the cause and effect between malnutrition and mild handicaps. But authorities do agree that "those children whose nutritional status was less-than-optimal also presented a 'less-than-optimal' profile for learning" (Jani and Jani 1974–75, 152).

In one study that attempted to isolate malnutrition from other environmental factors, Richardson, Birch, and Hertzig (1973), investigated the performance of children who had suffered severe malnutrition during childhood. When compared to classmates of the same age and sex, the malnourished children performed significantly lower on the Wide Range Achievement Test, teachers' evaluations, and class grades. As a result of comparing the malnourished children to their siblings who did not have a history of malnutrition, it was concluded that extreme malnutrition "may have been an additional factor contributing to the low cognitive functioning of the index children beyond the influence of the general social, physical, and biological background" (Richardson, Birch, and Hertzig 1973, 631).

Malnutrition can result from either internal or external causes. Internal causes of malnutrition include genetic metabolic defects such as PKU, genetic vitamin dependency conditions, stress, and an inability to absorb certain nutrients found in food (Jani and Jani 1974–75). Of the external causes of malnutrition, the major cause is inappropriate nutrient intake. Reasons for this poor intake include (Jani and Jani 1974–75, 155):

- lack of knowledge of good food patterns, e.g., skipping breakfast, or other meals;
- lack of concern about quality of food intake, e.g., the overuse of high-calorie, low-nutrient density foods;
- inappropriate food habits;
- intake of interfering substances, e.g., avidin, of raw egg white; and
- lack of food due to poverty or unavailability of foodstuffs.

These reasons for inadequate nutrient intake are supported by a recent study by Wilton and Irvine (1983), who compared the nutritional intake of socioculturally mentally

Poverty is an underlying factor in many of the negative variables associated with mild disabilities.

retarded children and children of low and average socioeconomic status. The results of this study were that the retarded group "showed significantly lower intakes of protein, fat, carbohydrate, kilocalories, iron, and thiamine than both non-retarded groups and significantly lower intakes of calcium, phosphorus, retinol, and ascorbic acid than did the average SES group" (Wilton and Irvine 1983, 82).

Poverty. Along with malnutrition, poverty or low socioeconomic status are frequently found. The close relationship between these two variables often makes it difficult to determine which factor is the more critical in causing mild handicaps. Using United States Department of Agriculture statistics, Perkins (1977) pointed out that the incidence of poor diets in American families was four times greater for families with incomes under $3,000 than for those with incomes over $10,000.

Poverty is associated not only with malnutrition but also with a host of other variables that could affect cognitive and behavioral development. These include poor maternal health, inadequate prenatal care, increased levels of infant mortality, poor health, and general environmental deprivation (Jani and Jani 1974–75). Poverty, therefore, is an underlying factor in many of the negative variables associated with environment and mild disabilities. In fact, when investigating the factors associated with variance in the prevalence of mental retardation, Baroff (1982, 133) stated that "the predominant source of variation is socioeconomic: parental occupation and education."

Abuse and Neglect. While the relationship between child abuse or neglect and handicaps has long been recognized, it often has been minimized as a cause, with more emphasis being placed on heredity and neurological theories (Money 1982). But recent interest in child abuse has focused new attention on the relationship between abuse and neglect, and learning and behavior problems. Abuse includes sexual abuse and physical abuse such as beating, lacerating, burning, breaking bones, near-drowning, poisoning, and sleep depriving (Money 1982). Frisch and Rhoads (1982) categorize abuse into (1) major physical, (2) minor physical, and (3) sexual and emotional. Neglect is divided into physical and other. Regardless of the method of categorizing abusive and neglecting behaviors, data suggest a relationship between abuse or neglect and disabilities.

Rose and Hardman (1982, 115) state, "It can be expected that in almost any group of physically abused children from 20 percent to 50 percent will have significant impairment of neurological function, ranging from severe to mild brain damage." Following an investigation of eleven funded demonstration programs for child abuse and neglect, Cohn (1979) concluded that abused children often:

- did not relate to their peers,
- did not interact well with adults,
- did not deal with frustration,
- had poor self-concept development,
- lacked the ability to give and receive affection,
- had a poor attention span, and
- showed other characteristics of general unhappiness.

Although the study did not find a general dysfunctional area, "deficits in the children's cognitive, language, and motor skills appeared widespread, as revealed through standardized tests of development" (Cohn 1979, 518).

To confirm the relationship between abuse and disabilities, Frisch and Rhoads (1982) altered the methodology of previous research and cross-checked the children referred to a learning clinic with those served by the regional child abuse center. Results indicated that learning-problem children on record at the abuse center numbered three-and-a-half times more than those that would be expected from the general population. The study indeed confirmed previous research supporting the relationship between abuse/neglect and mild disabilities.

Why some parents abuse their children has long been a mystery. Research reveals that abusive parents are more likely to have been abused children than parents who do not abuse their children. Other studies conclude that stress is related to child abuse. In a study by Egeland, Breitenbucher, and Rosenberg (1980), the role of stress and abuse was investigated. Results indicated that while most parents who suffer significant stress do not abuse their children, those who were abusive were also anxious and aggressive, interacted poorly with their children, and lacked a firm awareness and understanding of the problems experienced in parenting. Thus, the likelihood of abuse is affected by parental characteristics, child characteristics, and the social ecology (Frodi 1981).

Diet. In addition to developing fetuses whose mothers may be malnourished and children whose intake of various foods is inadequate and who lack the ability to utilize foods properly, some children simply do not ingest the appropriate food. Since both children and adults have nutritional requirements, it should not be surprising to link inadequate nutrition with certain behavior disorders (Cullinan, Epstein, and Lloyd 1983) and cognitive deficits. But the exact relationship between inadequacies of certain nutrients and these disorders is unclear.

Although equivocal, some research results indicate that certain vitamin deficiencies may be related to cognitive and behavior problems (Cullinan et al. 1983; Mercer 1983).

Table 3-6   Foods not Included in Feingold's Diet

Foods with Salicylates	Foods with Additives
tomatoes	luncheon meats
tomato products	hot dogs
pickles	margarine
apples	most butters
oranges	mayonnaise
peaches	mustard
plums	some commercial soups
prunes	manufactured candy
cherries	soft drinks
blackberries	colored cheeses
strawberries	cocoa
grapes	most manufactured ice cream
raisins	fish sticks
	powered puddings
	flavored yogurt
	jello
	cereals with artificial flavors
	toothpastes and powders
	most pediatric medications and vitamins

Source: D. Divoky 1978.

Those suggesting this etiological factor often recommend megavitamins. The success of using large doses of vitamins to treat learning and behavior problems, however, has not been substantiated. Such treatment represents state of the art, not scientific data (Silver 1975).

Still another focus on diet and learning and behavior problems is allergies. Allergies are abnormal responses to something to which most other individuals respond normally. Abnormal responses may result from such substances as food, chemicals, or inhalants. While the prevalence of allergies is not known, it has been estimated that as many as 60 to 80 percent of the people in this country have some allergic reactions to some food (Mayron 1979).

The individual most often identified with relating food allergies to behavior and learning problems was Feingold (1976). He believed that food additives and natural substances called salicylates were the primary causes of learning and behavior problems in children. The recommended therapy was to keep these children on a special diet, called the Kaiser-Permanente (K-P) Diet. This diet eliminates salicylates and substances with certain additives from the diets of these children. Table 3-6 lists foods included in these categories.

Feingold arrived at his recommendations based on his beliefs that hyperactivity and learning disabilities have increased rapidly during the past years as a result of food additives, the most common being synthetic colors and flavors. Children allergic to these additives can react in several different ways, some of which are listed in table 3-7. The K-P diet removes these additives and negates any adverse reaction (Feingold 1976), so hyperactivity and learning disabilities are reduced. Implementing the K-P diet "represents a radical change in how the child and perhaps the whole family will eat" (Cullinan et al. 1983, 282). Although the K-P diet is used by many families, recent studies by Spring and Sandoval have concluded that the K-P diet may help only a very

Table 3-7 Adverse Reactions Induced by Flavors and Colors

1. Respiratory
    Rhinitis
    Nasal polyps
    Cough
    Laryngeal edema
    Hoarseness (laryngeal nodes)
    Asthma
2. Skin
    Pruritus
    Dermatographia
    Localized skin lesions
    Urticaria
    Angioedema
3. Gastrointestinal
    Macroglossia
    Flatulence and pyrosis
    Constipation
    Buccal chancres
4. Neurological symptoms
    Headaches
    Behavioral disturbances
5. Skeletal system
    Arthralgia with edema

Reprinted, by permission, from B. F. Feingold 1976, 553.

small number of children experiencing hyperactivity and learning disabilities. In drawing this conclusion, these two authors suggested a moratorium on "further public advocacy of the Feingold hypothesis" (Spring and Sandoval 1976, 568). Some of the reasons for suspecting the diet are that the syndrome supposedly being treated occurs in many more boys than girls and that it is often manifested by only one member of a family (Silver 1975). Regardless of these concerns, and others expressed by professionals, the use of the K-P diet will likely continue because many parents and teachers report that children with learning and behavior problems have often benefited from the diet (Mayron 1979).

Other diet deficiencies have also been linked with learning and/or behavior problems. These include protein deprivation, zinc deficiency, magnesium deficiency, and low calcium levels (Mayron 1978). Although many professionals tie learning and behavior problems to these deficiencies, to date only limited reports have substantiated these relationships (Silver 1975).

Electromagnetic radiation. Although not well understood, evidence does link radiation from fluorescent lights and televisions to learning and behavior problems. After reviewing literature related to these factors, Mayron stated that "current knowledge implicates electromagnetic radiation in the radio frequency wavelengths as a cause of hyperactivity and perhaps lower academic achievement" (Mayron 1979, 502).

What must be emphasized is that many practices associated with suspected causes of learning and behavior disorders are unsubstantiated. The Feingold K-P diet is an excellent example. While research does not support the K-P diet as having a positive effect on learning and behavior problems in children, many parents try it anyway. The same can be said for other dietary interventions, hair analysis to determine trace elements, and exotic "cures" for children's problems. Professionals cannot tell parents not to try some of these remedies but they do have the responsibility to give parents the facts. Encouraging families to grope for cure-alls that have not been confirmed can only lead to additional problems and greater stress for the family.

Professionals—teachers, educational examiners, therapists, and administrators—must keep abreast of current research on these topics and be prepared to provide parents with complete, up-to-date materials and information. If parents are determined to try some unproven method, professionals should only provide accurate information and their best professional advice. The ultimate decision will be the parents'.

Psychological factors. The overall category of psychological factors can also lead to mild disabilities. Many authors describing the etiology of categorical groups have noted the relationship between psychological factors and disabilities. For example, Grossman (1983) includes a category of "following psychiatric disorder" as a cause for mental retardation. Other causes of emotional problems include family and school factors, self-concept, and economic disadvantage (Cullinan et al. 1983; Hallahan and Kauffman 1982). And, in describing the etiology of learning disabilities, family problems, emotional problems, and stress are also included (Mandell and Fiscus 1981; Reid and Hresko 1981).

Family Factors. Several factors within the family are related to disabilities. These include child-rearing practices, abuse, and maladjusted behavior learned from parents (Cullinan et al. 1983). While these can create learning and behavior problems in children, they are often temporary. The problems caused can be reversible if family factors change, if the child is no longer in the family environment, or if time has elapsed since the negative situations.

Child rearing is an obviously complex process. Unfortunately, of all the behaviors learned, how to raise children is not included. Individuals tend to learn how to be parents "on-the-job" (March and Price 1980). This unfortunate fact often leads to parenting skills that are less than optimal. Some of the many factors included in child rearing are depicted in figure 3-2. The complexity of the interrelationships among these factors is extensive.

Another family factor related to problems in children is premature separation from parents. While this may occur as a result of the death of a parent, or being given up for adoption, probably the major reason for premature separation from parents in this country is divorce. The current divorce rate in the United States is very high, causing a problem of major proportions.

Families also influence child development through role modeling. Studies have revealed that children tend to develop many of the same kinds of behavior patterns as those of their parents. This may reflect hereditary factors, or it may be the direct result of modeling the behavior of parents. Among the characteristics manifested in children and similar to those found in parents are criminal behavior, aggressive and abusive language, and phobic (Cullinan et al. 1983). This could lead to the conclusion that children with learning and/or behavior problems are also found in families where one or more other family members have the same disability.

Schools can also contribute to behavioral and learning problems. Often teachers are intolerant, stress overachievement, do not understand or want to understand a child's problems, and are biased against some children. These behaviors can lead to problems for certain students. While schools can add to an already disturbed child's condition, they can also contribute to the initial development of problems. This can occur as a result of the following behaviors (Hallahan and Kauffman 1982):

- teachers' insensitivity to individuality,
- teachers' requiring conformity to unnecessary rules and routines,
- too high or too low expectations,
- too lax, too rigid, or inconsistent disciplinary practices,
- communicating to the child his or her inadequacies, and
- reinforcement of inappropriate behaviors.

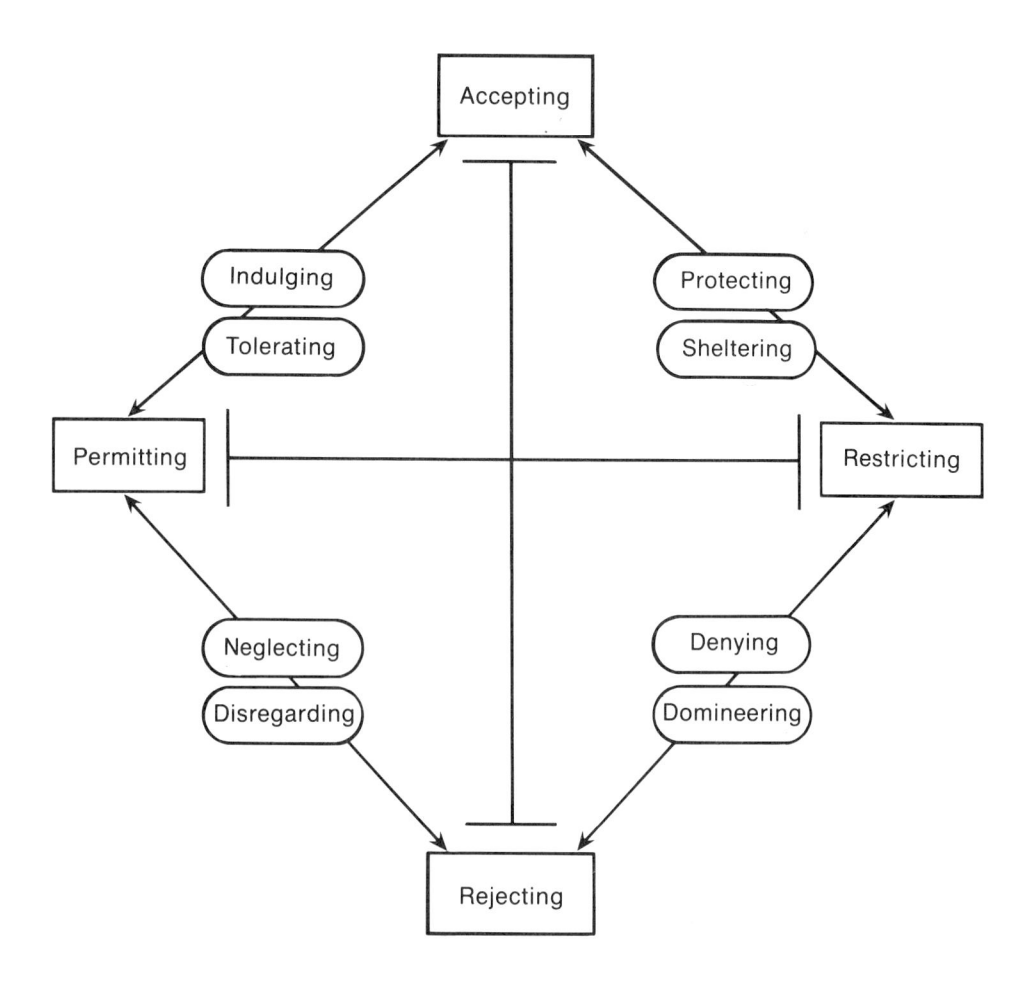

Figure 3-2 Factors included in child rearing. Reprinted, by permission, from Cullinan et al. 1983, 53.

The effects of the school environment on children have become more critical since the mainstreaming movement. Regular classroom teachers with negative attitudes toward mainstreamed handicapped children are likely to compound adjustment problems of these children by rejecting them and discriminating against them in a variety of ways. By doing nothing more than adding to a child's already negative self-concept, teachers can increase children's behavior and academic problems.

Self-concept. Most studies that investigate the self-concepts of disabled children have concluded that this group of children has more negative self-concepts than nonhandicapped children. The by-products of this negative self-attitude are often school failure and behavioral problems. However, no conclusive evidence indicates whether the behavioral/learning problems cause the negative self-concepts, or whether the negative self-concepts cause the behavior/learning problems (Cullinan et al. 1983). A complex relationship probably exists between mild disabilities and self-concept, where both variables initiate and reinforce the other.

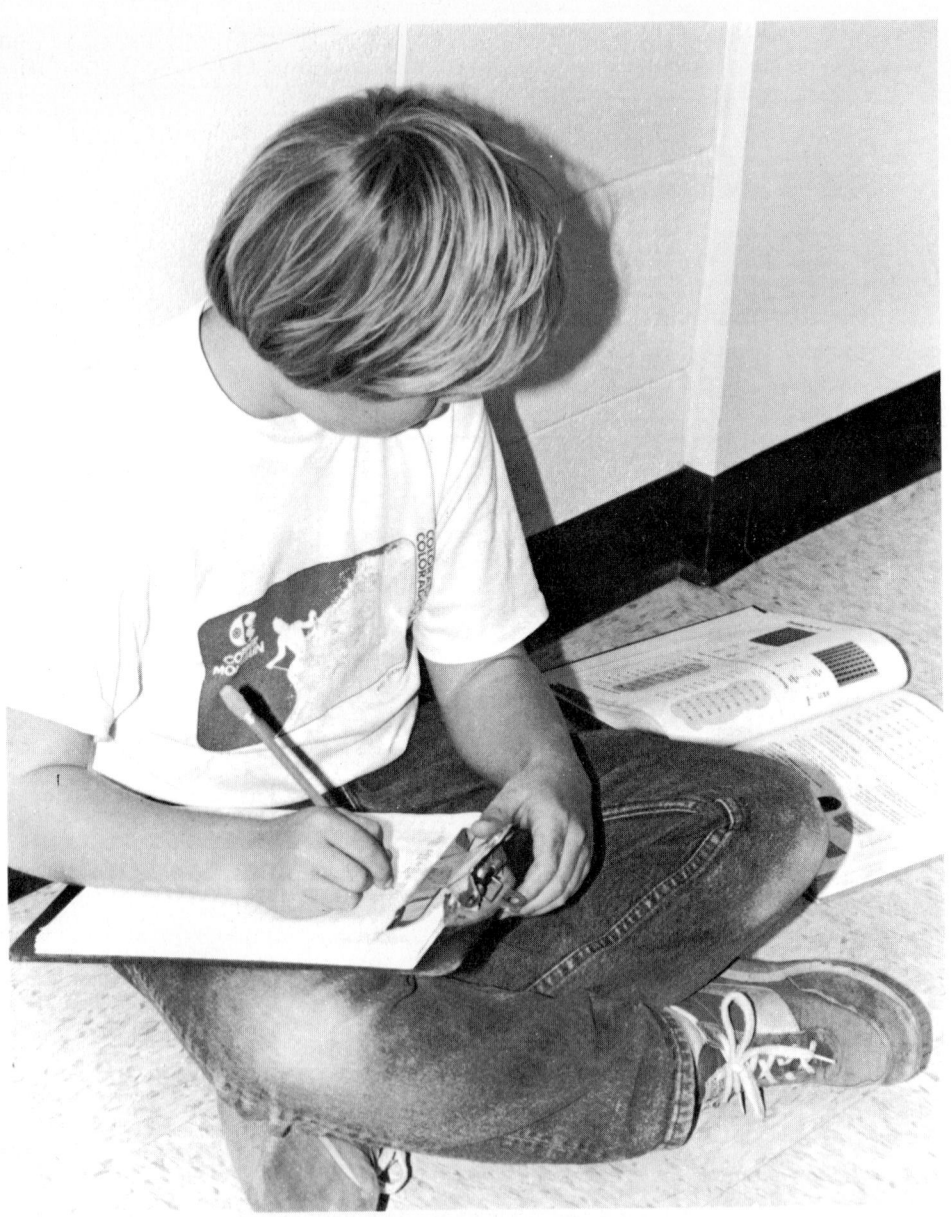

Expectations of teachers may contribute to learning problems in children and adolescents.

Stress, depression and anxiety. Three factors often associated with learning and behavior problems are stress, depression, and anxiety. Similar to the relationship between self-concept and problems, the relationship between these psychological factors and mild disabilities is unclear. While most would agree that learning and behavior problems can lead to these conditions, it is unclear how these factors cause learning and behavior problems.

Stress is either the "events that activate (and often overwhelm) the individual's coping resources, or the physical, social, or psychological disruptions that result"

(Cullinan et al. 1983, 58). While the exact relationship between stress, and learning and behavior problems is not understood, it has been pointed out that stress can lead to problems in thinking, confusion, and even depression (Cullinan et al. 1983).

Depression has also been linked to learning and behavior problems. In a study that investigated the relationship between depression and learning problems, Cullinan, Epstein, and Lloyd (1983) concluded that:

- incidence of depression in children is greater than previously reported;
- aggressive behavior is the primary reason depressed children are referred for special help;
- depressed children are often misdiagnosed as learning disabled;
- depressed children manifest learning problems as a result of lessened energy and attention; and
- segregating depressed children into classes for the learning disabled may increase negative self-concepts and result in deeper depression.

Anxiety, which often results from pressure, can lead to behavioral changes, including hyperactivity and lessened learning receptivity (Mayron 1978). Therefore, like stress and depression, anxiety may be either the result or the cause of a disability.

Other environmental causes. In addition to the factors discussed, other environmentally-related causes include the following:

1. lack of environmental stimulation (Reid and Hresko 1981; (Grossman 1983),
2. temperament (Cullinan et al. 1983; Ramey and Brownlee 1981; Hallahan and Kauffman 1982),
3. stability of the home (Ramey and Brownlee 1981),
4. mother's attitudes (Ramey and Brownlee 1981),
5. fluorescent lighting (Ott 1976; Mayron 1978), and
6. insufficient early perceptual motor experience (Ohlson 1978).

While these environmentally based factors can lead to mild handicaps in some children, they do not always result in negative manifestations. Many children grow up in poor homes with abusive parents and lack proper nutrition, yet they do not suffer negative effects. Others routinely ingest diets deficient in proteins, vitamins, and trace elements, yet suffer no noticeable side effects. Therefore, although environmental factors can cause mild handicaps in some individuals, they produce no ill effects in others. In addition to these environmental causes, many other ecological factors have the potential to cause disabilities—many of which are still unknown.

SUMMARY

This chapter presented an etiology system for the mildly handicapped. The initial section of the chapter focused on the purposes for studying the etiology of mild disabilities. While some professionals feel it is a waste of time for educators to study etiology, a teacher's understanding of the etiology of the mildly handicapped can be very beneficial in many ways, including the prevention of future cases of the disability and the determination of teaching techniques.

The next section of the chapter dealt with etiological systems for categories of handicapped persons, including the mentally retarded, learning disabled, and emotionally disturbed. These three groups are the primary types of individuals included in the noncategorical, mildly handicapped group. The methods of organizing etiologies include (1) when the disability occurs, (2) whether the disability is primarily the result of organic or environmental factors, and (3) which type is the causative factor.

The final section of the chapter presented an etiological system for the mildly handicapped. This system is based on the dichotomy of causes resulting from organic and biological factors and the environment. Major causes described in the organic and biological group included infections, drugs and poisons, physical injury, lack of oxygen, heredity and chromosomal abnormalities, biochemical disorders, and gestational irregularities. In the environmental area, specific etiological factors included psychological factors, nutrition, child abuse and neglect, poverty, and diet.

Finally, the role of heredity and environment as causes was discussed. While a controversy for the past several years concerns the "nature/nurture" issue, these two groups probably do interact in most conditions. The etiology of mild handicaps is simply too complex to state unequivocably that either heredity or environment is the etiological factor most often involved.

REFERENCES

Affleck, G., D. Allen, B. J. McGrade, and M. McQueeney. Maternal causal attributions at hospital discharge of high-risk infants. *American Journal of Mental Deficiency* 86, no. 6 (1982): 575–80.

Baroff, G. S. Predicting the prevalence of mental retardation in individual catchment areas. *Mental Retardation* 20, no. 3 (1982): 133–35.

Batshaw, M. L., and Y. M. Perret. *Children with handicaps: A medical primer.* Baltimore: Brookes Publishing Company, 1981.

Chaney, R. H. and R. K. Eyman. Etiology of mental retardation: Clinical vs. neuroanatomic diagnosis. *Mental Retardation* 20, no. 3 (1982): 123–127.

Cohn, A. H. Effective treatment of child abuse and neglect. *Social Work* 24 (1979): 513–19.

Cullinan, D., M. H. Epstein, and J. W. Lloyd. *Behavior disorders of children and adolescents.* Englewood Cliffs, N.J.: Prentice-Hall, 1983.

Divoky, D. Can diet cure the LD child? *Learning* (1978): 56–57.

Egeland, B., M. Breitenbucher, and D. Rosenberg. Prospective study of the significance of life stress in the etiology of child abuse. *Journal of Consulting and Clinical Psychology* 48, no. 2 (1980): 195–205.

Feingold, B. F. Hyperkinesis and learning disabilities linked to the ingestion of artificial food colors and flavors. *Journal of Learning Disabilities* 9, no. 9 (1976): 551–59.

Frisch, L. E. and F. A. Rhoads. Child abuse and neglect in children referred for learning evaluation. *Journal of Learning Disabilities* 15, no. 10 (1982): 583–86.

Frodi, A. M. Contribution of infant characteristics to child abuse. *American Journal of Mental Deficiency* 85, no. 4 (1981): 341–49.

Grossman, H. J., ed. *Classification in mental retardation.* Washington, D.C.: American Association on Mental Deficiency, 1983.

Hallahan, D. P., and J. M. Kauffman. *Exceptional children: Introduction to Special Education.* Englewood Cliffs, N.J.: Prentice-Hall, 1982.

Horwitz, A. L. The mucopolysaccharidoses: Clinical and biochemical correlations. *American Journal of Mental Deficiency* 84, no. 2 (1979): 113–23.

Houck, C. K. *Learning disabilities: Understanding concepts, characteristics, and issues.* Englewood Cliffs, N.J.: Prentice-Hall, 1984.

Jani, S. N. and L. A. Jani. Nutritional deprivation and learning disabilities—An appraisal. *Academic Therapy* 10, no. 2 (1974–75): 151–58.

Kirk, S. A. and J. C. Chalfant. *Academic and developmental learning disabilities.* Denver: Love Publishing Company, 1984.

Kirk, S. A. and J. J. Gallagher. *Educating exceptional children.* Boston, Houghton Mifflin Co., 1983.

Mandell, C. J. and E. Fiscus. *Understanding exceptional children.* St. Paul, Minn.: West Publishing Company, 1981.

Marsh. G. E., and B. J. Price. *Methods for teaching the mildly handicapped adolescent.* St. Louis: C. V. Mosby, 1980.

Mayron, L. W. Ecological factors in learning disabilities. *Journal of Learning Disabilities* 11, no. 8 (1978): 495–505.

Mayron, L. W. Allergy, learning, and behavior problems. *Journal of Learning Disabilities* 12, no. 1 (1979): 32–43.

Mercer, C. D. *Students with learning disabilities.* Columbus, Ohio: Charles E. Merrill Publishing Company, 1983.

Meyen, E. L. *Exceptional children and youth: An introduction.* Denver: Love Publishing Company, 1982.

Money, J. Child abuse: Growth failure, IQ deficit, and learning disability. *Journal of Learning Disabilities* 15, no. 10 (1982): 579–82.

Neisworth, J. T., and R. M. Smith. *Retardation: Issues, assessment, and intervention.* New York: McGraw-Hill, 1978.

Ohlson, E. L. *Identification of specific learning disabilities.* Champaign, Ill.: Research Press, 1978.

Ott, J. N. Influence of fluorescent lights in hyperactivity and learning disabilities. *Journal of Learning Disabilities* 9, no. 7 (1976): 417–22.

Perkins, S. A. Malnutrition and mental development. *Exceptional Children* 43, no. 4 (1977): 214–19.

Ramey, C. T., and J. R. Brownlee. Improving the identification of high-risk infants. *American Journal of Mental Deficiency* 85, no. 5 (1981): 504–511.

Reid, D. K., and W. P. Hresko. *A cognitive approach to learning disabilities.* New York: McGraw-Hill, 1981.

Richardson, S. A., H. G. Birch, and M. E. Hertzig. School performance of children who were severely malnourished in infancy. *American Journal of Mental Deficiency* 77, no. 5 (1973): 623–32.

Robinson, N. M., and H. B. Robinson. *The mentally retarded child.* New York: McGraw-Hill, 1976.

Rose, E., and M. L. Hardman. The abused mentally retarded child. *Education and Training of the Mentally Retarded* 16, no. 2 (1981): 114–18.

Siegel, E., and R. F. Gold. *Educating the learning disabled.* New York: Macmillan, 1982.

Silver, L. B. Acceptable and controversial approaches to treating the child with learning disabilities. *Pediatrics* 55, no. 3 (1975): 406–415.

Smith, C. R. *Learning disabilities: The interaction of learner, task, and setting.* Boston: Little, Brown & Co., 1983.

Spring, C., and J. Sandoval. Food additives and hyperkinesis: A critical evaluation of the evidence. *Journal of Learning Disabilities* 9, no. 9 (1976): 560–69.

Strauss, A. A., and L. E. Lehtinen. *Psychopathology and education of the brain-injured child.* New York: Grune and Stratton, 1947.

Thoene, J., J. Higgins, I. Krieger, R. Schmickel, and L. Weiss. Genetic screening for mental retardation in Michigan. *American Journal of Mental Deficiency* 85, no. 4 (1981): 335–40.

Umbreit, J., and L. S. Ostrow. The fetal alcohol syndrome. *Mental Retardation* 18, no. 3 (1980): 109–111.

Wilton, K. M., and J. Irvine. Nutritional intakes of socioculturally mentally retarded children vs. children of low and average socioeconomic status. *American Journal of Mental Deficiency* 88, no. 1 (1983): 79–85.

Chapter Four

ASSESSMENT OF THE MILDLY HANDICAPPED

CHAPTER OUTLINE

INTRODUCTION
PURPOSES OF ASSESSMENT
    Screening
    Identification
    Determination and Evaluation of Teaching Programs and Strategies
    Determination of Current Performance Level and Educational Need
    Decisions about Classification and Program Placement
    Development of Individual Educational Programs
CRITICISMS OF TESTING
LEGAL CONSIDERATIONS IN ASSESSMENT
    Nondiscriminatory Assessment
THE ASSESSMENT PROCESS
REQUIREMENTS FOR ADEQUATE ASSESSMENT
    Qualified Personnel
    Proper Selection and Use of Assessment Tools
CONSIDERATIONS IN ASSESSMENT
    Group versus Individual Tests
    Norm-Referenced and Criterion-Referenced Tests
    Test Environment
ASSESSMENT DOMAINS
PERSONNEL INVOLVED IN ASSESSMENT
INSTRUMENTS USED IN ASSESSMENT
    Intelligence Tests
    Achievement Tests
    Perceptual-Motor Tests
    Adaptive Behavior
    A Listing of Common Instruments
ROLE OF TEACHERS
SUMMARY

CHAPTER OBJECTIVES

After reading this chapter, you should be able to:
- Define assessment;
- List sources of assessment information;
- List and discuss the purposes of assessment;
- State the purpose of assessment;
- Describe the role of assessment in IEP development;
- List and describe criticisms of testing;
- Identify court cases that affected the development of assessment practices;
- Define nondiscriminatory assessment;
- Discuss procedures used to facilitate nondiscriminatory assessment;
- List and discuss requirements for adequate assessment;
- Define validity and reliability;
- List and describe personnel involved in assessment; and
- List and describe types of tests used in special education.

INTRODUCTION

The field of education seems to be greatly preoccupied with measuring skills, abilities, aptitudes, and interests of students at all levels. Educational testing is a multimillion dollar industry that has grown up around these practices, and it continues to grow as schools come under the scrutiny of the public, governmental agencies, and study groups. These tests are also employed to make policy decisions.

The school is constantly concerned with making judgments about student performance. This concern will increase as national examination scores become more important because state governments and local districts are holding schools more accountable for the "quality" of education. "Excellence" in education has become the slogan of the educational reform movement. Besides concerns about discipline, length of the school day, and teacher performance, the greatest concern is the "sliding" test scores in math and verbal areas on pre-college examinations. Standardized tests are relied upon heavily in our schools.

Testing and other forms of assessment are also used extensively in special education. In order to accomplish the legislative, moral, and professional mandate that mildly handicapped children are provided a free appropriate education at public expense, individual education programs must be developed for each child. This is due to the uniqueness of each individual and to the varying effects of the disability manifested. Before a disabled child can be served, he or she must be identified. Then strengths and weaknesses must be ascertained in order to develop an individual program that addresses the needs of the child. These actions cannot be completed without a comprehensive evaluation of the handicapped child. The information gained through such an evaluation can be used in the identification of a child with disabilities as well as in the development of an individual program.

Educational and psychological assessment of children with suspected or known disabilities is a prerequisite to appropriately serving these children in educational settings. Without such data, children may go unidentified, unserved, or inappropriately served. Assessment, a focus in education for many years, has a major role in special education. Without comprehensive, valid assessment information, the mandate to provide equal educational opportunities to disabled children cannot be accomplished.

Several terms used to discuss the assessment of handicapped children should be defined and clarified. **Assessment** can be defined as the process of collecting information that is used to make decisions about students (Salvia and Ysseldyke 1981). Sources of assessment information include (Salvia and Ysseldyke 1981):

- norm-referenced tests,
- criterion-referenced tests,
- observations,
- interviews,
- school records,
- medical evaluations, and
- social histories.

Assessment, therefore, is the collection of any information that might have relevance to educational decision making. It should be an ongoing process used not only to make initial decisions about children but also to determine on a regular basis changes in students or effectiveness of programs.

Testing, a term often used synonymously with assessment, is only one part of the assessment process. It "refers to the sampling of behaviors in students to obtain quantitative indices (that is, scores) of relative standings" (Salvia and Ysseldyke 1981, 135). While an important aspect of assessment, often too much emphasis is placed on the testing component. Unfortunately, many in our society and educational systems feel that tests and test scores can tell "everything-you-ever-wanted-to-know" about a particular child. Obviously, this is not the case, but this attitude does lead to many faulty conclusions. When used appropriately as one portion of assessment, test data can be invaluable; when used inappropriately, tests can be severely abused and lead to poor decisions that can very seriously affect children's lives.

Diagnosis is also a term used in the realm of assessment. Diagnosis can be defined as the effort to determine the etiology of a condition and the necessary interventions to be implemented (McLoughlin and Lewis 1981). Although necessary for some decisions, the actual etiology of a child's condition may be less important in planning and implementing the special education program than other information. When used in proper perspective, however, a diagnosis can be very helpful in the total educational program for a child.

Still another term often used regarding assessment is **evaluation.** Regulations implementing Public Law 94-142 define evaluation as:

> procedures used . . . to determine whether a child is handicapped and the nature and extent of the special education and related services that the child needs. The term means procedures used selectively with an individual child and does not include basic tests administered to or procedures used with all children in a school grade, or class. (20 U.S.C. 1415, 1415(c))

Throughout this text, the term *evaluation* will be used synonymously with assessment, as both are related to a broad gathering of information that is used to make educational decisions about handicapped children.

PURPOSES OF ASSESSMENT

Many textbooks and journal articles dealing with special education discuss the purposes of assessment. Aside from the need to document attempts to serve children and the belief that testing programs can benefit the educational process, a major purpose of assessment is to meet the requirements of federal and state laws. Public Law 94-142 and many state statutes require that schools conduct a comprehensive assessment of children before certifying their eligibility for special education services. This is the purpose that probably prompts much of the assessment done with handicapped children, but it is by far not the most important reason. Purposes of assessment that are more germane to educational services include (Taylor 1984):

1. screening and identification,
2. determination of teaching programs and strategies,
3. determination of current performance level and educational need,
4. determination of classification and placement, and
5. development of individual education programs.

Program evaluation is still another purpose of assessment. This purpose focuses on the entire special education program, or general education program, rather than on specific individuals. As related to special education, assessment is most often performed for gathering information about particular children. In the broadest terms, it is for identification, for diagnosis or eligibility, for some measure of the programs into which children and adults are placed, and for evaluation of individual progress.

Screening

Screening is a process of sorting large groups of subjects quickly, efficiently, and effectively into a separate pool of individuals with certain characteristics. In the case of special education, children are screened to find those who may have need of further investigation to determine the existence of behavioral, academic, or health disorders. Ideally, screening is a quick and inexpensive method of finding the smaller group of individuals within a population who either need additional, more intensive evaluation or who are "high risk" for manifesting disabilities. This is not likely to be a major concern at the secondary and post-secondary levels because persons with mild disabilities are usually known by then. At the elementary and preschool levels, however, screening is a very important aspect of the assessment program. Often screening efforts at these levels are the first opportunities to alert school personnel about the likelihood of a child's mild disability. Screening results do not determine that a child is handicapped—only the possibility that a handicap exists or could develop (Gearheart 1981).

Screening can be accomplished in many ways. Screening programs can emphasize formal screening instruments, such as behavior checklists, general achievement tests, or specific screening tests. The emphasis can also be on informal screening methods, such as observations by teachers and parents or an analysis of work. Regardless of the method or methods employed, screening is an integral part of the overall assessment program for a school. It is actually the first step in the assessment process for handicapped children (Taylor 1984). Comprehensive screening programs call attention to children who require more intensive assessment.

Identification

If the screening program indicates that a child has a problem, should be assessed further, or should be monitored closely because of a high risk of developing some disability, the child has been "identified." Identification based on screening information, therefore, could result in the child's being referred for additional assessment or simply monitored for various disorders. For some children, identification could actually lead to actions that may prevent disabilities. For example, children identified as "high risk" following kindergarten screening could be placed in a special first grade class designed to deal with specific developmental needs (Gearheart 1981). Such placement could even prevent future placement in special education programs.

Identification could also result in some negative actions. If teachers are aware that a child is "high risk" or has been identified as possibly having a disability, they could be biased in their interactions with the student. This could possibly cause the problem to become more pronounced. Despite such negative possibilities, the likelihood is much greater that positive actions will result from the identification process.

Determination and Evaluation of Teaching Programs and Strategies

It is very difficult to determine teaching programs and strategies for handicapped children without assessment data. It is a well-known fact that all mentally retarded children do not need the same type of instruction and may not respond to the same approach. Likewise, learning disabled children, emotionally disturbed children, and other disabled students are not likely to respond in the same ways to educational programs designed for a group or classification of handicapped individuals. All handicapped children are unique and require individual programming, so assessment data must be available for determining and evaluating teaching programs and strategies. The criticality of using assessment data for these purposes was pointed out by Smith when he stated, "To leap into suggesting an educational program before conducting as adequate a diagnosis as is needed will cause the teacher to fish around for what she supposes to be the kind of program each youngster needs, but without having proper documentation" (Smith 1974, 77).

Once programs and strategies have been identified, assessment data need to be continuously collected to verify that the child is making progress, that the program is effective. Without such ongoing verification, disabled children may spend an entire year in inappropriate programs that produce limited results. The effects of intervention plans must be monitored and evaluated to assure that handicapped children are, indeed, receiving appropriate assistance.

Just as special education teachers can use assessment data to assist in determining appropriate intervention strategies and the effectiveness of programs, regular classroom teachers can also use the data before a child is placed in special education (Taylor 1984). Evaluating educational programs, therefore, applies both before and after children are placed in special education classes.

Determination of Current Performance Level and Educational Need

Children classified as handicapped and served in special education programs must demonstrate an educational need for such services. In defining handicapped children, the regulations implementing Public Law 94-142 state that these are children whose disability results in a need for special education and related services (20 U.S.C. 1417(b)). Definitions of various handicapped children in the federal regulations consistently refer to the disability as "adversely affecting educational performance." Therefore, the child must have a need for special education before special services can be provided under Public Law 94-142. Assessment data corroborate this need. Before determining that handicapped children have a "need" for special education and related services, assessment data must provide the child's current educational performance levels. Without such data, it is very difficult to document that a need exists.

Some states have carried the federal regulations one step further and require that the disability manifested by the handicapped child result in an educational deficit, again an expression of "need." Without assessment data to indicate current functioning levels, need cannot be established and children are not eligible for special education programs.

Decisions about Classification and Program Placement

One of the major reasons for assessment is **classification.** What disability does the child manifest? The reasons for classifying handicapped children include the following:

- Classification of students is related to placement decisions.
- Classification of students facilitates communication among professionals.

- Classification meets legal requirements and enables students to be eligible for special education and related services.
- Classification of students provides data for requesting and receiving funding.

In some instances, determining the classification is easy; in others, the decision is very difficult. For example, with categorical classifications should a child be classified as mentally retarded or learning disabled when significant learning problems are manifested and the child's IQ is borderline for mental retardation? Although there is overlap, do those making the classification decision consider the bias that may result from using the "mentally retarded" label? Is the status of the child's family in the community a consideration?

Even more difficulty is often associated with classifying children by using a noncategorical or generic approach. When does a child stop being mildly handicapped and start being severely handicapped? Another dilemma often occurs when classifying children with behavioral and emotional problems. If a categorical classification is being used, is the child classified as emotionally disturbed or learning disabled, since many emotional problems result in academic problems? Although many states spell out criteria for each category, many children do not fit neatly into any *one* group. These difficult-to-classify cases require extensive assessment data to document the ultimate classification, which is somewhat subjective in many cases. Since the classification may affect the program provided, the decisions concerning classification are extremely important.

Classification of the child often affects decisions concerning placement. For example, certain educational placements might be considered appropriate for children classified as mildly handicapped or EMR, but questionable for the severely handicapped. Rarely are children classified as severely handicapped placed in resource rooms, while mildly handicapped children are most often placed in such settings. But the decision concerning where to place a child should be based on assessment data and should be made after development of the individual educational program. The particular classification of the child should not be the deciding factor. Still, in many cases, the label placed on a child is a major factor in the placement decision.

The data used to determine appropriate placement of a child can come from many sources. Knoff (1983) surveyed trainees and practitioners in special education and psychology to determine the sources of such information. Results indicated that the information rated as most important for placement decisions was obtained from classroom observations. Intelligence test results were rated only ninth out of sixteen sources. This is surprising since intelligence tests are given so much consideration in making some educational and labeling decisions. The fact that classroom observation was rated as the most important source of information is very positive. Such informal, subjective, and qualitative methods of data collection are often thought of as less important than standardized test results. In fact, observations can provide extremely useful information and the results of this study suggest that this type of data is being considered by many professionals. Table 4-1 gives the complete results from Knoff's study.

Regardless of the priority placed on various assessment information, data must be collected from a variety of sources and all relevant data must be considered. Multidisciplinary teams should keep in mind that decisions about disabled children are very critical and should be based on the best and most complete information possible. Anything less could result in inappropriate decisions that could have negative consequences for these children.

Table 4-1 Relative Order of Diagnostic Data On Importance to Final Placement Decisions

Diagnostic Data	Order	Mean Rated Importance	Standard Deviation
Classroom Observation	1	1.54	0.71
Receptive-Expressive Language	2	1.71	0.75
Interview with Child	3	1.74	0.78
Emotional Indicators	4	1.84	0.68
Social Skills Ratings	5	2.10	0.88
Visual-Motor Ability	6	2.19	0.94
Reading Grade Level	7	2.31	0.89
Math Grade Level	8	2.39	0.86
Intelligence Quotient	9	2.45	1.05
Chronological Age	10	2.75	1.11
Neurological Exam	11	2.78	1.13
Grade Retentions	12	2.90	1.11
Habitat	13	4.16	1.60
Income Level	14	4.79	1.40
Race	15	4.88	1.55
Sex	16	5.29	1.45

[a]Likert Rating Scale. —Extremely important; 2—Very Important; 3—Moderately Important; 4—Neither Important nor Unimportant; 5—Moderately Unimportant; 6—Very Unimportant; 7—Extremely Unimportant.

Reprinted, by permission, from H. M. Knoff 1983, 442.

Development of Individual Educational Programs

Public Law 94-142 requires an individual educational program (IEP) for every child served in special education programs. Certainly an important element in the development of an IEP is the utilization of assessment data. An IEP must contain the current functioning level of the child, as well as annual goals, short-term objectives, and services to be provided to assist the child in achieving the goals and objectives. Without adequate assessment information, valid IEPs cannot be developed. Assessment information is used to determine the goals of the child; from goals are derived objectives. Services provided the child are based on these goals and objectives. And finally, evaluations can be used to determine if the intervention program detailed in the IEP is effective (Deno et al. 1984).

Developing valid IEPs requires extensive assessment data. The procedures used to collect these data for the development and monitoring of IEPs should be (Deno et al. 1984):

- Valid,
- Sensitive to small adjustments made in teaching methods, motivational techniques, and administrative arrangements,
- Easy to administer,
- In parallel forms to allow frequent administration,
- Time efficient,
- Inexpensive,
- Unobtrusive, and
- Simple to teach.

Following initial development and implementation of IEPs, information collected through ongoing assessment can be used to monitor the effectiveness of the intervention program. This should prevent children from being served inappropriately for long periods of time. If evaluations determine that programs are ineffective, positive steps can be taken to modify programs and make them more beneficial.

CRITICISMS OF TESTING

Testing is only one component of assessment; however, it is the one component that is often overly emphasized in the assessment process. While an important aspect of assessment, the practice of using tests to evaluate students has many criticisms, including the following:

1. Testing practices foster undemocratic attitudes by their use to form homogeneous classroom groups that severely limit social, economic, and vocational opportunities.
2. Testing practices foster expectations such as a self-fulfilling prophecy that may ensure low-level achievement for children who score low on tests.
3. Tests represent an invasion of privacy.
4. Norm-referenced tests are not useful for instructional or teaching purposes.
5. Test measurements rigidly shape school programming, and instruction limits innovative change.
6. Test limitations on abilities assessed impair the changes in children that schools should be interested in producing.
7. Tests and testing practices foster a notion of children having a fixed entity or ability (for example, intelligence).
8. Tests or assessment procedures are conducted incompetently by individuals who do not understand exceptional children or who lack the ability to elicit an ability-level of performance that reflects the child's true ability.
9. Tests are biased against individuals of unique cognitive, linguistic, and affective learning styles (Swanson and Watson 1982, 6).

Although some of these criticisms are valid, when tests are given properly, and when test data are used appropriately, most of the criticisms are negated.

Valid assessment data must be available in order to accomplish the legal and moral objectives of providing appropriate educational programs for disabled children. Without such information, teachers are likely to grope about trying to find the right instructional level and the appropriate methods and materials. Although assessment information does not automatically lead to appropriate educational programs, it does give teachers the raw materials to develop appropriate programs. The criticisms described must be considered but should not dictate the elimination of testing.

LEGAL CONSIDERATIONS IN ASSESSMENT

As previously stated, one purpose of assessment is to satisfy the legal requirements imposed by legislation and litigation. Prior to the 1970s, assessment of handicapped children was often performed with limited legal restrictions. Evaluators often used single tests to make critical decisions about children; tests were often used on children who were not represented in the normative sample; individuals who administered tests often had limited knowledge of accommodating handicapped children during the testing; and labels dictated placement. Reevaluations were infrequent, and communication between the schools and parents concerning assessment was minimal (Martin 1982). In fact, many of the criticisms noted in the previous section were common.

Fortunately, the decade of the seventies brought significant changes to assessment practices. The forces behind these changes were litigation and legislation. Two court cases are vitally important in pointing out the inequities of testing for special education: *Larry P. v. Riles* (1972) and *Diana v. State Board of Education* (1973). Both cases focused on the assessment of minority children for special education eligibility, labeling, and placement. For example, in the *Larry P.* case in California, parents of black children who had been classified as mentally retarded claimed that this group of children was being labeled and placed in classes for the mentally retarded based on a single IQ test, which was discriminatory. A preliminary injunction was issued that prevented placement in such classes based on a single test (Martin 1982). The *Diana* case dealt with the placement of Mexican-American children in special education classes on the basis of IQ tests that had been standardized on children predominantly from the majority American culture. These cases made it increasingly apparent that assessment practices of schools were inappropriate for many minority children. As a result, dissatisfaction with standardized tests spread throughout the field.

A second factor that focused attention on assessment in special education was that parents were often denied access to their children's records. In response, the Buckley Amendment was passed in 1973 to guarantee the rights of parents to see the records of their children, including assessment information collected by the school (Martin 1982). Litigation dealing with single, often inappropriate tests to determine special education eligibility, and legislation mandating parental access to school records, minimized unfair assessment procedures. The passage of Public Law 94-142, however, had the most significant impact on the assessment of handicapped children. Not only did this legislative act deal with these two issues of litigation and legislation, but it also presented specific guidelines for the entire assessment process. Public Law 94-142 states that "Before any action is taken with respect to the initial placement of a handicapped child in a special education program, a full and individual evaluation of the child's educational needs must be conducted" (20 U.S.C. 1412(5)(c)).

Federal regulations implementing Public Law 94-142 also require that other safeguards be provided during the evaluation process. Many of these requirements relate directly to some of the criticisms previously cited. The regulations require the following evaluation procedures:

State and local educational agencies shall insure, at a minimum, that:

(a) Tests and other evaluation materials:
- Are provided and administered in the child's native language or other mode of communication, unless it is clearly not feasible to do so;
- Have been validated for the specific purpose for which they are used, and
- Are administered by trained personnel in conformance with the instructions provided by their producer;

(b) Tests and other evaluation materials include those tailored to assess specific areas of educational need and not merely those which are designed to provide a single general intelligence quotient;

(c) Tests are selected and administered so as best to ensure that when a test is administered to a child with impaired sensory, manual, or speaking skills, the test results accurately reflect the child's aptitude or achievement level or whatever other factors the test purports to measure,

When children and adults are evaluated, it is critical to select instruments which are nondiscriminatory.

rather than reflecting the child's impaired sensory, manual, or speaking skills (except where those skills are the factors which the test purports to measure);

(d) No single procedure is used as the sole criterion for determining an appropriate educational program for a child;

(e) The evaluation is made by a multidisciplinary team or group of persons, including at least one teacher or other specialist with knowledge in the area of suspected disability;

(f) The child is assessed in all areas related to the suspected disability, including, where appropriate, health, vision, hearing, social and emotional status, general intelligence, academic performance, communicative status, and motor abilities. (20 U.S.C. 1412(5)(c))

In addition to those specific requirements concerning assessment, parents of handicapped children must be involved in the process. The prior notice and consent requirements detailed in the due process rights of parents and children apply to assessment. In other words, parents must be asked for their permission to have their children tested and the assessment procedures must be explained to the parents in terms they can understand.

The requirements imposed by litigation and legislation may be viewed by many as excessive. However, compared to the lack of requirements that prevailed before the 1970s, and the resulting inequities, it should be clear that the current requirements are only an attempt to ensure adequate and fair assessment procedures. Assessment information is used in such critical decisions—classifying, placing, program development—that added safeguards are very necessary.

Table 4-2 Ways to Reduce Discriminatory Assessment

1.	Development of "culture-free" tests	Efforts have failed because learning occurs in environmental contexts.
2.	Development of "culture-fair" tests	Attempts to balance cultural content. Unsuccessful due to their being poor predictors of success.
3.	Development of "culture-specific" tests	Tests developed for specific cultural groups. These tests have low predictive validity.
4.	Use of Piagetian tests	Tests related to Piagetian developmental scales. Many of these items are also cultural-dependent.
5.	Linguistic translation of existing tests	Translates current tests into child's native language. This changes item difficulty and affects the norms.
6.	Alteration of administration procedures	Changes administration to make tests more fair to some groups. Prevents use of existing norms.
7.	Training children to take tests	Teaches test-taking skills. May be effective, but does not prevent bias in decision making.
8.	Use of pluralistic norms for current tests	Uses existing with pluralistic norms. Separate methods used to compute potential of various cultural groups. One problem may be the predictive validity to the majority culture.
9.	Criterion-referenced assessment	Measures mastery level of students in various areas. Problem with personnel and dollar resources involved in implementing system.
10.	Learning potential assessment device	Attempts to measure potential rather than stored information. Still a problem in biased instruments.
11.	Testing moratoriums	Discontinue testing temporarily. A ban would leave major decisions to subjective information.

Source: Duffey et al. 1981, 427–34.

Nondiscriminatory Assessment

A major requirement of Public Law 94-142 is that assessment be nondiscriminatory. While no specific definition of **nondiscriminatory assessment** nor suggested procedures for effecting nondiscriminatory assessment are provided (Taylor 1984), it is the obvious intent of the legislation that discrimination be eliminated from assessment. For example, tests must be administered in the child's native language.

Unfortunately, although "the legal status of nondiscriminatory evaluation is clear, the theoretical and technical status is uncertain at best" (Bailey and Harbin 1980, 594). Professionals cannot even agree on what should be included in nondiscriminatory assessment (Duffey et al. 1981). Until some agreement can be reached on what constitutes nondiscriminatory assessment, methods to eradicate the bias currently found in assessment will not be totally successful.

Many attempts have been made to remove the bias in assessment, ranging from the development of nonbiased tests to the total elimination of norm-referenced tests. Duffey et al. (1981) described eleven different methods to reduce discriminatory assessment. (See table 4-2.) Unfortunately, none of the approaches have been proven to eliminate all bias in the assessment.

Even attempting to reduce bias through simple methods has difficulties. For example, one obvious way to reduce the bias of assessing non-English or limited-English proficient students would be to conduct the assessment in the child's native language by

Table 4-3 **Stages of Assessment Related to Programming**

Stage	Major Activities
1. Screening and Identification	Students are identified as having various difficulties. Formal and informal screenings reveal this information.
2. Referral	If information substantiating the problem, child is referred for additional evaluation. Otherwise, the process may end at this stage.
3. Assessment	A comprehensive assessment is performed. Formal and informal methods are used.
4. Decision Making	A multidisciplinary team, using available assessment data from stage 3 determines if special education is required.
5. Program Design	Individual educational program is developed based on assessment data.
6. Evaluation	Ongoing assessment is conducted to monitor intervention plan.
7. Annual Review	End-of-the-year deliberations to determine if additional special programming is required during the next school year.

Source: McLoughlin and Lewis 1981.

an examiner fluent in the particular language. Unfortunately, the number of examiners with such bilingual skills is extremely limited (Langdon 1983). Some school-aged children with suspected disabilities speak languages rare in the U.S., such as Vietnamese. This presents major problems in conducting the assessment in the child's native language.

Implementing nondiscriminatory assessment is obviously much more difficult than accepting the idea that nondiscriminatory assessment should be used. It cannot be achieved simply by developing new test instruments (Bailey and Harbin 1980). Nor can the concept become reality while using the current norm-referenced tests and classification systems (Duffey et al. 1981). These actions alone do not guarantee movement toward nondiscriminatory assessment. Progress toward this concept may be achieved if the assessment procedures only discriminate regular or special education needs (Slate 1983) and include the use of criterion-referenced instruments (Duffey et al. 1981).

THE ASSESSMENT PROCESS

Assessment of handicapped children is an ongoing process, not a one-shot activity only designed to determine the eligibility and classification of children. The ongoing assessment process has several stages. McLoughlin and Lewis (1981) associate these stages with the total program to meet the needs of handicapped students. Table 4-3 depicts the stages of assessment and describes actions associated with each stage.

In assessing handicapped children, several considerations must be made. First, what kind of assessment data are needed? Salvia and Ysseldyke (1981) indicate various kinds of data, including:

- current information,
- historical information,
- direct information, and
- indirect information.

This information can be collected through observations, testing, or judgments (Salvia and Ysseldyke 1981). In some instances, certain kinds of data might be more beneficial than others. Each child being assessed may require slightly different assessment approaches. As a result, some professionals have emphasized the uniqueness of assessment by suggesting that an individual assessment plan be developed for each child. McLoughlin and Lewis (1981) indicate that such a plan must be established before an individual assessment can be performed.

REQUIREMENTS FOR ADEQUATE ASSESSMENT

Without adequate, comprehensive assessment data, the likelihood that handicapped children will be provided an appropriate educational program is lessened. Several important factors relate to valid assessment: qualified assessment personnel, adequate assessment tools, and nonbiased assessment (Bennett 1983).

Qualified Personnel

A basic assumption underlying adequate assessment of handicapped children is that the individuals conducting the assessments are qualified. Both Public Law 94-142 and the American Psychological Association (APA) *Standards for Educational and Psychological Tests* (1974) indicate that this is a basic requirement. Regulations implementing Public Law 94-142 state that tests must be "administered by trained personnel in conformance with the instructions provided by their producer" (20 U.S.C. 1412(5)(c)). The APA Standards (1974, 58–60) go into additional detail:

1. A test user should have a general knowledge of measurement principles and of the limitations of test interpretations.
2. A test user should know and understand the literature relevant to the tests he uses and the testing problems with which he deals.
3. Test users should seek to avoid bias in test selection, administration, and interpretation; they should try to avoid even the appearance of discriminatory practice.

Most states attempt to ensure the competence of test users by requiring that certified or licensed individuals administer certain tests. While this is a valid attempt to ensure quality, often tests are still administered by unqualified individuals (Salvia and Ysseldyke 1981).

The necessity for competent persons to conduct assessments of handicapped children should be obvious. Without adequate knowledge of proper test selection, administration procedures, and analysis of results, examiners may arrive at results that lead to improper identification, classification, and placement of children. Although requiring that only qualified individuals conduct assessments does not solve all problems associated with assessing handicapped children, it certainly is a basic requirement for adequate assessment.

Proper Selection and Use of Assessment Tools

Having qualified individuals to administer tests is related to this requirement. If those who conduct assessments are knowledgeable about tests, they should have the necessary skills to identify and to use only assessment tools that meet minimum technical

Teacher made tests can provide valuable information for developing individual programs.

requirements. Many tests are currently on the market; however, many of these tests are not technically adequate. Technical adequacy of tests is determined by reliability, validity, and norms (Ysseldyke and Algozzine 1982).

Reliability and Validity. Although many different criteria can be used to determine test adequacy, the two most often used are reliability and validity. **Reliability** indicates whether or not a test is stable. It reflects the consistency of a test score. The most commonly used reliability, test-retest, "is established by correlating the test results of a group of individuals with the same individuals' test results after a relatively short period of time (usually about two weeks, but time varies with the type of test)" (Taylor 1984, 66). A reliability coefficient, which ranges from 0 to 1.0, is a numerical index that indicates the reliability of the test. The closer the coefficient to 1.0, the more reliable the test. Salvia and Ysseldyke (1981) recommend that a test used to make individual diagnostic decisions should have a reliability coefficient of at least .90, while a reliability coefficient of at least .60 is required for tests used to make screening decisions.

Validity is the extent to which a test measures what it is supposed to measure. In other words, a valid math achievement test measures the achievement level of individuals in math. If a test is not valid, then totally inappropriate decisions could be made. A simple example would be the use of an invalid intelligence test to diagnose mental retardation. If the IQ test used really did not measure intelligence, then a wrong diagnosis could be applied to the child. It is imperative that tests are valid if decisions based on their results are used for special education issues.

Appropriate Norms. Norm-referenced tests allow the user to compare a child with children represented in the normative sample. Characteristics to be considered when determining the appropriateness of the norm sample include age, sex, race, geographic area (Taylor 1984), socioeconomic status, educational level, and ability level. The key in making such comparisons is that the child being evaluated is *comparable* to those represented in the sample. Comparing Mexican-American children to norms that were established using only white children is inappropriate. This was one of the major problems emphasized in the litigation that was discussed at the beginning of this chapter. By comparing minority children to norms that do not include such minority groups, invalid conclusions may be drawn, often leading to misclassifications and inappropriate placements.

The importance of these technical aspects of tests should be obvious, but many tests used regularly in public schools do not meet minimally acceptable levels of reliability, validity, and/or norms. Some of these tests with technical limitations can still be used; however, their weaknesses must be known by the users and considerations made during analysis of the results. The following frequently used tests have questionable validity and inadequate reliability (Salvia and Ysseldyke 1981):

- Developmental Test of Visual Perception
- Durrell Analysis of Reading Difficulty
- Full-Range Picture Vocabulary Test
- Gates-McKillop Reading Diagnostic Tests
- Gilmore Oral Reading Test
- Gray Oral Reading Test
- Illinois Test of Psycholinguistic Abilities
- Stanford-Binet Intelligence Scale
- System of Multicultural Pluralistic Assessment

CONSIDERATIONS IN ASSESSMENT

Individuals concerned with assessing handicapped children and children suspected of being handicapped must consider several issues in assessment. For example, of the hundreds of tests on any topic, which tests should be used? Should the tests be individual or group tests? Should they be norm-referenced or criterion referenced? Should tests be used that are easily administered and scored, or should other criteria be more important in test selection? These are some of the questions individuals responsible for assessment programs may have to answer in developing policies for assessing handicapped children. While most states provide guidelines on testing, they leave considerable decision making on these issues up to local districts.

Group versus Individual Tests

One of the first questions of assessment is whether to use group or individual tests. Most states require the use of individual tests when assessing children for special education. Although several group tests are often used, especially in the area of achievement testing, individual tests are generally considered better measures. Both types of tests have advantages. Table 4-4 describes some of these advantages and disadvantages. It is recommended that group tests be used for screening, general program planning, and

Table 4-4 Advantages and Disadvantages of Group and Individual Tests

Advantages	Disadvantages
Group Tests	
• Easily administered	• Often require reading skills
• Administered to large groups in one setting	• Prevent individual attention
• Require limited training to administer	• Limit observations by examiner
• Excellent for screening	• Often normed on volunteer groups
	• Provide insufficient data for many individual decisions
Individual Tests	
• Examiner can provide encouragement	• Require extensive training to administer, score, and interpret
• Examiner can make detailed observations	• Time-consuming
• Excellent for nonreaders	• One-on-one situation may actually increase anxiety
• Provide specific information for individual decisions	• Normative sample may be small
• Examiner can reduce anxiety	

program evaluation, while individual tests be used when planning individual educational programs (Salvia and Ysseldyke 1981).

Norm-Referenced and Criterion-Referenced Tests

Another major decision concerning testing is whether to use norm-referenced tests or criterion-referenced tests. **Norm-referenced tests** are tests that allow a student's score to be compared to an established comparative group, known as the normative sample. As previously discussed, this norm sample must be representative if the comparisons made are valid. Common interpretations of the results of norm-referenced tests are presented in age or grade equivalents. For the most part, norm-referenced tests "address the question of 'how much' rather than 'what' a person knows or can do" (Taylor 1984, 12). For example, if a child has a reading grade equivalent of 4.0, one only knows that, compared to other similarly aged children, the child can read on the fourth grade level. The score does not provide a great deal of information concerning intervention needs of the child. It only shows how the child's mastery level compares with that of other children.

Criterion-referenced tests differ significantly from norm-referenced tests because they do not result in scores for comparative purposes. Criterion-referenced tests describe what a person knows (Taylor 1984). They compare a student's performance to specific mastery levels, not to other students (McLoughlin and Lewis 1981). These tests are more beneficial in developing individual education programs because they provide specific information about a child's ability.

Although criterion-referenced tests are more beneficial in developing individual educational programs, too often norm-referenced tests are relied upon to provide most of the information. This results from states' requiring that certain norm-referenced tests be given to determine the child's eligibility for special education programs. Once these data have been collected, IEPs are often developed without significant amounts of additional assessment. The development of criterion-referenced tests is relatively new, so new, in fact, that firm guidelines have not been established governing their development (Swanson and Watson 1982). Many view the use of criterion-referenced tests as a major step forward in collecting appropriate assessment data on children. But until state departments of education control the test's use, it is unlikely that criterion-referenced tests will replace norm-referenced tests in the near future.

Test Environment

The time, place, and atmosphere in which the assessment is conducted are all important considerations in assessment. Without ample consideration of these aspects, invalid assessment data may be collected, which could lead to inappropriate decisions regarding handicapped children.

Time. Children should not be tested at a time of day when they expect and want to be somewhere else. If children in the second grade have a thirty-minute recess period beginning at 10:00 A.M., the child should not be pulled out of class at 9:45 A.M. for a two-hour assessment session and be expected to perform maximally. The child's schedule should be checked before the time of assessment is determined.

Place. Other than observations in "natural" environments, assessments should not be conducted in locations with major visual and/or auditory distractions. Although it may be impossible to locate a soundproof, visually distraction-free room, efforts can be made to utilize a room that minimizes distractions. Children seated in front of an open window hearing and watching other children on the playground cannot be expected to concentrate on the test items.

Rapport. The emotional climate surrounding the testing situation is important. Examiners who do not take the time to make students feel comfortable before popping questions are unlikely to bring out the maximum performance in the child. As part of the activities recommended to establish rapport prior to testing, McLoughlin and Lewis (1981) recommend that examiners discuss:

- length of test(s),
- activities involved,
- difficulty levels,
- confirmation of responses, and
- time requirements.

Making students feel at ease before subjecting them to a series of tests can greatly enhance the likelihood that test results will be a valid measure of true ability.

ASSESSMENT DOMAINS

Many domains can be assessed, but specific domains to be tested will be determined by the purpose of the assessment. A comprehensive listing suggested several years ago by the National Association of State Directors of Special Education is still useful in conceptualizing the comprehensive nature of assessment (Walker 1976):

A. Educational functioning
    1. Achievement in subject areas
    2. Learning styles
    3. Strengths and weaknesses

B. Social-emotional functioning
   1. Social/psychological development
      a. Attending/receiving
      b. Responding
      c. Valuing
      d. Organizing
      e. Characterizing
   C. Physical functioning
   1. Visual
   2. Hearing
   3. Speech
   4. Motor/psychomotor
      a. Gross motor
      b. Fine motor
   5. Medical health
   D. Cognitive functioning
   1. Intelligence
   2. Adaptive behavior
   3. Thinking processes
      a. Knowledge
      b. Comprehension
      c. Application
      d. Analysis
      e. Synthesis
      f. Evaluation
   E. Language functioning
   1. Receptive
   2. Expressive
   3. Nonverbal
   4. Speech
   F. Family
   1. Dominant language
   2. Parent-child interactions
   3. Social service needs
   G. Environment
   1. Home
   2. Interpersonal
   3. Material

PERSONNEL INVOLVED IN ASSESSMENT

If assessment of handicapped children is conducted as intended by Public Law 94-142, a great many individuals are involved in the process. The assessment of handicapped children could conceivably involve everyone associated with the child's educational program (Taylor 1984). Usually, the more information about a child, the more comprehensive the assessment. Although some of the information collected might prove invalid or unnecessary, having the information available gives the assessment team the option to consider the material.

Providing feedback to parents is an important aspect of the assessment process.

Obviously, several individuals should be involved in the assessment process. The child's teacher is a very important team member. Teachers are often the most critical team members since they are in a position to observe the child over an extended period of time. The child's teacher could be a regular classroom teacher, special education teacher, or both (Taylor 1984). Other likely assessment team members would be the psychologist or examiner who administers the formal test battery and someone representing the administration who is responsible for providing support for the team's decisions (Fiscus and Mandell 1983). The administrative representative might be the school principal, the director of special education for the district, the assistant superintendent for special programs, or someone else appointed to represent administrative interests.

Parents of the child being assessed also should be involved in the assessment process. Public Law 94-142 mandates significant parental involvement in the entire special education process. Although legislation mandates parental involvement and studies have revealed that involvement has increased, Halpern (1982) found that school personnel still do not actively seek information from the parents' perspective. If parental input is ever to be valued and available for assessment team consideration, school personnel must make an effort to acquire this information. Information from parents may be as valuable as that provided by teachers and evaluation personnel. Parental involvement in the assessment process can be helpful for many reasons (Fiscus and Mandell 1983):

- Parental involvement enables school personnel to better understand the needs of the child and family.
- Parental involvement is often necessary for full implementation of the child's IEP. If parents are involved in the assessment process, they may be more willing to assist in carrying out IEP activities.
- Involvement by parents makes them better understand the assessment process.

In addition to teachers, administrative personnel, and parents, other likely assessment team members are speech pathologists, medical specialists, physical therapists, and consultants. Composition of the team would depend on the suspected disability manifested by the child. For example, if a child with cerebral palsy were being evaluated, a physical therapist should be included.

Each member of the assessment team should be actively involved in the assessment process. Simply attending meetings is not enough. Team members must be able to discuss information gained through criterion-referenced tests, norm-referenced tests, and ecologically based assessments, and to "resolve the disproportionate impact, unique to that team of these assessments on the decision-making process" (Knoff 1983, 443). By gaining input from all team members, the entire team can more easily arrive at a consensus concerning the child's real needs.

INSTRUMENTS USED IN ASSESSMENT

A multitude of instruments are used in the assessment process. As previously noted, some of these are technically sound instruments, while others have technical limitations. Test users should take the responsibility of utilizing instruments that are reliable, valid, and appropriately normed. State departments of education are also responsible because they often provide schools with a list of instruments that can be used to determine the eligibility of handicapped children. Tests included on these lists should be technically sound.

Although many informal screening checklists and teacher-made, criterion-referenced tests are used in the identification of handicapped children, norm-referenced tests are still most often used in identification and program planning. Frequently used norm-referenced tests are (1) intelligence tests, (2) achievement tests, (3) perceptual-motor tests, and (4) measures of adaptive behavior.

Intelligence Tests

One of the most controversial issues in special education is the assessment of intelligence (Taylor 1984). At the heart of the debate is the definition of intelligence. Some definitions suggest that intelligence is a general concept, while others are more complex and describe intelligence as multifaceted. With such diverse opinions on the nature of intelligence, it is easy to understand the controversy that surrounds the testing of intelligence.

Intelligence testing is a very important area of assessment in special education. It is performed on children with suspected limited intelligence to document such limitations. For children exhibiting learning problems associated with processing deficits or emotional problems, intelligence tests substantiate that the problem is not the cause of limited intelligence but is due to other factors. For disability areas such as physical, visual, and auditory handicaps, intelligence testing can reveal that a lack of intelligence is not the primary problem of the child. Therefore, testing for intellectual level is done on most children in special education programs or those who have been referred for special education programs. Categorical definitions are used to certify the eligibility of children for special education; then intelligence tests are used to match children with some specific categories, such as mental retardation.

Intelligence testing is criticized primarily because of inappropriate decisions made about children based on intelligence tests (Taylor 1984). As a result of these criticisms, efforts are being made to ensure that classifying and placement decisions are not made based solely on the results of intelligence tests. Some of the safeguards included in Public Law 94-142 attempt to guarantee this.

There are basically two types of intelligence tests—group and individual. Group intelligence tests are generally used (1) to screen large groups of children and then identify those who require indepth assessments and (2) to determine the level of performance of a group of children (Salvia and Ysseldyke 1981). Group intelligence tests have the same advantages as other group tests; namely, they can be administered to large groups in one setting, are easily scored, and require limited training on the part of the person administering the test.

Group intelligence tests also have major limitations (Salvia and Ysseldyke 1981):

1. They are typically standardized by grade levels
2. The standardization sample is often not representative
3. Atypical students are often excluded from the normative sample

Limitations that apply to any group test also are present in group intelligence tests; namely, that monitoring individuals cannot be as extensive thereby limiting observation data; individual attention cannot be given; and students with limited reading ability may be at a severe disadvantage since most group tests are paper/pencil tests that require some reading.

Individual intelligence tests are primarily used to assess children for special education. Their use has been extensive in the past and will probably continue to be important, especially in determining eligibility and making classification decisions. Regardless of the criticisms of testing intelligence, when used properly, data from these tests can be beneficial. Past abuses of intelligence testing have most likely resulted from user error, not test error (Taylor 1984).

Individual intelligence tests have several advantages over group tests:

Individually administered tests of intelligence are a primary source of information concerning the intellectual strengths and weaknesses of children and adults.

- Examiners can closely monitor student performance and provide clarification
- Examiners can make detailed observations of the child during the testing
- Individual tests rarely require reading ability
- Examiners can vary the pace of the test
- Results are considered more valid than for group tests

The major disadvantages of individual intelligence tests are the time involved in administering them and the need to have well qualified, trained persons available to administer the tests.

Achievement Tests

One of the most common types of tests used in schools is the achievement test. As with intelligence tests, achievement tests are both individual and group. Results from group achievement tests are often used by the press, legislative bodies, and other authorities to judge the adequacy of education. Headlines in newspapers about decreasing or increasing group achievement test scores attract considerable attention, especially during the recent emphasis on education in this country.

While group achievement tests are frequently used with all school children, the use of individual achievement tests is primarily found in special education. Major purposes of these tests are (McLoughlin and Lewis 1981):

- To determine if there is a school performance problem;
- To determine current academic performance level;
- To determine a student's ability to learn in the regular classroom; and
- To determine the strengths and weaknesses of a student.

The two types of individual achievement tests are screening and diagnostic (Salvia and Ysseldyke 1981). The two most commonly used individual screening achievement tests are the Wide Range Achievement Test (WRAT) and the Peabody Individual Achievement Test (PIAT). Both instruments provide an overall picture of achievement in several academic areas, i.e., reading, math, and spelling. Diagnostic achievement tests are more subject-specific. For example, there are several diagnostic reading tests, diagnostic math tests, as well as diagnostic tests for language, spelling, and other academic skills.

Although individual screening achievement tests provide beneficial information in referral and program planning, results from these instruments alone are insufficient to make eligibility, classification, and programming decisions. In order to make such decisions, data from diagnostic tests must be considered because this information provides more detail on individual strengths and weaknesses. The information can be vital in developing intervention plans for handicapped children.

Perceptual-Motor Tests

Testing perceptual-motor skills has been a controversial issue in special education (Taylor 1984), but the actual assessment in this area has not been as controversial as the use of the resulting test data. For example, some intervention programs for children identified as learning disabled are based almost entirely on perceptual-motor skills (Siegel and Gold 1982). These programs contend that increased perceptual-motor skills will lead to academic remediation. While studies have shown that perceptual-motor training does improve those skills, evidence does not support its having a positive effect on academic achievement (Taylor 1984).

The three major purposes of perceptual-motor assessment are: (1) to screen large groups of children to identify those with perceptual-motor weaknesses; (2) to test children with learning difficulties to determine the extent of perceptual-motor problems; and (3) to diagnose brain injury (Salvia and Ysseldyke 1981). This third purpose is obviously the most controversial. Programs based on perceptual-motor intervention have become less popular during the past ten years, but the controversy continues over the place for perceptual-motor training in special education.

In the overall assessment of handicapped children, however, perceptual-motor testing should not be stressed. Although it does provide information related to skills in

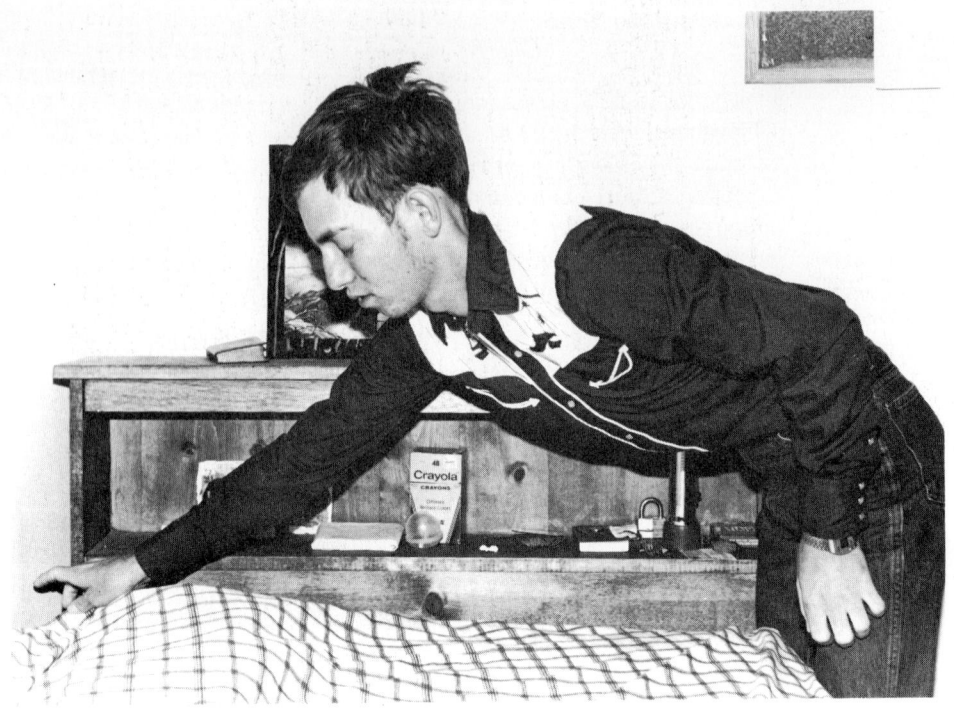

The assessment of adaptive behavior must be included as a part of the testing battery.

this area, research has not confirmed that remediation in perceptual-motor areas leads to academic remediation. As long as perceptual-motor tests are used, "The real danger [is] that reliance on such tests in planning interventions for children may actually lead to assigning children to activities that do them absolutely no good" (Salvia and Ysseldyke 1981, 347). If academic skill remediation is the goal for children, there is no substitute for direct remediation in specific academic areas (Siegel and Gold 1982).

Adaptive Behavior

A relatively new area included in many assessments of handicapped children because of legal mandate is **adaptive behavior.** Adaptive behavior includes age-appropriate behaviors expected of individuals from similar cultural and socioeconomic backgrounds. Adaptive behavior is included in many evaluations because of the American Association on Mental Deficiency (AAMD) definition of mental retardation, which is used by Public Law 94-142. The AAMD responded to criticisms of classifying children as mentally retarded by using only individual measures of intelligence. The belief that many IQ tests discriminate against minority and low socioeconomic children has also prompted inclusion of this concept in the definition. Examples of adaptive behavior provided by the AAMD include sensorimotor and self-help skills during infancy and early childhood, academic performance during the school years, and vocational and social adjustment for adulthood (Grossman 1983).

Often adaptive behavior scales are used to determine eligibility and classification of a child (Taylor 1984). The AAMD definition requires an individual to have deficits in adaptive behavior as well as low IQ scores, so the use of adaptive behavior measures is mandatory. Another major function of adaptive behavior scales is to provide useful information for programming, especially for children with more severe disabilities.

Since adaptive behavior is subjective, it is difficult to define and therefore difficult to measure (Taylor 1984). A major problem is "when is behavior adaptive (or maladaptive), and how does a student show a deficit in adaptive behavior?" (Ysseldyke and Algozzine 1982, 126) Establishing reliability and validity for adaptive behavior instruments has been a significant problem (Taylor 1984).

Thus, adaptive behavior must be measured to determine the eligibility for special education of some students, as well as their appropriate classification. Instruments used to determine adaptive behavior, however, are technically inadequate. Rather than over-emphasizing the instruments for measuring adaptive behavior, school officials would do better by subjectively considering the behavior of the child in various situations, with considerations given for cultural and socioeconomic status.

A Listing of Common Instruments

Below are some of the common instruments used in special education for the mildly handicapped. Of course, many instruments can be used in each category, but these appear to be used predominantly. Table 4-5 describes some of the commonly used instruments listed below.

Intelligence Tests
- Stanford Binet Intelligence Scale
- Wechsler Intelligence Scale for Adults—Revised
- Wechsler Intelligence Scale for Children—Revised
- Wechsler Preschool and Primary Scale of Intelligence

General Achievement
- Peabody Individual Achievement Test
- Wide Range Achievement Test

Reading Achievement
- Gilmore Oral Reading Test
- Gray Oral Reading Test
- Spache Diagnostic Reading Scales
- Woodcock Reading Mastery Tests

Arithmetic Achievement
- Key Math Diagnostic Test
- Stanford Math Test

Perceptual-Motor Tests
- Bender Visual-Motor Gestalt Test
- Developmental Test of Visual Perception
- Purdue Perceptual-Motor Survey
- Visual Motor Integration

Behavior Rating
- Burk's Behavior Rating Scales
- AAMD Adaptive Behavior Scales
- Devoreau Scales

ROLE OF TEACHERS

The assessment of handicapped children is an ongoing process involving many people. As previously discussed, regular and special education teachers should be involved in the process. Because of the extended periods of time they spend with children, teachers are in a unique position to provide assessment data to the assessment team.

The role of teachers in assessment often begins with monitoring children in the regular classroom. This might lead to referring a child for diagnosis. Teachers are then involved in the formal evaluation of the child by providing data to the assessment team

Table 4-5 **Characteristics of Some Common Instruments Used in Special Education Assessment Programs: Cognitive Academic Functioning**

Test	Description	Technical adequacy
Intelligence tests		
Stanford-Binet Intelligence Scale	Individual test that is not as widely used as in the past because of the increasing popularity of the WISC-R. It yields an MA with a deviation IQ of 100 having an SD of 16.	The 1973 revision reports no demographic data; validity and reliability are based on the prior standardization. Thus, the use of the test is risky because comparison of a subject's response to the norms of a different instrument is problematic.
Wechsler Intelligence Scale for Children–Revised	Consists of three scales: verbal, performance, and full scale. There are a total of 12 subtests, each with a mean of 10 and SD of 3. The mean for each scale is 100 with an SD of 15, a deviation IQ. The three scales and scatter of subtests are used for various interpretive approaches.	It was standardized on a large representative, stratified sample. The validity and reliability are considered very acceptable. Many uses by examiners to identify groups or process problems by profile or scatter analysis are not valid.
Slosson Intelligence Test	Short-form test comprised of items taken from other instruments. No age range is reported for the test.	The test yields a ratio IQ. Reliability and validity are unclear; the user can have no clear idea of who comprised the normative sample. The best use is for screening.
General achievement tests		
Wide Range Achievement Test (WRAT)	Comprised of three tests: reading, spelling, and arithmetic. Reading requires the identification of words, spelling involves writing words from dictation, and arithmetic is strictly computational. An evaluation may be quickly administered and scored. Grade equivalents, standard scores, and percentile ranks are provided. It is used for profile analysis comparison with the WISC-R, although no correlations or standard errors of the difference are reported.	The best use is for screening, especially because the test is too brief to indicate diagnostic information and may not reflect the actual skills taught by a school. Thus, the validity may be questioned.

Table 4-5 (continued)

Test	Description	Technical adequacy
Peabody Individual Achievement Test (PIAT)	Provides measures of mathematics, reading recognition, reading comprehension, spelling, and general information. It is arranged for easy presentation in a spiralbound book format that permits multiple choice pictures for response selection.	Test validity is a concern for the user depending on the nature of the actual curriculum. Reliability measures are low enough to recommend its use as a screening instrument. Standard error in some subtests at certain levels is large. Grade equivalents, percentile ranks, and normalized standard scores are available.
Reading achievement tests		
Woodcock Reading Mastery Tests	Consists of five separate tests: letter identification, word identification, word attack, word comprehension, and passage comprehension. The test was designed to serve as both a criterion- and norm-referenced instrument. There are two forms.	Normative sample is representative, and the validity is enhanced by the use of a criterion-referenced format. Reliability is weak in some subtests. The test yields age and grade scores, percentile ranks, standard scores, and mastery scores. Depending on the curriculum and the approach in assessment, the test may be used for placement and evaluation decisions.
Spache Diagnostic Reading Scales	Consists primarily in reading passages of increasing difficulty to examine reading comprehension and silent and oral reading. Supplementary tests are used for consonants, vowels, blends, syllables, and letter sounds.	There is no description of the consistency of the standardization group; the validity and reliability data are not adequate. Normative comparisons would be difficult to defend.
Arithmetic tests		
KeyMath Diagnostic Arithmetic Test	The authors base the test on developmental theory and include more skills than computation. There are 14 subtests within three process areas: content, operations, and applications.	The test is best used as a criterion-referenced instrument. Normative scores must be used with caution. The user can obtain scores in process areas, profiles of subtests, and behavioral statements.
Written expression		
Picture Story Language Test	Provides a basis for examining spontaneous written responses of a subject required to create a story about a picture. The response is examined in terms of productivity (length), correctness, and meaning.	Test is unique because it emphasizes actual production rather than recognition. Because of the undifferentiated nature of the written responses and questionable statistical properties, it is best used as an informal measure.

Table 4-5 (continued)

Test	Description	Technical adequacy
Language Illinois Test of Psycholinguistic Abilities (ITPA)	Consists of ten subtests, two of which are supplementary: it measures auditory-vocal and visual-motor modes of communication (channels); receptive, organizing, and expressive ability; and representation and automatic levels of language organization. The test has generated considerable controversy. The test yields a standard comparison profile, with a mean of 36 and a deviation of 10 considered to be remarkable. Age scores and quotients may be obtained from the test.	Norms are criticized because they are convenient rather than random and stratified. They also exclude minority and handicapped children. Validity has been questioned by a number of writers; there is considerable variability in the reliability. The greatest criticism has been of examiners who use the test to verify the existence of learning disabilities on the basis of subtest profiles not considered to be valid.

From Marsh, George E., II; Price, Barrie Jo; and Smith T. E. C.: Teaching Mildly Handicapped Children. *St. Louis, 1983. The C. V. Mosby Co.*

and participating in the team's deliberations. Finally, after the child has been identified and placed in a special education program, teachers must monitor student progress to determine the effectiveness of the intervention program.

Regular and special education teachers engage in both formal and informal assessment. Teachers may administer some norm-referenced tests to children. This is an activity often performed by special education teachers with children placed in special education programs. When administering norm-referenced tests, the teacher should remember the following points:

- Control the testing environment. Attempt to reduce visual and auditory distractions.
- Establish rapport with the child. Take a few moments to reduce the child's anxiety.
- Control the time of testing. Do not test children during normally scheduled recess, immediately after lunch, or during a period particularly enjoyed by the child.
- Be familiar with the tests used. Make sure that the administration of the tests has been practiced and that adequate materials are present and properly organized.
- Ensure the technical adequacy of tests. Before using norm-referenced instruments determine if validity, reliability, and the normative sample are sufficient.
- Follow directions for administration and scoring explicitly. If scores are to be compared with the normative sample, strict adherence must be realized. If the tests are being used as criterion-referenced measures, directions do not have to be followed, but scores should not be compared to the normative sample.
- Consider the socioeconomic and cultural background of the child during the analysis of the results.
- Do not overly emphasize the results from any one test.

Although teachers will be involved in collecting formal assessment data, a more

Table 4-6 Major Differences between Direct and Indirect Methods of Observation

Areas of Difference	Methods of Observation	
	Direct	Indirect
Characteristics	Observational schema	Question format
	Direct view of the student's performance	Prior or ongoing experience with student
	Immediate record of observation	Report based on summary of prior experiences
Examples	Counting the numbers of times student is out of his or her seat	Completing a questionnaire about a pupil's behavior
	Writing an account of a sequence of behavior	Keeping a diary on student performance
	Recording the antecedents and unsequences of a behavior	Describing a student's behavior to another teacher
Uses	Describing specific behavior	Obtaining an overview of behavior
	Planned report on student performance	Unexpected need to report on behavior
	Measuring change	Communicating to other professionals about a broad spectrum of behavior
	Selecting target behaviors and intervention strategies	Searching for clues for appropriate intervention strategies

Reprinted, by permission, from G. H. Guerin and A. S. Maier 1983.

likely role will be in the collection of informal assessment information. **Informal assessment** includes observations, interviews, and informal, criterion-referenced tests. Observations may be direct or indirect. In direct observations, teachers set out to observe a particular situation, for example, a handicapped child in a mainstream history class. The observer would focus on the particular child and make copious notes of the activities that occur. In indirect observation, teachers piece together various events that have been observed. There is no predetermined observation period when a particular child is observed and notes made, as in direct observation (Guerin and Maier 1983). (See table 4-6.)

Interviewing students is another method of acquiring substantial informal assessment data on children. When using this information-gathering method, teachers should keep the following in mind (Marsh, Price and Smith 1983, 65):

1. Communicate your genuine desire to gain information.
   a. Listen carefully.
   b. Encourage communication through verbal and nonverbal cues.
   c. Avoid "roadblocking" of sharing efforts (Don't "take the conversation away" from the respondent).
2. Be aware of all aspects of the informant's communication, including nonverbal or body language (posture, eye contact, and voice quality).
3. If possible, make the purpose of the interview clear to the respondent to reduce any anxiety or concern that there might be a hidden agenda.
4. At strategic points or particularly critical points summarize or restate what you believe you have heard; this gives the respondent an opportunity to clarify or modify any aspect of the response.

An important element in informal assessment, regardless of the methods used, is maintaining detailed, accurate records. Although teachers may think they will remember important details concerning a child's performance, it is likely that many important facts will be forgotten if unrecorded.

One method of record keeping is the use of an observation form. The teacher can construct it to meet the particular needs of a student. Observation forms may be for one brief observation period, an entire class period, or an entire day. (See figure 4-1.)

While participating as a member of the assessment team, teachers should ask questions and state their opinions concerning the child. They should discuss the technical adequacy of the tests and make sure cultural and socioeconomic factors are considered. Above all, teachers must not assume that all assessment data presented at the assessment conference is reliable and valid. Too often, teachers assume a low profile during the assessment process, allowing individuals who conducted the major portion of the formal assessment to dominate the proceedings. While this might be appropriate during some meetings, teachers must consider themselves capable of making a valuable contribution to the decision-making process. It is imperative that teachers be active participants. The professional responsibility of the teacher to the child involves not only instruction but also assessment. As a team member, teachers must contribute information, as well as respect and value information provided by other professionals. Open communication among team members, all team members, is critical (Fiscus and Mandell 1983).

SUMMARY

This chapter has focused on the assessment of handicapped children. Assessment is a major process in providing appropriate educational services. While testing is generally thought of as the primary focus of assessment, it is actually only one aspect of assessment. Other sources of information include observations, interviews, school records, medical evaluations, and social histories. Assessment is therefore multifaceted and conducted by all individuals involved in the education of the child.

Assessing children has several purposes. Foremost is the legal requirement imposed by Public Law 94-142. In order for children to be considered eligible for special education services, a comprehensive assessment of the child must be accomplished. This occurs during the screening and identification process. Other purposes are: (1) to determine the child's current level of functioning, (2) to determine the classification of the child, and (3) to develop an individual education program (IEP) for the child. Once the IEP is developed and implemented, assessment must be continued to monitor the effectiveness of the child's program. Results from this ongoing assessment could lead to continuation of the program or significant modification of the IEP.

Litigation and legislation, as they relate to assessment of handicapped children, were also discussed. Early litigation resulting from unfair assessment practices was presented, as well as the requirements regarding assessment as set forth in Public Law 94-142. Although not guaranteeing appropriate assessment, Public Law 94-142 attempts to ensure that fair, appropriate assessments are conducted. A primary focus of this legislative intent is to remove the discriminatory assessment practices often inherent in certain norm-referenced tests.

Adequate assessment has several requirements. These include the technical ade-

OBSERVATION FORM

Name _____

Location _____

Date _____ Time _____ Period _____

Teacher(s) Present _____

Student(s) Present _____

Scheduled Activity _____

Student's Behavior _____

_____

_____

_____

Antecedents to Behavior _____

_____

_____

General Comments _____

_____

_____

Observer _____

Figure 4-1 Observation Recording Form

quacy of tests and qualifications of persons administering tests. Individuals entrusted to administer, score, and interpret tests of handicapped children must be familiar with the instruments used, be aware of their technical adequacy, and understand nondiscriminatory assessment practices.

Many different areas should be assessed in handicapped children. These include educational functioning, socioemotional functioning, physical functioning, cognitive functioning, language functioning, family, and environment. Without information from these areas, a comprehensive assessment will not be accomplished.

The final section of the chapter focuses on the active role teachers must assume in the assessment process. Due to their frequent contact with students, teachers are in a unique position to provide substantial information necessary for adequate assessments.

Teachers cannot assume that others on the assessment team will question the quality of tests, the analysis of results, and the appropriateness of recommended educational programs. Teachers must be involved in the total assessment process.

REFERENCES

American Psychological Association. *Standards for educational and psychological tests.* Washington, D.C.: American Psychological Association, 1974.

Bailey, D. B., and G. L. Harbin. Nondiscriminatory evaluation. *Exceptional Children* 46, no. 8 (1980): 590–96.

Bennett, R. E. Research and evaluation priorities for special education assessment. *Exceptional Children* 50, no. 2 (1983): 110–17.

Deno, S. L., P. K. Mirkin, and C. Wesson. How to write effective data-based IEPs. *Teaching Exceptional Children* 16, no. 2 (1984): 99–104.

Duffey, J. B., J. Salvia, J. Tucker, and J. Ysseldyke. Nonbiased assessment: A need for operationalism. *Exceptional Children* 47, no. 6 (1981): 427–34.

Fiscus, E. D., and C. J. Mandell. *Developing individualized education programs.* St. Paul, Minn.: West Publishing Company, 1983.

Gearheart, B. R. *Learning disabilities: Educational strategies.* 3d ed. St. Louis: C. V. Mosby, 1981.

Grossman, H. J., ed. *Classification in mental retardation.* Washington, D.C.: American Association on Mental Deficiency, 1983.

Guerin, G. R., and A. S. Maier. *Informal assessment in education.* Palo Alto, Calif.: Mayfield Publishing Company, 1983.

Halpern, R. Impact of PL 94-142 on the handicapped child and family: Institutional responses. *Exceptional Children* 49, no. 3 (1982): 270–73.

Knoff, H. M. Effect of diagnostic information on special education placement decisions. *Exceptional Children* 49, no. 5 (1983): 440–44.

Langdon, H. W. Assessment and intervention strategies for the bilingual language-disordered student. *Exceptional Children* 50, no. 1 (1983): 37–46.

McLoughlin, J. A., and R. B. Lewis. *Assessing special students: Strategies and procedures.* Columbus, Ohio: Charles E. Merrill Publishing Company, 1981.

Marsh, G. E. II, B. J. Price, and T. E. C. Smith. *Teaching mildly handicapped children.* St. Louis: C. V. Mosby, 1983.

Martin, R. Legal issues in assessment for special education. In *Assessment in special education,* edited by J. T. Neisworth. Rockville, Md.: Aspen Systems Corporation, 1982.

Salvia, J., and J. E. Ysseldyke. *Assessment in special and remedial education.* Boston: Houghton Mifflin, 1981.

Siegel, E., and R. Gold. *Educating the learning disabled.* New York: Macmillan, 1982.

Slate, N. M. Nonbiased assessment of adaptive behavior: Comparison of three instruments. *Exceptional Children* 50, no. 1 (1983): 67–70.

Smith, R. M. *Clinical teaching: Methods of instruction for the retarded.* New York: McGraw-Hill, 1974.

Swanson, H. L., and B. L. Watson. *Educational and psychological assessment of exceptional children: Theories, strategies, and applications.* St. Louis: C. V. Mosby, 1982.

Taylor, R. L. *Assessment of exceptional students: Educational and psychological procedures.* Englewood Cliffs, N.J.: Prentice-Hall, 1984.

Walker, J., ed. *Functions of the placement committee in special education.* Washington, D.C.: National Association of State Directors of Special Education, 1976.

Ysseldyke, J. E., and B. Algozzine. *Critical issues in special and remedial education.* Boston: Houghton Mifflin, 1982.

Chapter Five

EDUCATING MILDLY HANDICAPPED STUDENTS: THE IEP PROCESS

CHAPTER OUTLINE

INTRODUCTION
UNDERSTANDING THE IEP PROCESS
    Child Find
    Referral
    Evaluation
LEAST RESTRICTIVE SETTING
    Service Models
    Placement Selection
WRITING THE IEP
    IEP Form
    Required Conference
    Relationship of the IEP to Daily Instruction
EVALUATION AND MONITORING
DUE PROCESS AND PARENTAL INVOLVEMENT
MAINSTREAMING
    Shared Responsibility: A Philosophy
    Shared Responsibility: The Reality
SUMMARY

CHAPTER OBJECTIVES

After reading this chapter, you should be able to:
- Describe the IEP process;
- Understand and explain the least restrictive setting concept
- List and describe the Cascade of Services Model;
- Describe the types of resource rooms;
- Know the components of an IEP; and
- Describe shared responsibility in providing educational services to handicapped children.

INTRODUCTION

As indicated in chapter 1, a major part of Public Law 94-142 is the **Individualized Education Program,** known as the IEP. The IEP is essential in efforts to provide handicapped students with a free, appropriate education delivered in the least restrictive setting. It represents the working mechanism through which student assessment is coordinated, evaluation data interpreted, placement selected, and daily instruction designed and evaluated. The IEP is really the skeleton around which educational services are developed; therefore, its meaning, intent, and components should be thoroughly understood.

A frequently quoted definition of the Individualized Education Program is that of Abeson and Weintraub (1977). See figure 5-1. That definition conveys a primary concept; namely, that the IEP is an educational plan to be developed for an individual child. The educational plan typically becomes equated with a form; however, that concept may be too limited in scope to accurately reflect the intent of Public Law 94-142. The form Abeson and Weintraub (1977) describe, completed in the process, is called the IEP. But the IEP form cannot accurately and appropriately be completed without a comprehensive process for gathering information and making decisions. Therefore, a more responsible approach is to view the IEP as a *process* rather than a product (Marsh, Price, and Smith 1983).

Conceptualizing the IEP as a process comprised of several stages seems to facilitate an understanding of the intent of the law and the regulations and requirements accompanying its implementation. However, perceiving the IEP merely as a form to be completed perpetuates the erroneous attitude that the assessment procedures, conferences, and parental interactions are simply "window dressing" to satisfy irrelevant governmental regulations. Therefore, the discussion of the IEP presented in this text will be structured around a conceptualization of the IEP as a process and will address the major stages in the total IEP process (figure 5-2).

Key Term	Meaning
Individualized	The educational program must be addressed to the educational needs of a single child rather than to a class or group of children.
Education	The program is limited to those elements of the child's education that are specifically special education and related services as defined by the law.
Program	The individualized education program is a statement of what will actually be provided for the child as distinct from a plan that provides guidelines from which a program must subsequently be developed.

Figure 5-1: Definition of the Individualized Education Program (IEP)
Source: Abeson and Weintraub 1977.

UNDERSTANDING THE IEP PROCESS

The major steps of the total IEP process are child find, referral, evaluation, placement, and service delivery. Each step includes key actions or events specifically required to guarantee that all intentions implicit in Public Law 94-142 and/or all requirements explicit in the implementation regulations are fulfilled. Each step is sequenced to aid educators in answering certain questions, as shown in Table 5-1 on the following page.

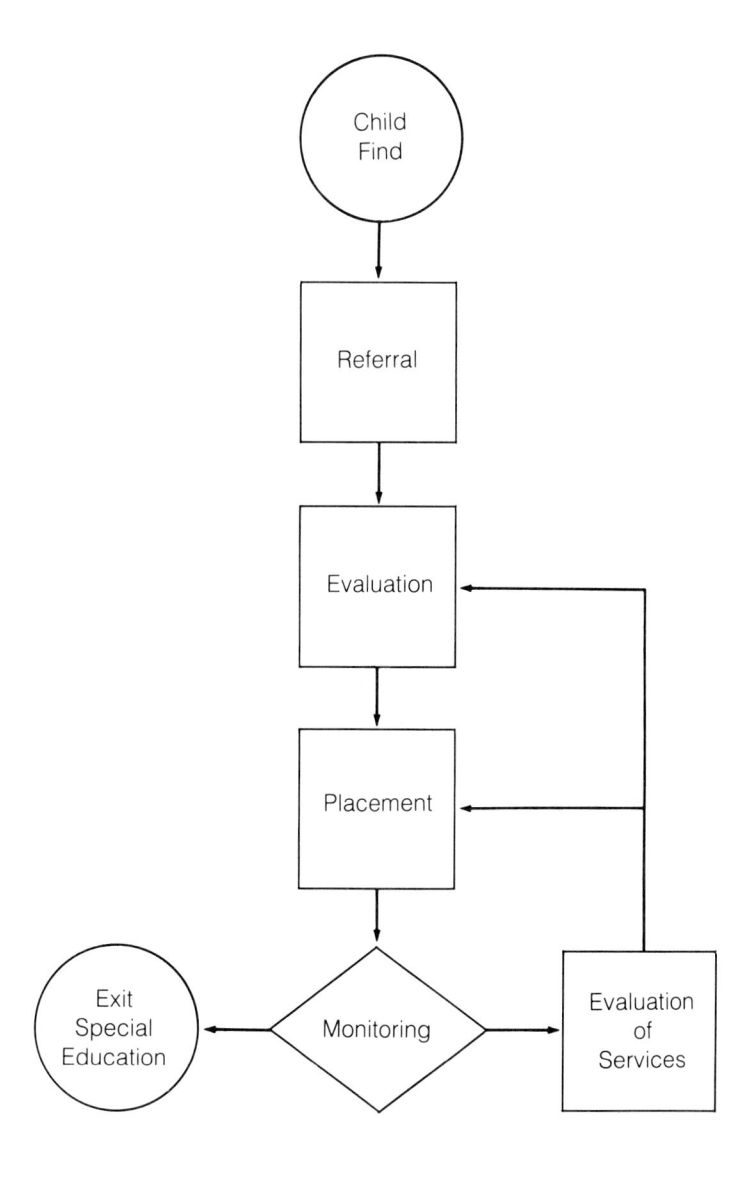

Figure 5-2: The Total IEP Process
Source: Podemski et al. 1984.

Table 5-1: Steps in the IEP Process and the Questions to Be Answered in Each Step

Step	Questions to Be Answered
Child Find	1. Are there children in the community who might be eligible for special services?
	2. Are there children needing special assistance who are not being served?
Referral	3. Does the child have a problem?
	4. What is known about the problem?
	5. Is the problem of such a degree or nature that it dictates the need for evaluation of the student?
Evaluation	6. Does a problem exist?
	7. If so, what is the precise nature of the problem?
	8. What is the primary handicapping condition?
Placement	9. What type of services should the child receive?
	10. What organizational plan is best to deliver the services needed?
Service Delivery (IEP Development)	11. What should the child learn?
	12. What strategies or materials should be used?
	13. Who will assume responsibility for delivering the instruction needed?
Service Delivery (IEP Evaluation)	14. Has the student learned what was identified in the IEP?
	15. If not, why?
	16. Do any changes need to be made in any part of the IEP?
	17. Have the responsibilities of the IEP been fulfilled?
	18. Does the child still need special services?

Child Find

The first step in the IEP process is described by the term **child find** (figure 5-3). Child-find activities identify children who have problems that interfere with academic achievement and school success; thus, they are eligible for services under state and federal laws. According to Public Law 94-142, such activities are the direct responsibility of local school districts. Child-find activities are conducted by school personnel, such as the special education supervisor or the school administrator responsible for supervising the special education program—a principal or assistant superintendent. The Department of Education in each state and various groups serving as advocates for handicapped students may provide assistance or guidelines for the child-find activities. Examples of child-find activities are described in table 5-2.

The basic outcome of child find is that all students who are potential candidates for special services are identified from the population pool of students in the community. Additional secondary outcomes within the community include increased awareness of special services available for handicapped students, the possibility of greater community involvement in various activities that support special education programs, and increased sensitivity to the needs and abilities of handicapped persons.

Referral

The purpose of *referral* (figure 5-4) is to state formally that a child is experiencing difficulties which significantly interfere with school performance. The referral may be initiated by (1) the child's teacher, (2) the parents, (3) other school personnel, or (4) specialists involved with the child through agencies or other contacts. The most common source of referral is the classroom teacher (Siegel and Gold 1982). Typical reasons cited for teacher-initiated referral include: "(1) inability to complete classwork, (2)

Table 5-2:	**Examples of Child Find Activities**

Screening Programs
Teachers are surveyed.
Kindergarten children are screened.
Student performance data are reviewed.

Public Information Programs
Community awareness programs are presented.
Health personnel are contacted.

Interagency Communications
Public agencies are surveyed.
Cooperative groups are informed and involved.

Faculty Interactions
Inservice sessions are conducted.
Faculty members are provided with information on services.

difficulty getting along with peers, (3) poor reading performance, (4) short attention span, and (5) level of learning far below grade level" (Marsh et al. 1983, 79).

Parent-initiated referrals are not as common as those initiated by teachers. Reasons cited in parent-initiated referrals often stem from serious deficits in achievement or from behavioral difficulties such as extreme reluctance to attend school. Referrals from other parties may be initiated because of behavior or performance outside of the classroom, conditions that may have implications for school behavior or achievement.

FACTORS INFLUENCING CHILD FIND

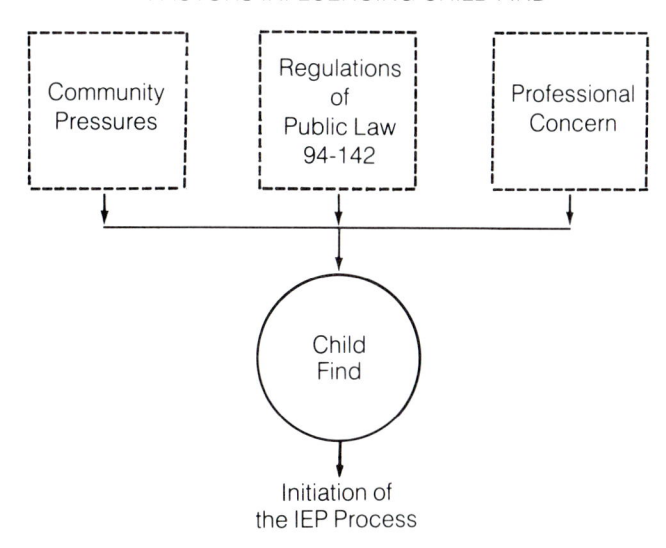

```
┌──────────────┐   ┌──────────────┐   ┌──────────────┐
│  Community   │   │ Regulations  │   │ Professional │
│  Pressures   │   │      of      │   │   Concern    │
│              │   │  Public Law  │   │              │
│              │   │    94-142    │   │              │
└──────┬───────┘   └──────┬───────┘   └──────┬───────┘
       │                  │                  │
       └──────────────────┼──────────────────┘
                          ▼
                       ( Child
                          Find )
                          │
                          ▼
                    Initiation of
                   the IEP Process
```

Figure 5-3: Child Find: Initial Step in the IEP Process

Child find activities are designed to identify children who may be eligible for special services.

All referring parties begin the referral process by contacting the appropriate school personnel, usually the special education supervisor or designated administrator. Parents frequently make the first contact about the problem with the classroom teacher or the building principal, who then, in turn, must contact the appropriate professional within the system. Each school district must have written referral policies and procedures governing the manner in which information about the problem is communicated to school personnel. The procedures vary somewhat among districts, but common to all is the use of a referral form, which allows the referring party to communicate succinctly in writing all relevant information about the "problem."

Referral Form. The referral form (figures 5-5 and 5-6) is extremely important in the IEP process because it is often the first official communication about the student and the possible problem. The referral form also serves to focus the attention and activities of school personnel on a single target, namely, to gather all information relevant to the problem. The form must be completed carefully and accurately with objective, specific data rather than broad, general terms such as hyperactive, underachieving, or disruptive. The latter terms do not mean the same thing to all professionals examining the referral form and therefore may not accurately communicate the necessary information. Data about the student and the problem, which are presented in precise language, make the referral process more time-efficient and effective. See table 5-3.

Table 5-3:	Referral Form Terminology
General	*Specific*
• hyperactive	• out of seat every ten seconds
• distractible	• average on-task behavior is two minutes
• too talkative	• physically attacks others
• aggressive	• completes papers only 25 percent of the time
• unmotivated	• lnot able to follow written instructions
• does not do well	

The special education supervisor or designated school administrator who receives the completed referral form is responsible for the following actions: (1) reviewing the information presented on the form; (2) contacting all involved professionals; (3) coordinating any type of informal evaluation required to validate or augment information presented, including examining school records or observing the child in various school situations; and (4) scheduling and conducting the referral conference (Howe 1981).

Referral conference. After the completion of the referral form and any informal evaluation activities, a conference (figure 5-7) is convened to provide a "forum for collective decision making concerning the student and the future actions to be taken to assist the student" (Marsh et al. 1983, 80). The conference must be attended by at least three professionals connected with the child's case, but the ideal referral team is comprised of all persons involved with the student or with services that might be considered relevant to the case. Table 5-4 is a listing of personnel who comprise the typical referral team.

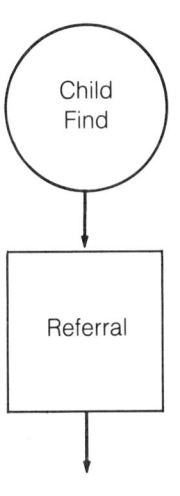

Figure 5-4: Referral as Part of the IEP Process.

Student referral

Student's name: _____ Parent/guardian: _____

Address: _____ Phone no.: _____

Birthdate: _____ Date of referral: _____ Grade: _____

Teacher: _____ School: _____

Reason for referral:

Social adjustment in classroom:

Areas of strength:

Description of academic performance:

Materials being used in academic areas:

Comments on general health-related conditions:

Other comments:

Figure 5-5: Sample Referral Form.

Student Referral

Date: _____ School: _____

Student: _____ Address: _____

Age: _____ Birthdate: _____ Parent/guardian: _____ Phone no.: _____

Grade: _____ Room: _____ Teacher: _____

Recent test scores:

    Name of test   Date given   Primary results

_____

_____

Specific area of academic weakness:

    Subject   Description of problem

_____

_____

Remedial assistance and approaches tried:

Check the space beside the statements that best describe the student:

Adjustment

__ poised   __ tense   __ moody   __ lazy   __ at ease   __ anxious

__ hostile   __ shy   __ depressed   __ sensitive   __ excitable   __ easily upset

__ cries often   __ unhappy   __ cheerful   __ cooperative   __ needs frequent reassurance

Responsiveness

__ alert   __ hyperactive   __ indecisive   __ deliberate

__ prompt   __ impulsive   __ withdrawn   __ daydreams

__ industrious   __ confused   __ hesitant   __ irrelevant or bizarre responses

Teacher opinions and behavior observations (please comment on the student's personality and general adjustment as you know him or her): _____

_____

_____

Figure 5-6: Sample Referral Form.

Relations with others:

___ outgoing, good natured ___ friendly ___ tolerant ___ jealous
___ independent ___ patient ___ has many friends ___ tactful
___ has few friends ___ enjoys group activities ___ plays alone ___ seeks attention
___ conscientious ___ very peer conforming

Effort and application:

___ careful ___ careless ___ distractible
___ spontaneous ___ creative ___ readily fatigued
___ gives up easily ___ works at fast pace ___ works at slow pace

Self-criticism:

___ extremely critical of self ___ boastful ___ downplays own inadequacies
___ healthy recognition of own mistakes ___ does not seem bothered by poor effort

Attention:

___ listens carefully ___ inattentive to most instructions
___ seems to understand most instructions ___ waits until instructions are complete
___ begins to work impulsively without listening to instructions

Perseverance:

___ works constructively on long tasks ___ easily distracted after short periods
___ does not complete many tasks ___ distracted only by unusual events

Motivation:

___ eager ___ resistant, sullen ___ guarded, suspicious
___ indifferent ___ apathetic ___ excessive concern with results

Verbalization:

___ talkative ___ expresses self well ___ difficulty in expression

Self-concept:

___ seems self-centered ___ forceful ___ submissive
___ seems self-confident ___ lacks self-confidence

How do you see this child? _____

Signature of referral party: _____

Figure 5-6 continued: Sample Referral Form.

```
         Initiation
            of
         Process
            |
            v
        Completion
            of
         Referral
           Form
            |
            v
         Addition
           Data
        Collection
            |
            v
         Referral
        Conference
            |
            v
         Outcomes
       /    |    \
      v     v     v
  Further  Formal  No Further
  Informal Evaluation Action
  Assessment
```

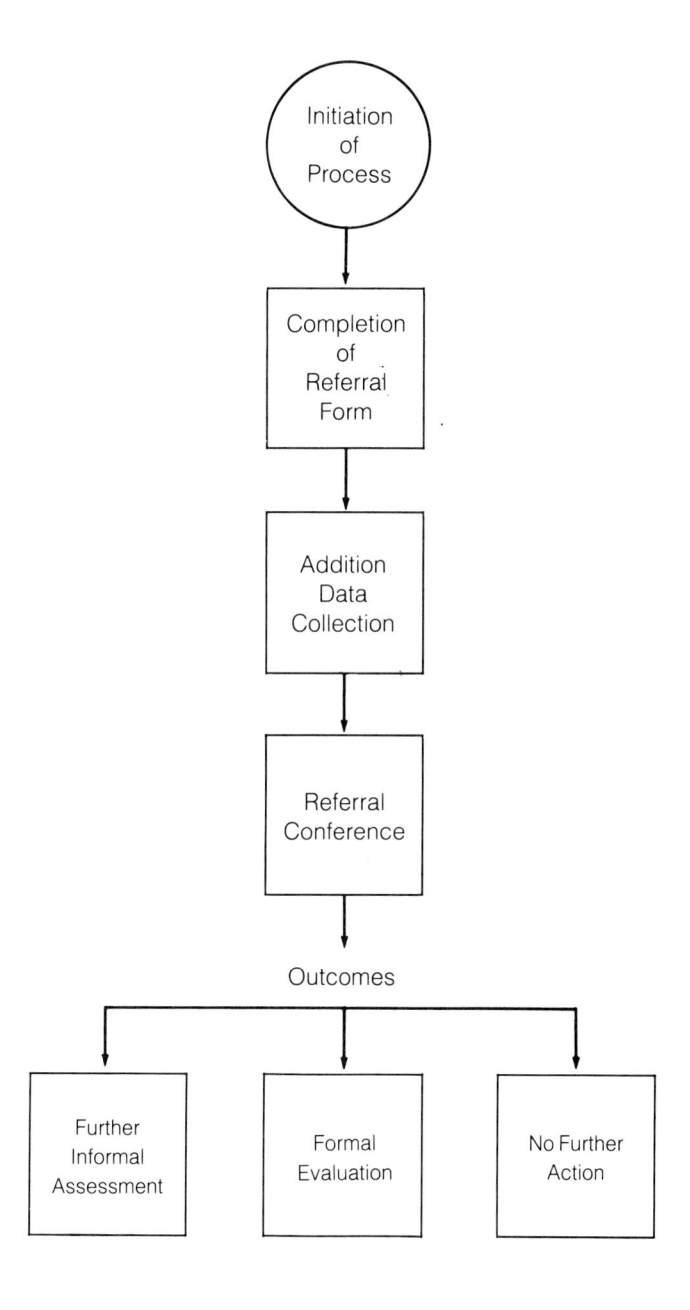

Figure 5-7: The Referral Conference as Part of the IEP Process.

Referral team members must collectively accomplish several tasks, including (1) validating the existence of the problem, (2) specifically describing the problem, and (3) making decisions on future actions to be taken on behalf of the student. Upon completion of the appropriate tasks are three possible outcomes of the referral conference: (1) further informal assessment, (2) formal evaluation, or (3) no additional

132 Mildly Handicapped Children and Adults

Table 5-4: **Referral Team Members**
Referring Teacher or Teacher of Appropriate Grade Level Building Principal or Designated Administrator Special Education Personnel Parent Child (when deemed appropriate)

evaluation or services required. In the case of either of the first two outcomes, the IEP process is continued to the next step, and student evaluation is begun. If the outcome is the determination that additional assessment activities are not necessary, the student is returned to the regular class and other actions are taken to address the situation.

Evaluation

The word *evaluation* is used to describe the procedures for determining "whether a child is handicapped and the nature and extent of the special education and related services the child needs" [*Federal Register,* (August 23, 1977): Vol. 42 No. 163]. Evaluation, frequently termed *assessment,* includes the collection of data that describes student performance. Evaluation activities include observation, testing, and other forms of information gathering, as described in chapter 4 of this text and depicted in figure 5-8.

Several salient points should be made about the evaluation of handicapped students:

1. Evaluation procedures should include measures of academic performance, intellectual capability, social functioning, language performance, and an individual history of the child.
2. Personnel involved in the evaluation process must follow the procedural safeguards specified in the *Federal Register,* (1977). (See chapter 4)
3. The evaluation team must document the presence or absence of a handicapping condition and certify the existence of a primary handicapping condition, that is, assign a label to the student.
4. The evaluation process is conducted by a team, guided by a designated school administrator (table 5-5).
5. The two possible outcomes of the evaluation process are (a) that special education services are needed or (b) that such services are not warranted.

Table 5-5: **Possible Members of the Evaluation Team**
Building Principal or Designated Administrator Special Education Personnel Referring Teacher Parent Psychologist, Psychometrist, Educational Examiner Speech Clinician and/or Audiologist Allied Health Personnel School Guidance Counselor Child (when deemed appropriate)

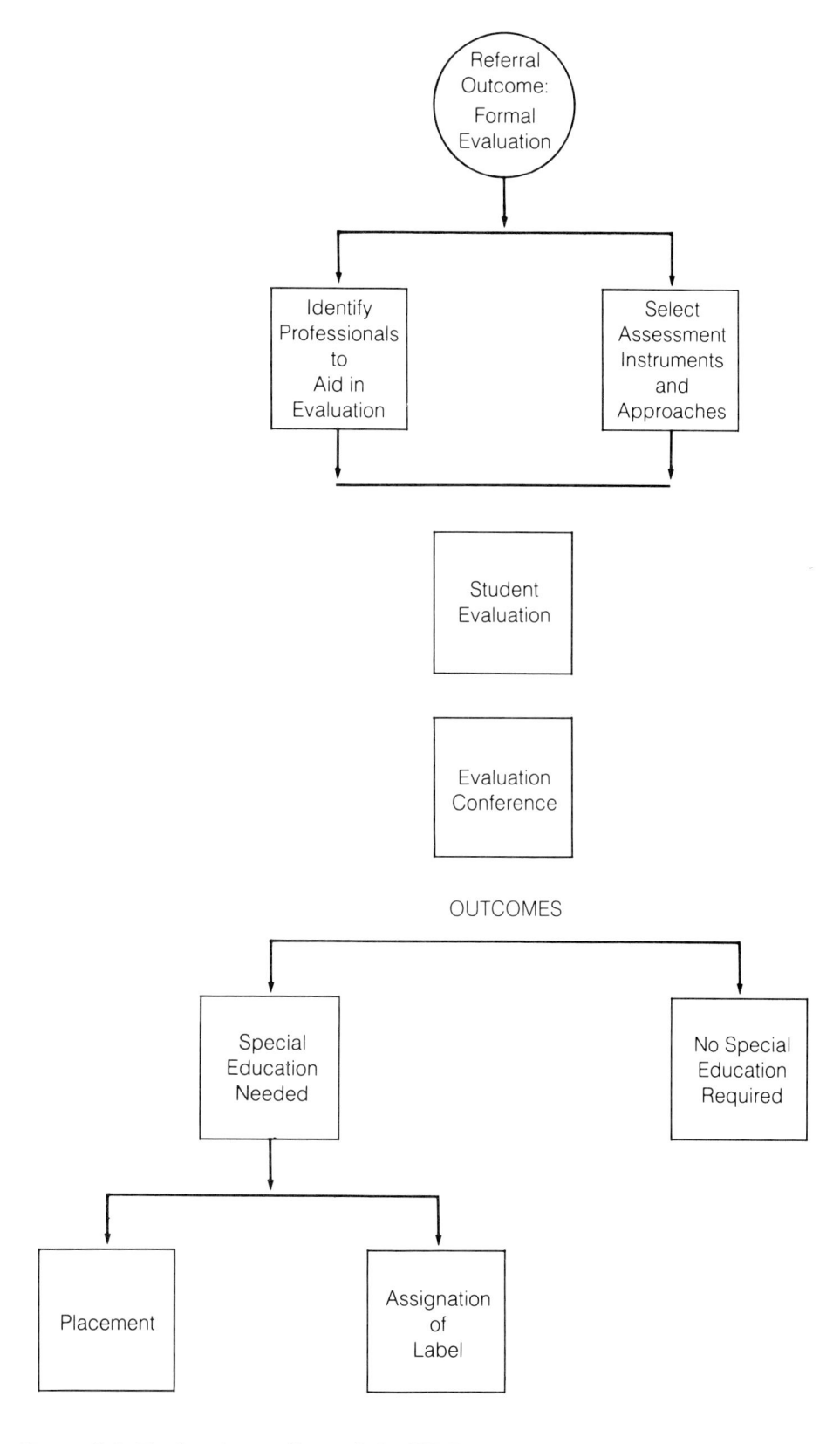

Figure 5-8: Evaluation as Part of the IEP Process.

HIGHLIGHT

State Programs Are Many and Varied

By Nancy Rubin

Amid rising concerns about the large number of children classified as learning disabled, confusion over eligibility requirements and shrinking funds, more schools and states are developing alternative programs as a screening device before referring a student to special-education services.

An example of how such programs work can be seen in this case from the Independence, Mo., school system: Early this year Cherie Toban, a third-grade teacher at the Middle Creek Elementary School in Independence, noted that one of her students, Cheriece Beem, was displaying puzzling gaps in her reading and math skills and seemed socially withdrawn. While the other students progressed rapidly through the multiplication tables, Cheriece forgot them soon after memorizing them. In addition, she read far below grade level, and demonstrated unusual difficulty blending vowel and consonant sounds. "She didn't have any of the qualities I normally associate with learning disabilities, but she was performing so far below grade level I wasn't sure," Mrs. Toban said.

Cheriece was removed from Mrs. Toban's class and placed in a nine-week alternative "Focus" program, where she received drill on basic language and math skills. Today, she has returned to Middle Creek Elementary and is performing well as a fourth-grader. "I had no idea about her previous difficulties," said Randall Kephart, her current teacher. "I see Cheriece as an average student, one who does satisfactory work, seems eager to learn and is well liked by her classmates."

Because the Federal definition of a learning disability has an educational rather than medical thrust and is based on a "severe discrepancy between achievement and ability," educators and school administrators are often caught in a dilemma about how to classify their underachievers. "Given the fact that the state of the art in identifying the learning-disabled child isn't as precise as we'd like, there are concerns about these 'borderline' children," said Dr. Martin Kaufman, director of educational services in the Office of Special Education Programs of the United States Department of Education. "More schools are beginning to ask themselves if they have exhausted what's reasonable and possible within regular education before placing a child in a special-education pull-out program."

After passage of Public Law 94-142, the Education For All Handicapped Act, the nation's learning-disabled population more than doubled, from 797,213 to 1,745,871, in the five years through 1981 82. Educators contend there are many reasons for this growth, most importantly compensation for earlier underidentification. "But there is also the fact that teachers often have no alternative for getting help for students who underachieve because they are slow learners, have behavior, environmental or cultural problems," observed Dr. James Chalfant, professor of special education at the University of Arizona. "There are thousands of children with learning or behavior problems so troublesome that teachers have few educa-

(continued)

Education Fall Survey *New York Times*, 11 November 1984, section 12.

tional options other than to refer them to special education."

In an attempt to screen dubious cases, state and local education boards have put into effect a variety of interim programs. Among the most popular are building-level support teams, or student-support teams as they are sometimes called, in which students with educational problems are evaluated by school-staff members or consulting teachers before being referred for special services. In 1980, California enacted legislation encouraging school districts to create such teams to evaluate underachieving students who did not appear to be learning disabled.

"Our hope is that the student-study teams will promote early identification of a child with potential problems and provide him with appropriate remediation," said Lou Barber, director of special education for the California Education Department. "If we can give students the skills, we believe it will help many stay in the classroom rather than be sent to special education."

In a similar effort, Vermont issued handbooks to its 277 school districts this fall recommending building-based support teams to its schools as a first step before a student is evaluated for learning disabilities. The Ohio Board of Education has also proposed regulations that ask schools to incorporate the building-level-team approach into its standard procedures prior to recommending a student for special education tests.

In September the Colorado Department of Education proposed rules for accreditation of its schools based on detailed reports of student outcomes. Schools will be asked to review the methods they use to help their underachieving students. While Colorado schools have used building-level conferences since 1981 to deal with underachievers, the new rules make those conferences part of a school's accreditation process.

Eight states have also begun to experiment with teacher-assistance teams, a peer-group brainstorming method that helps teachers struggling with underachievers. In a plan developed by Dr. Chalfant and Margaret Pysh, the classroom teacher presents a child's problems to three other teachers in a formal report form. After the team teachers study the child's work and observe him in the classroom, they meet with the classroom teacher and make recommendations. If these do not work within a reasonable time, the child is then referred to special-education services. The process has proved effective. A 1980 Federal Department of Education study on 15 demonstration teacher-assistance teams in Arizona, Illinois and Nebraska found that special-education referrals were cut by two-thirds.

One of the most important aspects of the program, according to Joseph Fisher, assistant superintendent of the Illinois State Board of Education, is that it is a pragmatic approach to students with learning difficulties. "T.A.T. is not an alternative to helping a child with learning disabilities, but a process to insure that all other regular academic avenues have been explored and attempted before that referral is made," he said. Dr. Fisher also noted that the T.A.T. approach was also less costly, time-consuming and stigmatizing to the child than an immediate referral to special education.

Other school systems, sensitive to the spiraling effects that early educational difficulties often have upon students, have created alternative classes for children within the regular system. One of the oldest is Project Read, an alternative language-arts curriculum established in the Bloomington, Minn., schools in 1970, which has recently been copied in Sarasota, Fla., and in Hemlock and Lansing, Mich. Based on the concept that a child with learning difficulties in

(continued)

> the first grade is likely to have future reading problems, Project Read routinely draws its population from children in the lowest first-grade reading groups.
>
> At Sea Cliff, L.I., the North Shore schools have also developed an early remediation program for low-achieving youngsters within the regular educational system. After a routine screening test, kindergarten youngsters found "at risk" for learning problems are placed in special classes where they are taught to read, write and spell through a multisensory approach. At the end of each year, the children are tested to measure their progress. Those who continue to have problems after the third grade attend regular classes but may also attend remedial-reading programs or other small-group instructional sessions.
>
> This year the New York City schools have also created a plan to deal with low achievers. Called the "program alternatives to special education," the $7 million plan provides funds to school districts to establish classes for children who are not achieving satisfactorily but are not believed to be learning disabled. "The idea is to give the child who isn't learning well an alternative between a class size of 35 and a referral to special education," explained Edward Sermier, chief administrator of the division of special education for the New York City schools. Mr. Sermier stressed that teachers could still refer any student for special-education evaluation whether he was in the alternative program or not.
>
> "If there's any nightmare that educators face," he said, "it's this kind of annual growth in the numbers of children being placed in special education as opposed to the other real issue — which is, how do we more effectively bring quality education into our classrooms?"

6. If the evaluation outcome is the documentation of a condition that requires special education services, the evaluation team must select the *least restrictive setting*, which is, in effect, the placement or type of service model through which the child will be served.
7. Parental consent *must* be obtained prior to formal assessment and prior to placement.

LEAST RESTRICTIVE SETTING

Services to handicapped students were traditionally selected from a limited array of approaches. The most common choices were residential care, enrollment in a special day school, and instruction in a self-contained classroom operated solely for handicapped students (Reynolds 1973). The selection of service was usually predicated on the label assigned. For example, the assignation of the label *mentally retarded* dictated a specific list of placements: sending the child to an institution or securing placement in a special class or school. With the advent of Public Law 94-142 in November 1975, however, came significant changes in service patterns for handicapped students (Cegelka and Prehm 1982). These included the development of placement options that were major alternatives to traditional organizational patterns (Turnbull and Turnbull 1978). The changes stemmed basically from the legal requirement that handicapped students be educated in the least restrictive setting.

As indicated in chapter 1, the phrase *least restrictive setting* is used to describe the instructional setting or organizational arrangement selected for each handicapped child in order to maximize the educational opportunities available to that student (Reid and Hresko 1981). As depicted in figure 5-9, the ideal placement procedure is for each student's case to be examined in light of the particular information gathered during the referral and evaluation activities, and for a determination to be made about the best placement for that student. Two important facets of this ideal process are (1) that the unique characteristics and needs of the child take precedence over the label assigned and (2) that the service options are infinite and not limited by availability of services.

Several points about this ideal process are important:

1. Two students bearing the same label (i.e., learning disabled) may be provided services through two totally different approaches because of the unique assessment profile of each student.
2. The determined placement is based on an examination of the student's needs rather than on a mere scanning of a list of options available in the community or district.
3. If the needed services are not presently available, the district must arrange to provide those services or develop a cooperative arrangement with another agency or district to see that the student receives the required educational opportunities.

Service Models

The ideal does not always materialize as a reality; this is also true of the concept of least restrictive setting. Following the passage of the law, special educators were confronted with the task of developing regulations and procedures for translating the concept of

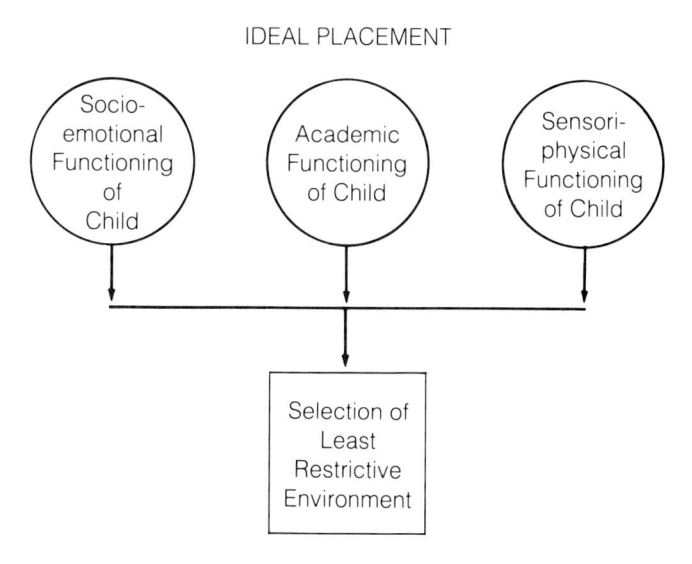

Figure 5-9: The Ideal in Placement Procedures.

least restrictive setting into placement and service practices. The model that closely paralleled the regulations and services is **Deno's Cascade of Services** (1970). See figure 5-10. It also figured prominently in the development of the guidelines. "The idea of the Cascade has been incorporated into federal and state laws and regulations governing special education and is the basis for implementation of the least restrictive environment principle" (Peterson et al. 1983, 404). Terminology (self-contained classes, resource room, etc.) and organizational structure of special education services in schools mirror the basic components and concepts of the Cascade; therefore, Deno's Cascade must be considered important in understanding least restrictive setting. These are the several significant, positive aspects about the Cascade of Services Model:

1. It aids conceptualization of a continuum of services (Podemski et al. 1984).
2. The intent of the Cascade is to present a base of service options for exceptional students (Merulla and McKinnon 1982).

CASCADE OF SERVICES

Least Restrictive

Regular Classroom

Regular Classroom With Assistance For Regular Teacher

Regular Classroom With Supportive Services For Child

Part-Time Special Class

Full-Time Special Class

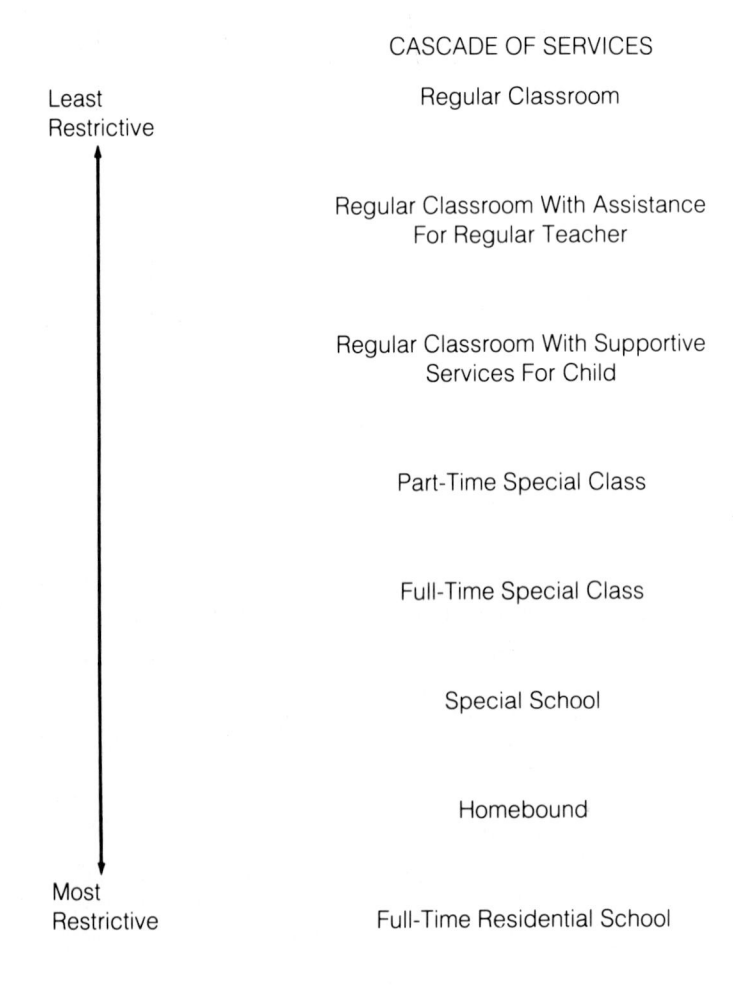

Special School

Homebound

Most Restrictive

Full-Time Residential School

Figure 5-10: Cascade of Services Model
Source: Deno 1970, 229–37.

3. The focus of the services is not on physical plant and other mechanical aspects of placement (Reid and Hresko 1981).
4. The emphasis of the model is on the appropriate assignment of special education students so that they eventually advance toward regular class placement (Cegelka and Prehm 1982).

Even though the Cascade of Services Model has played a significant role in the evolutionary process of least restrictive setting, some criticisms of it should be mentioned:

1. Implementation of Deno's procedures may be too limiting because of the lack of agreement about the precise nature of levels of disability (MacMillan 1977).
2. While flexibility and movement within the Cascade was the original intent of Deno, rules and organizational procedures may have converted the Cascade into a model too strict and precise to allow students to move freely along the continuum of services (Merulla and McKinnon 1982).
3. Some evidence encourages educators to question the existence of the distinctions conveyed by the model, such as the amount of integration involved in each level, the types of students served, and the differences in the allocation of time by teachers, thus presenting the model as operating somewhat differently than assumed in policy (Peterson et al. 1983).

Numerous and other models for continua of services have been proposed by Van Etten and Adamson (1973), and Berry (1974). However, since the Cascade of Services by Deno (1970) is considered one of the most prominent in special education service delivery (Peterson et al. 1983), the service models (Level IV, III, II, and I) considered the most prevalent in educating mildly handicapped are described in a discussion structured around the Deno model.

Full-time Special Class (Level IV). This approach is usually described as the self-contained special class model, a phrase which refers to an organizational strategy recognized as the traditional classroom found in American elementary schools. Some characteristics of the self-contained classroom might be considered ubiquitous, including: 1) one certified, special education teacher has primary responsibility for directing the instruction in the classroom, 2) most of the instruction is delivered within one classroom, 3) other services, such as speech, physical education, and music, may or may not be delivered by the special education teacher, but if not, they are still considered ancillary services to the self-contained program, and 4) the degree of individualization delivered to students pivots on the skills and motivation of the teacher and the diversity of materials and approaches employed within the classroom.

During the period 1950–1970, the self-contained, special classroom became the preferred organizational strategy for educating students with less severe types of handicapping conditions (Reynolds 1973). Preference for that model continued into the early 1970s, but it was beginning to lose support among parents and educators even before the passage of Public Law 94-142. Numerous hypotheses can be generated to explain the self-contained classroom model's apparent gradual loss of status, but the most logical would seem to include the following:

1. The population of students subsumed under the umbrella term *handicapped* was becoming increasingly diverse as students were identified as perceptually handicap-

> **Table 5-6: Summary of Possible Advantages and Disadvantages of the Self-Contained Classroom Model**
>
> *Advantages*
> 1. Full-time interaction with the teacher may allow more scheduling flexibility.
> 2. Students are able to spend more time in small groups with peers, which may foster friendships.
> 3. Parents may form closer relationships with one teacher than if they deal with several teachers.
> 4. Grouping for instruction may be easier to accomplish.
> 5. It may be easier for one teacher to assume complete responsibility for the student's performance.
>
> *Disadvantages*
> 1. The student's opportunities to interact with peers and other adults are restricted.
> 2. Teachers may be isolated from other staff members.
> 3. Opportunity is limited for special education students to have experiences with students of other ability levels.

Source: Cegelka and Prehm 1982.

ped, dyslexic, and learning disabled; these new subgroups presented a different profile of skills and needs than that of the mentally retarded, who comprised the bulk of the handicapped population prior to the 1970s.

2. Parents were becoming more actively involved in the education of their handicapped children, and often they objected to the isolation of these children from the mainstream activities of the school.

It is not particularly surprising that the loss of status experienced by the self-contained classroom model might have been predicated on attitudes and other social factors rather than on scientific research data. In fact, the establishment and maintenance of the self-contained model itself were not based on any clear-cut evidence of improved student learning! Apparently, the self-contained classroom came into favor as a result of the same societal influences that reduced its prevalence as an organizational pattern. Some distinct advantages and disadvantages of the self-contained classroom model are shown in table 5-6. It is an organizational model that will continue to exist in schools if present trends continue.

The self-contained classroom model commonly serves students who require full-time help. It is usually used as a structure for educating moderately or severely handicapped students; however, in some instances mildly handicapped students are educated in a self-contained classroom, either because it is considered the least restrictive setting for them or because it is deemed most expedient by the school administration. This last explanation is totally inappropriate and inconsistent with the intent of Public Law 94-142 and the concept of least restrictive setting, but the reality of implementation is that placement may result from just this motivation.

Part-time Special Class (Level III). The part-time special class is commonly called the resource room model and is significantly more integrated with the mainstream of the school than is the self-contained classroom. As stated earlier, the ultimate goal of special education services is the integration of handicapped students into the regular classroom. Therefore, the resource room might be considered a bridge between a self-contained class and full-time enrollment in a regular class. The resource room is a model through which students can receive special instruction part of the day and spend the balance of the day in the regular classroom setting with their peers.

Table 5-7: Types of Resource Rooms

Type	Description
Categorical	The children who attend are from one area of exceptionality.
Cross-Categorical	Children are assigned according to instructional level not label.
Noncategorical	Children in this model may or may not be labeled handicapped, but they do have mild or moderate learning and/or behavior problems.
Specific Skill Program	Teachers usually work on a specific skill area, typically with nonlabeled children who need assistance.
Itinerant Resource Teacher	Services are provided to more than one district, with the teacher serving part-time in each district.

Source: Wiederholt, Hammill, and Brown 1978.

Resource rooms can be varied, as indicated by Wiederholt, Hammill, and Brown (1978), who identify five types of resource rooms (table 5-7). But there are some definite commonalities among the resource room approaches, including those identified by Marsh and Price (1980):

1. The student divides the day between the resource room and the regular class.
2. Resource room scheduling is usually done so that only small groups of students are in the resource room at any one time.
3. Instruction is almost totally individualized and centers around the objectives and goals of the IEP for each child.
4. The focus of instruction may include remediation of student's basic skills or assistance in passing regular class subjects, an approached termed **accommodation.**
5. The teacher should be a certified special educator with experience and training in management of a resource room.
6. Successful resource room programs require extensive interaction and cooperation between the special education program and the regular classes of the building.

Resource room programs represent the major organizational approach used in junior high schools and secondary school programs. This structure is more compatible with the scheduling patterns found in most secondary schools and seems a more reasonable approach for adolescents. The resource room approach allows the teacher to aid the student in the particular areas requiring attention yet allows the adolescent to participate as much as the handicapping condition permits in normal high school classes and activities.

Even though conceptually the resource room model seems to offer extensive opportunities for mildly handicapped students, some practical considerations in the broad application of the resource room model include:

1. Teachers in resource room settings must have an extensive repertoire of skills (Sparks and Richardson 1981).
2. A high level of cooperation among teachers and students in the regular classes is required to make the resource room placement work effectively (Reid and Hresko 1981).
3. Teachers in resource settings must have clearly identified objectives for the program and a definite understanding of how the resource program fits into the overall structure of the school (Marsh et al. 1983).

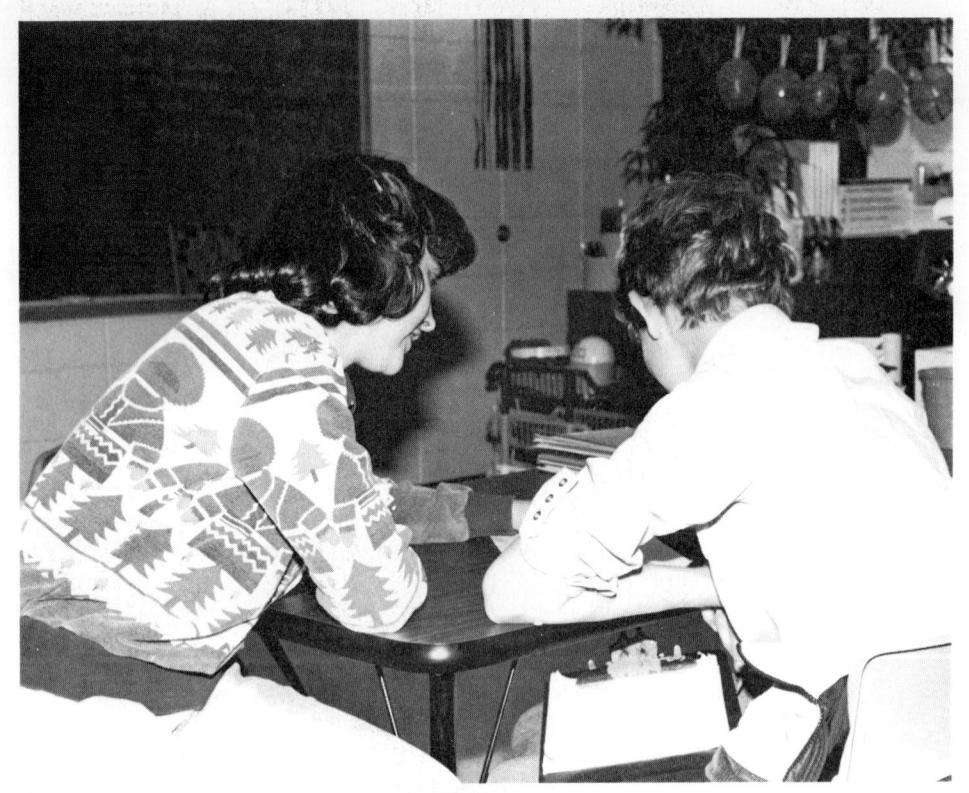

The resource room approach allows the teacher to aid the student requiring special attention.

4. School-wide support, especially from administrative personnel, is necessary in order to ensure that students served in a resource room are maximally integrated with the mainstream of the school and its activities (Podemski et al., 1984).

In spite of some practical concerns, the promise of the resource room setting has extensive support among special education professionals (Pasanella and Volkmor 1973; Hammill and Wiederholdt 1972; Sparks and Richardson 1981; Siegel and Gold 1982; Marsh et al. 1983) and the resource room model appears to be a popular administrative stragegy for serving mildly handicapped students (Podemski et al., 1984). Therefore, a section briefly reviewing the advantages and disadvantages of the resource room model are included in table 5-8.

Regular Class Placement with Supportive Services (Level II). One of the strategies subsumed under this arrangement is the itinerant teacher model, upon which school speech therapy programs are patterned. Another type of special services using this model is mobility training for visually impaired students in rural areas. The itinerant teacher, who could be called a traveling or circuit-riding teacher, works with handicapped students on a regular schedule of two or three sessions per week. While the typical itinerant teacher works directly with individual students, in some instances the itinerant teacher may work with small groups of children requiring the same type of remediation.

Table 5-8:	**Summary of Possible Advantages and Disadvantages of Resource Room Model**

Advantages
1. There are more opportunities to interact with peers.
2. Students can benefit from the expertise of several teachers.
3. The resource room is more compatible with secondary programming and organizational patterns.

Disadvantages
1. Coordinating services for students in this model can become very complex for the teacher.
2. Parents of students may have difficulty communicating with a broad range of teaching personnel.

Source: Cegelka and Prehm 1982.

Gearheart and Weishahn (1980, 32) state, "The itinerant teacher plan does not seem to be as practical as the resource room plan for students with learning disabilities, behavior problems, or limited intellectual ability because it does not provide intensive services on a daily basis." However, the itinerant teacher model is well-suited to serving students with low-incidence handicaps (visual impairments, health conditions, and hearing impairments) who might be included within the mildly handicapped category. This is especially true in rural, sparsely populated areas where the number of children with such conditions is extremely low.

Regular Class Placement with Minimal Support Services (Level I). This is the "most normal" of the organizational arrangements, allowing for maximum integration of handicapped students with the mainstream of regular education. The regular classroom teacher has primary responsibility for instruction of the handicapped student. The unique aspect of this approach is that any support required is provided to the teacher rather than directly to the child; assistance is delivered through a consulting teacher, assigned to provide consultation to the teacher.

While this is not among the most common models used to serve handicapped students, it is one that might be encountered in certain situations or locations. Periodically, variations on the model appear in limited practice in public schools or in the professional literature. It is important to note that recent economic developments have placed limitations on public education to such a degree that this model might occasionally be considered by administrators as a feasible means of serving mildly handicapped students. No matter how "reasonable" it might appear on the surface, however, cogent examination of the idea leads to the conclusion that the consulting teacher model is not appropriate as the primary means of serving all mildly handicapped students. A more acceptable approach is for the administrator considering alternatives to use the resource room model and employ teaching personnel with training and/or experience with the consultation process, considered a necessary resource teacher skill by some writers (Reynolds 1973; Montgomery 1978; Marsh et al. 1983).

Placement Selection

The selection of the least restrictive setting is very important and is given great attention in the IEP process. Most of what is written about least restrictive setting addresses the administrative aspects and deals with theoretical models. However, as Podemski et al.

Many mildly handicapped children can easily be accomodated in the regular class.

(1984, 2) state, "Regardless of what model is used to depict placement options, or to structure programming concepts for the administrator, the most important point to remember is that the needs of the individual child dictate placement and programming through the IEP."

WRITING THE IEP

After the evaluation process, the evaluation team must determine the existence of a handicap, assign a label to the primary condition, and select the least restrictive setting for the child. An additional responsibility is the development of the actual IEP. The written IEP is the guide for all personnel involved in delivering services to the handicapped student, the apex of the referral and evaluation processes. Torres (1977, 1) describes the IEP as "a management tool designed to assure that, when a child requires special education, the special education designed for that child is appropriate to his or her needs, and that the special education designed is actually delivered and monitored."

IEP Form

The implementation regulations of Public Law 94-142 require that specific components be included in the IEP form. (A sample form is shown in figure 5-11.) The precise form used is a matter of choice for the local school district, but it must contain the following components in some form and order:

- Statement of current level of functioning
- Specific description of services required
- Annual goals and short-term instructional objectives
- Least restrictive setting
- Projected beginning date and duration of services
- Evaluation criteria and procedures employed
- Evaluation schedule
- Assurance that the handicapped child is to be served in the least restrictive environment, integrated with nonhandicapped peers to the maximum degree possible

The form is carefully completed and kept in the student's records as part of the required administrative procedures. More importantly, the IEP guides the teachers involved with the student in designing daily instructional lessons. Because of its importance, the IEP is ideally developed by a team in a conference, not solely by the special education teacher.

Required Conference

The IEP conference must result in a written IEP that is signed by all participating persons. It must specify activities required to implement the educational program and identify the responsibilities of those involved in implementation. Members of the IEP conference team include the following:

- School representative(s)
- Parents
- Teacher(s)
- Child, when appropriate
- Other professionals involved with the case or the provision of services

Relationship of the IEP to Daily Instruction

A major component of the written IEP is the list of *instructional objectives* around which daily instruction is organized. The objectives guide the teacher in developing a daily schedule, selecting instructional materials, and planning instructional sequences. The time the child spends in instruction should be clearly related to the objectives specified in the IEP. The objectives are also the standards against which the school and governmental monitoring agencies measure the child's performance and the effectiveness of the instructional setting.

EVALUATION AND MONITORING

State and federal regulations require that each child's IEP be reviewed at least annually and revised if needed. This evaluation is conducted by a team of professionals, the parents, and if appropriate, the child. Ideally, the evaluation process is lead by the special education supervisor or designated administrator. It culminates in an evaluation

Classification _____

INDIVIDUALIZED EDUCATION PROGRAM

Child's Name _____ Birthdate _____ Age _____

School _____ Grade _____

Date of Referral _____ Date of Eligibility Determination _____

Date of Beginning Service _____ Anticipated Length of Service _____

A statement of the child's present levels of educational, psychological, and adaptive behavior functioning including strengths and weaknesses: _____

_____

_____

_____

Instructional Levels:
　Reading: _____
　Math _____
　Spelling _____

Justification for placement in special education: _____

_____

_____

_____

_____

IQ Range:
　Above Average _____
　Average _____
　Below Average _____
　(optional)

A statement of Annual Goals:	Specific educational and/or support services needed to meet annual goals:	Person(s) responsible to provide service(s):
_____	_____	_____
_____	_____	_____
_____	_____	_____
_____	_____	_____
_____	_____	_____
_____	_____	_____

Figure 5-11: Sample IEP Form.

A description of the extent of the child's participation in the regular classroom, including physical education activities:

_____

_____

_____

_____

Additional pertinent information as needed: _____

_____

_____

_____

Participant and anticipated involvement: _____

_____

EVALUATION/PLACEMENT TEAM MEETINGS and Participatnt Signatures and Titles		ANNUAL REEVALUATION
Date _____	Date _____	Date _____
_____	_____	_____
_____	_____	_____
_____	_____	_____
_____	_____	
_____	_____	Parent(s): _____
_____	_____	RECOMMENDATIONS:
_____	_____	_____
_____	_____	_____
_____	_____	_____
_____	_____	_____
_____	_____	_____

Figure 5-11 continued: Sample IEP form.

conference at which the written IEP is reviewed by all personnel responsible for educating the handicapped child. The effectiveness of every aspect of programming is examined, including the objectives, description of services and least restrictive environment, instructional procedures, and time lines for service duration.

Examination of the effectiveness of all aspects of the child's educational experience is essential, and the importance of the evaluation process cannot be overstated. The outcomes of the decision making conducted at the evaluation conference can have a profound, long-lasting impact on the life of the handicapped child. The potential impact should be obvious after reading this list of possible outcomes from the evaluation process and conference:

1. revision of the stated objectives
2. change in service delivery model used
3. modifications in instructional personnel responsible for services
4. changes in the roles played by related services such as speech therapy
5. alterations in the instructional procedures used (i.e., strategies and materials)
6. termination of services

Several important purposes for this evaluation and review requirement are (1) to ensure that the child does not become "stuck" in an educational program which does not change as the child grows and progresses, (2) to guarantee that all aspects of the IEP are being implemented as dictated by the IEP committee, (3) to allow parental feedback concerning the appropriateness of the program, (4) to require measurement of the child's progress toward the goals established in the IEP, and (5) to formally provide a mechanism for changing the objectives of the IEP. The evaluation conference also serves as the branching or looping point in designing services for handicapped students and accounts for the cyclical nature of the IEP process, as depicted in figure 5-12. The evaluation conference may be the termination point of required services for some students, but for others it may be the point at which the course of services is altered and attention directed to other points within the IEP process. In either event, the decisions made at the conference must not be taken lightly because, in effect, they dictate not only the immediate path of the child's education but also a part of the child's course through life.

DUE PROCESS AND PARENTAL INVOLVEMENT

Bersoff (1978) describes due process as having two significant components: the right to advance notice and the opportunity to be heard. One of the procedural safeguards in the IEP process is the guarantee that parental involvement will be secured at every juncture in the process. This parental or guardian involvement is part of the due process aspect of the law designed to protect the rights of the child and the family. This protection of rights through required parental involvement extends both to children being served in special education whose programs are being considered for revisions and to children not yet enrolled in special education but who are being evaluated for possible services (Howe, 1981).

Parental involvement may include (1) reviewing the child's records, (2) electing to have the child evaluated by a professional outside the school system, (3) participating in all decision making and assessment conferences, and (4) granting permission for assessment procedures to be conducted with the child. The school has several important responsibilities associated with parental involvement and due process, such as providing the parents or guardians with the following notifications:

1. written notice before making any change in the services to the child
2. written refusal of any request made by the parents

The school must also secure *written parental consent* before assessing the child and selecting or implementing placement. The guidelines associated with implementation of

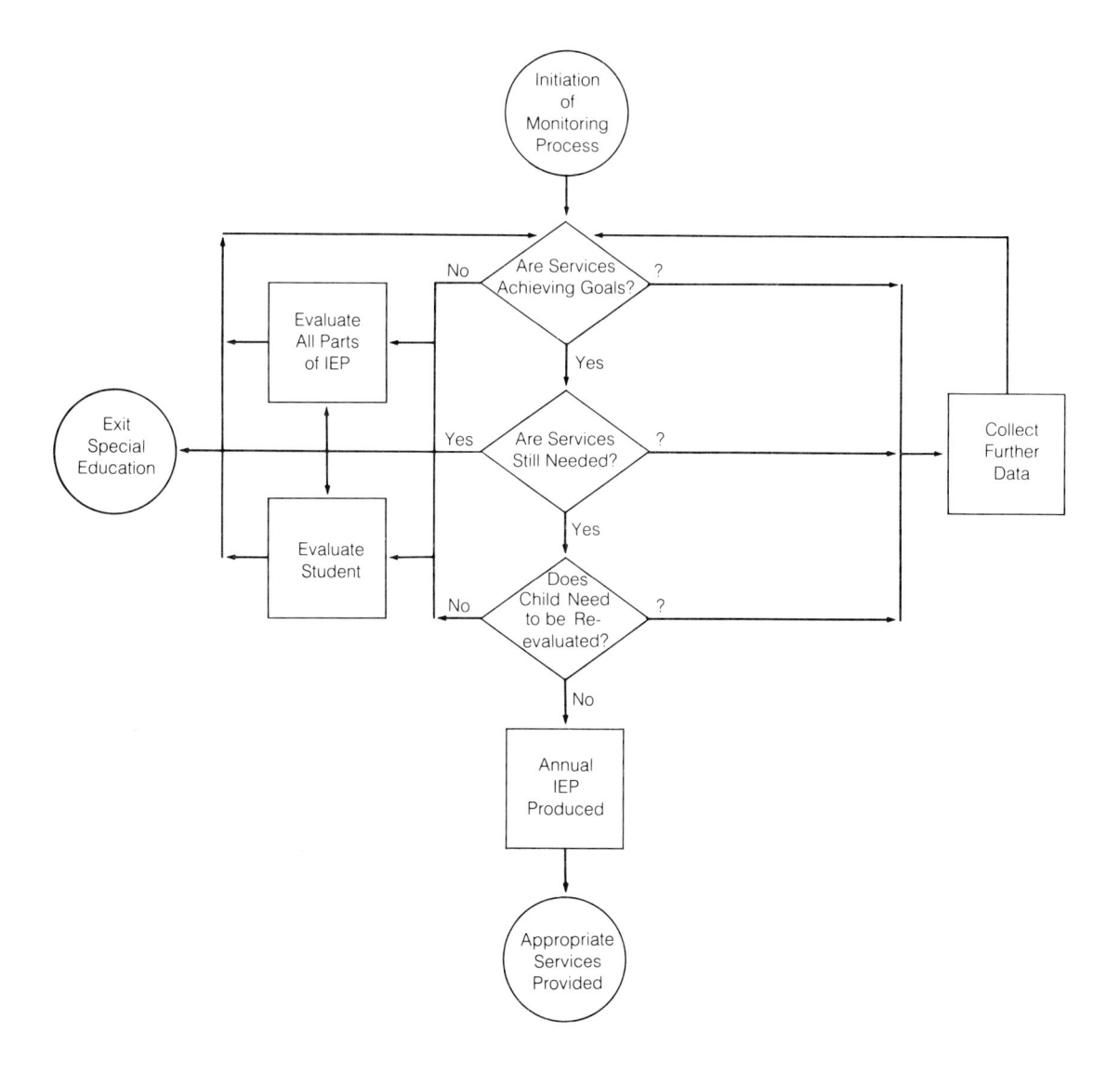

Figure 5-12: Evaluation of the IEP as Part of the IEP Process.

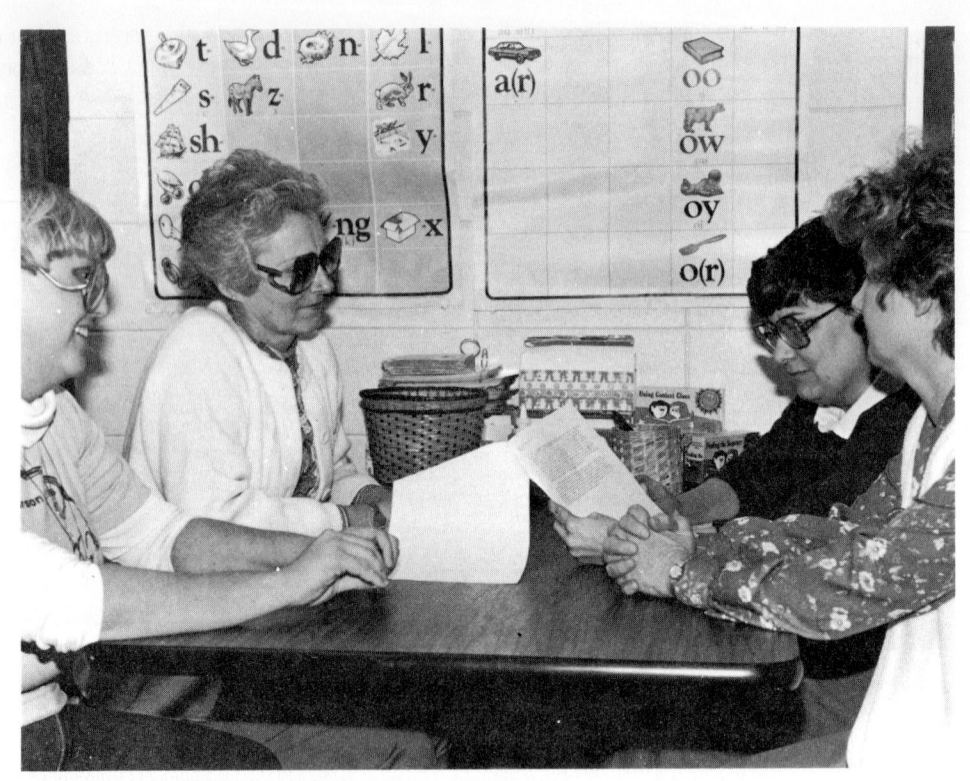

Parental involvement in the referral and placement process is mandated by law.

the IEP, provided by the Department of Education in each state, include the required parental consent and notification forms. The forms must be handled professionally and carefully in order to ensure that the rights of the student or the family are not abridged or violated in any manner.

MAINSTREAMING

"Mainstreaming is the educational arrangement of placing handicapped students in regular classes with their nonhandicapped peers to the maximum extent appropriate" (Turnbull and Schulz 1979). The concept of mainstreaming seems straightforward enough, but unfortunately, many educators initially attended more to the first part of the definition—"placing handicapped students in regular classes—than to the last part—"to the maximum extent appropriate." As a result, the misconceptions about mainstreaming were many:

1. All special education classes should be eliminated.
2. All handicapped students, regardless of the type of handicapping condition, should be placed in regular classrooms.
3. The classroom teacher should have total responsibility for teaching handicapped students in addition to the "normal," achieving students.

Time, experience, and inservice education have fortunately altered most of those early misconceptions about mainstreaming and its implications for the classroom teacher. It is now more accurately perceived as a concept defined in the unique context of each child's case. The degree of integration with "normal," achieving peers (mainstreaming) is different for each child and is determined by the particular skills and needs of the child.

Shared Responsibility: A Philosophy

Mainstreaming is predicated on the assumption that responsibility for handicapped students can be shared by all personnel associated with the educational process, not just the special educator. A critical partner in the process is the regular classroom teacher because, as indicated previously, mainstreaming usually means that the child's day is divided between special services and the regular classroom. An educational philosophy that all students are more alike than different makes such sharing of the responsibility of handicapped students totally feasible. Logic would also seem to support such an arrangement because, as was pointed out in the discussion of the Cascade of Services Model, students served through a more integrated mode are those considered able to manage to achieve in a "normal" environment, perhaps with a limited amount of special services (e.g., a resource room).

While the commonalities of all students are acknowledged, policymakers responsible for implementing mainstreaming perceived that classroom teachers might have concerns and negative attitudes when confronted with integrating handicapped students into the daily program. As a result, undergraduate teacher-preparation programs in elementary and secondary education have begun to offer coursework with the basic information needed by regular teachers to perform as part of the mainstreaming team. Entire courses or components of existing courses address topics such as definitions of areas of exceptionality, legal and ethical issues, the IEP, and responsibilities in mainstreaming. Future teachers are being exposed to such information in an effort to prepare them to understand mainstreamed students, the relationships among all educational components that mainstreaming requires, and the regulations and requirements imposed by state and federal agencies.

Mainstreaming of some students with particular types of handicapping conditions may require involvement from all school personnel, including certain specialists such as those shown in table 5-9. In order for handicapped students to be mainstreamed successfully, all professional parties must:

1. become informed about the student;
2. communicate openly and cooperatively with all other involved professionals and the parents;
3. assume that educational responsibility is to be shared by all school personnel, not just the special education teacher;
4. genuinely strive to see that the student feels accepted within the school environment; and
5. convey a sense of support and interest in the student and the educational program being implemented.

The IEP is at the heart of mainstreaming. It is the shared process and resulting document that weaves the various strands of the school into a common fabric to

Table 5-9: Other Professionals Possibly Involved in Services to Mildly Handicapped Students

Psychologists
Speech Therapists
Mobility Specialists
Librarians
Counselors
Medical Personnel
Audiologists
Curriculum Specialists
Physical Therapists
Occupational Therapists
Recreation Therapist

support the education of handicapped students. The IEP defines the daily educational activities for all parties and provides the objectives for each handicapped student. Even though the various segments of the school staff may not have frequent direct contact, as between the regular and special educator, the IEP and its objectives for the student enable all professionals to coordinate appropriate learning experiences toward the same end.

Shared Responsibility: The Reality

The implementation of mainstreaming became a reality in 1978 when Public Law 94-142 went into effect in the public schools. With its implementation came the need for extensive change in school personnel, including the following:

1. With the passage of the law and the advent of mainstreaming, handicapped students were no longer the sole responsibility of special education personnel, which represented a significant departure from tradition (Marsh, Gearheart, and Gearheart 1978).
2. Teachers' attitudes toward handicapped students and mainstreaming had to be altered (Larrivee and Cook 1979).
3. Mainstreaming required some skills that were not traditionally part of a classroom teacher's repertoire (Tymitz 1981).
4. School personnel had to devote time to mainstreaming and its accompanying required activities in addition to regular school duties (Robson 1981).
5. Serious misconceptions about the IEP and its role in education of the handicapped had to be addressed in teacher preparation and inservice education (Podemski et al., 1984)

The enactment of Public Law 94-142 may have occurred comparatively swiftly, but the changes in education it necessitated have not been accomplished that easily (Marsh et al. 1983). As stated earlier, coursework has been initiated for future classroom teachers in an effort to aid them in acquiring a better understanding of mainstreaming and the needed skills; however, surveys of institutions of higher education reveal that only fifteen states require such a course for all preservice educators (Smith and Schindler 1980).

The implementation of mainstreaming requires extensive cooperation and communication between professionals involved in the services. The needed level of interaction is not easily achieved because of a variance in philosophy among the professionals (Marsh and Price 1980) and because of mundane problems such as differences in daily schedules (National Education Association 1978). It is also difficult to achieve the type of team decision making required by mainstreaming because of the differing opinions of their roles espoused by professionals on the team (Fenton et al. 1979).

The final reality of mainstreaming is revealed by the misconceptions about IEP development, which appear to be prevalent among regular classroom teachers. Some of the misconceptions are (1) that the IEP is merely a form to be completed to comply with state or federal requirements, (2) developing the IEP is the job of special education personnel, and (3) the IEP describes only what the special educator has to do for the child and has no relationship to the rest of the instructional program. In all fairness to regular teachers, these misconceptions result from a lack of information not from a lack of interest in helping children. The significance of these misconceptions, however, is still great in terms of their potential interference with implementation of Public Law 94-142.

Until such time as the realities of mainstreaming are brought more in line with the philosophy of mainstreaming, the full promise of free, appropriate programming in the least restrictive setting cannot be delivered to handicapped students. The charge for bringing the promise to fruition rests not only with teachers and other professionals who are presently engaged in the educational process but also with those who will enter educational professions in the future.

SUMMARY

As indicated in previous chapters, Public Law 94-142, other laws and enactments, and the development of a substantial body of case law resulted in the mandate to provide handicapped students with free, appropriate public education in the least restrictive environment. Numerous implicit and explicit actions on the part of public schools had to be addressed by professional educator groups, state education departments, and federal governmental agencies such as the Office of Special Education. Regulations and guidelines had to be developed to translate the concept of free, appropriate education into practice. This chapter examined the regulations and the accompanying procedures employed in selecting appropriate educational placements for handicapped students as well as the service models typically used in educating mildly handicapped students.

The development of the Individualized Education Plan (IEP) was presented as a continuous process from child find through evaluation of the services provided. The chapter focused more on the provision of appropriate educational services than on the completion of the IEP form. The concept and practice of mainstreaming were defined and described as related to a least restrictive educational setting.

The chapter reviewed the underlying philosophy of mainstreaming and the realities encountered by school personnel involved with the delivery of a free, appropriate education on a daily basis. The difficulties associated with the synthesis of philosophy and practice were examined and strategies offered which may eliminate or at least reduce the potential for conflict between ideal and reality.

REFERENCES

Abeson, A. and F. Weintraub. Understanding the individualized education program. In *A primer on individualized education programs. See* Torres 1977.

Berry, K. *The guts to grow.* San Rafael, Calif.: Dimensions Publishing Co., 1974.

Bersoff, D.N. Procedural safeguards. In *Developing criteria for the evaluation of due process procedural safeguard provisions.* Washington, D.C.: Bureau of Education for the Handicapped, 1978.

Cegelka, P. T. and H. J. Prehm. *Mental retardation: From categories to people.* Columbus, Ohio: Charles Merrill Co., 1982.

Deno, E. Special education as developmental capital. *Exceptional Children* 37 (1970): 229–37.

Fenton, K. S., R. K. Yoshida, J. P. Maxwell, and M. J. Kaufman. Recognition of team goals: An essential step toward rational decision making. *Exceptional Children* 45 (1979): 638–44.

Gearheart, B. R. and M. W. Weishahn. *The handicapped student in the regular classroom.* St. Louis: C. V. Mosby, 1980.

Hammill, D. D., and J. L. Weiderholt. *The resource room: Rationale and implementation.* New York: Grune and Stratton, Buttonwood Farms Division, 1972.

Howe, C. *Administration of special education.* Denver: Love Publishing Co., 1981.

Larrivee, B., and L. Cook. Mainstreaming: A study of variables affecting teacher attitudes. *Journal of Special Education* 13 (1979): 315–24.

MacMillan, D. L. *Mental retardation in school and society.* Boston: Little, Brown & Co., 1977.

Mandell, C. J. and E. Fiscus. *Understanding exceptional people.* St. Paul, Minn.: West Publishing Co., 1981.

Marsh, G. E., C. Gearheart, and B. R. Gearheart. *The learning disabled adolescent.* St. Louis: C. V. Mosby, 1978.

Marsh, G. E. and B. J. Price. *Methods for teaching the mildly handicapped adolescent.* St. Louis: C. V. Mosby, 1980.

Marsh, G. E., B. J. Price, T. E. C. Smith. *Teaching mildly handicapped children: Methods and materials.* St. Louis: C. V. Mosby, 1983.

Merulla, E. and A. McKinnon. "Stuck" on Deno's Cascade. *Journal of Learning Disabilities* 15 (1982): 92–96.

Montgomery, M. D. The special educator as a consultant: Some strategies. *Teaching Exceptional Children* 10 (1978): 110–112.

Education for all handicapped children: Consensus, conflict, and challenge. Washington, D.C.: National Education Association, 1978.

Pasanella, A. L., and C. B. Volkmor. *Coming back . . . or never leaving.* Columbus, OH: Charles E. Merrill, 1973.

Peterson, R. L., R. H. Zabel, C. R. Smith, and M. A. White. Cascade of services model and emotionally disabled students. *Exceptional Children* 49 (1983): 404–410.

Podemski, R., B. J. Price, T. E. C. Smith, and G. E. Marsh. *Comprehensive Administration of Special Education.* Rockville, Md.: Aspen Systems Corporation, 1984.

Reid, D. K. and W. P. Hresko. *A cognitive approach to learning disabilities.* New York: McGraw-Hill, 1981.

Reynolds, M. C. Staying out of jail. *Teaching Exceptional Children in all America's Schools.* Reston, VA: The Council for Exceptional Children, 1977.

Reynolds, M. C. Changing Roles of Special Education Personnel. Paper presented to UCEA, 1973.

Robson, D. L. Administering educational services for the handicapped: Role expectations and perceptions. *Exceptional Children* 47 (1981): 377–78.

Siegel, E. and R. Gold. *Educating the learning disabled.* New York: Macmillan, 1982.

Smith, J. E., Jr., and W. J. Schindler. Certification requirements of general educators concerning exceptional pupils. *Exceptional Children* 46 (1980): 394–96.

Sparks, R. and S. O. Richardson. Multicategorical and cross-categorical classrooms for learning disabled students. *Journal of Learning Disabilities* 14 (1981): 60–61.

Torres, S., ed. *A primer on individualized education programs for handicapped children.* Reston, VA: The Foundation for Exceptional Children, 1977.

Turnbull, A. P., B. B. Strickland, and J. C. Brantley. *Developing and implementing individualized education programs.* Columbus, OH: Charles E. Merrill, 1978.

Turnbull, A. P. and J. B. Schulz. *Mainstreaming handicapped students: A guide for the classroom teacher.* Boston: Allyn and Bacon, 1979.

Turnbull, H. R., and A. Turnbull. *Free appropriate public education: Law and implementation.* Denver: Love Publishing, 1978.

Tymitz, B. L. Teacher performance on IEP instructional planning tasks. *Exceptional Children* 48 (1981): 258–60.

Wiederholdt, J. L., D. D. Hammill, and V. Brown. *The resource teacher: A guide to effective practices.* Boston: Allyn and Bacon, 1978.

Van Etten, G., and G. Adamson. The fail-safe program: A special education service continuum. In *Instructional objectives for exceptional children,* edited by E. N. Deno. Reston, VA: The Council for Exceptional Children, 1973.

Chapter Six

PRESCHOOL MILDLY HANDICAPPED CHILDREN*

*This chapter is written by Anna C. McFadden, University of Missouri, Columbia, Missouri.

CHAPTER OUTLINE

INTRODUCTION
EARLY IDENTIFICATION
    Problems in Early Identification
THE IDENTIFICATION PROCESS
    Child-Find
    Screening
    Diagnosis
    Assessment
PROFESSIONALS INVOLVED WITH IDENTIFICATION
    Medical Personnel
    Public School Personnel
    Other Professionals Involved with Identification
SERVICE DELIVERY: MODEL PROGRAMS
    Home-Based Models
    Home and Center-Based Model
    Center-Based Models
CURRICULAR APPROACHES
    Normal Development Model
    Behavioral Model
    Cognitive Developmental Model
BARRIERS TO PRESCHOOL SERVICES
    Legislation
    Funding
    Socioeconomic Structure
SUMMARY

CHAPTER OBJECTIVES

After reading this chapter, you should be able to:
- Understand and list assumptions underlying early intervention for mildly handicapped children;
- Describe problems associated with early identification of mildly handicapped children;
- Describe the identification process for preschool mildly handicapped children;
- State the roles of various professionals in the assessment of young handicapped children;
- Describe various models for providing services to mildly handicapped preschool children; and
- State barriers to preschool services for the mildly handicapped.

INTRODUCTION

The importance of preschool experiences and their effects on learning and school achievement are widely supported in professional literature (Kirk 1958; Bloom 1964; White 1975; Lazar and Darlington 1979). They have also been accepted by the general public, as evidenced by the support accorded Head Start since its inception in 1965 (Caldwell 1973). Mori and Olive capture the significance and potential impact of preschool experiences in their statement: "Clearly, when various environmental variables are manipulated, critical developmental milestones can be accelerated or retarded" (Mori and Olive 1980, 4). Of course, the desired result of preschool experiences is accelerated learning and achievement.

Acceptance of the Mori and Olive statement makes it logical to assume that the effects of preschool experiences may be even more significant for children with handicapping conditions, a contention supported not only by child development specialists but also special educators (Kirk 1958; Cook and Armbruster 1983). Awareness of the need for and importance of preschool services for handicapped children has captured greater public attention since P.L. 94-142 was passed. The intent of this law and its regulations is to provide every handicapped child from the age of three to twenty-one a free, appropriate public education. The delivery of special education services to young handicapped children, known as *early intervention,* represents a specific component of the Education of All Handicapped Children Act (P.L. 94-142).

EARLY IDENTIFICATION

All state departments of education direct local school districts to conduct *child-find activities.* These activities have several purposes, including:

1. to identify children who would benefit from special services, and
2. to locate children who are not being appropriately served.

For the preschool population, the first purpose—*identification*—is the cornerstone of services. The term *early intervention,* used to describe preschool special education services, means that by increasing efforts at the preschool level, intervening, as it were, may reduce or eliminate the need for services at later points in the child's life.

While there can be no doubt as to the value of early intervention, its merits are based upon two assumptions: (1) *that children requiring early intervention can be accurately and consistently identified,* and (2) *that the diagnostic process will result in interventions or treatment programs that will eliminate or reduce the effects of the condition.* Examination of these two assumptions reveals some discrepancies between the ideal and reality, as reflected by the questions raised in relation to these assumptions (table 6-1).

The assumption that children requiring early intervention can accurately and consistently be identified requires that practitioners be able to compare children to a *performance standard.* There must be not only a clearly stated and recognizable standard but also *valid and reliable instruments and procedures* that can be used in the identification process. In the case of children exhibiting severe discrepancies and difficulties, these aspects may not be quite so significant in initiating early intervention. In the case of the more mild, less obvious conditions, however, the need for standard and reliable, valid instruments becomes central to bringing the promise of early in-

Table 6-1: **Assumptions Underlying Early Intervention and Possible Questions Raised**

Assumption	Questions Raised
1. Children requiring early intervention can be accurately and consistently identified.	• Is there a clearly stated standard against which to judge preschool children? • Can valid and reliable instruments be used to identify preschool students who might benefit from early intervention?
2. The diagnostic process will result in interventions or treatments that will eliminate or reduce the effects of the condition.	• Can specific interventions be definitely matched to the label or condition? • Is the diagnosis directed to the assignment of a label or to a treatment?

tervention to fruition. As mentioned earlier, *identification* is the cornerstone of these services, making this first assumption, that children can be accurately and consistently identified, one which should be neither taken lightly nor routinely accepted without question.

The second assumption underlying the acceptance of early intervention is that the diagnostic process will result in interventions which will eliminate or reduce the effects of the condition. This is commonly called the *medical model,* meaning that examination of a set of symptoms will, through certain deductive analyses, lead to a specific set of treatments. As indicated in table 6-1, this assumption raises several practical questions. For example, have any treatments and/or interventions definitively demonstrated that they have this desired effect on preschool children who have been identified? In the case of more severely handicapped students, such evidence seems to exist (Bender and Valletutti 1976; Kirk 1958; Safford 1978), especially in areas such as language (Bricker and Bricker 1974) and physical development (Lillie 1968). However, clear and specific relationships do not always exist between the condition identified and the treatment and/or interventions employed. For instance, identifying a child as learning disabled does not automatically dictate a specific treatment approach (Marsh, Price, and Smith 1983). Therefore, educators and other professionals involved in early intervention must make every effort to address the questions associated with this assumption.

Problems in Early Identification

The realities of identifying preschool children with mild handicaps can be awesome, regardless of the intentions of the law, educators, parents, and other advocates. These realities include *referral* of such preschoolers, *involvement* of appropriate professionals in the identification process, and *proper diagnosis* (table 6-2). While these realities exist in the identification process for all mildly handicapped children (Marsh, Price, and Smith 1983), they seem to be exacerbated in the case of preschool children (Safford 1978).

Sources of Referrals of Preschoolers. As indicated in table 6-2, getting referrals of preschool children may represent a significant problem in early identification efforts. *There is no single professional responsible for directing the daily, educational activities*

Table 6-2: Problems in Early Identification

Problem	Contributing Factors
Sources of Referrals of Preschoolers	• No single professional is responsible for directing the daily educational activities of preschoolers. • Parents might appear to be the logical source but may not realize or be able to admit that a problem does exist. • Unless the family is receiving services from some social service agency, social workers may not have enough contact to refer a preschool child. • Social workers typically have greater interaction with lower socioeconomic families, so referrals from other income groups are less likely.
Involvement of Appropriate Professionals	• Preschool programs may be staffed by a variety of personnel depending upon the sponsoring agency or organization. • Identification requires a team approach, typically found only in conjunction with public school programming or extensive preschool services in an agency or comprehensive private school.
Diagnosis of Preschoolers	• Typically most states have screening programs for school-age children. • *Lack of clear and definite standards* against which to measure a child's performance is a major complicating factor in diagnosis of a child not yet in school. • Parents or other adults dealing with preschool programs may not have access to instruments to identify high-risk students. • Parents may not have a conceptual standard of what is "normal" or "appropriate." • There is a possible negative effect of labeling or mislabeling a preschool child.

of preschoolers. For school-aged children, classroom teachers have responsibility for referring children who have a suspected handicap. However, for preschool children from birth to age five, especially those not enrolled in a formal educational program, a professional may not be available to assume such a responsibility.

Parents may not realize or be able to admit that a problem does exist (Turnbull and Turnbull 1978) and therefore do not seek professional assistance for their preschooler. Sadly, there are even those parents who Schulz says do not "feel it [an educational program] is worthwhile" (Schulz 1978, 31), but these parents are few in number.

The two primary stimuli for referrals of preschool children who might benefit from early identification are (1) state and local child-find activities such as those mandated by P.L. 94-142, and (2) efforts of parents who are concerned that their child is not developing normally. In this last instance, parental concern may be based on a discrepancy, real or imagined, between their child's development and that associated with the normal developmental milestones, differences among siblings in terms of development, and/or observable difficulties in performance. Regardless of the reason for the parental concern, these parents begin attempting to locate information and/or assistance in dealing with the child, prompting a referral.

Parents may not have the knowledge of child development necessary to identify a handicapped child.

Although less common than parental or school related referrals, activities conducted by social workers as part of other social services for a family or its members may result in referral of preschool children. Social worker initiated referrals appear to occur most often with children from low socioeconomic homes. Unless social workers or other agency representatives are involved with the family, however, some children may go unreferred and therefore undiagnosed; in these instances, no services will be provided to the child.

> **HIGHLIGHT**
>
> ## Spotting Problem and Setting a Course
>
> By Betty Osman
>
> Although a child's learning problems are usually identified first in school, parents frequently suspect very early that "something isn't quite right," perhaps even before their children are old enough to go to school. They may notice that Jimmy at 6 months rarely sleeps through the night and has a hard time settling into a routine. At 4, he still can't count to three or remember color names. Betsy's second-grade teacher complains to her parents that she can't sit still in class and her writing is messy; while Joey, the class clown in sixth grade, never finishes an assignment and says he hates school.
>
> Although the parents of these children may sense that something is the matter, they sometimes keep their concerns to themselves. Perhaps they do not want to admit — even to themselves — that anything is wrong, but more likely lack confidence in their own judgment and do not know where to go for help. So they wait for the school to tell them what they already suspect.
>
> When parents sense a problem, they should not deny it or let themselves be falsely reassured. Most learning disabilities do not disappear. Early intervention, though, can minimize difficulties that develop in school — and save both child and family years of frustration. But each child must be measured against himself rather than compared to others.
>
> The diversity of learning disabilities makes them hard to pinpoint. There is no single pattern of learning or behavior that signals their presence at any age. There are a few early signs and symptoms, but no parent should scrutinize a young child for evidence of a learning problem or predict difficulties merely because a toddler cannot count to three or put a puzzle together. Each child has a different developmental profile.
>
> An early sign of potential learning disabilities is difficulty with language. When a child's speech is significantly delayed, or his "baby talk" persists for an inordinately long time, it may presage later problems in reading, spelling and writing. If a child is not talking by the age of 3, a speech and language evaluation is probably warranted to determine the reason.
>
> At the age of 4, for example, Tony was an independent youngster. He could dress himself, write his name and copy a triangle. He did not speak very much, though, and when he did he was almost impossible to understand. His attempts to describe an experience usually ended in his crying in frustration. Danny, on the other hand, could express himself adequately at age 4, but did not seem to listen or remember what was said to him. His mother wondered if his hearing was all right. It actually was, but both Tony and Danny had learning disabilities that affected them in different ways.
>
> Another sign of a learning disability can be when a child assiduously avoids puzzles, cutting and coloring in the early years. This may indicate that his fine motor coordination is not up to par. Difficulty with handwriting and written work in school
>
> *(continued)*
>
> Education Fall Survey *New York Times* 11 Nov. 1984, Sec. 12.

may follow. And when a child who couldn't wait to start school comes home every day moody and irritable — and complains of stomach aches only on school days — he may be signaling that he is having trouble learning. If he says he hates to read, it may be because he can't. "It's boring" can usually be translated to mean "it's too hard."

Learning disabilities are not necessarily confined to academic subjects. There is also a social side. Many youngsters have as much trouble making friends as they have with their homework. Reading facial expressions and body language can be as confusing to a learning-disabled child as reading numbers and words, and paying attention in a game can be as challenging as concentrating in a history lesson. For example, a child's inability to concentrate or display of particularly erratic behavior may signify learning disabilities. If he never seems to finish a project and can't even sit through a television program, he may have a short attention span that will surely affect his social relationships as well as his work in school.

What should parents do if they suspect that their child might have a learning disability? For a child who attends school or even a day-care program, the teacher is the first person to consult. If parents and teacher agree that there is cause for concern, the child can be referred for a psychoeducational assessment. The referral can be made by teachers and parents, or parents may pursue a referral alone— they know their children, and should trust their intuition if they suspect a problem. In most instances, the testing can be carried out by a school psychologist or learning-disability specialist, and under Federal law must be initiated within 60 days. The same ruling applies to pre-school programs that are within a state's public school system.

However, if a pre-schooler is not enrolled in a school program, parents should consult their family physician or pediatrician. If the response is "He's just immature, he'll outgrow it," they should seek further advice. Most likely there are diagnostic services available at a nearby medical center, university or family agency. A psychologist or therapist who specializes in learning disabilities could also be helpful.

Many changes occur within the family of a child found to be learning disabled. The child no longer bears the burden alone. Although the learning problems may be most apparent in the classroom, a child's family can begin to spread a support cushion; there is much they can do to alleviate a child's anxiety and make life easier for all members of the family. A few suggestions follow:

An honest discussion of the problem with the child clears the air. Children need to know the truth in language they can understand. They'll have less frightening fantasies if they know the reason for their difficulties. Also, brothers and sisters may become unexpected allies if they are informed and can understand.

Daily routines provide stability and organization for "L.D." youngsters who typically feel lost in time and space. A regular time for homework, television and dinner and a special place for books and games takes the guesswork out of living and reassures the child who needs to feel more secure.

Finding a child's area of competence outside his academic subjects provides an ego boost for a youngster who does not feel good about himself in the classroom. Collecting rocks or becoming the neighborhood ornithologist can give him the status he needs among his peers. And if he is a talented artist or a good athlete, those activities should be encouraged, even if it means somewhat less time for studying.

A child with learning problems needs

(continued)

to feel accepted, to know that his parents care about him as a person, not just as a student. A child who is frustrated during the school day needs to be listened to when he comes home — with empathy and support rather than criticism or blame. How parents feel about a child helps determine how that child feels about himself.

Along with acceptance, honestly given compliments encourage growth and self-esteem that is necessary for a healthy adjustment in life. Children need to know what is good about themselves as well as what their problems are.

The child in the family with learning disabilities is not the only one who needs help. Parents also need to be understanding and supportive. It takes both patience and stamina to be the parent of a child with a handicap, and there is too little help available from overworked professionals. Recognizing their needs, parents around the country have formed grassroots organizations to provide information, advocacy and support, allowing parents to share their experiences and problems.

Parents of children with learning disabilities face many difficult decisions with which they may need help. Should our child be in the "mainstream" or in special education? Do we need a tutor or can he manage alone? Is the reading program at school adequate — and is he progressing? They may not be prepared to make these decisions alone. Conferences at school can help parents keep abreast of their child's individual program and his progress, but if they continue to have questions or doubts they may also want to consult an outside counselor or therapist for a second opinion — and to help with the more difficult decisions that must be made.

To really help parents and children with learning disabilities, professionals in medicine, education and psychology need to work together to assist parents in early identification and treatment. They must also help parents understand their own feelings and accept those of their children; parents can be their children's greatest resource for learning and living.

Involvement of Appropriate Professionals. Unlike elementary and secondary schools, programs for preschool children (normal and otherwise) are quite varied in nature, purpose, and focus. Some programs are primarily day care with the emphasis on nutrition, socialization, and physical development. Other programs emphasize activities that are quite "school like" or considered preparatory for academic achievement (*Newsweek* 1983). The diversity of the programs results in an extremely broad range of professionals subsumed under the heading of service providers for preschool programs, as shown in table 6-2. This diversity represents a major problem in efforts to implement early identification of preschool children. Professionals such as preschool educators and child-development specialists are expected to be part of the staff in preschool programs; but others who are involved often come from a wide variety of backgrounds, including medicine, social work, psychology, and physical education, depending upon the location of the program and its source of funding. For example, preschool programs may be associated with churches, colleges and universities, hospitals, and private business. Each of these preschool programs may have significantly different purposes, procedures, and employee profiles. This diversity of personnel may make it even more difficult to convene a team of specialists for preschool identification unless, as in some states, public school personnel assume that specific responsibility and/or provide the leadership required.

Diagnosis of Preschoolers. One of the major realities (table 6-2) confronted by professionals attempting to identify preschool children with mildly handicapping conditions is the *lack of clear and definite standards* against which to measure children's performance, as suggested in the discussion of the assumptions underlying early intervention (Ellis and Cross 1977). Even though standards of performance in elementary and secondary schools are often implied and general rather than specifically stated, performance norms do seem to be more observable and consistent there than at the preschool level. For example, in elementary and secondary schools, achievement data and other types of standardized assessments can be used to measure certain areas of performance; these can also be coupled with classroom performance data provided by the teacher.

Parents or other adults dealing with preschool programs may not have access to screening programs and instruments developed to identify high-risk students, considered so critical to early intervention. Even though many of the screening programs have flaws and may be of questionable reliability and validity, especially if inappropriately used, they can provide something of a rough estimate of performance.

Another complicating aspect of identification for referral of preschoolers is that parents may not have a conceptual standard of what is "normal" or "appropriate," especially if this is their first child (Keeffe 1984). Even when there are other children, lengthy time intervals may have colored the memory's conceptual standard. Peer performance or normative data as a standard for evaluating preschool performance may not be readily available to the adults associated with the child. At best, they usually rely on nebulous "norms" predicated on the behavior and performance of other children they have reared or with whom they have been associated. These standards are probably imprecise and biased, complicating identification even more.

A second problem associated with diagnosis is the *possible negative effect of labeling or mislabeling* a preschool child (Cook and Armbruster 1983). Negative effects which may be produced include the following: (1) identification of children who are experiencing developmental lags rather than those with actual handicaps that impede learning and will not be eliminated or reduced by special programming; (2) inappropriate assignment of a label which results in an intervention not consistent with the nature of the child's problem; (3) alteration of parental and professional expectations, causing further developmental delays in the child (i.e., labeling a child as mentally retarded may result in lower expectations of parents and teachers and delivery of inappropriate interventions); and (4) development of a self-fulfilling prophecy in preschool children identified and assigned a label. These children may begin to behave in the way they perceive their parents and other family members view them.

THE IDENTIFICATION PROCESS

The identification process for preschool children incorporates many of the same general steps and procedures used for locating the school-aged population requiring special education services: child-find, screening, assessment, diagnosis, and placement. Some aspects and problems within the identification process are unique to the preschool program. These will be presented through the discussion, but the reader is expected to be somewhat familiar with the general procedures described in an earlier chapter.

Child-Find

Each state department of education is required by P.L. 94-142 to conduct a Child-Find Project to identify children who might benefit from special education services but are presently unserved and children who are not being appropriately served. Typically, the emphasis in most states is on locating school-aged children rather than preschool children (Lessen and Rose 1980). Several explanations may be suggested for the focus of attention on school referrals instead of early intervention:

1. Each state has its own eligibility age for receiving special education services
2. Not all states have state enactments which require preschool services to be delivered even if children are identified
3. Some states have rather "undeveloped" systems of preschool education, reflecting a more fragmented population and unstructured administrative organization than that of schools

One of the major results of the discrepancies among states is that while the type of child-find activities for preschool handicapped children may not vary significantly from one state to another, the expected outcomes, goals, and even effects may be different. Child-find activities in most states include conducting a public awareness campaign to inform parents about the services available from their local school district and other state and community agencies. Media such as television, radio, newspaper, brochures, and posters are also used to find possible high-risk children who will be referred for further evaluation and perhaps special education services.

Screening

Screening is the assessment or examination of a large group of students to identify those most likely to be "high-risk." The screening process is the initial step in the assessment process. The results of screening should identify children who have a possible problem requiring further evaluation. *The results of screening should not be used to label a child or to develop an intervention program.* Instead, results should *only* be used to guide further investigative efforts on behalf of the preschooler.

Professionals who comprise the screening team may use a variety of strategies to gather information about the child. These may include using instruments specifically designed for this purpose. Several basic screening instruments for preschool children are described in table 6-3. In addition, professionals may also collect various kinds of data relevant to their own discipline and cadre of professional skills. For example, social workers or psychologists may contribute important socioemotional information collected in natural settings (Spaulding 1980) or physicians and/or nurses may report on nutrition and medical histories (Anspaugh, Gilliland, and Anspaugh 1980). In any event, whether specific screening instruments are used or other types of data are collected and reported, only pertinent information should be shared, and it should be contributed as objectively as possible to avoid some of the potential problems identified earlier.

Table 6-3 Screening Instruments

Instrument Name	Description of Test	Age Range	Intended User
1. Denver Developmental Screening Test	Consists of 105 items in the four areas of fine motor, gross motor, personal-social and language skills	Birth to 6 years	Preschool and trained paraprofessionals
2. Developmental Indicators for the Assessment of Learning (DIAL)	Screening test for identifying preschool children with learning problems	2½ to 5½ years	Preschool teachers
3. Developmental Activities Screening Inventory (DASI)	A nonverbal measure which identifies major developmental skill deficits requiring remediation. Can be used with hearing impaired and learning disordered; adaptions for physical and visual impaired are possible	6 to 60 months	Preschool teachers
4. Developmental Screening Inventory	Individual administrative instrument which assesses abnormal development in gross and fine motor, language, and personal-social skills	1 to 18 months	Preschool teachers
5. Boyd Develpmental Progress Scales	Consists of 150 items in developmental areas related to adaptive behavior and activities of daily life; parent interview items are included	Birth to 8 years	Professionals from any of the disciplines working with the child
6. Aldern-Boll Development Profile	217 items in the developmental areas of gross motor, fine motor, receptive and expressive language, cognitive, self-help and personal-social skills	Birth to 9 years	Examiner/Interviewer; caregiver
7. Minnesota Child Developmental Inventory	320 items in the developmental area of gross motor, fine-motor, receptive and expressive language, self-help, social-perceptual and situation comprehensive skills	1 to 6 years	Parents
8. Brigance Diagnostic Inventory Early	A criterion referenced inventory that determines developmental levels in the areas of psychomotor, self-help, communication, general knowledge, comprehension, and academic skills	0 to 7 years	Teacher or trained paraprofessional
9. Learning Accomplishment Profile	A developmental checklist to assess language, cognition, self-help, gross motor, and fine motor skills	0 to 6 years	Teacher or trained paraprofessional
10. The Portage Guide to Early Education	A criterion referenced checklist to assess cognitive, self-help, motor, language, and socialization skills	0 to 6 years	Teacher or trained paraprofessional

Source: J. H. Meier 1976.

Diagnosis

The purposes of diagnostic procedures include the following (Ellis and Cross 1977):

1. to determine whether a problem does exist,
2. to clarify the cause of the problem,
3. to develop an intervention plan, and
4. to determine the most appropriate services for the child.

Examining these purposes reveals that diagnosis is much more specific than screening and should be carried out by a multidisciplinary team; members of the team should be selected on the basis of the child's suspected handicap. The team may involve a variety of trained professionals such as physician, social worker, psychologist, teacher, and speech therapist. After the relevant information has been obtained and analyzed, a conference should be arranged with the parents and the multidisciplinary team to discuss placement, educational programming, service options, and treatment plan. The previously mentioned problems associated with preschool identification, including lack of specific personnel to direct the referral effort and wide diversity of personnel associated with preschool programs, often make achieving the desired quality of diagnostic procedures difficult.

Assessment

The purposes of assessment include the following:

1. to determine a child's specific strengths and weaknesses,
2. to determine a child's level of functioning in various developmental areas, and
3. to identify the child's learning traits.

The resulting information is used to develop instructional objectives and goals for the child's curriculum as specified in the child's IEP. Fulfilling the purposes of assessment in terms of preschool handicapped children requires extremely competent personnel because of the difficulties which may be encountered in attempting to identify and quantify strengths and weaknesses in a child who has not yet achieved great language facility (Cook and Armbruster 1983).

The most commonly used procedures in assessment of preschool children are: (1) *criterion-referenced measurements* and (2) *informal assessment techniques* (Ellis and Cross 1977). "A criterion-referenced test is based on the sequence of skills in a particular area of the school curriculum and is used to determine a student's mastery of skills without any reference to norms" (Marsh, Price, and Smith 1983, 23). "An informal test is typically one that is devised by teachers or others in a particular setting for evaluating student behaviors in many domains" (Marsh, Price, and Smith 1983, 24). The popularity of these two approaches may be attributed to any one or more of these explanations:

1. Both approaches allow personnel to evaluate the child, using an established level of performance as a standard
2. Both can be conducted more easily within the organizational structure of a preschool than informal testing
3. Both can be used in a more "non-pencil-and-paper" manner than can formal, normed tests

Informal assessment techniques are useful with preschool children.

Assessment can also involve the use of procedures such as anecdotal records, observational reports, daily logs, video tapes, Piagian concept testing, and norm referenced tests (Marsh, Price, and Smith 1983). Although norm referenced tests are not usually used with this population, they might be used to gather useful information for the preschool teacher and/or other professionals involved with program development for the preschool child (Cook and Armbruster 1983). A variety of assessment instruments in various developmental areas, which can be employed with preschool children, are described in table 6-4.

PROFESSIONALS INVOLVED WITH IDENTIFICATION

The identification of preschool, mildly handicapped children may involve a host of professionals, including pediatricians, obstetricians, dentists, public health nurses, social workers, ministers, public school personnel, and parents. Other participants may include Head Start and public day care center personnel, neighbors, and other family members (especially grandmothers).

Many of these professionals will be able to provide information about one or more aspects of the child's performance but no one can provide a complete picture; the identification process really produces a composite profile of the child, reflecting a sum of all the parts contributed by the various professionals involved with the child.

Table 6-4 **Assessment Instruments**

Instrument Name	Developmental Area	Description of Test
Bayley Scales of Infant Development	Infant Development	A motor and mental scale of over 200 items (2 to 30 months)
Cattell Infant Intelligence Scale	Infant Development	Yields a mental age score which may be converted to an Intelligence Quotient (3 to 30 months)
Gessell Development Test	Infant Development	Measures developmental age in motor, adaptive language, and personal-social behavior
McCarthy Scales of Children's Abilities	Intelligence Development	Yields a general cognitive index with scores for verbal, quantitative, perceptual, memory, and motor areas (2½ to 8½ years)
Stanford-Binet Intelligence Scale	Intelligence Development	Yields a mental age which may be converted to an Intelligence Quotient (2 to 18 years)
Wechsler Pre-school and Primary Scale of Intelligence (WPPSI)	Intelligence Development	Yields a verbal and a performance score (2 to 6 years)
Utah Test of Language Development	Language Development	Assesses expressive and receptive language skills (1½ to 14½ years)
Houston Test of Language	Language Development	This test has two forms: assesses the language of children from birth to six years; measures reception, conceptualization, and expression
Pre-school Language Scale	Language Development	Assesses auditory comprehension ability; includes a section on articulation (1½ to 7 years)
Bayley Scales of Infant Development	Motor Development	Contains a motor development section to assess degree of body control, coordination of large muscles, and fine motor skills (2 to 30 months)
Development Test of Visual Motor Integrations	Motor Development	Assess the degree to which visual-perception and motor behavior are integrated, test consists of 24 geometric forms to be copied by the child (2 to 15 years)
Development Test of Visual Perception	Motor Development	Assesses the development of perception in children (eye-hand coordination, figure-ground perception, form constancy, position in space, and spatial relations (3 to 9 years)

Source: N. H. Fallen and J. E. McGovern, 1978.

Medical Personnel

Typically, medical personnel provide information concerning the child's sensoriphysical performance and development. Medical histories, including achievement of major developmental milestones by the child, may be included for review by the evaluation team. In addition, prenatal data describing the mother's pregnancy and perhaps genetic information may figure significantly in evaluating a preschool child.

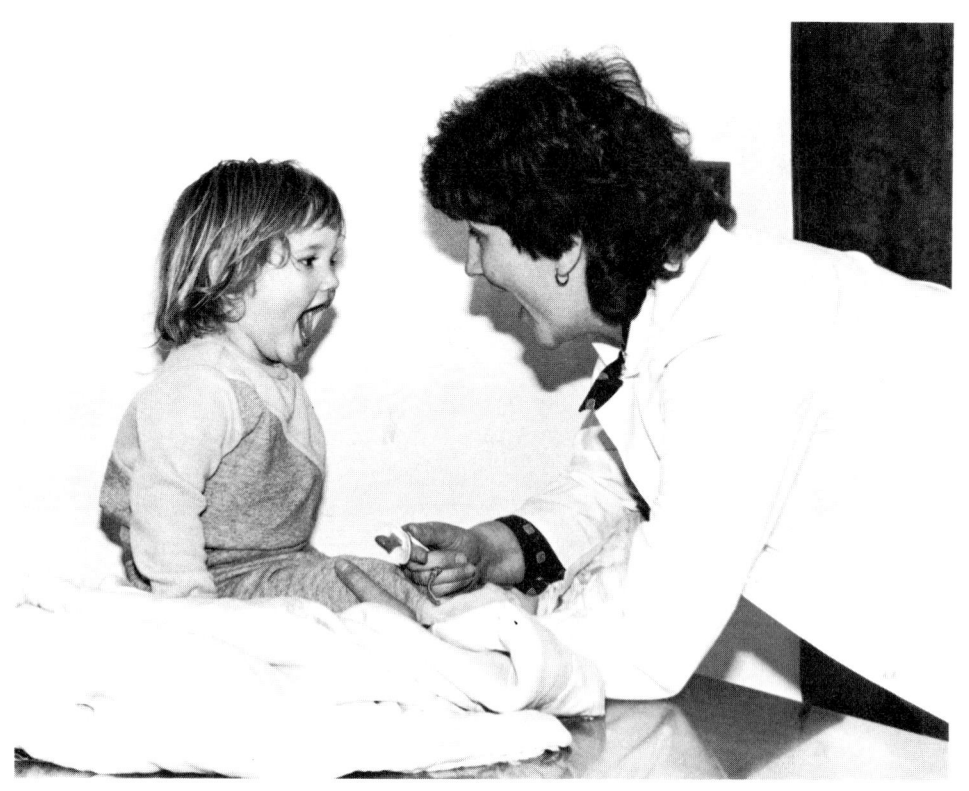

Medical evaluations provide information on sensory and motor performance and development.

A growing body of research concerns allergies and their relationships to development and learning. As knowledge in this area increases, medical personnel may be more able to describe these conditions and their effects on achievement and to relate their medical treatments, such as drug therapy, to educational programming.

Obstetrician. The initial identification of a possible disability may be made by an obstetrician (Fallen and McGovern 1978). While a severe handicap may be clearly identifiable at or prior to birth, the obstetrician may also become aware of a mild disability as early as the first few months of pregnancy through such techniques as amniocentesis and ultrasound echograms. Amniocentesis is a process by which the amniotic fluid around the fetus is tested to determine if certain types of conditions exist that may result in the newborn child's being handicapped. Ultrasound echograms are used to reveal multiple fetuses, orthopedic impairments, and physical abnormalities that may need special treatment at the moment of birth. As technological advances are made in the area of medical research and early diagnosis, the possibility that family physicians will be involved with preschool identification is increased significantly.

Pediatrician. The traditional role of the pediatrician has become more demanding and complex due to the significant developmental and associated health problems of handicapped children (Howard 1982). Many pediatricians have become specialists in the area of handicapped children to meet the growing demands of this population and their families. The pediatrician may play several roles, including these described by Howard (1982):

1. aiding the parents during the initial diagnostic period,
2. helping the parents through the various consultations with other medical specialists,
3. guiding them in understanding the diagnostic results of laboratory tests,
4. assisting the family in adjusting to the fact that their child has a handicap,
5. answering any questions the family may have regarding the child's present and future medical problems, and
6. aiding the family in learning to become competent and confident in interacting with their child.

After the identification of a handicapped child, the pediatrician may suggest an early intervention program to the parents. It will be necessary for the pediatrician to collaborate regularly with the intervention program's staff of educators and therapists, parents, and social workers in order to provide constant exchanges of information. The pediatrician must provide information regarding medical factors that may have an effect on the child's behavior and development, and continually review the course of intervention for the child.

Nurses. Nurses may be some of the most actively involved medical personnel associated with handicapped preschool children, particularly public health nurses and pediatric nurses. The public health nurse may observe a child in a health clinic or in the home, often as a result of involvement with the family through one or more forms of agency services. The pediatric nurse may have the opportunity to observe a child in the pediatrician's office, the hospital nursery, or a clinic. The pediatric nurse may prove a valuable resource because of extensive experience with the peer group, which has allowed the nurse to develop a conceptual standard against which performance can be judged.

Public School Personnel

Teachers in public school preschool programs are constantly involved in activities with the children, activities that can contribute data important to the identification of handicapped children. Teachers have the advantage of observing children on a daily basis as compared to other professionals who may be involved with the child on a more limited and less frequent schedule. The preschool teacher is also able to observe various aspects of the child's performance within the natural context of the age cohort, a better standard for interpreting the data. Teachers are also in a unique position because they are able to attend to the child's performance in terms of several important variables, such as demonstrated mental ability, sensoriphysical development, and social-emotional functioning. Other professionals are usually concerned with only one specific area of development such as physical problems. This explains why teachers in some areas have been asked to assist in massive screening and public awareness programs (Cook and Armbruster 1983).

Other Professionals Involved with Identification

Depending upon the nature of the suspected handicapping condition, other professionals may be involved with the identification process. This involvement may result from other problems encountered by the family such as financial or adjustment problems, which mean interaction with agency personnel or other professionals. The following section reviews the possible involvement of professionals such as social workers and ministers; the list of those included here for discussion is certainly not all-inclusive but instead reflects those most commonly expected to have involvement.

Social Worker. The social worker may play an important role in early identification of a handicapped preschool child as a result of involvement with the family. Other problems, especially in those families with low socioeconomic status, may require the attention of the social worker, who may then become a frequent observer in the home. Because of this interaction with the family in the home environment, the social worker may be able to detect any atypical behaviors and then make the proper referral for assessment, evaluation, and placement (if needed) for the child. The social worker may also be able to identify an inappropriate environment in which a handicapped, preschool child may be living. The parents may have inadequate skills due to their socioeconomic status or minority group status; they may also be observed by the social worker to have inadequate training and to be unable to provide intellectual stimulation needed by the handicapped child. It is these parental inadequacies in infant stimulation that may affect the child's mental, psychological, and social development (Fallen and McGovern 1977). The social worker may refer the family and child to other professional sources for training in intervention strategies to be implemented in the home environment. The social worker may also be involved in explaining, monitoring, or evaluating the progress made in a home-based service delivery model.

Ministers. Ministers may routinely visit the homes of their church members and may also make special visits because of particular events, such as the birth of a child. Therefore, ministers, like social workers, may have the opportunity to observe both the child and the family and to provide insight into the needs of all parties. The minister also may be able to recognize abnormalities in the preschool child and to aid the family in securing appropriate professional help, including referral for assessment, evaluation, and intervention.

Obviously, many ministers are not professionally trained in identification and social work. However, by virtue of their position in the community and their relationship to the family, they may be able to initiate services for children who would not otherwise come into contact with professionals, and therefore would not be identied until much later. The role of ministers should be recognized as a valuable link between the child and family, and the professionals in the community who may be able to provide services.

SERVICE DELIVERY: MODEL PROGRAMS

Service delivery model is a phrase that refers to the environment in which a child with special needs will be placed to receive services. The determination of the most appropriate means of delivering services to handicapped students is a decision that should be predicated on several important variables, including:

1. information about the child's handicapping condition,
2. geographical considerations,

3. the program's theoretical basis, and
4. the available service model options.

The delivery system models may be categorized into *home-based, center-based,* and those in *hospital settings*; these three general categories are described in table 6-4. There can be many combinations such as home and center-based or home followed by center-based models. A brief review of the major service delivery models and the primary curricular approaches within each model will aid the reader in understanding programming provided to preschool handicapped children. In addition, a description of exemplary preschool programs within each delivery system will be included to illustrate the most salient features of each approach.

Home-Based Models

The basic intent of home-based programs is to offer a means through which professionals or paraprofessionals train parents in the home environment to provide services to the handicapped child. These home visitors/trainers visit the homes regularly for several purposes, including:

1. to act as consultants,
2. to evaluate the success of the intervention, and
3. to make regular assessments of the child's progress.

Many home-based programs have programming objectives for children from birth to three years of age (Karnes and Zehrbach 1977). Research results suggest that these programs are more effective in stimulating the development of the child than are center-based programs, although home-based programs require more staff, time, and monies (Karnes and Teska 1975).

Exemplary Home-Based Programs. Several home-based programs have developed unique expansions of the basic intent of typical home-based instruction. The *Portage Project* in Wisconsin serves preschool children from birth to six years with a variety of handicapping conditions and is one of the major models of home-based programs. *Portage Project* staff develop training objectives employing behavior modification strategies to be used with the children in their own homes. The trained professionals and paraprofessionals of the project staff spend an hour and a half per week with each family member, teaching them new skills and defining goals for the next week for which the family is responsible (Shearer and Shearer 1976).

Another exemplary home-based program is *The Project Casa* program in San Antonio, Texas; it has a homebound component which utilizes high school students, working in pairs under the supervision of a homebound teacher. The program uses secondary school students to extend the potential impact of professionals associated with the project.

The typical approaches used in such home-based programs include (1) regular visits to the home by the project team to demonstrate interventions and to confer with the parents, and (2) less frequent visits by the project team with other forms of assistance from volunteers and others who visit regularly to follow up on the visits by the professionals. Other homebound programs include weekly consultation visits and even cassette tape instructions for parents on how to work with their children (Karnes and Zehrbach 1977).

An early intervention program based in the home of the handicapped preschool child has several advantages:

1. The house is the child's natural environment.
2. The parents are the first teachers and are trusted by the infant or child.
3. Other family members such as brothers, sisters, or perhaps grandparents have more opportunity to interact with the child for the purposes of social contact and instruction and can, therefore, become involved in the program for the child. These "significant others" can play an important role in the child's growth and development (Heward, Dardig, and Rosett 1979).

Home Followed by Center-Based Model. Home-based followed by center-based programs begins with a sequence of home-based instruction for the parents of children, usually from birth to three years of age. The next step in the program is for parents to enroll their child in a center-based preschool program; planning and accomplishment of the transition is guided by staff from the home-based program. Such sequential programs provide services from a variety of staff personnel that may include occupational therapists, physical therapists, speech and language pathologists, psychologists, and nurses. Home trainers continue to work with the family and the child in the home setting but under the direction of the center-based program staff so that services are consistent and compatible. A prime objective of the center-based program is to secure parental involvement through a number of approaches such as group meetings and individual conferences (Karnes and Zehrbach 1977). Through other activities such as parent workshops, parent education, monitoring, and referrals, other children in the family also receive indirect services, which is considered a valuable by-product of center-based or home-based services.

Home and Center-Based Model

This combined service delivery model provides services to the child and family and is coordinated between an instructional center and the child's home. Parents may receive training at the center in addition to home visits from teachers who conduct parent conferences, observe parent-child interactions, and educate parents about the teaching methods appropriate for their child (Heward and Orlansky 1980). Staff members at the instructional center may consist of educators, psychologists, speech and language therapists, and social workers. Their responsibilities reflect their various areas of professional expertise and provide the multidisciplinary foundation upon which daily programming for the child and the family is formulated. Some home and center-based programs focus on a variety of handicapping conditions such as multihandicapped, bilingual instruction and low-incidence handicapping conditions, rather than on a program for just one type of handicapping condition such as mildly to moderately multihandicapped.

One important aspect of this delivery model is its effort to establish interventions that will carry over from the center to the home environment. Feedback from the home program may also be reflected not only in changes made in the home-based strategies but also in the program developed and delivered by the professionals within the center. In this model direct parental involvement is obtained through group meetings, parent conferences, and workshops to construct materials and make policies.

An important aspect of the center based program is to establish interventions that will carry over into the home environment.

Exemplary Home and Center-Based Programs. A review of preschool programs of this type reveals several efforts considered typical of this approach; these are the following:

1. The PEECH Program (Precise Early Education of Children with Handicaps), The University of Illinois, in which handicapped children are placed with nonhandicapped children who act as models; and
2. The Chapel Hill Project, North Carolina, and PEEP (Preschool and Early Education Project), sponsored by Mississippi State University at Starkville, which utilizes data collection of the child, role playing, videotaping and observational techniques to train parents.

Center-Based Models

This intervention program is carried out in a special educational setting outside of the home. The setting may be part of a hospital complex, a special day care center, or preschool. The major emphasis is on parent teaching at the center (Karnes and Zehrback 1977). One important aspect of a center-based program is the opportunity for a team of specialists from different fields such as medicine, education, physical and occupational therapy, speech therapy, and others to observe the child and to cooperate in the intervention and continued assessment of the child. The children also often benefit from the specialized equipment which is housed at the center. This equipment could not be brought to the home as in other model delivery systems.

A possible disadvantage of this program model is that staff members may only rarely visit the child's home, but they do encourage the parents to use what they have learned in the home environment. While it is accepted that carryover of intervention techniques by the parents is important and may be beneficial to other siblings in the family, there is still not as much opportunity for supervision of parents as they implement the strategies at home as is true of more home-related models. The children served in this model spend a specified number of hours at the center on a daily or weekly basis.

CURRICULAR APPROACHES

The method of organizing what to teach, how to teach, and when to teach is referred to as a *curriculum* (Mandell and Fiscus 1981). With the advent of early childhood education, it is essential that current circular approaches be defined and a review of their effectiveness be discussed because some curricular approaches may be indiscriminately applied to the handicapped preschool population. The following section identifies the three basic models/approaches used with preschool handicapped children.

Normal Development Model

This is the approach to instruction that is used in most public school systems (Anastasiow 1977). A major goal of this model is *conformity to normal guidelines of development.* Long lists of skills considered reflective of normal development have been generated by curricular specialists. Such skill lists include an appropriate age at which the child is normally expected to achieve these milestones.

One of the major weaknesses of this model is the total reliance upon these normal guidelines of development. Children in this model might rarely receive instruction or assistance from a teacher other than at an average pace of development, and the teacher probably would not try to improve the child's skills at a pace faster than normal (Anastasiow and Mansergh 1975). Thus, this model has limited applicability to the education of preschool handicapped children.

The classroom in the normal developmental model includes different areas for play such as fine and gross motor activity centers and a center for housekeeping. A unit approach is used, which focuses on a range of activities around a central theme. The classroom experiences are intended to teach children how to behave in school, how to participate in school related activities and tasks, and how to obtain and master the concepts taught in school. During the majority of the instructional day, the teacher supervises group activities rather than provides direct instruction. Individualized instruction is generally not utilized in this model (Anastasiow 1977).

Behavioral Model

This program's major emphasis is on direct instruction in academic skills such as concept formation, number concepts, socioemotional development, and language development. In this model verbal interaction with the teacher is the primary method of accomplishing the predetermined behavioral and skill objectives specified for the child. This model does not rely on the principles of child development but rather on the subject matter to be taught, which is deemed to be important by the culture in which one lives (Karnes and Teska 1975; Anastasiow 1977). Thus, the young handicapped child can experience success in this program by achieving at an individual pace of learning.

Another major objective in this model is changing a child's behavior through the use of sequenced instruction and reinforcers, both primary and secondary. This objective is accomplished through the use of a teaching strategy termed *teacher directed*, in which the teacher presents the lessons to small groups of children. The behavioral model has been demonstrated to be applicable to preschool children with special needs/impairments as well as those children with extreme behavior problems (Anastasiow 1977).

Cognitive Developmental Model

The foundation for the cognitive developmental model is Jean Piaget's research and theory. This approach assumes that all children go through a series of sequential and orderly stages of development. Piaget's theory postulates that the child is an active learner in the environment, and the child's intelligence is constructed from the nature of his or her experiences. According to Piaget, the four stages of development through which all children pass are:

1. sensorimotor (0 to 2 years of age),
2. preoperational (2 to 5 years of age),
3. concrete operations (5 to 12 years of age), and
4. abstract reasoning (12 years of age to maturity).

Throughout each of these stages of development, the teacher in the cognitive developmental model will provide classroom experiences appropriate for each of the child's developmental stages. According to Anastasiow and Mansergh (1975), a theory of affective development to serve as a companion approach to the cognitive programming has not been clearly specified, although the cognitive developmentalists do assert that affective development is probably fundamental to healthy cognitive functioning.

BARRIERS TO PRESCHOOL SERVICES

Although federal legislation such as P.L. 94-142 has been vital in making early childhood education for the handicapped a national concern, numerous barriers still exist that prohibit the provision of services to preschool handicapped children in some states. Obviously there may be cultural, religious, or other somewhat obtuse reasons why preschool programming has not reached the pinnacle desired by many professionals. Among the myriad of barriers that might be suggested, legislation, funding, and socioeconomic structures are three of the most obvious impediments to services.

Legislation

It is the intent of P.L. 94-142 and its enabling regulations to provide a free, appropriate public education to every handicapped child from the ages of three to twenty-one. It is this Education for All Handicapped Children's Act that provided the impetus for state departments of education to serve the previously unserved preschool population (McGovern, Draper, and Vacca 1978). However, *any state that has a law excluding children of preschool age does not have to educate or provide services to this population.* This exclusionary statement means that, in fact, some states are *not* required to serve preschool handicapped children because it is, in essence, against *another* law to provide services to preschoolers, meaning services of any kind.

The lack of state legislation defining preschool handicapped children also presents another legislative barrier to services to preschool handicapped children. Without such enabling legislation at the state level, preschool handicapped children are not entitled to the same benefits as other handicapped school-aged children (nondiscriminatory testing, parental involvement, IEPs, due process, etc.) Results of a study conducted by Lessen and Rose (1980) indicate that only 57 percent of the forty-four states that responded to their questionnaire had a specific definition for preschool handicapped children or had provisions for identifying this population.

Funding

Special incentive grants have been designed and are available from the federal government to encourage all states to implement P.L. 94-142 and to provide services and education to every preschool handicapped child. The government will authorize up to three hundred dollars a year for each preschool handicapped child between the ages of three and five that the school serves. However, funds or incentive grants are *not* made available for the preschool handicapped child in the birth to three years of age range, but it is this age range that is known to be critical to later development. Unfortunately, many states are reluctant to provide state funds to support early identification, intervention, and services to this age population when their own state laws exclude this population from services.

Socioeconomic Structure

Parents with low socioeconomic status and limited educational background may not be aware that they have a handicapped preschool child or that the family and child are in need of services. Also, such families may not be aware of how to locate services for their child or how to contact the various agencies in the community; this lack of knowledge of social services may function as a major barrier between the family and child and the needed services.

SUMMARY

Early childhood education for handicapped preschool children has two major purposes: to identify and to provide services to this population as soon as possible. Some states have laws excluding services to children, both normal and handicapped, of preschool age. Federal legislation has designed special incentive grants to promote awareness of the need for early identification of preschool handicapped children, and to encourage those states to make services available to this population.

A wide range of professionals should be involved in the identification of a preschool handicapped child. Identification teams might include physicians, social workers, and public school personnel. The numerous problems in identifying handicapped children include the effects of labeling, mislabeling, the failure to identify a child who needs special services, and the use of norm-referenced tests, which compare the handicapped child's scores with the norms of those children of the same group but who are not handicapped. Once a child has been identified as high-risk in screening, assessment to determine the child's handicapping condition or deficit areas in development is the next step.

A variety of service delivery models such as home-based and center-based programs have been developed to provide services for the preschool handicapped child. The determination of the most appropriate means of delivering services to this population is based on the child's handicapping condition, geographical variables, the program's theoretical basis, and the available service model options in the community.

Several different curricular approaches are used with preschool handicapped children, most of which use normal development as the standard against which the child is measured. Such approaches provide a program in which handicapped preschool children can achieve an appropriate education. Barriers to providing services to preschool handicapped children still exist in some states as a result of conflicting legislation, funding problems, and familial factors such as socioeconomic structures.

REFERENCES

Anastasiow, N.J. Strategies and models for early childhood intervention programs in integrated settings. In *Early intervention and the integration of handicapped and nonhandicapped,* edited by M. J. Guralnick. Baltimore: University Park Press, 1977.

Anastasiow, N.J. and G. P. Mansergh. Teaching skills in early childhood programs. *Exceptional Children* 41, no. 5 (1975): 309–316.

Anspaugh, D. J., M. Gilliland, and S. J. Anspaugh. The student with epilepsy. *Today's Education* 69 (1980): 78–86.

Bender, M., and P. T. Valletutti. *Teaching the moderately and severely handicapped,* vol. 1. Baltimore: University Park Press, 1976.

Bloom, B. S. *Stability and change in human characteristics.* New York: Wiley, 1964.

Bricker, W. A., and D. D. Bricker. An early language training strategy. In *Language perspectives: Acquisition, retardation, and intervention,* edited by R. L. Schiefelbusch and L. Lloyd. Baltimore: University Park Press, 1974.

Caldwell, B. M. The importance of beginning early. In *Not all little wagons are red,* edited by J. B. Jordan and R. F. Dailey. Arlington, VA: Council for Exceptional Children, 1973.

Cook, R. E., and M. A. Armbruster. *Adapting early childhood curricula: Suggestions for meeting special needs.* St. Louis: C. V. Mosby, 1983.

Ellis, N. E., and L. Cross. *Planning programs for early education of the handicapped.* New York: Walker and Company, 1977.

Fallen, N. H., and J. E. McGovern. *Young children with special needs.* Columbus, Ohio: Charles E. Merrill, 1978.

Heward, W. L., J. C. Dardig, and A. Rossett. *Working with parents of handicapped children.* Columbus, Ohio: Charles E. Merrill, 1979.

Heward, W. L., and M. D. Orlansky. *Exceptional children: An introductory survey to special education.* Columbus, Ohio: Charles E. Merrill, 1980.

Howard, J. Role of the pediatrician with young exceptional children and their families. *Exceptional Children* 48, no. 4 (1982): 316–22.

Karnes, M. B., and R. R. Teska. Children's response to intervention programs. In *The application of child development research to exceptional children* edited by J. J. Gallagher. Reston, VA: Council for Exceptional Children, 1975.

Karnes, M. B., and R. R. Zehrback. Alternative models for delivering services to young handicapped children. In *Early childhood education for exceptional children*, edited by J. Jordon, A. Hayden, and M. Wood. Reston, VA: Council for Exceptional Children, 1977.

Keeffe, S. D. Parents are people too! *Exceptional Children* 17, no. 1 (1984): 59–66.

Kirk, S. A. *Early education of the mentally retarded*. Urbana: University of Illinois Press, 1958.

Lazar, I., and R. Darlington. *Lasting effects after preschool.* (OHDS 79-30179). Washington, D.C.: Administration for Children, Youth and Families, Office of Human Development Services-Department of Health, Education and Welfare, 1979.

Lessen, E. I., and T. L. Rose. State definitions for preschool handicapped populations. *Exceptional Children* 46, no. 6 (1980): 467–69.

Lillie, D. L. Effects of motor development lessons on mentally retarded children. *American Journal of Mental Deficiency* 72 (1968): 803–808.

McGovern, J. E., D. A. Draper, and R. S. Vacca. Introduction. In *Young children with special needs. See* Fallen and McGovern 1978.

Mandel, C. J., and E. Fiscus. *Understanding exceptional people.* New York: West Publishing Co., 1981.

Meier, J. H. Screening, assessment, and intervention for young children at developmental risk. In *Intervention strategies for high risk infants and young children*, edited by T. D. Tjossem. Baltimore: University Park Press, 1976.

Mori, A. A., and J. E. Olive. *Handbook of preschool special education.* Rockville, Md.: Aspen Publications, 1980.

Newsweek, 10 January, 1983.

Saffort, P. L. *Teaching young children with special needs.* St. Louis: C. V. Mosby Co., 1978.

Shearer, D. E., and M. S. Shearer. The portage project: A model of early childhood intervention. In *Intervention strategies for high-risk infants and young children*, edited by T. D. Tjossmen. Baltimore: University Park Press, 1976.

Schultz, J. The parent-professional conflict. In *Parents speak out: Views from the other side of the two-way mirror. See* Turnbull and Turnbull 1978.

Spaulding, R. L. *C.A.S.E.S. Manual.* San Jose, Calif.: San Jose State University, 1980.

Turnbull, A. P., and H. R. Turnbull, *Parents speak out: Views from the other side of the two-way mirror.* Columbus, Ohio: Charles E. Merrill, 1978.

White, B. *The first three years of life.* New York: Prentice-Hall, 1975.

Chapter Seven

ELEMENTARY-AGED MILDLY HANDICAPPED CHILDREN

CHAPTER OUTLINE

INTRODUCTION
CHARACTERISTICS AND NEEDS
    Academic Characteristics and Needs
    Social/Emotional Characteristics and Needs
THE ELEMENTARY SCHOOL
    Elementary School Administration
    Organizational Arrangements
    School Policies
    Curriculum
    The Regular Classroom
EDUCATING MILDLY HANDICAPPED CHILDREN IN REGULAR
   ELEMENTARY SCHOOLS
    Accommodative Strategies
    Teaching Strategies for Specific Subjects
SUMMARY

CHAPTER OBJECTIVES

After reading this chapter, you should be able to:
- List and describe the academic characteristics of mildly handicapped children in elementary schools;
- Identify social and emotional characteristics of elementary-aged mildly handicapped children;
- Describe the role of elementary school administrators in special education;
- Discuss the importance of regular elementary teachers in special education;
- Describe teaching methods for mildly handicapped children; and
- Discuss ways to improve social and emotional characteristics of mildly handicapped elementary-aged children.

INTRODUCTION

Beginning elementary school is an exciting time for most children; it is a period when new friends are developed (Drew, Logan, and Hardman 1984), academic growth achieved, and physical growth and maturity accomplished. Unfortunately, for many mildly handicapped children, the excitement quickly turns to frustration and failure. Mildly handicapped children often meet their first difficulties in the elementary grades. Some of these children are not identified before they enroll in school, but they soon come to the attention of parents and teachers because of their academic or behavior problems.

Many children begin the elementary school years with the requisite skills for academic progress. They often have adequate information-processing skills, and some even have the ability to interpret print and spelling (Smith 1983). For many mildly handicapped children, however, problems begin almost immediately. The inabilities to attend, concentrate, manipulate a pencil properly, and learn to read are often the first signs that a child may have a problem (Lerner 1985). These may lead to academic failure and behavior problems.

During the later elementary years, problems with peer acceptance, self-concept, and more extensive behavior control may develop. The ability to make and keep friends becomes increasingly difficult with age (Lerner 1985). These problems are often the result of failure in academic work during the early elementary years. The elementary school, therefore, is a critical period for mildly handicapped children. During these years students with disabilities may become frustrated with failure, develop poor social relationships, fall further and further behind academically, and eventually give up, stop trying, and become behavior problems.

Professionals in elementary schools must intercede in these cases and prevent such negative consequences. Comprehensive educational programs for mildly handicapped elementary-aged students can greatly facilitate positive development of these students. If resource room teachers work closely with regular elementary teachers and have the support of the administration, they can greatly lessen the impact of mild disabilities during the elementary years. In some cases where appropriate services are provided, children identified as mildly handicapped during the elementary school years may even be able to leave the elementary school without any deviant label; they may be totally assimilated into the regular school program.

CHARACTERISTICS AND NEEDS OF ELEMENTARY-AGED MILDLY HANDICAPPED CHILDREN

The two major areas in which elementary-aged children are expected to excell are academic skills and social/emotional adaptability. For mildly handicapped children, both of these domains can be troublesome.

Academic Characteristics and Needs of Mildly Handicapped Children

Several studies have determined that children with mild disabilities often experience academic failure. Indeed, academic underachievement is a leading characteristic of mildly handicapped children. Research has not been conducted with subjects generically labeled "mildly handicapped;" however, research does show that the academic inabili-

Many mildly handicapped children are first identified because they have great difficulty paying attention in the classroom.

ties of children with categorical labels are similar to those of the mildly handicapped. For example, Neisworth and Greer (1975) found major similarities in distractibility, discrimination, motivation, and retention in both learning disability and educable mental retardation groups.

Learning disabled children have long been associated with academic underachievement. However, the other two major categories of handicapped children in the mildly handicapped category, namely, educable mentally retarded and emotionally disturbed, have also been linked to academic deficits (Hallahan and Kauffman 1977; Gajar 1979). IQ scores have been shown to be positively correlated with academic achievement. Studies investigating the mean IQ scores of educable mentally retarded children, learning disabled children, and emotionally disturbed children have found that all three groups have mean IQ levels that are below average (Epstein and Cullinan 1983; Gajar 1979; Gajar 1980; Hallahan and Kauffman 1977). This suggests the likelihood that academic achievement is below average for all three groups of children.

Specific academic areas that prove problematic for mildly handicapped students include reading, handwriting, written expression, spelling, and mathematics (Lerner 1985; Smith 1983; Drew et al. 1984). These, of course, are the basic instructional areas in elementary schools. Students having problems in these areas are often referred for special education and are formally identified as disabled—that is, *mildly handicapped* in states that serve children noncategorically, or *mentally retarded* or *learning disabled* in states that serve children categorically.

HIGHLIGHT

Showcasing Talent Among Disabled

By Herman Wong,
Times Staff Writer

The setting in the Anaheim Convention Center lobby was makeshift and audience members drifted in from meetings and exhibitions, but the performers easily took command of the situation.

From theatrical fables to renditions of Broadway show tunes, the acts—the Williams School Puppeteers, Carl Harvey Singing Choir and Hope Music Makers—delighted the noon-hour crowd with their unmistakable artistic prowess.

The achievement was no small feat, since the members of these student ensembles from Orange and Los Angeles counties are all severely disabled.

The program at the convention center Wednesday opened A Very Special Arts Festival, which is out to demonstrate that people who are physically and mentally handicapped can also possess significant—even exceptional—creative talents.

More than 500 disabled persons have been performing this week at the convention center in conjunction with the 63rd annual convention of the Council for Exceptional Children.

(The council is a national organization that deals with educational issues pertaining to both the disabled and the mentally gifted. The convention has been attended by nearly 8,000 teachers, psychologists, other professionals and parent advocates.)

"We've made great strides in the past several years. People are increasingly accepting the concept that the disabled should be—and can be successfully—integrated into the mainstream school and job programs," said Phyllis Berenbeim, the Orange County Education Department official coordinating this week's festival.

The programs this week make up the second statewide festival, and Berenbeim noted, "When it comes to numbers (of arts festivals for the disabled), California is one of the most active in the nation."

(Berenbeim also coordinates the annual Orange County version of the festivals. The next one, to feature 300 performers, is set for May 18 at Brea Mall. Other programs, especially art exhibits, have taken place at the Orange County Hall of Administration, and in connection with the Orange County Fair.)

"The growing recognition of these (arts) festivals is a greatly encouraging sign to us. The arts are being seen as an absolutely essential tool for reaching the fullest potential of these (disabled) people," Berenbeim added.

Tonight, beginning at 7:30, is "Festival Gala Evening" at the Anaheim Hilton Hotel (admission is free), with guest stars such as actor William Allen Young and singer Bob Schneider. The closing program will start at 10 a.m. Saturday at Disneyland. Several ensembles of disabled performers—including the Hi Hopes, singers and musicians from Anaheim, and Frances Blend School ballet troupe, from Los Angeles—will perform at both programs.

The festivals first took hold in the mid-1970s, when large-scale versions were staged at the John F. Kennedy Center for the Performing Arts in Washington, D.C. The movement is spearheaded by a Ken-

(continued)

Los Angeles Times, 19 April 1985, Part VI

nedy Center affiliate, the National Committee, Arts for the Handicapped, chaired by Jean Kennedy Smith.

Nationally, the Very Special Arts Festivals organized on a statewide level now number more than 450. The first in California took place in the fall of 1981. It was organized by Orange County-based groups and staged at the Sheraton-Anaheim Hotel, Anaheim Plaza and Disneyland. This week's festival is again sponsored by Orange County groups, the state Department of Education and the Kennedy Center committee.

Although the 1985 festival did not have nearly as many discussion-demonstration sessions as the one in 1981, a few sessions this week dealt with the teaching of arts to the disabled. These workshops, part of the Council for Exceptional Children convention, included demonstrations by the Saticoy Ballet Company of North Hollywood and the Singing Hands troupe of Santa Ana.

Disabled participants also came from Bellflower, Ontario, Santa Barbara, Santa Maria, Visalia and Watsonville. Some of the drawings, paintings and paper sculptures exhibited were done by disabled artists from Arizona, Colorado, Nevada, New Mexico, New York and Wyoming.

The mood of the opening program Wednesday was a typical overflowing of enthusiasm, from both performers and audience.

On the bill that day:

- A demonstration by four students from the Huntington Beach Union High School District of the use of computers in art, such as in landscapes and depictions of sea life. They are the students of Robert Garcia, of the school district's Guidance Center for the developmentally disabled.
- Songs by the Hope Music Makers, from Anaheim Union High School District's Hope Special Education Center. The group of 20 developmentally disabled singers is directed by Karen Provensen.
- The Carl Harvey Singing Choir, a 45-member group from the Santa Ana Unified School District's center for the physically handicapped conducted by Marge Osborn. (The choir has been invited to perform in New York at the International Symposium of Music Education for the Handicapped in August, and the group needs to raise $30,000 to pay for the trip.)
- The Williams School Puppeteers, a troupe of physically handicapped players from Downey led by Peggy Hooberman-Lenz. They performed "The Three Little Hawaiian Pigs and the Magic Shark."
- The Williams School children's reactions to the presentations seemed to speak for all the ensembles:

When their show was over, the 10 puppeteers were wheeled out from behind the curtains to acknowledge the applause. Some of the students were grinning; others looked a bit shy.

"This is always a big moment for them, to be recognized in such a warm way for their abilities," said Hooberman-Lenz. "It never fails to be something special for them—for *all of us.*"

Children who are identified in the elementary school as having academic deficits and formally classified as handicapped require special education and related services. Without such assistance, many of these children become chronic school failures and may develop behavioral and emotional problems. With special education and related services, it is hoped that many of these children will be able to overcome their disability or at least achieve at their optimal levels of performance.

Social/Emotional Characteristics and Needs

As with academic problems, many elementary-aged mildly handicapped children experience social/emotional problems. Although personality and adjustment problems are often thought of as only affecting children classified as emotionally disturbed, children with other mildly disabling conditions also develop these characteristics. While social and emotional problems are not considered the primary problems facing mildly mentally retarded and learning disabled children, they are often present.

For many mildly handicapped children, social/emotional problems develop in the elementary grades. This could result from several factors, including:

- teachers who do not understand the limiting effects of disabilities,
- parents who demand too much, and
- peer rejection.

Learning disabled children may be judged negatively by teachers (Garrett and Crump 1980), may be rejected by their nonhandicapped peers (Scranton and Rykman 1979), and may do poorly in social situations (Lerner 1985). Children with academic deficits due to mental retardation may be rejected by both frustrated teachers, as well as nonhandicapped peers. They have a higher incidence of emotional problems than nonretarded children (Drew et al. 1984).

School personnel must address the social and emotional problems of mildly handicapped children. In fact, these problems often must be dealt with before any significant progress can be made with academic remediation. Peer and teacher rejection, often compounded by parent rejection, can lead to very low self-concepts, which can greatly affect academic performance.

Well-adjusted children have skills that enable them to deal with a wide variety of social situations. These include "(a) an expectation that they can take personal initiative in a situation and gain a favorable outcome; (b) a sensitivity to others' feelings and perspectives; (c) the ability to set a clear goal, consider alternative actions that might lead to the goal, and consider various possible consequences; (d) the ability to plan specific steps to reach a goal; (e) the behavioral repertoire needed to implement their plans; (f) the persistence to continue using their problem-solving skills in the face of obstacles; and (g) the ability to refine their problem-solving strategies in light of experience" (Elias and Maher 1983, 341). Many mildly handicapped children do not possess these skills, but with appropriate training they can learn them. With these skills, handicapped children are less likely to be rejected, and therefore, they will be better able to adjust to the school environment.

THE ELEMENTARY SCHOOL

Elementary-aged mildly handicapped children have to function in the elementary school environment. This environment is where they receive their basic educational program, remedial programs, and opportunities for social interaction. The environment of the elementary school is crucial for optimal development of mildly handicapped children and is a major factor in the success of these children.

The elementary school and the regular classroom have a great deal more significance for mildly handicapped children now than before mainstreaming. The education of this group of children has become a shared responsibility between regular and special educa-

Rejection of mildly handicapped children by their non-handicapped peers may result in isolation and feelings of loneliness on the playground.

tion teachers because these children receive a portion of their educational program in regular classrooms. The elementary school environment plays a major role in the development of mildly handicapped children.

Elementary School Administration

The administration of elementary schools is a vital element in all activities of the school. While local boards of education set policies for schools, and superintendents and other

> **Table 7-1. Competencies Needed by Regular School Administrators**
>
> Assuring due process
> Interpreting federal and state laws
> Using appropriate leadership styles
> Showing that records comply with confidentiality and due process
> Resolving conflicts among program personnel
> Using evaluation data to make individual program revisions
> Determining staff functions and qualifications

Source: Nevin 1979.

central office staff oversee the implementation of these policies, building principals are ultimately responsible for policy implementation.

As a result of mainstreaming, special education is a major responsibility of principals (Davis 1980), so their role in special education is crucial. Principals now spend a great deal of time, an average of 14.6 percent of the school day, dealing with special education issues. In order to accomplish the many administrative tasks associated with special education, principals need certain competencies. See table 7-1.

Organizational Arrangements

Elementary schools are organized along two basic lines: vertical and horizontal. Vertical organization is the school plan that determines who enters school, when he or she enters school, and the procedures for determining progress through the school (Ragan and Shepherd 1977). The two most often used vertical organizations are graded schools and nongraded schools. In graded schools, students progress from grade to grade, based primarily on chronological age. This contrasts with nongraded schools, where continuous-progress education is the aim. Students in this organization progress through the school's curriculum at their own pace. While there are advantages and disadvantages to both the graded and nongraded organization, only about 10 percent of the elementary schools utilize the nongraded format (Ragan and Shepherd 1977).

Horizontal organization is the distribution of students and teachers into units or groups. Self-contained classrooms and departmentalization are the two primary modes of horizontal organization. In self-contained programs, students spend the majority of the school day in one classroom with the same teacher. In a departmentalized scheme, students rotate among teachers for various subjects, similar to the way students go from class to class at the secondary level. The organizational patterns of schools have implications for special education. See table 7-2.

School Policies

Policies of elementary schools have great impact on mildly handicapped elementary-aged students. For example, the policy on discipline could directly relate to the method used to manage the behavior of disabled students with behavior problems. If schools have a policy that a particular act automatically leads to a particular disciplinary response, special education teachers may be hampered in individualizing discipline for students whose primary problem area is aberrant behavior.

Besides the policy on discipline, policies on other areas could affect handicapped pupils in the elementary schools. These include scheduling, attendance, homework, test

Table 7-2. **Organizational Patterns and Possible Implications for Special Education**

Organizational arrangements	Relevant characteristics	Possible implications for special programs
Graded school	Curriculum is strongly tied to grade level. Progress is measured against grade level standards.	Skill instruction may have to be carefully structured to mesh with grade-level content so that program is viewed as compatible. For example, special teacher would need to secure copy of a curriculum guide, content area skills list, or teacher's manuals to attempt to integrate skills taught in special program with those emphasized in regular classroom. Materials selected for special program may need to be similar to those used in some classrooms yet not exact duplicate. For example, child mainstreamed in second-grade classroom may be aware of type of workbook used in first grade. Thus, special educator will want to select a different set of workbooks or other materials that are compatible yet not clearly identified with a grade. Assignation of grades may be an important issue, requiring special educator to deal with pressure to conform to strict grading policy based on test results. It may also be more difficult for special teacher to reconcile individual focus of program with group standards emphasized in school.
Nongraded school	Curriculum is viewed as total body of skills through which students progress at individual rate. Recording and reporting of student progress is done more frequently and on more individual basis. Instructional experiences are varied.	Mainstreaming may be more easily accomplished because of absence of grade-level concern when searching for "appropriate" mainstream placement. A comprehensive skills list comprising all content to be taught should be more readily available. Special educator should secure list, thus making it easier to make content consistent between special class and regular classroom. Participation in IEP process may be more easily achieved because of individual focus of school; teachers may be more receptive to interaction with special teacher. Special educator may have more instructional flexibility in terms of materials used and objectives addressed. Social experience designed to foster learning and emotional growth may be more acceptable.

(continued)

Table 7-2. (continued)

Organizational arrangements	Relevant characteristics	Possible implications for special programs
Self-contained classroom	One teacher has primarily instructional responsibility. Students form peer groups within their own class. Teachers generally appear to form strong personal bonds with students in their classes.	Instructional interface may be more difficult to achieve because teachers are unaccustomed to coordinating their program with other instructional components. Mainstreaming may require more effort from special educator, since students may not be easily accepted by regular class students and may face more social barriers. Teachers can provide detailed information on regular students, such as interests, attitudes, and abilities, thus aiding special teachers because of almost total instructional control of classroom teacher.
Departmentalized	Teachers tend to have subject-matter emphasis. Teachers deal with more students.	Special educators may find less support and interest in area of student social growth. Handicapped students may be under greater pressure to perform to group standards in handling course content.

Source: Reprinted by permission, from G.E. Marsh, B.J. Price, and T.E.C. Smith, 1983, 144–45.

taking, standardized tests, suspension, and expulsion. Table 7-3 describes the ways these policies could impact on mildly handicapped students.

Curriculum

The curriculum of the elementary school is very important. It is not a simple listing of courses, but the total set of student experiences for which the school takes responsibility. This includes formal courses, school sponsored clubs, and athletics; these informal learning experiences are as important as formal classroom activities (Ryan and Cooper 1980).

The curriculum is derived from many different sources, including the community, subject-matter specialists, and students. It is in a constant state of flux, never static for long periods, but changing as a result of external influences. The curriculum of the school reflects the attitudes, values, and concerns of the society and therefore changes as these variables change. Although the curricula of elementary schools vary somewhat, they usually include certain basic academic subject areas. Table 7-4 describes the basic subject areas commonly found in the academic curriculum of most elementary schools.

The Regular Classroom

Most mildly handicapped students in elementary schools spend at least a portion of each school day in **regular classrooms,** receiving instruction from **regular classroom teachers.** As a result, the regular classroom environment is critical to the success of

Table 7-3. **Impact of Policies on Mildly Handicapped Students**

Policy Area	Impact on Mildly Handicapped Students
Discipline	Rigid disciplinary codes impact greatly on special education. School officials must realize that handicapped children should not be disciplined for actions that are a direct result of their disability. On the other hand, handicapped students should be responsible for their actions and should receive equal punishment for actions not related to the disability.
Expulsion and Suspension	As with other disciplinary methods, suspension and expulsion of handicapped students must take into consideration the nature of the disability and its relationship to the misbehavior. Suspensions are not considered a change of placement for handicapped students, but expulsions are and must be accompanied with proper due process proceedings.
Attendance	Most schools have strict policies related to attendance requirements. As a result of some handicapping conditions causing students to miss class days, some special considerations should be made.
Scheduling	Policies on scheduling might require students to enroll in a minimum number of classes. Since some mildly handicapped students need significantly more time to make progress, some modifications of scheduling policies might need to be made.
Standardized Tests	Some schools now require students to pass certain standardized tests before being promoted. Unique needs of many mildly handicapped students should be considered related to passing standards as well as test taking procedures.

mildly handicapped students. Within this regular classroom setting are several variables that impact on mildly handicapped students, including the teacher, classroom environment, and peers.

Regular Classroom Teachers. Regular elementary classroom teachers are key individuals in the success of mildly handicapped students. If regular classroom teachers support mainstreaming and accommodate these mildly handicapped students, the chances of

Table 7-4. **Basic Subject Areas Found in Most Elementary Schools**

Language Arts
  Reading
  Writing
  Spelling
  Listening
Science
Mathematics
Social Studies
  History
  Geography
Arts
  Music
  Art

Regular classroom teachers who can adapt the curriculum to maintain interest and involvement in the classroom are important for the mildly handicapped child.

their experiencing success are greatly enhanced. However, regular classroom teachers who are not supportive of mainstreaming and who do not want handicapped students in their classrooms diminish the likelihood of success for these students.

For regular classroom teachers to be successful with mainstreamed handicapped children, they need certain competencies. They must (1) understand "normalization" and mainstreaming, (2) understand the nature of handicaps, (3) have positive attitudes, (4) utilize proper resources, (5) use appropriate teaching techniques, (6) create a positive environment, (7) understand various learning styles, (8) effect positive classroom management techniques, (9) effectively use individualized educational programs, (10) communicate with students, teachers, and parents, (11) assess student needs, (12) determine student progress, and (13) perform administrative duties (Goldhammer, Rader, and Reuschlein 1977).

Teacher attitudes are also related to the success experienced by mainstreamed handicapped children. Teachers with negative attitudes toward handicapped children are likely to reject these students, while teachers with positive attitudes are more likely to make the necessary accommodations for their success. Chapter 10 discusses the role of attitudes in dealing with the mildly handicapped.

Teaching Methods. Instructional methods in regular classrooms are important for handicapped children. If teachers use a lecture approach (teaching to the group as a whole), handicapped children are at a disadvantage. Teachers should take into consideration individual students' strengths and weaknesses. Learning styles, preferred learning modalities, and simple variables such as location of the student in the classroom should be considered by teachers. While elementary teachers use several different teaching styles and methods, the key is to consider the individual needs of students. If regular classroom teachers are flexible and willing to make some accommodations for mildly handicapped students, the chances of these students' succeeding will be much greater.

Role of the Regular Teacher. As previously discussed, regular classroom teachers are key individuals in the successful integration of mildly handicapped students in regular classrooms. With their support, chances of student success are increased; without their support, success is less likely. Teachers perform many roles in the classroom: planner of instruction, facilitator of learning and instruction, and evaluator of learning and instruction (Jarolimek and Foster, 1976). Additional skills of the teacher of handicapped students include:

- acting as a team member on the multidisciplinary team that plans and implements instruction for the handicapped child,
- advocating for handicapped children when they are both in the classroom as well as outside of the classroom,
- counseling parents of handicapped children,
- individualizing instruction for handicapped children,
- understanding and abiding by due process procedures required by federal and state regulations, and
- being innovative in providing equal educational opportunities for handicapped children (Marsh, Price, and Smith 1983).

Classroom environment. The classroom teacher usually determines the environment of the classroom. Does the teacher have an open, trusting environment, or is the teacher continuously suspicious of all students, thinking they are always trying to "get by with something"? Does the teacher expect students to be always on task and recognize individuals only when they behave inappropriately, or does the teacher positively reward appropriate behavior, and when possible, ignore inappropriate behavior?

The teacher sets the tone. Variables in the classroom environment that appear to have the most effect on students are the following:

1. Definition of a "good" student. Teachers like some pupils better than others. This is probably determined by the values held by a teacher related to what constitutes a "good" student. If mildly handicapped children are considered capable of being classified as "good" students, then their chances for successful integration in the regular classroom are improved.

2. Classroom rules. Classroom rules are a part of the total set of expectations by which students must abide. Depending on the classroom rules, some mildly handicapped students have an easy or a difficult time meeting required rules.
3. Student-teacher interactions. Teachers vary considerably in their amount and time of interactions with students. Some want a great deal of interaction, while others reject interaction as bordering on being too friendly. The amount of interaction between teachers and mildly handicapped students can affect the anxiety levels of the students.
4. Student-student interaction. Interactions among peers is as important for children as interaction with adults. For mainstreamed handicapped children, peer acceptance is very important. If students feel they are rejected, they are more likely to withdraw or become acting-out behavior problems. Teachers should encourage positive student-student interactions. (Marsh et al. 1983)

EDUCATING MILDLY HANDICAPPED CHILDREN IN REGULAR ELEMENTARY SCHOOLS

Mildly handicapped elementary-aged children have specific needs that schools should address. The most widely used service delivery model for mildly handicapped students in elementary schools is the resource room (Marsh et al. 1983). Although all states serve mildly handicapped children in resource rooms, the nature of resource rooms varies greatly (Friend and McNutt 1984).

Friend and McNutt surveyed all fifty states and the District of Columbia to determine the status of resource rooms. The following conclusions were reached based on the study:

- All states and the District of Columbia use the resource room model to serve mildly handicapped students
- All states serve learning disabled, mildly mentally retarded, and emotionally disturbed children in resource rooms
- The majority of states use a combination of resource room types, with the most frequently reported combination being categorical, multicategorical, and itinerant
- Some states serve as many as 98 percent of all handicapped students in resource rooms, while others serve only 17 percent of handicapped students in resource rooms
- Eighteen states reported that students could spend up to half of the school day in the resource rooms, 17 states indicated other time maximums, while 14 states indicated that there were no time specifications concerning resource room placement (Friend and McNutt 1984)

The **resource room model,** therefore, is the most popular model for serving mildly handicapped children in public school programs. As a result of the resource room being used so extensively, regular classroom and special education teachers need to work together to provide appropriate educational programs.

HIGHLIGHT

Day Camps Proving Boon to Handicapped

By Sharon Johnson

James Greene, an 11-year-old from Auburn, N.Y., spent last summer learning to swim and ride a pony at Freedom Day Camp in his hometown. What was unusual about the experience was that James is afflicted with Perthes' disease, a degenerative hip ailment that makes it necessary for him to use a wheelchair and leg braces.

"Day camp opened a new world for him," said his mother, Eunice Greene. "It showed him that he can do things that other kids do."

An increasing number of handicapped children are having such summer experiences, according to experts. More handicapped children are enrolled in day camps, they say, because the supervised activities help them retain what they have learned in school, develop new skills and make friends.

Some parents also prefer day camp to residential camp because they believe day camp is less disruptive to their children's lives than living away. Like sleep-in camps, day camps also give parents some free time to pursue their own interests and help young people considering careers in special education decide if they really like to work with the handicapped.

Dr. Toni Haas, director of the National Information Center for Handicapped Children and Youth in Roslyn, Va., said: "Nobody knows how many of the 4.2 million handicapped schoolchildren in the United States attend day camp, but the number has been growing during the last decade. Since 1975, handicapped and regular kids have spent more time together in school because Federal legislation requires that handicapped children be placed in the least restrictive environment. That attitude has been carried over to the summer, with many handicapped youngsters now attending camps for regular children."

For example, about 2,000 handicapped youngsters are expected to attend Y.M.C.A. day camps across the nation this summer. In New York City, the Children's Aid Society predicts that 250 handicapped youngsters will be among the 1,200 campers in its day program.

"There is a new attitude among parents and camp administrators today," said C. Warren Moses, director of city and county branches for the Children's Aid Society. "An increasing number of people believe that handicapped children should be exposed to situations that challenge them physically and intellectually. And so they are sending their kids to camp."

Elaine Giannettino, director of the Lakes Region of the Easter Seal Society, at Auburn, which sponsored the Freedom Day Camp, agrees. "Summer can be a terrible time for a handicapped child if he has to stay at home where there is nothing to do but watch soap operas on television," she said. "Unlike normal children, the physically impaired cannot jump on their bikes and go to the shopping center when they want to see their friends. The 24-hour presence of kids with serious handicaps can take a heavy toll on parents and children."

Children with a variety of mild handicaps are being integrated into regular day-

(continued)

New York Times, 15 April 1984, page 11.

camp programs. For instance, the Children's Aid Society has accepted children with orthopedic handicaps, learning disabilities such as dyslexia and emotional problems.

"In most cases, all it takes to accommodate these kids is some ingenuity in adapting the program or the facilities," Mr. Moses of the Children's Aid Society said. "Children in wheelchairs concentrate on the upperbody movements in our dance classes, and we try to avoid using buildings that have stairs."

Having the handicapped children attend camp with normal children is advantageous, according to Grace Reynolds, director of the Y.M.C.A.'s Office of Special Populations, because "it shows them that they have more in common than differences." They make new friends and develop new interests, she said.

Sometimes the stereotypes about the abilities of the handicapped also disappear. Mrs. Reynolds cited the example of normal children at a Y.M.C.A. day camp who learned to appreciate the talents of an orthopedically handicapped camper who excelled in music.

There are also more specialized day camps today for those with severe handicaps such as autism, profound mental retardation and cerebral palsy. The camp programs for the severely impaired, unlike those for normal and mildly impaired children, often stress education, self-care, speech and prevocational training for older youngsters.

Providing day-camp services for handicapped youngsters poses some challenges, however. The lack of transportation, inadequate funding and architectural barriers were the major problems cited by 61 agencies across the nation that were surveyed in 1978 by Dr. John A. Nesbitt, professor of special recreation at the State University of Iowa. "Although the handicapped represent about 10 percent of the population, they don't receive 10 percent of the public and private dollars spent on recreation," Dr. Nesbitt said. "The agencies told us that they would like to do more for the handicapped but simply did not have the money."

Handicapped campers pay from $20 to $50 a week, about the same as those without handicaps, according to interviews with various agencies.

Finding and training people who can meet the needs of the handicapped is another challenge, Dr. Nesbitt said. Day camps that serve the handicapped usually need more counselors because handicapped children usually require more supervision and assistance. Sometimes the counselor-child ratio is as low as 1 to 1 rather than 1 to 10 as it is with normal children. More nurses and sometimes physicians, physical therapists and speech teachers must be employed to accommodate the severely impaired.

Like many camps for handicapped children, the Easter Seal Society's Freedom Day Camp recruits counselors who have handicaps themselves to serve as role models for the children. Handicapped counselors sometimes come up with ideas for solving problems that might not otherwise occur to their able-bodied counterparts. For example, one counselor who had an orthopedic problem designed a device that enabled children with orthopedic handicaps to bowl.

Operation Fun, a camp for 400 handicapped children in Brooklyn and Queens that is sponsored by Catholic Charities and Builders for Families and Youth, recruits volunteers as counselors. Many of them discover that they like working with the handicapped so much that they go on to pursue careers in special education.

Finding a suitable camp for a handi-

(continued)

> capped youngster is easier today because organizations such as the American Camping Association offer a free service to assist parents. Karenne Bloomgarden, executive director of the New York section of the association, said: "About 60 day camps that belong to our section are accepting the handicapped because we made a special effort to acquaint directors with these children's needs. Many camps for regular children can be easily adapted to accommodate these children."

For mainstreaming and the resource room model to be effective, several different actions must occur: (1) development of criteria for mainstreaming, (2) preparation of handicapped students, (3) preparation of nonhandicapped students, (4) communication among educators, (5) evaluation of student progress, and (6) inservice training (Salend 1984). Since regular classroom teachers and special education personnel must work closely, communication and training are key elements in the success of mildly handicapped children.

If regular classroom teachers are expected to teach mildly handicapped students in regular classrooms, they must be familiar with effective teaching methods for these children. They must be able to use proper academic remedial techniques and to know how to deal with behavior problems (Campbell, Dobson, and Bost 1985). Unfortunately, many regular elementary classroom teachers do not feel adequately prepared to deal with mainstreamed mildly handicapped children. In a study that determined the issues expressed by elementary classroom teachers concerning mainstreaming, Schultz determined that many of the teachers involved in the study "felt a lack of expertise in accounting for individual differences as related to curriculum and instruction" (Schultz 1982, 367). This feeling of inadequacy must be alleviated with better inservice and preservice training. Even with qualified, trained regular classroom teachers, special education personnel must be available to provide support and assistance.

Accommodative Strategies

Probably one of the best ways to assist mildly handicapped children in regular elementary classrooms is to make accommodations in the environment, curricula, and teaching methods. Many different methods can accommodate the needs of mainstreamed children. See table 7-5.

Teaching Strategies for Specific Subjects

The elementary school curricula usually include a variety of subjects and experiences for children. Four specific areas often stressed are reading, written expression, math, and social/emotional skills. The following are some suggestions for teaching specific subjects to mildly handicapped students. The discussions are not intended to be all-encompassing but should provide a brief description of some of the methods appropriate for teaching mainstreamed handicapped children.

Reading. Teaching children to read has been considered a primary responsibility of schools for many years (Lerner 1985). Reading is a very complex process. One of the main characteristics among mildly handicapped children, including those categorically

Table 7-5. **Accommodative Strategies**

Strategy	Description
Outlines	Simple course outlines assist pupils in organizing notes and information.
Study Guides	Expanded outlines. Provide specific information such as assignments and evaluation criteria.
Advance Organizers	A set of questions or other guides indicating the most important parts of reading assignments.
Audio-Visual Aids	Overhead projectors, films, film strips, and chalkboard are examples. Reinforce auditory information and enable students with auditory deficits to access information.
Varying Instructional Strategies	Alternative teaching strategies enable students to utilize their most efficient learning style.
Seating Arrangement	Place students in locations that minimize problems. Examples: close to front of class for children with auditory and visual problems; away from other children for students with behavior problems; away from windows and doors for those with distractibility problems.
Tape Recorders	Using tape recorders can greatly benefit children with visual problems, memory problems, reading problems, etc. Taped textbooks, tests, and lectures can facilitate learning.

Source: Marsh, Price, and Smith, 1983.

labeled learning disabled, mildly mentally retarded, and emotionally disturbed, is reading deficiency. Problems in learning to read often result from a multitude of behaviors. See table 7-6.

Reading has two basic components: word recognition and reading comprehension (Lerner 1985). Mildly handicapped children may have difficulties with either or both of these components. These difficulties may cause reading errors that vary considerably from child to child. But the majority of errors include (Smith 1983):

- omitting letters, syllables, words, or word endings,
- inserting extra words or sounds in words,
- substituting words that look, sound, or have similar meanings,
- mispronouncing letters,
- reversing words, letters, or syllables,
- transposing the order of words,
- repeating words, using the wrong inflection, or using inappropriate dialects.

One of the tasks of teachers is to identify the type of problem experienced by the child and then determine appropriate educational intervention strategies. Without assessment data, inappropriate remediation could be implemented. The type of reading problems can be determined by administering norm-referenced tests, criterion-referenced tests, and informal reading inventories, by collecting anecdotal information, or by making observations. One advantage of the informal reading inventory is that it enables teachers to see how children perform in real reading activities (Klesius and Homan 1985), whereas norm-referenced tests only indicate how a child performs in comparison with a normative sample.

Table 7-6 Behaviors of Children with Reading Problems

Characteristics	Comments
Reading Habits	
Tension movements	Frowning, fidgeting, using a high-pitched voice, and lip biting.
Insecurity	Refusing to read, crying, and attempting to distract the teacher.
Loses place	Losing place frequently (is often associated with repetitions).
Lateral head movements	Jerking head.
Holds material close	Deviating extremely (from 15–18 inches).
Word Recognition Errors	
Omissions	Omitting a word (e.g., Tom saw a cat).
Insertions	Inserting words (e.g., *The dog ran* [fast] *after the cat*).
Substitutions	Substituting one word for another (e.g., *The house horse was big*).
Reversals	Reversing letters in a word (e.g., *no* for *on*, *was* for *saw*).
Mispronunciations	Mispronouncing words (e.g., *mister* for *miser*).
Transpositions	Reading words in the wrong order (e.g., *She away ran* for *She ran away*).
Unknown words	Hesitating for 5 seconds at a word he cannot pronounce.
Slow choppy reading	Not recognizing words quickly enough (e.g., 20–30 words per minute).
Comprehension Errors	
Cannot recall basic facts	Unable to answer specific questions about a passage (e.g., *What was the dog's name?*).
Cannot recall sequence	Unable to tell sequence of story read.
Cannot recall main theme	Unable to recall the main topic of the story.
Miscellaneous Symptoms	
Word-by-word reading	Reading in a choppy, halting, and laborious manner (e.g., no attempts are made to group words into thought units).
Strained, high-pitched voice	Reading in a pitch higher than conversational tone.
Inadequate phrasing	Inappropriately grouping words (e.g., *The dog ran into* [pause] *the woods*).

Source: Reprinted, by permission, from Mercer 1983, 309.

Table 7-7 briefly describes the several methods of teaching reading. These are all appropriate for mildly handicapped elementary-aged children.

Written Expression. During the school years, writing skills are important because so much evaluation relates to written responses. Later, adults must be able to express themselves in many day-to-day activities such as writing letters, completing job applications, and making simple lists. Several components of written language can cause problems for mildly handicapped children, including (1) handwriting, (2) spelling, and (3) written expression (Marsh et al. 1983).

The first skill that must be mastered in order to express thoughts in writing is handwriting. Many skills are necessary for handwriting. These include prerequisite skills such as being able to touch, reach, grasp, and release objects, and actual writing skills such as grasping writing objects and copying letters (Payne, Polloway, Smith, and Payne 1977). Informal assessment is usually the method used to determine which handwriting skills are deficient in students. Although formal, more standardized tests are available to ascertain writing skills, they are probably less effective than informal methods.

Table 7-7 **Teaching Strategies for Reading**

Approach	Description
Basal Reading Series	Using a series of interrelated books and supportive materials. Books are graded readers that increase in difficulty of vocabularly, content, and skill development.
Phonics Methods	Students learn isolated letters and sounds and then blend them into words.
Linguistic Approach	Focuses on decoding using the sound system of the English language. Differs from the phonics approach in that individual letter sounds are not learned in isolation.
Language Experience	Reading is considered an extension of language arts. Reading skills linked to listening, speaking, and writing. Materials are the stories of students.
Individualized Reading	Builds on students' individual interests. Students read in books suited to their needs and interests.
Computer Instruction in Reading	Uses computer programs to teach initial reading skills.
Special Remedial Reading Approaches	Includes many different reading programs designed to remediate various reading problems. Includes multisensory approaches of Fernald and Gillingham; DISTAR; the Rebus Program, Glass Analysis; Initial Teaching Alphabet; and others.

Source: Lerner 1985.

In teaching writing at the elementary level, the initial decision is whether to teach printing or cursive writing first. Although printing is taught first in most elementary schools, some research suggests that teaching cursive first does not have negative effects on children and, in fact, has some advantages. These include helping children with transpositions and letter reversals (Marsh et al. 1983; Larson 1970; Early, Nelson, Kleber, Treegoob, Huffman, and Cass 1976). Teachers should determine on an individual basis the most appropriate approach. This can be accomplished using norm-referenced tests, criterion-referenced tests, and teacher-made tests. Probably the best method of determining appropriate intervention techniques is through informal observation.

Specific teaching techniques to improve handwriting vary according to the cause of the writing problem. After determining the underlying cause, teachers should develop strategies that will assist in remediating these problem areas. Examples of remediation include the following:

- stringing beads to develop fine eye-motor skills
- walking in straight lines or circles to develop an awareness of figures and improve concepts of left and rights, forward and backward
- making figures in sand with finger paint or on sandpaper to help make figures without guides (Marsh et al. 1983)

Poor spelling has long been noted to be a characteristic of children with disabilities. Spelling has been called "the invention of the devil." Noting this, Lerner (1985) states that spelling is difficult because (1) creativity and divergent thinking are not helpful; (2) only one pattern of letters is correct; (3) there is not a consistent pattern of spelling in English; (4) spelling words is more difficult than reading; and (5) peripheral clues that aid in reading are not available in spelling.

Once the types of spelling errors have been determined by using either formal, norm-referenced tests or informal teacher-made instruments, remediation of spelling skills can

While there are a variety of special programs available to teach basic skills, teachers must still be creative in their use of learning activities.

be initiated. Mercer (1983) describes five major spelling instruction approaches used in schools. These include the rule-based method, where emphasis is placed on the rules governing the spelling of the majority of words; the multisensory approach, which stresses the use of visual, auditory, kinesthetic, and tactual modalities; and the study-test method, where students are given a pretest, then must study the words missed on the pretest before they are given a post-test. In addition to these three methods, some teachers use fixed and flow word lists. This method usually provides students with a weekly word list for study in preparation for testing at the end of the week. Finally, imitation methods require the child to spell words orally and in writing after the teacher has provided correct word models.

Many students have difficulties in expressing themselves in writing. Being able to write and spell does not automatically lead to good **written expression** skills. "Written expression reflects a person's level of comprehension, concept development, and abstraction" (Mercer 1983, 296). Because written expression requires the assimilation of several skills, it is probably the most likely problem students have in communication (Lerner 1985).

Written expression includes ideas, how ideas are written, the choice of words used to express ideas, and punctuation. First efforts of written expression are not "masterpieces." Rather, students need to learn from each of their efforts; critiques should be timely and understandable, and lead to improved products.

Methods of improvement rely on teaching the basic components of written expression. These include punctuation and capitalization, vocabulary and grammar, and sentence and paragraph writing (Marsh et al. 1983). Students must be encouraged to write and their efforts must be reinforced. There are few "canned" programs for teaching written expression; teachers must use their own creativity and ingenuity. One method currently being tested as an aid to teaching writing skills is the microcomputer (Rosegrant 1985). Regardless of the method or methods used by teachers, writing is a skill that can be learned by most students. It is as important for mildly handicapped children to master written expression skills as it is for nonhandicapped children.

Math. Math has been referred to as the universal language, symbols that can be understood by individuals who speak different languages (Lerner 1985). Along with reading, writing, and spelling, math is a subject area that frequently causes problems for mildly handicapped children.

Problems in math can be recognized at an early age. For example, preschool children who have difficulties sorting objects by size, matching objects, understanding numbers, and understanding the general concepts of counting may be the same children who have difficulties with computation during elementary school (Mercer 1983).

Skills required for mathematical operations definitely develop sequentially. Arithmetical concepts that develop in accordance with Piagetian theory are described in table 7-8. Learned concepts build on each other to enable higher mathematical reasoning and operations.

Students who experience math problems display certain characteristics, including disturbances of spatial relationships, disturbances of motor and visual-perception abilities, language and reading problems, poor concepts of direction and time, and memory problems (Lerner 1985). School personnel must diagnose the basis of the problems and intervene with appropriate remedial activities.

Remediation of math problems should focus on basic math facts, computational processes, and application (Marsh et al. 1983). Innumerable methods are used to teach these skills. What teachers must consider is that the math curriculum is a continuum of sequential skills in which lower level skills must be learned before higher level skills. Although there will be some variation, the following indicates the skills learned at various grade levels:

- Kindergarten   Basic number meanings, counting, classification, seriation or order, recognition of numericals, writing of numbers.

Table 7-8 Arithmetical Concepts in Accordance with Piagetian Theory at Specific Ages

Age	Concepts	Age	Concepts
3 to 5 years	Rudimentary concepts of more, bigger, smaller, etc. One-to-one correspondence	6 to 7 years—cont'd	Multiplicative relationships Mastery of geometrical forms
6 to 7 years	Cardinality Ordinality Conceptualization of a set Joining sets Place value Addition Concept of equivalency Conservation of number Reversibility Rational counting Transitivity Subtraction Part-to-whole fractions	8 to 9 years 10 to 12 years	Parallelism Three-attribute classification Associative property of addition Distributive property of multiplication Commutative property of addition Fractions Percentages Proportions Probability Conservation of weight and volume Geometry

Source: Reprinted, by permission, from Marsh, Price, and Smith 1983.

- Grade 1   Addition through 20, subtraction through 20, place value of 1s and 10s, time to the half-hour, money, simple measurement.
- Grade 2   Addition through 100, subtraction through 100, ordering of 0 to 100, skip counting (by twos), place value of 100, regrouping for adding and subtracting.
- Grade 3   Multiplication through 9s, odd or even skip counting, place value of 1,000s, two- and three-place numbers for addition and subtraction.
- Grade 4   Division facts, extended use of multiplication facts and related division facts through 9s, two-place multipliers.
- Grade 5   Fractions, addition and subtraction of fractions, mixed numbers, long division, two-place division, decimals.
- Grade 6   Percents, three-place multipliers, two-place division, addition and subtraction of decimals and mixed decimals, multiplication and division of decimals and mixed decimals by whole numbers (Lerner 1985, 445).

Many different commercial math programs are designed for remediating math deficits. Teachers must determine which, if any, of these programs meet the needs of individual children. Often teacher-made materials and approaches work as well as commercial programs. Regardless of the type of programs selected, they must (1) be individualized, (2) be based on individual math skill levels, and (3) consider a combination of other variables, such as maturation level, readiness level, intellectual level, and motivation.

Social/emotional skills. Mildly handicapped children have difficulties in the area of social acceptance. This has been documented in the various categories of handicapped children frequently included in the generic, mildly handicapped group. For example, Lerner 1985) noted that learning disabled children often do poorly in social situations and that many of them have problems in meeting the social demands placed on them by peers and adults. Drew et al. (1984) stated that mentally retarded children in schools are rejected by both peers and teachers, that they have more emotional problems than their nonhandicapped peers, and that they are socially inadequate. All three of the major groups of children classified as mildly handicapped—learning disabled, mildly mentally retarded, and emotionally disturbed—experience social and emotional problems.

Too often, programming for these problems is a crisis-oriented approach; that is, techniques are not used to deal with problems until they are manifested. Proponents of social and affective programming have long argued for preventive actions that would build positive social and emotional skills and limit the problems that develop from these weaknesses (Elias and Maher 1983).

Lerner (1985) lists the following characteristics of social problems among disabled children:

- lack of judgment
- difficulties in perceiving how others feel
- problems in socializing and making friends
- problems in establishing family relationships
- social disabilities in the school setting
- poor self-concept

The ability of children to understand themselves evolves over time. Self-concept, for example, should not be considered a simplistic view of self, but rather an understanding that develops through a series of progressive stages (Coleman 1985). As a result, educators must develop long-term strategies for dealing with inadequacies in social and emotional development. One such strategy is cooperative group tasks. After orchestrating cooperative group tasks between disabled and nondisabled students, Anderson (1985) concluded that the cooperative group activities had a positive effect on peer acceptance and cooperation.

Another strategy advocated by some professionals is the social-cognitive problem-solving approach (Elias and Maher 1983). Using this method, students view video tapes and then discuss and role play various social situations. Although not billed as a panacea, Elias and Maher do state that the approach represents a "viable, flexible, and educationally sound means of approaching a significant imminent need: how to promote the social and affective development of our children" (Elias and Maher 1983, 344).

Many commercial kits are available for teaching and strengthening social skills; however, good teachers often do things in the classroom that have the same positive effects. Regardless of the program used, the child's social and emotional status must be considered; this is one area of the school curriculum that should not be overlooked just because it is nonacademic.

SUMMARY

Many children classified as mildly handicapped, whether their categorical labels are mental retardation, learning disability, or emotional disturbance, experience both academic and social problems.

The second section presented a description of the regular elementary school, classroom, and teacher. With the advent of mainstreaming, the importance of these factors for mildly handicapped children has greatly increased. For example, prior to mainstreaming mildly handicapped children into regular classrooms, regular classroom teachers had very little contact with this group of students. Since federal and state laws have mandated mainstreaming, however, regular classroom teachers have become partners in the education of these children.

Several variables in the elementary school impact on handicapped children. These include administration, organizational arrangements, curriculum, and school policies.

The final section of the chapter dealt with the education of mildly handicapped children in elementary schools. General accommodative strategies were discussed, as well as specific techniques for teaching these children reading, writing, spelling, and math. Finally, methods of dealing with social and emotional problems were discussed.

The chapter on elementary-aged mildly handicapped children emphasized the role shared among all school personnel in the provision of appropriate educational programs for these children. Regular classroom teachers and special education teachers must work together in order to appropriately serve mildly handicapped children. The support of administrators is also a key factor in enabling these children to experience success in elementary school.

REFERENCES

Anderson, M.A. Cooperative group tasks and their relationship to peer acceptance and cooperation. *Journal of Learning Disabilities* 18, no. 2 (1985):83–86.

Campbell, N.J., J.E. Dobson, and J.M. Bost. Educator perceptions of behavior problems of mainstreamed students. *Exceptional Children* 51, no. 4 (1985):298–303.

Coleman, J.M. Achievement level, social class, and the self-concepts of mildly handicapped children. *Journal of Learning Disabilities* 18, no. 1 (1985):26–30.

Davis, W.E. Public school principals' attitudes toward mainstreaming retarded pupils. *Education and Training of the Mentally Retarded* 15, no. 3 (1980):174–78.

Drew, C.J., D.R. Logan, and M.L. Hardman. *Mental retardation: A life cycle approach.* 3d ed. St. Louis: C.V. Mosby, 1984.

Early, G.H., D.A. Nelson, D.J. Kleber, M. Treegoob, E. Huffman, and C. Cass. Cursive handwriting, reading, and spelling achievement. *Academic Therapy* 12, no. 1 (1976):67–74.

Elias, M.J., and C.A. Maher. Social and affective development of children: A programmatic perspective. *Exceptional Children* 49, no. 4 (1983):339–46.

Epstein, M.H., and D. Cullinan. Academic performance of behaviorally disordered and learning-disabled pupils. *Journal of Special Education* 17, no. 3 (1983):303–307.

Friend, M., and G. McNutt. Resource room programs: Where are we now? *Exceptional Children* 51, no. 2 (1984):150–155.

Gajar, A. Educable mentally retarded, learning disabled, emotionally disturbed: Similarities and differences. *Exceptional Children* 45, no. 6 (1979):470–472.

Gajar, A. Characteristics across exceptional categories: EMR, LD, and ED. *Journal of Special Education* 14, no. 2 (1980):165–173.

Garrett, M.K., and W.D. Crump. Peer acceptance, teacher preference, and self-appraisal of social status among learning disabled students. *Learning Disabilities Quarterly* 3, no. 3 (1980):42–48.

Goldhammer, K., B.T. Rader, and P. Reuschlein. *Mainstreaming: Teacher competencies.* East Lansing, Mich.: Michigan State University, 1977.

Hallahan, D.P., and J.M. Kauffman. Labels, categories, behaviors: ED, LD, and EMR reconsidered. *Journal of Special Education* 11, no. 2 (1977):139–48.

Jarolimek, J., and C.D. Foster. *Teaching and learning in the elementary school.* New York: Macmillan, 1976.

Klesius, J.P., and S.P. Homan. A validity and reliability update on the informal reading inventory with suggestions for improvement. *Journal of Learning Disabilities* 18, no. 2 (1985): 71–76.

Larson, C.E. Teaching beginning writing. In *Building handwriting skills in dyslexic children*, edited by J.E. Arena. San Rafael, Calif.: Academic Therapy Publications, 1970.

Lerner, J. *Learning disabilities: Theories, diagnosis, and teaching strategies.* 4th ed. Boston: Houghton Mifflin Co., 1985.

Marsh, G.E., B.J. Price, and T.E.C. Smith. *Teaching mildly handicapped children: Methods and materials.* St. Louis: C.V. Mosby, 1983.

Mercer, C.D. *Students with learning disabilities.* 2d ed. Columbus, Ohio: Charles E. Merrill, 1983.

Neisworth, J.T., and J.G. Green. Functional similarities of learning disability and mild retardation. *Exceptional Children* 42, no. 1 (1975):17–21.

Nevin, A. Special education administration competencies required of the general education administrator. *Exceptional Children* 45 (1979):363–65.

Payne, J.S., E.A. Polloway, J.E. Smith, and R.A. Payne. *Strategies for teaching the mentally retarded.* Columbus, Ohio: Charles E. Merrill, 1977.

Ragan, W.B., and G.D. Shepherd. *Modern elementary curriculum.* New York: Holt, Rinehart, and Winston, 1977.

Raske, D.E. The role of general school administrators responsible for special education programs. *Exceptional Children* 45, no. 8 (1979):645–46.

Rosegrant, T. Using the microcomputer as a tool for learning to read and write. *Journal of Learning Disabilities* 18, no. 2 (1985):113–115.

Ryan, K., and J.M. Cooper. *Those who can, teach.* Boston: Houghton Mifflin Co., 1980.

Salend, S.J. Factors contributing to the development of successful mainstreaming programs. *Exceptional Children* 50, no. 5 (1984):409–416.

Schultz, L.R. Educating the special needs student in the regular classroom. *Exceptional Children* 48, no. 4 (1982):366–68.

Scranton, T.R., and D.B. Ryckman. Sociometric status of learning disabled children in an integrative program. *Journal of Learning Disabilities* 12 (1979):402–407.

Smith, C.R. *Learning disabilities: The interaction of learner, task, and setting.* Boston: Little, Brown & Co., 1983.

Chapter Eight

MILDLY HANDICAPPED ADOLESCENTS

CHAPTER OUTLINE

INTRODUCTION
THEORIES OF ADOLESCENCE
    Developmental Theory
    Psychoanalytic Theory
    Evolutionary View
    Biological Explanation
THE ADOLESCENT SUBCULTURE
    Influences of the Peer Culture
    Peer Membership and the Handicapped
SPECIAL PROBLEMS OF ADOLESCENCE
    Drug Abuse
    Alcoholism
    Running Away
    Stealing
    Pregnancy
    Suicide
EDUCATIONAL NEEDS OF HANDICAPPED ADOLESCENTS
    Service Models
CAREER DECISIONS
SUMMARY

CHAPTER OBJECTIVES

After reading this chapter, you should be able to:
- Define adolescence;
- List and discuss the major tasks of adolescence;
- Identify the major theories of adolescence;
- Describe the adolescent subculture;
- Describe problems affecting mildly handicapped adolescents;
- Identify educational needs of mildly handicapped adolescents;
- Discuss secondary programming for mildly handicapped adolescents.

INTRODUCTION

Adolescence is a term heard frequently in the American culture; it is used to convey a number of concepts and attitudes as well as to describe events and actions. The adolescent period has been described as (1) the transitional period between childhood and adulthood, (2) the period during which an emotionally immature person reaches the final stages of physical and mental development, and (3) the period of attainment of maturity. Konopka identifies **adolescence** as "one of the most significant stages in the development of each individual. In adolescence, the person moves into being part of a *new* generation, no longer a child" (Konopka 1983, 391). While general statements abound, a definitive description of adolescence is elusive. As Gallatin points out, "it *is* difficult to specify what the experience of adolescence contributes to the human cycle" (Gallatin 1975, 12). However, a review of the literature addressing this stage of human development reveals that several important developmental tasks may be associated with this period (Erikson 1950; Havighurst 1951). The major tasks of adolescence have remained fairly constant since its initial recognition in the literature of the 1950s.

1. Creation of a sense of sexuality as part of a personal identity
2. Development of confidence in social interactions
3. Infusion of social values into a personal code of behavior
4. Acceptance of biological changes
5. Attainment of a sense of emotional independence
6. Contemplation of vocational interests
7. Identification of personal talents and interests
8. Awareness of personal weaknesses and strengths
9. Development of sexual interests with non-family members
10. Development of peer relationships
11. Completion of formal educational activities
12. Preparation for marriage, parenting, and adult relationships

While these tasks are central to the period as it typically occurs in all adolescents, they may take on even more significance for students identified as handicapped. The "firsts" and "problems" of adolescence may magnify already complex situations for handicapped adolescents and may require the intense concern of special educators (Anastasiow 1983). Table 8-1 reviews these tasks and presents possible complicating questions associated with a variety of handicapping conditions that may exist among handicapped adolescents. These questions may not have clear and definite answers, but they must be considered when contemplating the question, are the developmental tasks more significant and difficult for the handicapped adolescent:

THEORIES OF ADOLESCENCE

There appears to be a consensus among writers concerning several important points related to adolescence, including the following:

1. Adolescence is a period within the lives of young people which is accompanied by significant change
2. Students' bodies change, sometimes drastically in terms of proportion
3. This period of biological change represents the onset of puberty

Adolescence is a difficult developmental period that may present special problems for the mildly handicapped.

4. These significant physiological transformations are due to an alteration in glandular activity, which causes change and stimulates the development of secondary sexual characteristics and sexual drives (Marsh and Price 1980)

Agreement cannot be reached, however, on some important points involved in the study of adolescence; namely, the explanation of the changes in observed behavior and

Table 8-1. **Developmental Tasks and Resultant Questions**

Developmental Tasks	Questions to Consider
1. Creation of a sense of sexuality as part of a personal identity	• How is this affected by the presence of a physical handicap? • Does poor school performance and low social status impact this?
2. Development of confidence in social interactions	• Do negative classroom experiences play a role? • Is social inadequacy assumed by others to be an automatic result of being handicapped?
3. Infusion of social values into a personal code of behavior	• Are handicapped students often protected by adults to such a degree that they do not have experiences which allow them to develop a sense of what social values exist? • Does the handicap and/or others' reaction to it prevent experimentation with social behavior?
4. Acceptance of biological changes	• Are handicapped students denied accurate information about their own bodies and sexual maturity? • Is it sometimes difficult for handicapped students with lower intellecutal performance to glean information by osmosis or to comprehend the information?
5. Attainment of a sense of emotional independence	• Are handicapped students given the same opportunity as other adolescents to make their own decisions? • Is it more difficult for a handicapped adolescent to deal effectively with emotion?
6. Contemplation of vocational interests	• Are handicapped students limited in vocational choices because of preconceived notions of their ability? • Are vocational training options too tightly tied to labels and not to true individual ability?
7. Identification of personal talents and interests	• Is it more difficult for handicapped students to identify positive traits within themselves as a result of negative events experienced?
8. Awareness of personal weaknesses and strengths	• Do students focus more on their limitations than strengths? • Do handicapped students have an inaccurate self-concept?
9. Development of sexual interests with non-family members	• Is it more difficult to develop heterosexual contacts if the adolescent is handicapped? • Do public prejudices serve as barriers to the development of sexual interests?
10. Development of peer relationships	• Are there fewer opportunities for handicapped adolescents to develop peer relationships? • Are some students isolated socially by the limitations of their label more than by the actual effects of the condition?
11. Completion of formal educational activities	• Has P.L. 94-142 increased the likelihood of this? • Should handicapped students receive special diplomas which identify them as handicapped?
12. Preparation for marriage, parenting, and adult relationships	• Do handicapped students receive information concerning family responsibilities? • Do some community attitudes operate against adolescents so that adult relationships are difficult to achieve?

Table 8-2. **Summary of Theories of Adolescence and Possible Significance to Educators**

Theory	Possible Insights to Aid Educators in Understanding Adolescent Behavior
Developmental Theory	• Developmental tasks can provide at least a rough standard for evaluating progress within the adolescent period. • Developmental tasks might also be considered in designing high school experiences, which facilitate student efforts to accomplish the tasks.
Psychoanalytic Theory	• Interactions with adolescents may be viewed in light of the internal struggle underway. • Confrontive behaviors and otherwise "difficult behaviors" might be viewed more as a symptom of the change taking place rather than as an interpersonal problem between teacher and student.
Evolutionary View	• Its concrete explanation of the adolescents as "sometimes adults and sometimes children" would seem to give some validity to such observations on the part of the educators.
Biological	• Future, biological explanations of adolescence may become more important because, unlike many of the other theories, this one may result in the development of practical methods for aiding the student in dealing with such pressures of adolescence as chemical interventions.

the underlying causes. As a result of this lack of consensus, a number of theories attempt to explain adolescence and its changes such as those observed in personality and behavior.

The following section summarizes the major theories of adolescence. Table 8-2 describes some of the possible implications each theory might have for educators.

Developmental Theory

This view of adolescence by Havighurst (1951) is predicated upon the importance of the developmental tasks (listed in table 8-1) that are considered necessary in the socialization process of becoming an adult. One of the major strengths of this particular theory of adolescence, at least in the eyes of educators, is that those developmental tasks can provide a rough standard for evaluating progress within the adolescent period. These same developmental tasks might also be considered in designing a high school experience that can facilitate student efforts to accomplish the tasks.

One of the major aspects of Havighurst's developmental theory is the emphasis on adolescence as a "formative period" in the development of vocational options. The premise is that from age ten to fifteen the student must acquire the basic habits of industry and learn to organize time and energy to complete assignments and responsibilities. Between the ages of fifteen to twenty-five, the student focuses on acquiring an identity as a worker, choosing and preparing for an occupation. Beyond age twenty-five, the task is to become a productive person, mastering the skills of one's occupation. This particular aspect of the theory, coupled with the tasks presented earlier, gives insight into the developmentalist explanation of the adolescent period.

Adolescents acquire basic habits of industry and learn to organize time and energy.

Psychoanalytic Theory

The psychoanalytic theory of adolescence from Freud describes the adolescent period with terms such as *storm and stress, turbulence, re-emergence,* and *resurgence of primitive instincts.* According to this theoretical explanation of adolescence, the primary adjustment problem for adolescents is accommodation of the re-emergence of suppressed sexual instincts (these instincts had been controlled in childhood as a result of the incomplete resolution of the Oedipal complex). More plainly stated, this view perceives adolescence as a period of renewed struggles that have long existed within the individual.

This explanation implies that adolescence is the resolution point for many of the unanswered or unresolved issues that were temporarily addressed in earlier stages of life and therefore, with their re-emergence, can be expected to be turbulent and stress ladened. Advocates of the psychoanalytic theory postulate that the adult adjustment that results from the resolutions achieved during adolescence more directly reflects childhood than adolescence itself. It is almost as if the adolescent period is the point at which feelings, values, and attitudes begun in early childhood are finally rejected, accepted, or altered.

The primary source of the stress is described as the struggle created by the imbalance resulting from biological change within the system. Primitive drives are rekindled; greater effort is then required to control them, and more attention must be paid to the drives that need checking and restraint and those that do not. This is the classical explanation of the adolescent who is aggressive, troubled, and in constant conflict with the environment; this adolescent is a reflection of the internal struggle underway over primitive instincts, outside pressures, and a desire to be an adult in complete personal control.

Educators often describe adolescents as troubled, aggressive, erratic, unpredictable, and, in general, combative with adults. Therefore, this particular theory may have significance for educators because its proponents hypothesize that it is normal for the adolescent to exhibit these characteristics, which reflect the struggle going on within the youth. This theory might aid educators in understanding the process underway and might help them keep the interactions with adolescents in perspective. The "difficult behaviors" could then be viewed more as a symptom of the change taking place rather than as an interpersonal problem between teacher and student.

Evolutionary View

In this approach to explaining adolescence, Darwin's theory of evolution is used as the basis for understanding. The originator of this particular view is Hall (1904). In his work, Hall draws parallels between the stages of adolescent development and those recorded in the evolution of mankind, which have brought the human race to the present point of civilization. Hall describes the period of adolescence as similar to that period of time when man made the transition from savage to civilized participant in society, including the wide variance of behavior from base pursuits to lofty ideals.

While this theory and its accompanying explanations have not received wide acceptance, the depiction of adolescence as a period of variance with wide emotional and behavioral swings persists. Educators might find some benefit in examining this evolutionary theory of adolescence because of its concrete explanation of the struggle between previous, lower level stages of function and the acquisition of a new, higher level of performance on the part of the individual. The description of adolescents as "sometimes adults and sometimes children" would seem to reflect this growth process and give some validity to such observations by educators. Therefore, rather than viewing adolescents who exhibit such behaviors as troublesome, they might be seen as attempting to mesh the previous types of survival behavior with the new and more complex demands of adulthood.

Biological Explanation

In recent years our society seems to have become increasingly interested in the relationship between certain biological aspects of functioning, and observed behavior and personality. For example, the relationship between red dye and child behavior, the behavioral effects of certain types of allergies, and the causative impact of diet on behavior of students have been reported in professional literature. While not much has been produced in the way of conclusive findings and there is, as yet, no wide acceptance of some of the hypothesized causative relationships, interest in investigating such areas is growing.

This interest in biological explanations of behavior extends to the study of adolescence. Researchers investigating adolescence in terms of biological change are exploring physiological explanations for the behavior of adolescents, such as an increased or altered hormonal activity (Kulin 1974) and the growth stages of the brain (Dobbing and Smart 1974).

Future educators can expect to have access to more extensive research findings concerning the relationship between biological conditions within the individual's body and the observed behavior of that person. Emerging technology will enable researchers to investigate biological functioning in humans with greater precision and scope. Also, increased interaction between psychologists and others interested in behavior, and scientists and other professionals interested in human biology, will produce a larger body of information from which the educator can draw. It would seem reasonable to say that in the future, biological explanations of adolescence may produce practical methods for assisting the changing adolescent and for fostering understanding from those around the student.

THE ADOLESCENT SUBCULTURE

Peer relationships among adolescents, including mildly handicapped students, have received intense attention from researchers and educators (Coleman 1971; Kronick 1978; Alley and Deshler 1979; Marsh and Price 1980; Zigmond and Brownlee 1980). Obviously, "peer acceptance is of paramount importance to most high school students" (Hallahan and Kauffman 1982, 126). The degree to which this emphasis on peer relationships detracts from society's goals for youth is debatable. If, as Coleman (1971) states, peer relationships and values are detrimental to societal goals, then the issue of the existence of an adolescent subculture extends beyond the realm of educating mildly handicapped adolescents and impacts all aspects of adolescent education. Whether or not peer relationships produce such a negative effect must be decided in light of other important information; namely, that the adolescent's peer group provides emotional support and social feedback.

The question must be raised, Haven't such types of criticism traditionally been leveled at the emerging generation of adults by members of the current adult generation? Our present society seems to believe that young people were different in the "good old days"! Examination of today's social and economic conditions suggests, however, that these very conditions may contribute to an adolescent subculture; namely, that youth of today do not join the work force until much later in life than the youth of a few decades ago (Kett 1977). Thus, adolescents are kept more economically dependent upon their families now than in the earlier years of this century. On the other hand, today's youth have more freedom in some areas such as dating, travel, and leisure time. This produces conflicting messages: increased freedom but decreased economic independence. It is conceivable that in industrialized Western societies the peer subculture is nourished by the adult environment and the intermediate status awarded to adolescents; they are allowed some privileges previously available only to adults and yet they are barred from such adult areas as income earning and civic responsibility. This contradictory treatment may lead to establishment and maintenance of an adolescent subculture.

The effects of an adolescent subculture should be evaluated in terms of the overall impact on the adolescents as a group and as individuals within that group. The peer culture can provide adolescents with an environment of support and understanding of the bodily changes and emotional changes underway. It does not seem reasonable to assume that peer influences are always negative and counter to those of society; such sweeping generalizations would not seem appropriate or acceptable to future educators. Many examples within society illustrate the potential for positive effects, such as scouting, 4-H, team sports, honor societies, and letter clubs. Many of these groups engage in activities designed to model appropriate citizen participation. Therefore, future educators might consider the influence exerted by the peer culture as a potential medium for *positive* interactions and effects.

If, as Hallahan and Kauffman state, peer acceptance is critical to adolescence, then the importance of joining the peer subculture is even more significant for handicapped adolescents seeking acceptance (Marsh and Price 1980). Unfortunately, if our secondary schools are the lonely places described by Bloom (1978, 574), membership in the peer subculture and its various cliques within a school may not be available to handicapped students. This membership may be denied because of the peer culture's intolerance of those who are, in some way, "different." In fact, Skrtic (1980) reports that LD adolescents perceive less approval and more disapproval from teachers in the classroom and are less happy there than non-LD students. Bryan (1975; 1976) has stated clearly that LD adolescents are not well-liked by peers and adults. They tend to have difficulty relating to others. Kronick (1978) has contended that psychosocial deficits of learning disabled students are manifested independently of academic failure. Others argue that these students have no noticeable social problems (Schumaker, Sheldon-Wildgen, and Sherman 1980). In any event, until further research clarifies this issue there is sufficient reason to believe that handicapped students may be denied membership in a peer group because they look different, function differently academically, or in some manner violate one or more of the norms of the peer culture.

Influences of the Peer Culture

Peer influences can be observed in a number of areas of adolescent life. Ideally, educators responsible for special education students acknowledge these influences, and the educational program reflects strategies to aid in attaining membership. Some of the most prominent manifestations of peer influence are discussed in this section in order to aid the reader in understanding how the handicapped student might encounter difficulty in meeting conformance requirements for peer membership.

Dress Codes. One of the most obvious influences of the peer subculture is in dress codes. Expectations concerning dress have always played an important part in achieving membership in a peer group. Examples of required conformity in recent years include:

1. length of hair for boys,
2. length of skirts for girls,
3. jeans,
4. designer jeans, and
5. "preppy" clothes with designer labels.

The ability of handicapped students to meet peer conformance requirements in terms of dress is affected by several familial factors, including (1) economic status, (2) religious beliefs, (3) attitudes, and (4) awareness of trends. Additionally, some mildly handicapped students may be unaware of subtle dress requirements for peer membership and therefore, unknowingly, may fail to meet the standards. They simply don't know what is "in."

Slang Expressions and Gestures. Each group of adolescents seems to have its own unique expressions, jokes, gestures, and even movements. The dynamic nature of these is illustrated by the fact that some high school principals consistently ask new teachers to prepare a list of "in" words to be circulated among older faculty members! There is nothing more amusing to a group of adolescents than hearing an adult use a phrase that dates the adult, making him or her "out of it." Keeping up with what is "in" and what is "out" is not always easy, especially for mildly handicapped students. They tend to lag somewhat behind other students and therefore are susceptible to acquiring phrases and/or words which are "on their way out." Using outdated terms or expressions can contribute to their feeling of being on the outside and can even make them the subject of peer ridicule and criticism.

Dating and Sexual Behavior. To some degree, the peer culture can determine the dating patterns of its members. For example, trends toward single couple dating or double dating are dictated by the groups. Also dating and matchmaking are affected by peer group membership; for example, in some settings, dating from another school is just not done. In other situations, dating from a different age group may or may not be acceptable. The degree and nature of sexual activity also result from peer standards. In some cliques, sexual activity produces increased peer status while in others the opposite may result. Mildly handicapped students may misunderstand some of the talk among peers and even risk misinterpreting the banter that accompanies dawning sexual awareness. This creates the possibility for mildly handicapped students to be the object of teasing, cruel practical jokes, and other forms of negative attention. Therefore, because of the preoccupation of adolescents with sex and their own awareness of sexual development, mildly handicapped students must be aided in their attempts to deal with peer influences.

Peer Gathering Places. The peer group will dictate the appropriate places to go to "see and be seen." All adults can recall a particular drive-in restaurant, drive in movie, city park, bowling alley, country music saloon, or video arcade where adolescents convened as if by invitation or decree. To gather elsewhere would result in an individual or group's being identified as outside the culture or even labeled as such.

Peer Membership and the Handicapped

Research studies have been undertaken to develop a data base from a wide range of variables associated with mildly handicapped adolescents (specifically, those labeled *learning disabled*) and their environment in secondary schools (Schumaker et al. 1981). The variables in the research design included family factors, use of support services, academic performance, and social factors. The studies addressing social factors produced one significant finding concerning the status of handicapped adolescents, in this case the learning disabled, and their interactions with peers; namely, that these students reported being asked to go somewhere with a friend less frequently than other students (Deshler et al. 1980). It can be hypothesized that while peer relationships are extremely important in

Dating and other social activities may be complicated by mild disabilities. The peer culture can determine the dating patterns of its members.

adolescence, they may be even more important to handicapped students and, at the same time, more difficult to achieve. Educators should consider the importance of peer group membership when contemplating the education of handicapped students. Also, consideration should be given to the possible implications of student failure to "belong," including the following:

1. Dropping out of school becomes a greater possibility for students who are social isolates, with little peer interaction (Marsh and Price 1980)
2. Adolescent suicide may be linked to feelings of insecurity and a lack of warm, giving friendship (Konopka 1983)
3. School can become an extremely unpleasant experience and can result in a lack of involvement or withdrawal from the learning process (Gardner 1974)
4. Value patterns, attitudes, and behaviors of adolescents aged fifteen or more are retained through adulthood (Bachman et al. 1978)

Classroom research using observational techniques to collect data on the social behavior of handicapped adolescents, specifically learning disabled students, has produced findings which indicate that such students are not necessarily social isolates in the classroom setting (Schumaker et al. 1980). Fafard and Haubrick (1981) reported research results which would tend to support the premise that "making friends" may not be easy for this general group of adolescents, and that "making friends" at school is the preferred avenue to peer acceptance for this group. These studies would make it reasonable to

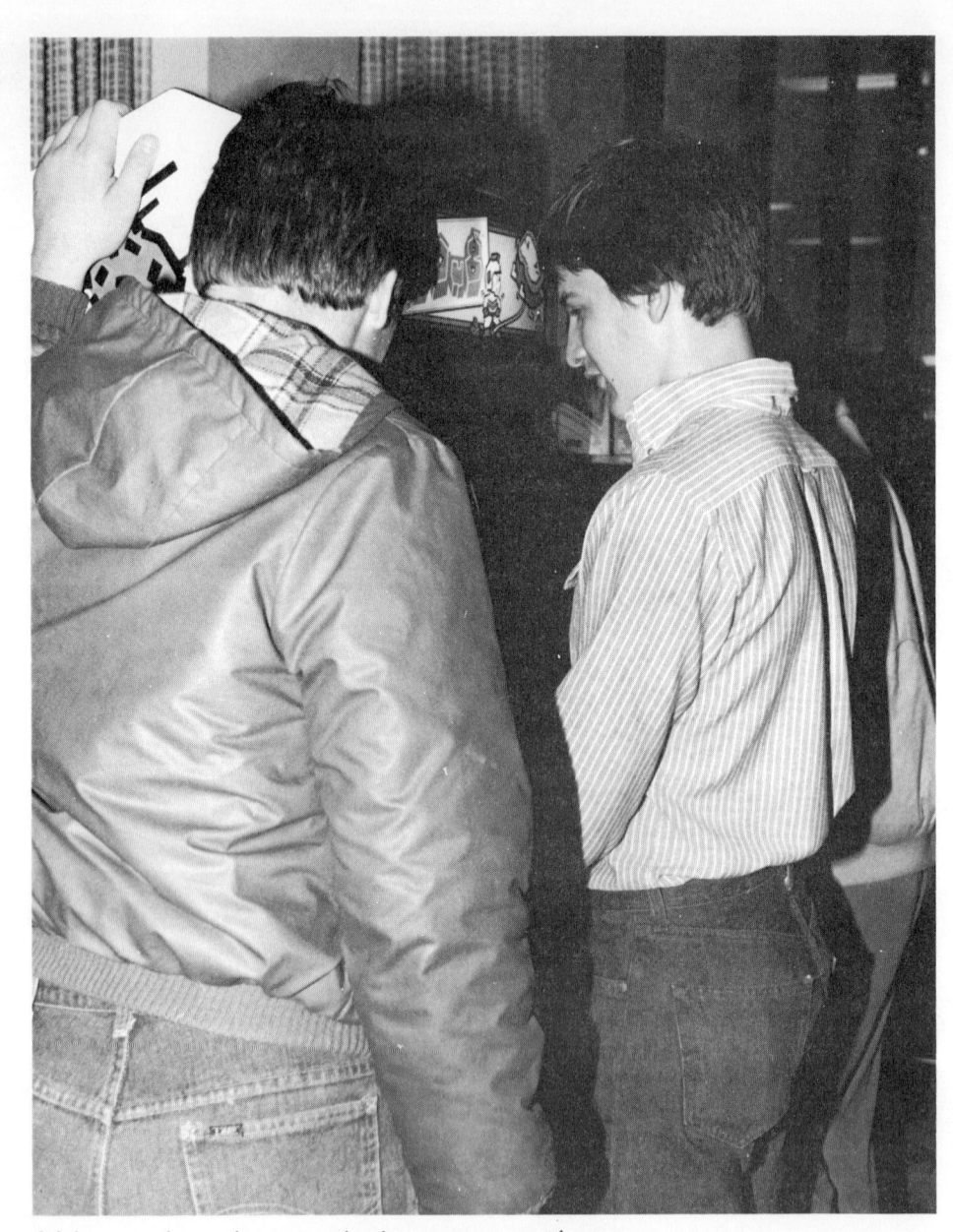

Adolescents often gather in specific places to interact with peers.

assume that many of the social limitations in interactions with peers are manifested in social situations outside the context of the classroom, in the form of membership in formal and/or informal peer groups. Therefore, special educators and other professionals involved in educating handicapped adolescents are urged to help students become members in one or more school groups or organizations to gain peer membership (Marsh and Price 1980).

Being an "outie" in high school can have not only obvious effects during high school but also rather subtle effects visible even in people who complete school and achieve measures of success in adulthood. Many adults can trace aspects of their self-concept, motivation, and general self-confidence to high school and its accompanying peer experiences.

SPECIAL PROBLEMS OF ADOLESCENCE

Adolescence, as a period of storm and stress, is expected to be accompanied by some special problems. The severity and frequency of these problems is a very individual matter, somewhat dictated by the environment of the adolescent and by a vast range of other influences. Comparative data on the prevalence of these problems in handicapped and non-handicapped secondary students are not readily available for a number of reasons:

1. Identification procedures vary among states and school districts, making it difficult to definitively state that the labeling process consistently produces a population exhibiting a common set of behaviors; that is, the placement of a label may reflect procedural differences rather than actual student differences.
2. Data are not systematically reported on many of the problems associated with adolescence.
3. Students who are labeled as mildly handicapped by schools may be more frequently involved with various types of support services than normal achieving students and therefore may go "on record" more often as having problems.

Obviously, *the problems associated with the period of adolescence occur among non-handicapped adolescents as well as those identified as mildly handicapped.* However, it is important to acknowledge this statement to prevent the misconception that these problems are unique to handicapped adolescents.

Drug Abuse

Drug abuse is defined as the use of drugs contrary to medical and legal regulations and/or norms. Professional and popular literature presents data supporting the contention that drug abuse exists in all segments of our society, crossing barriers of race, socioeconomic status, age, and geographic location. Of particular interest are the estimates of drug use among high school students, which range as high as 80 percent (Millman 1978). Drugs used by adolescents include marijuana, hashish, and cocaine, with marijuana reported to be the most common.

It is sometimes postulated that drug abuse is correlated with feelings of rejection and isolation (Bronfenbrenner 1972) and peer pressure (Warner and Swisher 1975). If this is true, mildly handicapped adolescents might be especially vulnerable to drug abuse. Since the underlying characteristic of mildly handicapped students is failure to perform satisfactorily in academic classes, either because of information deficits or behavioral impairments, it might also be hypothesized that negative experiences in the school setting and general feelings of failure might contribute to the likelihood that handicapped adolescents would try various drugs as a means of coping. Marsh and Price report an example of such use. "One teacher related to us that she was certain that one student made a concerted effort to smoke a marijuana cigarette before his English class because it made him mellow enough to make it through the hour" (Marsh and Price 1980, 69). All of this speculation concerning causes of drug abuse does not constitute positive proof that mildly handicapped students engage in drug abuse extensively. In fact, it might be more accurately assumed that they employ drugs for a variety of reasons *just like their non-handicapped peers*.

Alcoholism

The news media, popular magazines, parent groups, community service organizations, and youth groups have begun to draw national attention to the problem of alcoholism among adolescents. Frequently seen in the media are reports of volunteer groups offering "no questions asked" assistance to adolescents in an effort to prevent drinking and driving; adolescents can call one of these groups for volunteer transportation home without hassle. The existence of such groups underscores just how widespread is alcohol abuse among the youth of today. While precise data are not available, it is estimated that over one million teenagers drink to excess (Unger 1978). Estimates are not available on what proportion of this group is identified as handicapped, but it is reasonable to assume that mildly handicapped students are represented.

Causative factors underlying the abuse of alcohol are shrouded in inconclusive research, speculation, and complex interrelated behaviors. Therefore, as in the case of drug abuse, no definitive statement can be made concerning the precise relationship between the existence of an identified handicap and the tendency toward alcoholism. Those same pressures that contribute to other types of social deviancy, such as feelings of failure, anxiety, and alienation, could be considered potential causes for alcoholism among handicapped students.

Running Away

Missing teenagers appear to have become a common feature in this country, especially since the 1970s. Runaways, as they are called, are sought by their families through various approaches, including the mass media strategy of running ads in underground newspapers. McFadden (1983) reports that this approach and others, like the use of a no-charge telephone number, may be used to achieve several purposes:

1. to let the family know that the adolescent is safe,
2. to allow the adolescent to maintain contact with the family,
3. to allow the teenager access to support when needed, and
4. to provide a "fail safe" or emergency resource for help.

The percentage of runaways who are identified as mildly handicapped is unknown. According to reports by McFadden (1983), observations and opinions of teachers of behaviorally disordered and/or learning disabled students suggest that these two types of students probably are more likely to run away than those with lower levels of intellectual functioning (EMR). The pressures confronted by these two segments of the mildly handicapped population may prove overwhelming and so contribute to the desire to avoid further contact with school and parents.

Stealing

Stealing as an adolescent problem typically takes the form of shoplifting, which is reported to exceed one billion dollars annually. While adolescents appear to engage in many forms of stealing, such as car theft, pickpocketing, and hubcap stealing, shoplifting is the major theft problem. Economic need and the desire to possess certain items do not seem to be the primary causes for teenage shoplifting; rather, the sense of adventure and the challenge of the process appear to be the major causes (Marsh and Price 1980). Since the occurrence of shoplifting does not appear to be more prevalent in lower income groups, this latter explanation might be related to the student's need for recognition and sense of success. Such conclusions concerning cause and effect are strictly speculative, however, and should be tempered with cautions about the effects of value systems and definitions of what constitutes success. Therefore, it cannot immediately be assumed that adolescents who are failing in school or in social situations with adults or peers are natural candidates for shoplifting. No such association can be made. The point to be made here is that stealing, particularly in the form of shoplifting, is a problem of national economic significance and is also an area of concern for professionals involved in the education of adolescents.

Pregnancy

Anastasiow (1983) states that 1.2 million young girls become pregnant and bear over 550,000 babies each year. Dealing with these numbers is overwhelming, but such statistics dilute the impact of the event on the life of a young girl. Childbearing and, more particularly, child rearing is not an easy undertaking, even under the best of circumstances. There is always concern, anxiety, and stress. To couple these and other parenting problems with the difficulties of adolescence is to almost certainly assure extreme emotional and financial pressure. As Anastasiow states, the young girl may be isolated from family and friends and "sink into a morass of helplessness and frequent childbearing" (Anastasiow 1983, 397). Anastasiow explores the outcomes of teen pregnancies in terms of the effects on the baby and the potential for reduced functioning in such offspring; however, the concern in this chapter is with the mother and the long-term effects of teenage childbearing.

Newsweek reported that "between 1970 and 1982, the number of one-parent families headed by never-married women rose by a startling 367 percent" (*Newsweek*, 17 January 1983, 27). In the same issue the following facts were reported:

1. The number of illegitimate births among teenagers jumped from 199,900 in 1970 to 271, 801 in 1980.
2. Among white teenagers, 33 percent of all births were illegitimate
3. Among black teenagers, 86 percent of all births were illegitimate

The article cites possible causes for these statistics, including greater sexual activity among today's teenagers, a change in society's attitudes toward unwed mothers and their offspring, and increased willingness to report illegitimate births. However, *Newsweek* presents other causative factors which are extremely significant to future educators. Dr. Kristin Moore, social psychologist on the staff of the Urban Institute in Washington, claims that adolescents with high expectations for a successful future are less likely to have illegitimate children than those with lower aspirations. She infers that "the absence of good schools and solid job prospects may help to explain the particularly high rate of births" (*Newsweek*, 17 January 1983, 27).

If the hypothesis presented in *Newsweek* can be accepted, then girls experiencing failure in school and in their social context may have a more negative outlook about the future and so be considered higher risks than other girls. If this is the case, future educators must assume some of the responsibility for attempting to break the cycle of events. As

Anastasiow (1983) suggests, the special educator must become aware of the existence of adolescent sexual activity and deal with it and its consequences realistically. Again, *no clear-cut statement can be made about the proportion of the population of teenaged, unwed mothers who are identified as mildly handicapped.* Teenaged pregnancy must be more accurately viewed as a problem of adolescence, shared by both handicapped and nonhandicapped students.

Suicide

Suicide among adolescents has been recorded throughout history, even in the works of Shakespeare. Its long existence, however, has not dulled the staggering sense of waste and sadness felt each time it occurs. Unfortunately, adolescent suicide is not rare or isolated. Marsh and Price (1980) report the following facts concerning the prevalence of adolescent suicide:

1. An average of thirteen adolescents commit suicide each day
2. Suicide is the third leading cause of death of persons aged fifteen to twenty-four
3. Adolescents committing suicide come from a cross section of the population, from all races and socioeconomic groups.

What are the causes of adolescent suicide? This question has been investigated in the past and will undoubtedly be the object of future research. To date, no clear and precise answer can be given, but several causes associated with our society and this decade can be suggested, including:

1. a pervading concern about "the bomb" and nuclear warfare,
2. an unhappy contemplation of "what is life?",
3. an inability to deal with death, illness, injury and/or injustice,
4. a need for family,
5. familial mistreatment such as beatings or incest,
6. high expectations and pressures to succeed,
7. prejudices within our society, and
8. a lack of warm, giving friendship (Konopka 1983).

The final three items from the list could be particularly significant for the future educator who might be able to prevent them in the school setting. The use of planned intervention and informal personal intervention might be beneficial for any student, but especially for the mildly handicapped.

Special educators should be particularly sensitive to the fragility of the adolescent being, in spite of the rather tough and resistant front that might be presented. Awareness of underlying pain, anger, guilt, stress, feelings of worthlessness, anxiety, and self-hate may help educators to identify suicidal tendencies before they come to fruition. The following poem by an eighteen year old expresses the feelings that may precede adolescent suicide:

> Will it make a difference, world,
> when I am gone?
> I think not.
> You will go on, day after day,
> never giving me a second thought.
> What then, do I owe you?
> Who will ever shed a tear for me? (Konopka 1983, 390)

HIGHLIGHT

Case Study of One Teen-Ager's Victory

By Sharon Johnson

Educators have made steady progress in developing techniques for dealing with learning disabilities. Witness the case of Jane, from Greenwich, Conn., at 15 years old the quintessential American teen-ager—surrounded by friends and involved in a multitude of school activities. The slim brunette skis, reads novels and is an expert in pop music. A diligent student, she earns B's and C's and is planning a career as a veterinarian's assistant or as a hair stylist.

For all her accomplishments, Jane suffers from a moderate learning disability that often prevents children from achieving academically and interferes with their social development. "Jane has difficulty understanding abstractions, a common language disability that makes it difficult to learn to read and to acquire basic skills in mathematics," said Patricia Hiles, coordinator for elementary special education who helped diagnose Jane's condition in 1974. "Like so many people who suffer from learning disabilities, she also has less severe problems that have necessitated special education. Over the years, she has been given help in speech to eliminate a stutter, writing to help her with letter formation, and physical education to make her steadier on her feet."

The first signs of Jane's disability appeared when she was 4 years old. Her teacher at a private nursery school noticed that she had difficulty counting, making simple analogies and differentiating between objects. The teacher, who had attended a training program to alert nursery school teachers to signs of learning disabilities in young children, suggested to Jane's parents that they have her tested by the school district. The parents agreed.

The evaluation consisted of an interview with the parents to determine the child's medical and family history, observing Jane completing various educational tasks and the administration of the Houston Test of Language Development, the Peabody Picture Vocabulary Test and the Beery Visual Motor Integration Test.

The findings were that Jane's level of general information and use of language was below expectation, that she had difficulty copying designs and that her speech had a sing-song quality — further signs that she might have a learning disability. The social workers, the speech and language expert and the parents decided that on the basis of the evaluation that it might help Jane to remain in nursery school for an extra year.

"We generally don't like to retain youngsters, but we thought that an extra year might help her grow up so that she could do well in kindergarten," Mr. Hiles said. "We took a middle ground approach: We said that this is where she is right now and this is what we hope that the extra year will accomplish. We didn't want the parents to become overly optimistic and think that Jane would overcome all her problems in one year or so pessimistic because they had received a long-range prediction about the number of years of special education she might require."

A year later, Jane was re-evaluated by the same experts and it was decided by the parents and the school to place her in a reg-

(continued)

Education Fall Survey *New York Times* 11 Nov. 1984, Sec. 12.

ular kindergarten class. "Halfway through the year, we and her teacher realized that the regular class was not working out," said Jane's mother. "The other kids would be working on their alphabets and Jane would be sitting there sucking her thumb."

Another extensive evaluation was made, including the administration of the Stanford-Binet Intelligence Test, the McCarthy Scale of Children's Abilities, the Bender-Gestalt perception test and the Rorschach personality test. All the tests showed that Jane ranked within the average range of abilities, but needed special work in language development because she had difficulty understanding and using abstractions.

Her parents and the school staff agreed that Jane required special education for her language disability, so in February 1977, she was placed in a "self-contained" kindergarten.

"One of the goals of our self-contained classes is to give students as much of the regular curriculum as they can possibly handle," said Marie S. Bierman, director of pupil personnel. "To accomplish this, we use different materials, methods, and classroom modifications."

In Jane's case, her instruction in reading in the elementary grades had to be adapted because she needed more concrete examples of what words signify than did pupils in the regular classes who were better at abstraction. Her teacher used a linguistic reading series and showed her lots of pictures to illustrate vocabulary. Jane had more drills to reinforce what she was learning than did the pupils in the regular classes.

Because Jane's motor skills were weak, her early teachers also worked with her on letter formation. For a short time, she was placed in an adaptive physical-education class to improve her gait.

In first, second, and third grade, she studied art and music with pupils in the regular classes because the Greenwich public schools are committed to the principle of "mainstreaming."

By fifth grade, Jane had made such strides in overcoming her disability that she could study science and social studies with pupils from the regular classes as well. "Jane is one of our success stories," said Mrs. Hiles. "Each year pupils do. Her social development also was good. She became less withdrawn and began to make friends."

In September 1982, Jane entered junior high school where she was enrolled in even more mainstream classes. In seventh and eighth grades, she was enrolled in a self-contained English class but by ninth grade, her reading skills had improved so much that she was able to be placed in a regular class. Pat Brennan, her current English teacher, thinks it was a good placement. "Regular classes have helped increase her sense of self-esteem," she said. "She is now reading 'Of Mice and Men' and all the other novels the other students do."

Jane still needs special help, however. It is difficult for her to write essays and so she takes part in the learning-resource center where she and the teacher work on developing topic sentences.

"Students at this age often do not know how to structure their learning and in Jane's case, this difficulty is more pronounced," said Jean Goebelbecker, the learning-resources-center teacher. "She and I work out strategies such as writing out definitions of terms so that she can prepare for tests in subjects like science."

For three years Jane has had the same adviser — Josephine Gleeson — who has given her help in math, her weakest subject. Twice a week, she receives speech therapy for a stutter. She and two other girls also work on inductive reasoning and other skills in these sessions.

"We do a lot of role-playing to teach these children how to become their par-

(continued)

ents," explained Pat Ginsberg, a speech and language pathologist. "We work on how they will handle social situations like asking a teacher for help or returning an item to the store so that they will feel more comfortable and hopefully more fluent."

Jane's parents and school officials are exploring what kind of curriculum Jane should pursue in high school. One possibility is a career program. Another is a mainstream academic program with special help from a resources room, and still another is a special mainstream program in English and social studies.

"Jane has lots of options," said Myra Burstein, coordinator for special education at the secondary level. "She has come a long way since her disability was discovered and she has a bright future."

EDUCATIONAL NEEDS OF HANDICAPPED ADOLESCENTS

American education has come under increasing fire during the decade of the eighties. For instance, *Newsweek* carried a three-part series in 1981 on the status of public education, including *Why Public Schools Are Flunking?* It reported that public schools were losing public confidence and support. A Gallup Poll in 1982 indicated that the predictions of the media were coming true. In 1983, President Ronald Reagan appointed the National Commission on Excellence to examine the status of public education and its products: students and graduates. That commission's report, *A Nation at Risk: The Imperative for Educational Reform,* presented fuel for the fires of discontent with public education, and in the eyes of some critics, it proved the public's worst fears—that our schools *are* inferior. The media coverage of the public school situation then moved from questioning to conveying a sense of urgency, as demonstrated by the *Newsweek* article *Saving Our Schools: A Scathing Report Demands Better Teachers and Tougher Standards* (9 May 1983).

All of these trends and events have contributed to the momentum toward increased standards and accountability. Throughout this decade, schools have initiated actions to stem some of the criticism and to correct what the public perceives as weakness. For example, competency testing has become widespread; many schools require students to demonstrate competency in order to graduate. These and other actions have produced some unusual sets of circumstances for mildly handicapped students and generated several important issues for the schools. Some of the most pertinent issues are summarized in table 8-3.

Even in the face of these and other unresolved issues, mildly handicapped adolescents must be educated, and secondary school special education programs must achieve that end. The Office of Special Education, Department of Education, state departments of education, teacher preparation programs, and professional organizations such as the **Association for Children with Learning Disabilities** (ACLD) and the Council for Exceptional Children (CEC) are all involved in determining organizational structures and administrative plans to design and develop appropriate educational settings for mildly handicapped secondary students. Exactly how mildly handicapped adolescents should be educated is a matter for discussion and differences within the field of special education. The reasons for some of the debate on how to plan and implement secondary special education programs stem from the following:

Table 8-3. Issues Surrounding Standards

Issues	Possible Implications for Mildly Handicapped Adolescents
Increased student standards required for graduation	• More pressure will be exerted on handicapped students to conform to norms. • More emphasis will be placed on test taking. • Student performance differences will become more pronounced and an increasing source of undesirable attention. • Special education students may find high school diplomas more unobtainable. • Students may be awarded amended or equivalent certificates instead of regular diplomas.
Extracurricular Activities	• Special education students may not be allowed to participate in extracurricular activities. • These activities may not be available to all students because of economic constraints and school policies, thus removing possible incentives for some students to remain in school and to achieve peer status.
Increased number of required math and science courses	• Mildly handicapped students may be confronted with an increased number of "solids" that must be included in the special education program. • Mildy handicapped students may fall victim to increased prejudices against inefficient readers.
Increased grading requirements	• Less opportunity may be given for individual variances in learning style.

1. Historically special education programs were primarily elementary school programs because older students moved to other models or services or dropped out of school prior to reaching high school
2. Many of the professionals within the field of special education received training and experience in the elementary model
3. The major secondary model for handicapped students traditionally was a work-study program, primarily for retarded students
4. Research concerning the effects of various types of secondary school programs is still somewhat sketchy because of the relative newness of such programs
5. Model programs and teacher-preparation programs with specific coursework in the area of secondary school services have only become common since the late 1970s.

Thus, the early secondary programs for students exhibiting mild handicaps tended to model elementary school programs. This did not prove satisfactory because of the obvious differences between elementary and secondary schools. In addition, the students served were significantly different and so presented different problems. Also, the goals of elementary programs, namely, basic skills, were not appropriate for secondary school programs. Therefore, trends within recent years have been toward the development of programs specifically designed to meet the needs of adolescent students identified as mildly handicapped.

Table 8-4. **Summary of Service Models**

Service Model	Description
Remedial Model	• Includes activities, techniques, and practices directed primarily at eliminating or strengthening the basic source(s) of a weakness that interferes with learning. • Includes goals designed to *alter the learner* in some way so that he or she can take advantage of the educational program provided.
Compensatory Model	• Includes any approach to education of the handicapped that emphasizes coping strategies to *circumvent the learning deficit* of the learner and *modify the environment* to promote learning. • Includes goals that would focus on the acquisition of content information.
Vocational Model	• Includes prevocational and vocational training programs such as work study. • Includes programs designed for handicapped students, which lead to immediate or short-range employment.

Service Models

The typical secondary school has a curricular pattern with three strains: *general* curriculum which is the traditional liberal arts curriculum, *basic* curriculum which is a diluted version for less academically talented students, and *vocational* education. The special education program for mildly handicapped adolescents must mesh with this organizational structure. Because of the diversity of performance capability and behavioral patterns of the student population in programs for the mildly handicapped, developing a program that meets their needs *and* conforms to the organization of the school can be complex. Marsh and Price cite the following questions for special educators and curriculum developers:

1. What kinds of special education services should be delivered?
2. What should be the balance between special education and the general curriculum?
3. How should the special education program be organized for effective and efficient instruction of the mildly handicapped?
4. What should be the educational outcomes for mildly handicapped students? (Marsh and Price 1980, 8).

The answers to these questions can guide educators and administrators in the development of a secondary special education program for mildly handicapped students, but the answers may not be easily provided. Even so, the organizational patterns for secondary special education programs are still limited to three basic types: remedial, compensatory, and vocational. These three categories reflect the major approaches to programming and illustrate the primary differences among professionals responsible for training and program development. The overview of these approaches presented in table 8-4 includes some of the more salient differences in the approaches.

No one type of program can be deemed the most appropriate. As indicated by the list of questions above, each circumstance and context must be considered. Resources must be evaluated, goals for students determined, and long-term outcomes of the program selected. The decision as to what type of program will be operated within a particular school system is a matter of local determination (Podemski et al. 1984). Therefore, the future educator may find a number of varied arrangements for structuring the secondary school education of mildly handicapped adolescents.

CAREER DECISIONS

Like all youth, mildly handicapped students reaching adolescence are confronted with major decisions about their future. Upon completion of secondary school, students must make decisions rather than simply follow a predetermined plan. As secondary programs for mildly handicapped students have become available, some of these students have sought to continue their education at postsecondary institutions (Dexter 1982). This slowly increasing group of students is now beginning to consider professional careers, in contrast to the typically lower level jobs previously pursued by the handicapped with milder conditions (Fafard and Haubrich 1981). Growing numbers of mildly handicapped students, especially those labeled as *learning disabled*, are enrolling in institutions of higher education. Few of the colleges and vocational schools, however, provide specialized programs for such students (Kahn 1980). Many students also encounter difficulties in postsecondary settings because of the absence of the support system provided through secondary school special education programs (Lorterman 1978). Even so, the numbers of students desiring such postsecondary experiences are growing, and it can be anticipated that their ranks will continue to increase, reflecting the growth of programs at the secondary school level.

Obviously, not all mildly handicapped students should be encouraged to attend a postsecondary institution, just as perhaps not all non-handicapped students should be so urged. It would be just as inappropriate, however, to assume that *none* of those students enrolled in special education should be encouraged or allowed to pursue postsecondary education. Previous chapters with descriptions of the general characteristics of this category of students showed that many of these students do indeed have average or above average intellectual capabilities. Therefore, suggesting that they might continue their formal education does not seem irrational or unreasonable.

As technology advances, the future career opportunities of mildly handicapped students will continue to change. Microcomputers, voice synthesizers, and other such technological innovations may significantly alter the expectations of adults. Emphasis on the retention of literal, factual information may be reduced. In some cases, a reduced focus on reading ability and new areas of professional development might be suitable for the mildly handicapped. While all of this is accurately termed speculation, the promise of brighter careers for mildly handicapped adolescents should be a goal of all professionals involved with their education. Perhaps this list of cautions and admonitions will assist future educators in their pursuit of optimal career preparation for mildly handicapped adolescents:

1. Mildly handicapped students should *not* be denied access to formal postsecondary programs simply because of the existence of a special education label
2. Students served in secondary special education programs should *not* be "tracked" into a particular program based upon the label assigned to the program and/or the individual

> **HIGHLIGHT**
>
> # Many Colleges Now Offer L.D. Programs
>
> By Bob Weinstein
>
> Landmark College, a new school for learning-disabled students, will open in Putney, Vt., next September on the site of defunct Windham College. The school, according to its president, James Olivier, will take 150 students "with average to above-average I.Q.'s, who don't have a primary emotional problem and who are diagnosed as being dyslexic or as having a specific learning disability."
>
> Landmark will become one of several colleges that accommodate learning-disabled students, who are in turn being identified in elementary and secondary schools in ever-increasing numbers. Most colleges have at least some services for the learning disabled, some have special programs that involve sizable proportions of the student body, and some, like Landmark, make the education of learning disabled their focus.
>
> "We are looking for students," said Mr. Olivier, "who have a true clinical disability who have never received specific remedial help." Landmark will offer two programs: a precollege skills-development program in basic skills and a two-year college program. The cost will be $17,000 a year, all of which is tax-deductible, according to Mr. Olivier.
>
> "Ninety-five percent of the colleges in this country provide some type of facilities for L.D. students," according to Jane E. Jarrow, executive director of the Association of Handicapped Student Services Programs in Post-Secondary Education, in Columbus, Ohio.
>
> According to United States Department of Education statistics, 5 percent of the school-age population has learning disabilities. The legal basis for servicing the learning disabled is Section 504 of the Rehabilitation Act of 1973 (Public Law 93-112), which requires that public and private organizations receiving Federal funds not discriminate in any way against handicapped persons. All institutions must provide appropriate facilities, programs, instruction and procedures for evaluating handicapped students.
>
> An example of the second category of colleges, those that offer special programs for the learning-disabled, is Curry College in Milton, Mass., which has been running a learning-disabled program since 1970. Its director, Dr. Gertrude Webb, describes it as designed for students who are "college able and language-disabled." About 10 percent of Curry students are in the program.
>
> "If they didn't have problems getting their ideas on paper, they probably could go to any college in the country," Dr. Webb said. "We take students on the basis of their high abstract reasoning and help them understand those strengths so they can use them effectively. They're taught techniques and strategies so that they can capitalize on their strengths and cope with their weaknesses." Curry's students are fully integrated into the college, taking the same courses as everyone else. "There is no labeling of our L.D. students," she explained. "We help them learn and move toward competence and independence." On top of tuition, Curry charges $1,100 a semester for its supportive services.
>
> Adelphi University has had a learning-disabled program since 1979, when 19 stu-
>
> *(continued)*
>
> Education Fall Survey *New York Times* 11 Nov. 1984, Sec. 12.

dents were enrolled, that features a dual focus: educational and social. Fred Barbaro, its director, said that "both components are equally important for students who are different from the general student body." A major goal, said Dr. Barbaro, a professor of social work, is "not only to enroll students but to graduate them."

The school, employing both special-education teachers and social workers, intervenes in all areas that have an impact on student performance. For example, conflict-resolution sessions are held with students and their roommates, who generally do not have a learning disability. Private counseling is provided to students as well as their parents. Students pay a $2,000 surcharge over the tuition of $5,114 to take part in the highly individualized program. In addition, a $500 one-time charge is assessed for a five-week preprogram skills course.

A daily summer diagnostic skills session has been adopted, with modifications, from the Curry College program. Among the courses taught are techniques for memory improvement, the use of recordings for the blind, development of writing skills, techniques for planning research papers and note-taking techniques.

Upon acceptance to the program, two weekly individual tutoring sessions are mandatory, given by an educator with a master's degree in special education. Each student sees a social worker one hour a week privately and one hour in group.

Another school with a program for learning-disabled students, the College of the Ozarks in Clarksville, Ark., this fall accepted 54 new students, who were assigned an individual program coordinator. In phase one of the program, according to Betty Robertson, director of the college's Special Learning Center, students she described as "very dependent" see their coordinator daily. Those with severe learning disabilities, who need more individual services, may go all through college in phase one. Among the accommodations granted them are tutors who read to them to clarify assignments and transcribe notes that are then photocopied for students' use. Total annual tuition cost is $4,600.

Another small, independent school, Barat College, in Lake Forest, Ill., focuses on language remediation. An additional support service for the 26 students in the program includes the Write Wing, in which individual help is given in writing skills. According to Dr. Pamela Adleman, acting director of the program, learning-disabled students are assessed a one-time $450 diagnostic fee, as well as a surcharge over the general tuition of $4,995. The surcharge is $1,000 a semester in the first year, $650 in the second year and $350 in the third year. A one-time diagnostic testing fee is also charged.

While many institutions go beyond mere remedial classes, a 1980 survey of postsecondary programs for the learning disabled found that only 14 of the 121 institutions that accepted such students said they provided more than a basic tutorial program. The study was undertaken by Dr. Barbara K. Cordoni of Southern Illinois University.

Few Ivy League schools, for example, make provisions for the learning disabled. Harvard has some learning-disabled students but stresses that they must meet school requirements; it does not provide any special services. Brown has a dyslexic students' association, but it maintains traditional admissions procedures for all students.

Suzanne Harmon, deputy director of Closer Look, an information center in Washington, D.C., for learning-disabled students and their parents, cautioned: "These programs are not appropriate for every L.D. student. There are a lot of schools providing services for them; the trick is finding the right one."

3. Assumptions should *not* be made concerning the upper ability limits of individual students based upon exhibited performance and/or assigned labels
4. Students should *not* be misled about their ability to perform and to achieve financial success and economic independence, by establishing goals either too high or too low.

SUMMARY

The purpose of this chapter has been to present an overview of the population identified as mildly handicapped adolescents. This group of handicapped students presents an interesting and complex mixture of the characteristics associated with being an adolescent and being handicapped. Because these students are identified as mildly handicapped and do not exhibit conditions considered extreme or severe, they may be expected to grapple with the problems of adolescence without in-depth support or without an understanding of the compounding effect of a learning or behavioral deficit. Most of these students do not *look* handicapped and their particular problem may not visibly set them apart from their peers. Thus, they may be expected to conform to standards that are beyond their capability.

At the same time, the nature of their handicap, academic and/or behavioral, may make conformance even more difficult than would normally be true for adolescents. For example, peer acceptance may be denied because of a student's failure to comprehend social standards and requirements for peer membership. Academic policies of the school may also deny students access to social activities normally given great weight by secondary school students.

This chapter reviews some of the major theories of adolescence and many of the problems specific to the period of adolescence, including stealing, pregnancy, running away, and suicide. Discussions of the problems and how they relate to the handicapped population are included. Also included in this chapter are descriptions of the primary organizational patterns around which secondary school special education programs are structured along with explanations of the goals and outcomes expected from each.

The chapter concludes with information concerning career options of mildly handicapped adolescents, including postsecondary educational opportunities. The inclusion of this topic reflects the recognition that with the proliferation of secondary school special education programs will come increased expectations and opportunities for mildly handicapped adolescents entering the work force and postsecondary education.

REFERENCES

Alley, G., and D. Deshler. *Teaching the learning disabled adolescent: Strategies and methods.* Denver, Colo.: Love Publishing Co., 1979.

Anastasiow, N.J. Adolescent pregnancy and special education. *Exceptional Children* 49, no. 5 (1983):396–401.

Bachman, J., P. O'Malley, and J. Johnston. Dogmatic teens. *Human Behavior* 7, no. 10 (October 1978):32.

Bloom, B. S. New views of the learner: Implications for instruction and curriculum. *Educational Leadership* 35, no. 7 (April 1978):563–76.

Bronfenbrenner, U. Childhood: The roots of alienation. *National Elementary Principal* 52, no. 2 (1972):22–29.

Bryan, T. 1975. Strangers' judgement of children's social and academic adequacy: Instant diagnosis. Reported in D. Kronick. An examination of psychosocial aspects of learning disabled adolescents. *Learning Disability Quarterly* 1 (1978):86–93.

Bryan, T. Peer popularity in learning disabled children. *Journal of Learning Disabilities* 5 (1976):307–311.

Coleman, J. S. The adolescent subculture and academic achievement. In *Readings in adolescent psychology,* edited by M. Powell and A. H. Frerich. Minneapolis: Burgess, 1971.

Deshler, D.D., J. Schumaker, M.M. Warner, G. Alley, and F. L. Clark. An epidemiological study of learning disabled adolescents in secondary schools: Social status, peer relationships, time use and activities in and out of school. Research Report no. 18. Institute for Research in Learning Disabilities. Lawrence, Kans.: University of Kansas, 1980.

Dexter, B.L. Helping learning disabled students prepare for college. *Journal of Learning Disabilities* 15, no. 6 (1982):344-46.

Dobbing, J., J. Smart. Vulnerability of the developing brain and behavior. *British Medical Bulletin* 30, no. 2. (1974):164-68.

Erikson, E. H. *Childhood and society.* New York: Norton, 1950.

Fafard, M., and P.A. Haubric. Vocational and social adjustment of learning disabled young adults: A follow-up study. *Learning Disabilities Quarterly* 4 (1981):122–130.

Gallatin, J.E. *Adolescence and individuality: A conceptual approach to adolescent psychology.* New York: Harper and Row, 1975.

Gardner, W. *Children with learning and behavior problems: A behavior management approach.* Boston: Allyn and Bacon, 1974.

Hall, G.S. *Adolescence: Its psychology and its relations to physiology, anthropology, sociology, sex, crime, religion and education.* New York: Appleton-Century-Crofts, 1904.

Hallahan, D.P., and J.M. Kauffman. *Exceptional Children.* 2d ed. Englewood Cliffs, N. J.: Prentice-Hall, 1982.

Havighurst, R.J. *Developmental tasks and education.* New York: Longman, 1951.

Kahn, M.S. Learning problems of the secondary and junior college learning disabled student: Suggested remedies. *Journal of Learning Disabilities* 13, no.8 (1980):445–49.

Kett, J.F. *Rites of Passage.* New York: Basic Books, 1977.

Konopka, Gisela. Adolescent suicide. *Exceptional children* 49, no. 5 (1983):390–394.

Kronick, D. An examination of psychosocial aspects of learning disabled adolescents. *Learning Disability Quarterly* 1 (1978):86-93.

Kulin, H.E. The physiology of adolescence in man. *Human Biology* 46 (1974):133–43.

Lorterman, A.S. College composition and the invisible handicap. Paper presented at 29th annual meeting of the Conference on College Composition and Communication, March 1978, in Denver, Colorado. ERIC Document Reproduction Service no. ED 168 016.

McFadden, A.C. Behaviorally disordered adolescents and teenage problems: Some observations. Columbia, Mo.: University of Missouri, 1983.

Marsh, G.E., II, and B.J. Price. *Methods for Teaching the Mildly Handicapped Adolescent.* St. Louis, Mo.: C.V. Mosby, 1980.

Millman, R.B. Drug and alcohol abuse. In *Handbook of treatment of mental disorders in childhood and adolescence,* edited by B.B. Wolman. Englewood Cliffs, N.J.: Prentice-Hall, 1978.

Newsweek, 17 January 1983, 27.

Podemski, R., B.J. Price, T.E.C. Smith, and G.E. Marsh. *Comprehensive Administration of Special Education.* Rockville, Md.: Aspen Systems Corporation, 1984.

Schumaker, J.B., J. Sheldon-Wildgen, and J.A. Sherman. An observational study of the academic and social behaviors of LD adolescents in the regular classroom. Research Report no. 22. Institute for Research in Learning Disabilities. Lawrence, Kans.: University of Kansas, 1980.

Schumaker, J.B., M.M. Warner, D.D. Deshler, G.R. Alley, and F.L. Clark. An epidemiological study of LD adolescents in secondary schools: Data Base. Research Report no. 31. Institute for Research in Learning Disabilities. Lawrence, Kans.: University of Kansas, October 1981.

Skrtic, T. The regular classroom interactions of learning disabled adolescents and their teachers. Research Report no. 8. Institute for Research in Learning Disabilities. Lawrence, Kans.: University of Kansas, 1980.

Unger, R.A. The treatment of adolescent alcoholism. *Social Casework* 59, no. 1 (1978):27–35.

Warner, R.W., and J.D. Swisher. Alienation and drug abuse: Synonymous? In *Contemporary adolescence: Readings,* edited by H. Thornburg. Monterey, Calif.: Brooks/Cole, 1975.

Zigmond, N., and J. Brownlee. Social skills training for adolescents with learning disabilities. *Exceptional Education Quarterly* 1 (1980):77–83.

Chapter Nine

MILDLY HANDICAPPED ADULTS

CHAPTER OUTLINE

INTRODUCTION
NEEDS AND CHARACTERISTICS OF MILDLY HANDICAPPED ADULTS
    Social Adjustment
    Vocational Opportunity and Adjustment
    Community Acceptance
    Other Problems
SERVICES FOR MILDLY HANDICAPPED ADULTS
    Education
    Vocational
    Housing Services
    Recreation and Leisure Time Opportunities
    Self-Help Groups
THE ELDERLY MILDLY HANDICAPPED
    Characteristics of the Aged Disabled
    Needs of the Elderly Disabled
SUMMARY

CHAPTER OBJECTIVES

After reading this chapter, you should be able to:
- Describe the needs and characteristics of mildly handicapped adults;
- Identify problems associated with social adjustment of mildly handicapped adults;
- Discuss vocational problems experienced by mildly handicapped adults;
- Define normalization;
- Apply normalization to services for mildly handicapped adults;
- Describe educational programs for mildly handicapped adults;
- List rehabilitation services provided by state agencies to mildly handicapped adults;
- Identify purposes of self-help groups for mildly handicapped adults;
- Define the elderly mildly handicapped; and
- Describe problems and needs of the mildly handicapped adult.

INTRODUCTION

Mildly handicapped children grow up to become adults. In some cases, the disabilities experienced by mildly handicapped children cause minimal problems in adulthood. For other adults, however, disabilities that caused problems during the school years continue to limit individual potential. The view of some professional educators that mildly handicapped children do not have problems as adults may result from "assumptions made about the future functioning of an individual student based on present behavior, school achievement, and physical characteristics; a lack of knowledge—or worse, a lack of concern—about the future adult world of school-aged children; and the assumption that since the adult with a disability is more or less absorbed into society, the educational system has done its job in providing adequate preparation for emergence into that area" (Best 1978, 152).

Unfortunately, many assumptions about the lack of problems experienced by mildly handicapped children when they become adults are invalid; adults with disabilities often have problems. Just because they are not required to complete academic work does not mean that they are easily assimilated into society and require no further assistance. For some, quite the contrary exists. Mildly handicapped adults face problems in many areas, including community adjustment and acceptance, employment, recreation, living arrangements, mobility, and peer relations. And these problems are experienced by many categories of disabled persons. Adults with visual impairments, hearing impairments, and mental disabilities face the obvious problems, but individuals with disabilities considered less severe or related only to academic work also experience problems as adults. A recent study investigated the adjustment of adults who were previously identified as learning disabled. It was found that the learning disabled group, when compared to a nonlearning disabled population, (1) had lower mean job status, (2) was less involved in social or fraternal activities, (3) had been convicted of a crime more often, and (4) had fewer plans for future educational activities (White et al. 1982). These results indicate that a handicap such as learning disabilities, which is primarily considered a school-aged problem, may continue to cause significant problems for adults.

Federal and state legislation, litigation, advocacy groups, and professionals have attempted to alleviate many of the problems faced by handicapped adults. The major federal legislation enacted to deal with some of these problems is the Rehabilitation Act of 1973, with Sections 503 and 504 being particularly important. Section 503 deals with affirmative action in the employment of handicapped persons, while Section 504 prohibits discrimination against individuals solely for reason of their handicap. Of the two sections, 504 is broader because it prohibits discrimination in education, housing, health care, and employment, whereas Section 503 is only related to employment (Ochoa 1977). Section 504 is civil rights legislation to protect the rights of the handicapped. As a result of its passage, discrimination against handicapped individuals is prohibited. While not solving all the problems experienced by this group, Section 504 does attempt to reduce these problems and to guarantee equal opportunities.

Unfortunately, legislation alone cannot guarantee equal treatment and nondiscrimination, nor can it solve other types of problems that must be dealt with by the handicapped adult group. Studies investigating the status of adults with disabilities have often revealed negative findings: unemployment, underemployment, low socioeconomic status, lack of socialization and recreational opportunities, and rejection by members of the community. Indeed, some problems such as poor peer acceptance can never be "legislated away." Instead, educators must do a better job in preparing handicapped children for adulthood during the school years. No longer can teachers and other professionals assume that the problems experienced by handicapped children will disappear when they leave school and become adults. Nor can it be assumed that agencies designed to serve the adult handicapped will take on the responsibility or that legislation will correct all problems. Educators and other school personnel must understand the problems faced by handicapped adults and initiate programs during the school years that will lessen or eliminate these problems.

NEEDS AND CHARACTERISTICS OF MILDLY HANDICAPPED ADULTS

Social Adjustment

One of the major problems faced by disabled adults is social adjustment, including social acceptability and social competence. Social competence can be defined as "getting along with people, communicating with them, and coping with the frustrations of social living" (Schulman 1980, 285). Everyone needs to feel socially competent and accepted. When nonhandicapped persons move into new neighborhoods, they frequently feel anxious and uneasy until friendships and relationships are established. Once friendships are established, many of these uneasy feelings disappear. In school, teachers often structure situations to ensure that handicapped children experience some degree of social acceptability. In the community, however, handicapped adults do not have this externally arranged structure and therefore may find themselves feeling isolated and lacking friends. These negative feelings only hinder adequate social adjustment.

Several studies have revealed the social rejection of persons with disabilities by the nondisabled sector. A follow-up study of learning disabled students after high school found that the nondisabled adults belonged to more community clubs and groups than the learning disabled group; they were also more active in social, fraternal, and recreational activities (White et al. 1982). In another post-school follow-up of learning disabled students, Fafard and Haubrich (1981) found that the former students indicated normal social activities. However, further investigation revealed that these former students identified the family and school as the places where social activities occurred. Since the former students were no longer in school, the results seem to indicate that going outside the family and school for social activities was difficult. Other studies investigating the social adjustment of learning disabled adults found a continuation of social maladjustment (Spreen 1976) and social-emotional immaturity (Wender 1976).

Studies investigating the social adjustment of mildly mentally retarded individuals have also revealed problems. For example, Peterson and Smith (1960) found that smaller numbers of mentally retarded adults marry than nonretarded persons, and the divorce rate for the retarded group was much higher than in the nonretarded population. Mentally retarded adults also have been found to experience greater legal problems than their nonretarded peers. In a recent study using participant-observation, Edgerton (1981) studied forty-eight mildly mentally retarded Caucasian adults from middle class families and found:

- a wide variability in crime and deviance among the sample,
- approximately one-third of the sample was not engaged in any form of criminal or serious deviant behavior,
- approximately one-third had been involved in minor legal offenses,

- approximately 20 percent had committed serious legal offenses, and
- aggressive behavior toward others was exhibited by fifteen of the forty-eight persons in the sample.

If problems with the legal authorities can be considered an indication of adjustment problems, these results suggest difficulties for mildly retarded adults. But they also show that many retarded individuals can live in communities within the guidelines of legal restrictions and not violate social and legal rules.

Mentally retarded adults, therefore, appear to experience social adjustment problems. Robinson and Robinson suggest that many of these problems may be due to "limited budgets, rejection by nonretarded individuals, restricted opportunities for social contacts, self-imposed isolation because of low self-esteem, and lack of skill in the use of leisure time" (Robinson and Robinson 1976, 467). Still another reason for problems in social adjustment may be the constant threat of failure (Schulman 1980). Once failure occurs, there may be a tendency to avoid situations where failure could be repeated, thereby starting a cycle of avoiding social situations for fear of failure.

Other types of disabled adults also experience social adjustment problems. For example, it has been concluded from many research studies that children with emotional problems have difficulty in being accepted by their nonhandicapped peers. For the most part, they are social outcasts. Often, this characteristic carries over into adulthood, with several authors having determined that many emotionally disturbed children are not able to outgrow these negative characteristics before becoming adults (Hallahan and Kauffman 1982).

Because social and personality development depends on verbal communication, many hearing impaired individuals have difficulty in the area of social adjustment. Since language is so central to most of the social interactions that occur among adults, it should not be surprising that individuals with language barriers have difficulties in social adjustment (Hallahan and Kauffman 1982).

Vocational Opportunity and Adjustment

As with social adjustment, mildly handicapped adults often experience significant problems in the vocational area, including vocational opportunities and adjustment. Despite these problems, many mildly handicapped adults are capable of achieving vocational success.

Once in the labor market, mildly handicapped adults have the potential to make excellent employees. Crain (1980) did a follow-up study of 130 mildly mentally retarded high school graduates. The subjects were from the graduation classes of 1962, 1965, 1968, 1971, 1974, and 1977. Results indicated that approximately two-thirds of the subjects were in the civilian labor force, comparable to the number of nonhandicapped adults. Of those in the labor force, 7.9 percent were unemployed, which again compares favorably with the unemployment rate for all workers. Average income of the group was $7,280, with only one of the working individuals earning an income below the poverty level.

Several other studies have also concluded that mildly mentally retarded individuals experience vocational success, especially if they have had appropriate pre-vocational training (Chaffin et al. 1971; Strickland 1967; Kelley and Simon 1969; Brolin and Kokaska 1979). Mildly mentally retarded adults, therefore, are capable of successful employment if given the opportunity and appropriate training.

Mildly handicapped adults have the potential to become excellent employees.

The literature also suggests that other types of mildly handicapped adults are capable of achieving successful employment. Moores (1982) indicates (1) that hearing impaired individuals are as capable of handling work situations as their hearing peers; (2) that deaf workers have been rated as good to superior; and (3) that communication has been the major obstacle to vocational upward mobility and advancement. As a result of a doubling of postsecondary programs for deaf individuals during the 1970s, the many vocational options currently available range from vocational training to graduate education programs.

Visually impaired individuals have also experienced vocational success. Kirchner and Peterson (1980) studied the occupational status and earnings of approximately 1,500 working-aged visually impaired individuals. Results revealed the following:

- Professional, technical, managerial, clerical, and sales jobs were held by 62 percent of the sample with some college or higher education
- Thirty-seven percent of those with some college training held blue collar jobs, such as craftsman, laborers, and farmers
- In 1975, 61 percent of the visually impaired persons in the sample were employed more than half the year.

While these figures do not compare favorably with individuals without disabilities, they do reveal that adults with vision problems can function well in the labor market.

Although many mildly handicapped adults are capable of vocational success, some are not afforded the opportunity to demonstrate their abilities. Obstacles such as personal appearance and other aesthetic factors (Ohshansky 1973), and work attitudes and motivation (Stewart 1977) often preclude success. T.E.C. Smith (1981) conducted a study to determine the concerns of potential employers of mentally retarded individuals. Results showed that while most employers surveyed indicated that they had jobs capable of being performed by these individuals, certain prerequisite skills were still required of all applicants, such as the ability to complete a job application satisfactorily. Therefore, mildly handicapped adults, even those with average to above average intelligence and the necessary job skills, may not be able to get a job without being able to read and successfully complete a job application. For too many mildly disabled individuals, job applications "often appear to be a frustrating jumble of small spaces and difficult words" (McGee 1981, 152). Unfortunately, the ability to do a job is not always the critical element in whether or not disabled individuals have the opportunity to work. Other less important skills such as completing job applications may preclude job success.

Learning disabled individuals also experience vocational problems. In the study by Fafard and Haubrich (1981), results indicated that approximately one-third of the individuals who had graduated or left high school held full-time jobs, with the remaining two-thirds employed only on a part-time basis. While a later study by White et al. (1982) indicated a higher employment rate among former learning disabled students after high school, the mean job satisfaction of this group was significantly lower than the nonhandicapped population. In summarizing the vocational possibilities of learning disabled adults, Siegel and Gold (1982) suggest a wide range of vocational possibilities ranging from a beginning level of sheltered workshops to high-skill jobs.

In addition to vocational problems experienced by adults with cognitive and intellectual deficits, other individuals may have problems because they look different, have mobility problems, have visual or hearing difficulties, or experience psychological disturbances. Adults with visual disabilities have been shown to be good employees but often receive less than optimal treatment in the labor market. Kirchner and Peterson (1980) studied approximately 1,500 visually impaired individuals of working age (18–64) and determined the following about employment status:

- A smaller percentage of visually impaired adults are in the labor force than their sighted peers
- Jobs obtained by visually impaired adults have less permanence than jobs secured by sighted individuals
- Skills and training gained through higher education are less likely to bring higher occupational status for them than for sighted persons
- Higher occupations have less financial pay-off than for sighted peers
- Seniority has less impact on salary than it does for sighted individuals

These findings substantiate the fact that getting a job does not alleviate discrimination and differential treatment; they also reveal that visually impaired adults may suffer substantial underemployment. This does not need to be the case. Given that problems such as mobility in the work area can be overcome with appropriate mobility training (Larson and Johnson 1981), visually impaired adults can make excellent employees and should be provided opportunities and rewards commensurate with their abilities.

Hallahan and Kauffman report that hearing impaired individuals may also experience vocational problems. While studies have shown that these individuals make good employees, they are often unemployed or underemployed. Also, as a group hearing impaired adults "are overrepresented in manual trades and underrepresented in professional and managerial positions" (Hallahan and Kauffman 1982, 270). The major problem of adults with hearing problems that affects employment is communication. Without

Table 9-1 Federal Legislation Relating to Employment of the Handicapped

Act	Description
1948 Amendment to the Civil Service Act (PL 80-617)	Prohibits discrimination in the federal Civil Service for physically handicapped individuals.
Rehabilitation Act of 1973 (PL 93-112, 516) Section 501	Requires departments in the executive branch to submit affirmative action plans for the hiring, placement, and advancement of handicapped persons.
Section 503	Requires contractors with contracts in excess of $2,500 to include in the contract an affirmative action provision; contractors with contracts for $50,000 or more who have 50 or more employees must prepare and utilize an affirmative action plan.
Section 504	Prohibits discrimination against handicapped persons in a variety of settings, including employment, by programs receiving any federal financial assistance.
Education for All Handicapped Children Act of 1975 (PL 94-142)	Each recipient under this legislation is required to make positive efforts to employ and advance handicapped individuals.
Developmentally Disabled Assistance Bill of 1974 (PL 94-103)	Recipients shall take affirmative action to employ and advance handicapped persons.
Vietnam Era Veteran's Readjustment Act of 1974 (PL 93-508)	Requires federal agencies and contractors with contracts over $10,000 to implement affirmative action in hiring qualified veterans of the Vietnam era and all disabled veterans.
Randolph Sheppard Act Amendments of 1974 (PL 93-516)	Gives priority to blind persons licensed by the state to operate vending facilities on federal property.
Wagner - O'Day Act	Establishes a committee for the purchase of goods and services by the government from disabled persons.

Source: Guidelines for disabled persons subject to discrimination in employment. AMICUS[1] (1976):29.

verbal communication skills, these individuals are at a significant disadvantage in the "world of work."

For physically disabled adults, certain vocations are automatically ruled out. For example, a quadriplegic would be limited in jobs requiring fine manual dexterity and speed, but this individual could overcome problems associated with quadriplegia and become an excellent college professor. Regardless of job success experienced by some physically handicapped adults, many are unemployed as a result of social and emotional problems (Hallahan and Kauffman 1982), discrimination, or a lack of job skills.

Legally, equal employment opportunity for the handicapped must exist. Recent federal legislation, the Rehabilitation Act of 1973, has focused on the civil rights of handicapped individuals, including their rights to equal vocational opportunities. Section 503 of the act requires that employers take affirmative action to employ individuals with disabilities. The section does not dictate what steps must be implemented to assure affirmative action, only that it be implemented by employers with government contracts over $2,500. Employers covered would include those which provide goods and services to the government, such as contractors and construction companies. Section 504 applies to all recipients of federal financial assistance, which includes loans, contracts, or other forms of funds (Ochoa 1977). Both sections of the act should provide some safeguards to handicapped job seekers. In addition to sections 503 and 504 of the Rehabilitation Act of 1973, other federal legislation has been passed related to the employment of the handicapped. See table 9-1.

Table 9-2 State Statutes Regarding Employment

State	Type of Statute	State	Type of Statute
Alabama	CS, WCL	Maryland	HRC, CS, WCL, PS
Alaska	HRC, CP, COA, WCL, PS	Massachusetts	FEPC, CP, WCL
Arizona	WCL	Michigan	HRC, WCL
Arkansas	WCL	Minnesota	HRC, CP, COA, CS, WCL, PS
California	FEPC, CP, WCL, PS	Mississippi	WCL, PS
Colorado	WCL, PS	Missouri	WCL
Connecticut	HRC, WCL	Montana	HRC, CP, COA, CS, WCL, PS
Delaware	WCL, PS	Montana	HRC, CP, COA, CS, WCL, PS
District of Columbia	HRC, CP, COA, WCL, PS, CS	Nebraska	FEPC, CP, CS, WCL, PS
Florida	WCL, PS, CP	Nevada	FEPC, COA, WCL
Georgia	CS, WCL	New Hampshire	HRC, CP, WCL, PS
Hawaii	FEPC, CP, CS, WCL, PS	New Jersey	HRC, CP, WCL
Idaho	HRC, CS, WCL, PS	New Mexico	HRC, WCL, PS
Illinois	EOL, FEPC, WCL	New York	HRC, CP, COA, CS, WCL
Indiana	HRC, WCL, PS	North Carolina	CS, WCL, PS
Iowa	HRC, WCL, PS	North Dakota	WCL, PS
Kansas	HRC, CP, WCL, PS	Ohio	HRC, CP, WCL
Kentucky	EOL, COA, CP, WCL, HRC	Oklahoma	CS, WCL
Louisiana	WCL, PS	Oregon	FEPC, WCL, PS
Maine	HRC, COA, WCL, PS	Pennsylvania	HRC, CP, COA, WCL

State legislation supplements federal laws in prohibiting discrimination in employment. Table 9-2 summarizes the types of legislation each state has adopted to prevent job discrimination.

Unfortunately, federal and state legislation alone does not ensure equal employment opportunities. While laws go a long way to promote equality, disabled adults still experience a great deal of discrimination. Professionals, including special educators and rehabilitation counselors, and advocacy groups must play an active part in guaranteeing employment opportunities.

Some advocates for employment opportunities for handicapped individuals suggest that the best way to ensure equal opportunities in employment is to amend Title VII of the Civil Rights Act of 1964. This action is recommended because the Civil Rights Act has been in existence for nearly twenty years and has greatly facilitated equal opportunities for other minority groups (Megivern 1983).

Although legislation requires equal employment opportunities, and research has shown that many mildly disabled persons are capable of competitive employment, job opportunities are not always afforded this population. When made available, jobs are often in low-skill areas that actually produce underemployment of the disabled indi-

Table 9-2 (continued)

State	Type of Statute	State	Type of Statute
Rhode Island	HRC, WCL, PS	Vermont	EOL, COA, WCL
South Carolina	WCL, CS	Virginia	EOL, COA, CS, WCL
South Dakota	WCL	Washington	HRC, CP, WCL, PS
Tennessee	EOL, WCL, PS	West Virginia	HRC, CP, WCL, PS
Texas	EOL, CP, COA, WCL	Wisconsin	FEPC, COA, CS, WCL
Utah	WCL, CS, PS	Wyoming	WCL, PS

Key:

FEPC — A Fair Employment Practices Commission is a body established by statute to investigate, review, and resolve complaints of discrimination in hiring, dismissal, and terms and conditions of employment.

HRC — A Human Rights Commission (or Civil Rights Commission) is a body established by statute to investigate, review, and resolve complaints of unlawful discrimination in housing, public accommodations, education, employment, and other areas.

EOL — An Equal Opportunity Law is a civil rights statute which may or may not provide for administrative enforcement, a criminal penalty, or a private cause of action.

CS — A Civil Service statute is a law which affects only all or part of those persons employed by the state civil service system. Some states which do not have a statute prohibiting discrimination do have an administrative policy to that effect.

WCL — A White Cane Law is a statue designed primarily to define the rights and responsibilities of blind persons, particularly in relation to the use of white canes and guide dogs. In some states, it has been broadened to include other handicapped persons as well.

PS — A Policy Statement is a statute which says that nondiscrimination is the official policy of the state, but provides no enforcement mechanism.

COA — A Cause of Action is the right of an aggrieved person to bring a lawsuit for unlawful discrimination, either as an exclusive remedy or in addition to an administrative remedy.

Source: State statutes regarding employment. AMICUS[1] (1976):30–35.

viduals (Muraski 1982). This is a result of several factors, including negative attitudes, outright discrimination, and a lack of certain skills viewed as prerequisites by many employers. Negative attitudes can be changed, and discrimination can be confronted in the courts; but a lack of skills must be addressed in the educational settings serving mildly handicapped students and adults.

Several studies have pointed out deficient areas in job seeking skills and on-the-job behavior that should be addressed in educational or training programs. First, individuals must know how to locate jobs that they are capable of performing. Being able to read want ads, contact employment agencies, and apply for vocational rehabilitation services are important in locating job vacancies. After appropriate jobs are found, mildly handicapped persons need certain skills such as completing job applications and performing well in interviews. Hill, Wehman, and Pentecost (1980) investigated the job interview skills of mentally retarded adults and determined that they lacked certain interview skills such as orientation to the interviewer, good posture, and proper verbal responses. The study did find, however, that following a treatment program, these skills could be taught to retarded adults. There are many school programs that focus on these areas. One such program for disabled adolescents described by McGee (1981) includes vocabulary training, completing job application forms, pursuing classified job ads, and role playing job interviews.

It should be noted that many mildly handicapped adults do not experience significant vocational problems. Many find appropriate employment and are successful employees without assistance. Others, unfortunately, require either pre-job assistance or on-the-job assistance. For this group of mildly handicapped adults, being able to find appropriate employment, perform the necessary pre-job skills successfully, and finally perform adequately on the job present major problems.

Community Acceptance

As previously discussed, mildly handicapped adults frequently experience problems in the areas of social and vocational adjustment. One problem encountered by many of these individuals, which is related to both social and vocational adjustment, is community acceptance. Often, handicapped adults are rejected by peers, employers, and persons in authority roles in the community. In order for mildly handicapped adults to become contributing, adjusted members of communities, they must be accepted by other community members. Unfortunately, this acceptance has not always been the case.

One area of community acceptance is housing; mildly handicapped adults require equal opportunity in housing. In one study conducted by Trippi, Michael, Colao, and Alvarez (1978), housing proved discriminative toward mentally retarded adults. Potential landlords were queried about their vacant rental units by supposedly nonhandicapped persons and persons calling on behalf of a mentally retarded individual. Based on the information given to the callers, the authors concluded that only one out of one hundred subjects was interested in renting to a mentally retarded individual. In a similar study conducted at a later date, Margolis and Charitonidis (1981) found more positive results: over 70 percent of the subjects were willing to rent their units to mentally retarded adults.

Smith, Liska, and Smith (1980) replicated the Trippi et al. study using blind individuals as the handicapped group rather than the mentally retarded. Although the results were not nearly so discouraging, the conclusion was still that significant housing discrimination existed toward blind persons. In the replication, nearly 40 percent of the subjects were not interested in renting to blind individuals. While there are laws requiring equal opportunities, discrimination is often difficult to prove. The real concern is that discrimination, which results from negative attitudes, does exist. For mildly handicapped adults to be accepted in communities with appropriate housing opportunities, these negative attitudes must change.

Another area that reflects community acceptance of mildly handicapped adults is the attitude of community members toward *group homes* and other community living arrangements. Several studies have revealed that group homes for handicapped adults often face significant opposition from potential neighborhood members (Landesman-Dwyer 1981). A study by Sigelman (1976) determined that slightly less than half of the adults questioned were in favor of a living facility for mentally retarded individuals in their neighborhood. Other studies, however, have revealed that community attitudes toward residential programs for mentally retarded persons were not negative, and in some cases were positive (President's Committee on Mental Retardation 1975; Kastner, Repucci, and Pezzoli 1979). After reviewing the literature on community acceptance, Sandler and Robinson (1981) concluded that although attitudes toward living programs for the mentally retarded are often negative in the beginning, these attitudes have a tendency to become positive following the opening of the facility.

Participating in recreational activities is an important part of community acceptance.

One of the arguments often voiced by community members in opposition to community living facilities for the mentally retarded is the impact such programs have on property values. A recent study that investigated this issue, however, revealed that community-based residential facilities for mentally retarded adults did not have a negative effect on property values. In fact, in two of the neighborhoods studied, property values actually increased (Wiener et al. 1982).

Another area related to community acceptance is recreational activities. Leisure time is a problem for many mildly handicapped adults since many of these individuals have been sheltered a great deal during their years in the home. During working hours, activities are structured; however, after working hours individuals living independently must fend for themselves in the utilization of their free time. Since mildly handicapped adults are often rejected by their nonhandicapped peers, the problem of what to do during leisure time is even more difficult.

The two basic barriers to recreation for mildly handicapped adults are architectural and attitudinal. Architectural barriers, while not affecting all mildly handicapped adults, are a major problem for some physically handicapped individuals and visually impaired persons. For these groups, architectural barriers are often the most common obstacle for recreation (Murtaugh 1978). In many public facilities, federal laws now require accessibility for the handicapped. However, for nonpublic facilities such as movie theaters accessibility may not be legally mandated. Many individuals in wheelchairs simply do not go to movies because there is no place for them to park their chairs without being in the aisle or sitting immediately in front of the screen.

Attitudinal barriers also prevent many mildly handicapped adults from enjoying recreational activities. In some cases, even though architectural barriers are not present, individuals are denied admission to facilities because owners and managers fear for their "safety" and the liability involved. Although most handicapped adults are perfectly capable of taking care of their own needs, this safety excuse is often used to deny their participation in certain activities (Murtaugh 1978).

Other Problems

In addition to problems of social adjustment, vocational opportunity and adjustment, and community acceptance, mildly handicapped adults may experience a multitude of other problems. Some of these are related to social and vocational adjustment and community acceptance, while others act independently on the lives of these individuals. Problems range from alcohol abuse among mentally retarded persons to hyperactive behavior among adults with emotional disorders. Table 9-3 describes some of these problems and the category of disabilities affected.

As a result of the problems facing mildly handicapped adults, various programs and services are necessary to facilitate the assimilation of these individuals into communities. Without such services, many mildly handicapped adults are not able to achieve their maximum level of success, nor to live as independently as possible. This leads to more dependence on society, which is costly in terms of both dollars and manpower. More importantly, however, is the fact that without appropriate services many mildly handicapped individuals live less than optimal lives.

SERVICES FOR MILDLY HANDICAPPED ADULTS

With proper services, many mildly handicapped individuals can become productive members of our society and experience as normal a life as possible. This goal, to experience life in a normal or near normal manner, is the current philosophical base for many of the services for handicapped individuals, both young and old, mild and severe.

Normalization "implies that the handicapped ought to be able to live a life as equal as possible to a normal existence and with the same rights and obligations as other people. The handicapped are also to be accepted with their exceptionalities when these cannot be remedied" (Juul 1978, 326). The concept, therefore, is simply to do the things necessary to make life for individuals with handicaps as near normal as possible through advocacy, litigation, legislation, and personal actions. Normalization entails providing opportunities to enable handicapped individuals to move from "marginal societal positions to more normal environments" (Mandell and Fiscus 1981, 154).

The philosophy of normalization can be implemented in many ways. In the area of education, normalization is realized through mainstreaming, that is, placing handicapped children in regular classrooms as much as possible. The current trend of mainstreaming was legislated by P.L. 94-142. For adults, normalization focuses on equal opportunities in education, training, housing, employment, recreation, and leisure time. In addition, guaranteeing legal rights and providing services required to facilitate normal living are also included. The types of normalization activities and services depend on the nature of the disability. For example, adults with reading problems do not require normalization activities in the area of housing because they look and behave "normally" and do not need housing modifications. Those with mental disabilities and mobility problems due to

Table 9-3 Problems Experienced by Handicapped Adults

Group	Problem
Mentally Retarded	Obesity (Jackson and Thorbecke 1982) Alcohol abuse (Krishef and DiNitto 1981) Stress (Matson 1982) Limited guardianship (Mesibov et al. 1980)
Learning Disabled	Memory problems (Wordern, et al. 1982) Auditory language deficits (Blalock 1982) Auditory perceptual disorders (Hasbrouck 1983) Excess Emotional Strain (Geib et al. 1981)
Hearing Impaired	Stress for families of deaf adults (Moores 1982)
Visually Impaired	Shopping needs (Inana 1980) Mobility on the job (Larson and Johnson 1981) Equipment, transportation, volunteer and recreational services (Delaney and Nuttall 1978)

paralysis would require supportive services and housing accommodations. Therefore, the type of disability manifested by adults will dictate the normalization activities that must occur in order to foster "normal" living.

Normalization is more than a philosophy; it requires such services as the following:

- vocational rehabilitation
- vocational training programs
- educational programs
- counseling services
- advocacy services
- community living programs

While not all adults with mild disabilities will become totally independent with such services, their level of independence will be higher. This means that they will require less from society, contribute more to society, and indeed experience a more normalized life.

Education

Mildly handicapped adults require assistance in post secondary education. Post secondary education programs enable many mildly handicapped adults to become qualified for appropriate employment. Several colleges and universities encourage the participation of individuals with disabilities by providing support services. These programs are targeted for all types of mild disabilities, including mental retardation, learning disabilities, hearing and visual impairments, and physical handicaps. Specific reasons for which mildly handicapped adults enter college programs include (1) preparation for a specific career, (2) basic educational or adult living skills, (3) leisure education, and (4) it is the thing to do (Jones and Moe 1980). These reasons are very similar to those of nonhandicapped adults who attend college.

Post secondary educational programs vary significantly, based on the target group being served and the philosophy of those implementing the program. Gearheart (1980) describes three types of programs offered by colleges and universities for handicapped students. These include (1) the adaption of materials, teaching methods, and the physical

252   Mildly Handicapped Children and Adults

Community colleges and universities are developing special programs for meeting the needs of the mildly handicapped.

facilities to accommodate attendance by students; (2) special college programs for specific types of disabilities, such as programs for the hearing impaired, and (3) programs offered at colleges and universities, which are not really credit programs but provide training to handicapped individuals through a specially designed program on a college campus.

Many colleges and universities provide services that would be classified as the first type described by Gearheart, namely, accommodation. Accommodation can occur as a result of an individual professor's actions, or through a coordinated comprehensive program. Accommodative strategies may include the following:

- special reading instructional programs
- study skills classes
- guidance and counseling during scheduling
- the use of tape recorders for lectures
- talking books for visually impaired and reading disabled students
- alternative testing procedures by instructors
- peer tutoring
- interpreters for hearing impaired students
- ramps and other provisions to ensure accessibility for mobility impaired students

These modifications or accommodations enable many mildly handicapped individuals to experience success in college and university classes without additional services. One specific disability group that has recently attracted a great deal of attention at the college level has been learning disabled students and others who have deficits in basic skills. The number of programs for these students on college campuses has increased greatly during the past ten years. Reasons for this increase include (1) efforts by learning disabled adolescents and adults, their parents, and professionals in the field of learning disabilities, and (2) Section 504 of the Rehabilitation Act of 1973 (Vogel 1982). College programs for students with reading and other basic skill problems range from minimum advising services to a full range of assessment and programming services. A survey of programs in community colleges in California found that services offered included (1) tutorial support by a learning disabilities specialist, peer tutor, aide, or faculty member, and (2) counseling in academic, personal, and career areas—both internal and external to the specialized program (Ostertag et al. 1982). These services help to meet the following needs of learning disabled adults in higher education:

- assessment
- academic advising
- effective study habits
- written language skills
- social/interpersonal skills

While many programs provide for some of these needs, prospective students with learning disabilities and similar problems should inquire about specific programs. Cordoni (1982) provides a list of sources of information concerning college programs for students with learning disabilities:

ACLD List of Colleges, Universities, and Trade Schools ($1.00)
   Association for Children & Adults with Learning Disabilities (ACLD)
   4156 Library Road
   Pittsburgh, PA 15234

Joy: A Guide to Post-secondary Educational Opportunities for the Learning Disabled Student (No Cost)
   Time Out to Enjoy, Inc.
   113 Garfield Street
   Oak Park, IL 60304

Directory of College Programs for Learning Disabled Students (No Cost)
   Carol Hopkins, Admission Counselor
   Loyola Academy
   Wilmette, IL 60091

National Directory of Four Year Colleges, Two Year Colleges and Post High School Training Program for Young People with L.D. (No Cost)
   Partners in Publishing
   Box 50347
   Tulsa, OK 74150

Visually impaired students also receive specialized services on many college campuses. Gearheart states that "for the most part, college programs for the blind are much more satisfactory than those for students with other types of disability" (Gearheart 1980, 438). This is probably because of the exposure received by blind individuals and the strong lobbying groups that have advocated special services for these individuals.

Programs for students with learning and visual problems are primarily general programs that serve all types of disabled individuals. For example, most students with reading problems would be able to benefit from such programs. Different from these general, support programs are those included in the second type of college program described by Gearheart (1980). These are special programs designed for specific disabled groups. The disability group that has often been the recipient of these programs is the hearing impaired. This group of college students has its own college, Gallaudet College in Washington, D.C. While this is the only college in the United States that strictly caters to the hearing impaired, several other colleges offer programs designed to provide services for this group. In most instances, these services include interpreters, which may be provided in conjunction with a rehabilitation agency.

The first two types of programs described by Gearheart (1980) are designed for academically able students who can achieve success with the accommodations provided through the special program. The curriculum remains the same, with services designed to facilitate accessing the program and earning a regular college degree. The third type of program offered through a college or university is a special program that involves the development of a special curriculum. These programs, while not actually college credit programs that lead to a regular degree, are supported by the college or university. One program designed for mentally retarded and orthopedically impaired individuals was started at the central campus of Broward Community College in Fort Lauderdale, Florida, in 1974. This program enables students to earn college credit, participate in student services, and use all college services. The curriculum has grown from such areas as vocational adjustment, personality insights, leisure time, and home management, to basic business, food and nutrition, and cosmetology (Wood et al. 1977). Similar programs exist on many college campuses.

Special programs on college campuses are often initiated by staff from a sheltered workshop, adult developmental center, or group home. While all of these programs are not on campus, the trend seems to be to locate them there and provide student services to program participants. A common problem is that many of the students in these programs are not taking advantage of some of the campus courses and services that would be beneficial and that are a major goal of the program (Jones and Moe 1980). Still, the potential is there for such involvement, and the trend appears to be in that direction.

Another area related to educational services for mildly handicapped adults is pre-college preparation. While many handicapped individuals can experience college success, their chances for success may be increased significantly if they are provided with pre-college preparation. Many programs prepare individuals for college work. These programs are usually short-term in nature and focus on study skills, reading remediation, and other areas where assistance may increase the chances of success in the college classroom. One program described by Martin, Martin, and Hapeman (1978) attempts to prepare visually impaired students for college by providing high school students between their junior and senior years with an opportunity to complete college courses. After the coursework, the students have the option of keeping the credit and grades earned, or expunging the courses from their records. The program, offered by Northern Illinois University and the Illinois Division of Vocational Rehabilitation, was found to increase the readiness skills of the students in the areas of communication, studying, personal-social, and mobility. In addition to various colleges offering similar programs, several agencies, including the Chicago Lighthouse for the Blind and the Arkansas Enterprises for the Blind, also provide college preparation training for visually impaired students (Martin et al. 1978).

Many secondary school programs focus on preparing mildly handicapped students for college-level courses. These programs emphasize study skills, career counseling, and survival skills, including test-taking tips and time management. These programs usually serve mildly handicapped students—those who are mildly disabled but who possess the necessary academic skills and motivation to be successful in post secondary education programs. Since the number of agencies that provide such college preparation programs is limited, the obvious place for such programs would be high school special education classrooms.

Vocational

Mildly handicapped adults also need assistance in vocational activities. While specific needs vary from individual to individual, they often include vocational and career guidance, pre-vocational training, vocational training, and other supportive services provided by rehabilitation agencies that facilitate vocational success. As with other needs and services, all individuals who fall under the rubric of mildly handicapped do not require the same vocational services. On the one hand, disabled individuals with average or above average intellectual levels and intact physical abilities may need only minimal guidance, accommodation during training, and equal opportunities for vocational success. At the other extreme, mildly handicapped adults with below average intellectual levels or those with physical impairments may require extensive services. The type of program needed by mildly handicapped adults therefore is varied. Gearheart (1980) indicates that the following variables are among those that should be considered in determining the type of vocational program required:

- type of handicap or disability
- age of the individual
- intellectual level of the individual
- previous education and/or vocational training

Vocational Education. Vocational education programs can be found in most schools and have the aim of preparing individual students in specific job skills. Since many mildly handicapped students do not attend college, vocational education classes would seem to be an ideal curricular option. Unfortunately, many mildly handicapped adolescents do not have access to vocational education. Although vocational programs should be able to serve learning disabled students, many problems such as attitudes, personnel preparation, funding, and interagency cooperation often prevent learning disabled students from accessing these programs (Greenan 1982). This is also often true for other types of mildly disabled students. For example, many physically handicapped students cannot benefit from vocational education because equipment is not modified for their use, or the vocational programs are physically inaccessible. These limitations are often present for visually impaired students too. The conclusion is that "many youths need vocational classes at the high school level but are not receiving them" (D'Alonzo 1983, 55). While all the information presented thus far appears negative, some positive vocational programs for mildly handicapped students do facilitate vocational success as adults. Chapter 12 will present information concerning vocational educational programs for these children.

Vocational Rehabilitation. A major service provided to handicapped adults is vocational **rehabilitation.** The first government program designed to provide vocational assistance to disabled individuals in the United States was the Soldier's Rehabilitation Act of

1918, which was passed to serve disabled veterans from World War I (Snell 1983). State agencies now provide rehabilitation services, which include the following:

1. Medical examinations to determine the extent of disability
2. Medical assistance to limit the disabling condition
3. Prosthetic devices
4. Vocational evaluation and guidance
5. Psychological evaluation
6. Vocational training
7. Basic living costs during training
8. Job related equipment and licenses
9. Job location
10. Job follow-up (Brolin 1976)

The primary professional in the vocational rehabilitation agency is the vocational **rehabilitation counselor,** whose role is to carry out all the services provided by the agency for individuals on a case load. In addition to ensuring the provision of needed services, vocational counselors should be aware of the job opportunities in the community, requirements for local jobs, and agencies and groups that provide services and training (Best 1978). The vocational rehabilitation counselor, therefore, is the core of the rehabilitation agency and the direct service individual responsible for meeting individual client needs.

Vocational rehabilitation agencies provide vital services to mildly handicapped adults. Without this vocationally oriented support service, many mildly handicapped adults would never reach their potential for employment or independence. With vocational rehabilitation services, many of these individuals receive the necessary evaluation, training, placement, and follow-up to facilitate employment and social success. Even disabled groups not traditionally served by vocational rehabilitation, such as learning disabled individuals, are currently eligible for services. Vocational rehabilitation, therefore, is available for all of the acknowledged handicapped groups and is a great factor in successful employment and independence for these individuals.

Even though these agencies provide such vital services, they are not above criticism. Some of the major criticisms of state rehabilitation agencies include: (1) the vast amount of paperwork required for services, (2) the time required for medical and other evaluation personnel to complete evaluations that determine eligibility and services, (3) the overloaded counselors, (4) the lack of funds during the latter part of the funding cycle, and (5) the emphasis on case closures (Brolin 1976). Despite these criticisms, vocational rehabilitation agencies provide quality services for many disabled adults. Without such agencies, handicapped adults would be served through public service programs that do not encourage independence, or these adults would have to struggle without any assistance.

Organized Work Settings. Many mildly handicapped individuals require a specialized work setting because their disability is such that it prevents success in the competitive labor market. Major types of specialized settings include *sheltered workshops, work-activity centers,* and *rehabilitation workshops.* While primarily thought of as programs that serve only mentally retarded and more severely disabled individuals, many sheltered workshops and work-activity centers also serve visually impaired, emotionally disturbed, and physically disabled persons. For example, approximately 3 percent of the rehabilitation closures for visually impaired adults were in sheltered workshops (Kirchner and Peterson 1980).

Sheltered workshops are designed for disabled individuals who cannot function in competitive employment but who can develop competitive employment capabilities. Workshops should provide therapeutic activities designed to develop vocational readiness (Snell 1983). Some sheltered workshops are designed to provide short-term opportunities for individuals in transition to competitive employment, while others are considered long-term options for less capable individuals who may not quickly acquire the skills necessary for competitive employment. For most mildly handicapped adults, sheltered workshops are a transition to competitive employment. And many mildly handicapped adults will not require any placement in a sheltered workshop.

Work-activity centers focus on less capable, more severely disabled individuals. In conjunction with the work setting, social and personal adjustment training is emphasized because individuals served in these centers may require extensive training in these areas. Most mildly handicapped adults, however, will not require services in a work-activity center.

Besides work-activity centers and sheltered workshops, another specialized work setting is the rehabilitation workshop. While this term has been used synonymously with sheltered workshop, the term currently refers to a different specialized setting—one where the emphasis is on evaluation, work adjustment, training, and placement, while the sheltered workshop is considered a place of employment for sheltered employees (Brolin 1976). Rehabilitation workshops can do the following:

- offer a simulated work environment
- provide job experiences and trials in a controlled setting
- provide many work options
- provide the opportunity for clients to try out before actual competitive job placement
- provide an accepting environment designed to determine individual strengths and weaknesses
- offer a trained staff who specialize in vocational development and who are aware of community jobs (Brolin 1976).

Many mildly handicapped adults do not require specialized work settings. For this group, rehabilitation agencies emphasize finding an appropriate job and providing follow-up services after job placement. For those with deficits requiring additional work experience, however, specialized settings provide an excellent opportunity to move toward independence.

Housing Services

As previously stated, not all mildly handicapped adults need housing services. Many can assimilate into normal housing patterns in communities without special assistance or accommodations. Some mildly handicapped adults, however, do require assistance in housing. While most mildly handicapped adults are capable of community living, historically some of these individuals have been institutionalized. This group, primarily composed of those individuals with mental disabilities, may require extensive services in the area of housing. The current trend in serving mildly handicapped individuals who have been institutionalized or face institutionalization is a method of implementing the normalization philosophy. Three basic components are included in deinstitutionalization:

1. Preventing the institutionalization of disabled individuals
2. Moving individuals from institutions to community living facilities

258 Mildly Handicapped Children and Adults

3. Establishing a community support network to provide supportive services for disabled individuals in the community (National Association of Superintendents of Public Residential Facilities for the Mentally Retarded 1974).

While the idea of deinstitutionalization has been around for decades, the current emphasis began with the landmark court case of *Wyatt v. Stickney* in 1972 (Scheerenberger 1981). In this case it was argued that individuals residing in institutions for the mentally retarded were entitled to certain habilitation and treatment. The court ruled that the plaintiffs had been denied habilitation, and ordered the implementation of a detailed set of standards that would guarantee the adequate habilitation of residents at the Partlow State School and Hospital in Alabama.

The current deinstitutionalization movement has significantly reduced the population of public residential facilities for the mentally retarded. Figure 9-1 shows the average daily population of public residential facilities from 1970–1971 until 1980–1981. There was an obvious depopulation trend during these ten years. Without exception, the average daily population declined indicating the persistence of the population trend. This

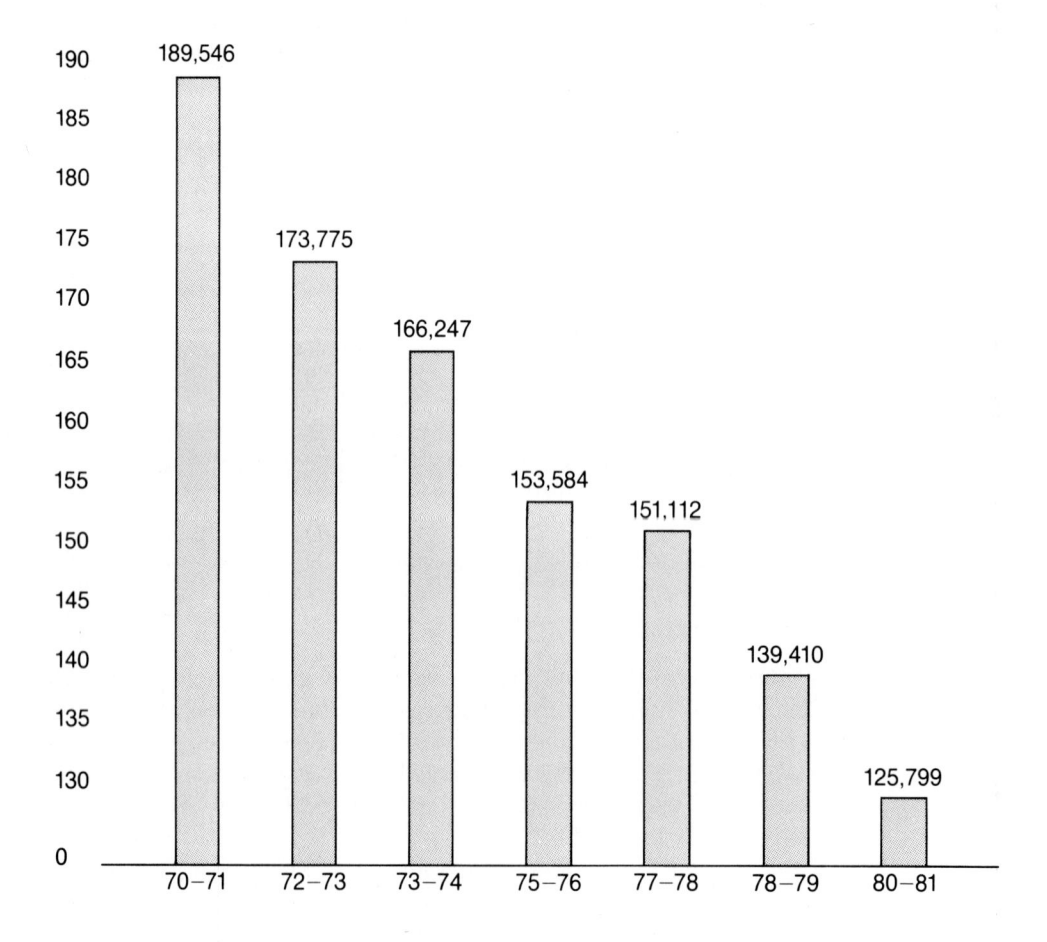

Figure 9-1 Average daily population of public residential facilities from 1970–1981 (Scheerenberger 1982).

Group homes provide support for mildly handicapped adults in independent living situations.

trend began in 1967 when the population of retarded individuals peaked at 194,650 (Lakin et al. 1982).

Simply removing individuals from institutions is not the only aspect of deinstitutionalization. Just as important is the provision of services in the community, both to prevent institutionalization and to provide support for individuals who have moved from institutions into the communities. While various support systems typically exist in communities, often these systems must change in order to meet the needs of the deinstitutionalized population, as well as to prevent institutionalization. A study by Intagliata, Kraus, and Willer (1980) showed the impact of deinstitutionalization on the community-based service system through the following observations:

- Agencies served a larger portion of formerly institutionalized individuals
- Agencies served individuals with lower intellectual levels
- Formerly institutionalized individuals required services similar to those not institutionalized, but the services needed to be more intensive
- Special programs were needed to provide appropriate services for the lower functioning individuals

Therefore, even in communities where support services are present, these services often must change in order to meet the needs of deinstitutionalized individuals.

Community living services and support services must be present to meet the needs of mildly handicapped adults. In the area of housing, **group homes** are often used to meet the needs of this population. Community residential facilities include many forms of

> **HIGHLIGHT**
>
> ## 'Life Styles': A Place Where People Are Learning To Live
>
> Simply called *"Bill"* after its main character, a recent television movie about a mentally handicapped man learning to live independently after being institutionalized for much of his life touched the heartstrings of American viewers.
>
> Those kind of dramatic stories—about developmentally disabled people finding a way to lead their own lives—are unfolding daily at a publicly funded Fayetteville home called "Life Styles" where 67 people have undergone training since 1976.
>
> The newest chapter in the Life Styles story concerns the construction, beginning this June, of a 12-apartment complex at the intersection of Porter Road and Sycamore Street in Fayetteville. Funded largely by the Department of Housing and Urban Development, the complex will be a learning center for mentally disabled people.
>
> "Some Life Styles residents have lived the majority of their lives in Arkansas institutions for the mentally retarded," director Carol Hart says. "Because of the opportunity provided here, many are now able to live in their own apartments and hold jobs in communities throughout Northwest Arkansas."
>
> Life Styles, Mrs. Hart comments, is a part of a strong national movement to provide better living alternatives for people with developmental disabilities. And, she adds, the movement reaps dividends for taxpayers.
>
> The cost to house one person during 1984 in an Arkansas institution for the mentally retarded for a one-year period was $30,000, she says.
>
> "This cost is reduced to $10,000 a year at Life Styles, with each resident contributing $2,000 annually towards room and board expenses," she says. "Most residents remain in the program for one to two years and then become taxpayers themselves, supporting programs like Life Styles."
>
> People in the program learn skills which most people take for granted: home management, personal care, job readiness, social development, money management, survival academics and community awareness. They might start with a simple task, like frying an egg, and gradually work to learn all the things needed to work and live on their own, Mrs. Hart says.
>
> *Northwest Arkansas Times*, 31 March 1985, Vol. 117 No. 287.

housing arrangements, varying in size, staff, services provided, ages served, and disabilities served (Bruininks et al. 1981). Although these facilities serve disabilities ranging from borderline to severe, most serve populations that are primarily mildly handicapped.

A lot of research concerns the effectiveness of community residential facilities and the variables related to successful placement in such programs. A recent study by Jacobson and Schwartz concluded that while personal characteristics alone are not powerful predictors of successful community placement, they are associated with placement success to some "degree" (Jacobson and Schwartz 1983, 5). The study also found that "more capable" handicapped adults are more likely to have problems in group homes than "less

Table 9-4   State Zoning Laws

State	Facility	No. Residents	Type of Residents	Zone Permitted
California	Family care home Foster home Group home	6 or less	Mentally disordered or otherwise handicapped, or dependent or neglected children	Single/Family
Colorado	Group home	8	DD	Single/Family
Michigan	Residential facility	6 or less	Persons in need of supervision or care	Single/Family
Minnesota	Group home Foster home	6 or less	MR or physically handicapped	Single/Family
	Residential facility	7–16		Multiple family
Montana	Community residential facility: group, foster, or other	8 or less	DD or handicapped	Single/Family
New Jersey	Group home	12 or less	Children	All
New Mexico	Community residences	10 or less	Mentally ill or DD	Single/Family
Ohio	Family home Group home	8 or less 9–16	DD	Single family Multiple family
Rhode Island	Any type	6 or less	MR	All
Virginia	Family care home, foster home, group home	not specified	MR & DD	Appropriate private residential districts
Wisconsin	Child welfare agency Group foster home for children Adult residential	8 or less 9–15 16 or more	All children or adults	All residential zones

Source: State zoning laws regulating group living facilities in the community, AMICUS[3] (1978):38–39.

capable" handicapped individuals. Other variables related to community living success or independence include age (Seltzer et al. 1982), total residential environments (Seltzer 1981), sensorimotor and work skills, appropriate behavior, family involvement, and gender (Schalock et al. 1981). Therefore, these variables should be considered when making placement recommendations.

Before community placement can be successful, the community must accept the presence of the living facility. It has already been noted that many neighborhoods reject the presence of such a program. They have negative attitudes toward group homes and other community living facilities; they also discriminate against disabled individuals in regards to housing (Trippi et al. 1978; Smith et al. 1980), so successful integration into the community may be difficult. Another barrier to community living programs is zoning. Although many zoning regulations were established to ensure the safety and health of communities, they are often overly restrictive and prevent the establishment of community residences for disabled individuals (Disabled citizens in the community, 1978).

Two types of ordinances, single-family dwelling ordinances and exclusionary zoning ordinances, cause the problems. Two approaches to overcoming these barriers include challenging the ordinances in court and creating state legislation to prevent local communities from maintaining discriminatory zoning regulations. By 1978, eleven states had such legislation, with eight additional states considering similar legislation (Disabled citizens in the community, 1978). Table 9-4 describes some of the state zoning laws.

Recreation and Leisure Time Opportunities

As was detailed in the problems section of this chapter, mildly handicapped adults often have difficulties in recreation and leisure time activities. Problems either result from discrimination, inaccessible facilities, or a lack of accommodations. Some disabled adults may not have the intellectual capacity to participate in activities requiring considerable cognitive abilities. Those with physical problems may not be able to get into facilities because of barriers. Individuals with vision problems may not be able to utilize facilities because of their vision loss and the corresponding lack of physical accommodations. Hearing impaired individuals will be at a loss at movies or even when watching television without captions.

Services designed to alleviate some of these problems may be initiated by agencies, schools, self-help groups, individuals, or even private enterprises. An example of a school's effort to accommodate handicapped individuals in recreation was described by Slaney (1980). The Plano School District in Texas adapted a nature trail for use by visually impaired persons. Adapting the trail included reviewing available information concerning environmental education for the visually handicapped; establishing markers and trail guides; developing materials available in Braille, large and regular print, and on tape; and developing a guide for use by teachers. With such modifications, many recreational facilities can become usable by the visually impaired, without a great deal of dependence on sighted assistants. Similar adaptions can be made at zoos (Mobilizing for a barrier-free zoo, 1974), where physical barriers are removed for mobility disabled individuals, listening posts are established for nonreaders, and Braille maps are displayed for visually impaired adults.

While many actions can be made at individual recreational sites, states can also undertake steps to make entire public recreational facilities accessible and usable for handicapped individuals. The Illinois Department of Conservation has established six goals to implement statewide accessible recreational facilities:

- Goal One—reduce attitudinal barriers at all staff levels
- Goal Two—make accessible all basic facilities, such as parking areas, drinking fountains, bathrooms, etc.
- Goal Three—make accessible all general recreation facilities, including picnic areas, fishing and camping areas, nature trails, etc.
- Goal Four—modify facilities with historical, natural, or cultural significance in such a way as to ensure accessibility while preserving special features
- Goal Five—disseminate information to the public concerning accessible facilities
- Goal Six—provide limited special programs for handicapped and aging individuals (Illinois is revamping its outdoor recreational resources, 1978).

The department developed a five-year plan to accomplish these goals. Following full implementation, public recreational facilities in Illinois should provide equal recreational opportunities for all citizens of the state.

Numerous other options are available for making recreational facilities more usable for handicapped individuals. Dr. John Nesbitt, Chairman of the Subcommittee on Employment of the Handicapped in 1978, believes that equal opportunity in recreation is a *right*, not a privilege (Recreation: The final dimension, 1978). All efforts should be made to ensure that right.

Self-Help Groups

Another service utilized by mildly handicapped adults is not provided by any agency, institution of higher education, or community. This service, self-help groups, is provided by disabled individuals themselves. The purposes of such groups include "self-help seminars, group activities, dissemination of information, and social opportunities" (Cordoni 1982, 534). Often disabled adults realize that the persons most likely to understand their problems and provide the necessary support to overcome these problems, especially psychological problems associated with a disability, are other similarly disabled individuals. This concept of people with problems helping others with similar problems has a long history. One only has to look at Alcoholics Anonymous, Weight Watchers, and abused women's groups to realize the magnitude of these types of support groups.

Many mildly handicapped adults have realized that support received from others like themselves is often more germane to their problems than support received from "outsiders." For example, learning disabled adults continue to need counseling and emotional support, even after the school years (Geib et al. 1981). Self-help groups can provide support these individuals need. Johnson (1981) describes a self-help group for learning disabled adults, and indicates that these types of groups have specific benefits:

- Groups of individuals with common problems can combine efforts to find ways to help themselves
- Motivation is present to find out about each others' problems
- Information concerning various methods of overcoming problems is shared
- The realization that everyone in the group has similar problems encourages group sharing.

These benefits of self-help groups for the learning disabled are fairly generalizable for other types of mild disabilities. The key seems to be that individuals with similar problems feel more comfortable talking about their situation in self-help groups than they would in a setting with individuals who are not as "tuned in" to their problems and needs. As stated by Johnson in talking about the self-help group for learning disabled adults, "the LD adult can report from the 'firing line'" (Johnson 1981, 439).

There are currently many self-help groups for learning disabled adults. The following is a partial list (Cordoni 1982):

YACLD
210 Wick Ave.
Youngstown, Ohio 44503

Time Out to Enjoy, Inc.
113 Garfield St.
Oak Park, IL 60304

Marin Puzzle People, Inc.
1368 Lincoln Ave.
San Rafael, CA 94901

A National Network of Learning Disabled Adults
P.O. Box Z
East Texas State University
Commerce, TX 75428

Association of Learning Disabled Adults (ALDA)
P.O. Box 9722
Friendship Station
Washington, D.C. 20016

Institute for LD
313 Caruth-O'Leary Hall
University of Kansas
Lawrence, KS 66103

Pennsylvania ACLD Youth and Adult Section
1108 Mayberry Lane
State College, PA 16801

LAUNCH, Inc., The Coalition of LD Adults
Department of Special Education
East Texas State University
Commerce, TX 75428

Adelphi Learning Disabled Adult Organization
Adelphi University
Garden City, NY 11530

Phoenix, AZ Sunshiners
2701 E. Camelback Road
Phoenix, AZ 85061

Groups similar to self-help groups for adults with learning disabilities have been successful with other types of disabled individuals. In a recent study, Jaureguy and Evans (1983) studied the effects of short-term counseling using the telephone with visually impaired adults. The main methodology was group self-help, with the telephone being the medium of delivery. After eight sessions, individuals in the experimental group were found to have significantly more social involvement and increased levels of daily living skills than did a matched control group not involved in self-help. These results suggest that self-help groups can have a positive effect on visually impaired adults, even when the sessions are held over the telephone.

The next goal is to increase the number of self-help groups available. Although the growth of such groups has been rather rapid (Cordoni 1982), there is still a severe shortage. In describing methods for expanding self-help groups, Johnson (1981) suggests that groups be established in conjunction with government agencies, and that professional organizations become more involved. While not a panacea for many of the problems experienced by disabled adults, self-help groups may fill a void left by agencies and other professional service groups, and therefore increase the likelihood of maximum independent living.

THE ELDERLY MILDLY HANDICAPPED

Adults with disabilities have problems different from those of disabled children. Likewise, older disabled adults have unique problems. Just as children grow up to become disabled adults, disabled adults grow older and become aged. The problems associated with aging are often compounded with disabilities. Not only are elderly individuals faced with health problems, financial problems, and psychological problems, but *elderly handicapped* persons have to deal with the problems associated with their particular disability.

Research on aging is a relatively new field, with the study of the aged disabled being even more recent (Hardman et al. 1984). During the past several years, however, research on this topic has been growing in prominence and is becoming "an increasingly sophisticated field of research inquiry" (Hoyer et al. 1984, 48). There are several reasons for this recent interest. First of all, our society is getting older (Hardman et al. 1984). As medical technology increases the life expectancy of the population and as birth rates decline, the proportion of the population considered elderly is growing. The simple fact that more and more individuals fit into the elderly population supports increased scientific interest and inquiry.

A second reason for the growth in research on aging is increased interest by various professionals in the elderly population. For example, various medical conditions primarily associated with old age have become topics of interest, such as Alzheimer's disease. Sociologists and social workers are interested in the aged, and psychologists are becoming more interested in the psychology of aging. Even politicians, sensing a growing constituency group, have become interested in older Americans. Regardless of the reasons, however, it is an established fact that increased, improved research with older persons should continue (Hoyer et al. 1984).

Aged, disabled individuals present unique problems for service providers. Not only are the problems of old age present, but they are compounded by problems associated with various disabilities. The lack of research into the aged disabled is the result of several factors. First, there is little consensus on who makes up the elderly disabled (Drew et al. 1984). A lack of general understanding of who constitutes the aged group limits research. Several reasons contribute to this lack of clarity, including the limited research and the fact that "aging is a fluid concept" (Hardman et al. 1984, 464). For example, ages that have been arbitrarily used to denote the elderly mentally retarded include 40 and 55 years (Drew et al. 1984). There is little consensus concerning when one becomes "old." It thus appears that one of the reasons for limited research into the aged disabled population is a lack of definition of the population, and one of the reasons for this lack of definition is limited research. The cycle must be broken with basic studies, even if the definition of the population changes.

Characteristics of the Aged Disabled

The aged, disabled population is heterogeneous, making it very difficult to ascertain the general characteristics of the group. Many older disabled individuals, however, experience major problems. For example, in describing the elderly mentally retarded, Schulman indicated that this group "usually [has] no children, no retirement pensions, and low social security coverge because of their limited prior earnings" (Schulman 1980, 152). Individuals classified as learning disabled in school continue their problems into adulthood and old age. Blalock (1982) investigated the characteristics of adult learning disabled individuals and found that they often have problems in oral language, reading, writing, math, orientation, social perception, thinking and reasoning, and attention. The problems manifested by the adult learning disabled are rarely remediated and only become more of a handicap as individuals progress through adulthood and become a part of the elderly population.

General characteristics of the aged, which also apply to disabled older persons, include mobility problems, memory deficits, senility, depression, overweight, and sensory impairments. Psychological problems such as depression are often found in elderly individuals; this population appears to be very susceptible to psychiatric problems (Waxman et al. 1984). When disabling conditions such as mental deficiency, perceptual and learning problems, and physical disorders are added to these general characteristics, the problems may be difficult to overcome.

Needs of the Elderly Disabled

All elderly individuals need certain services. These may include financial assistance, medical intervention, disease prevention, psychological and psychiatric services, and general social services. Elderly disabled individuals also need these services, but often to a greater degree. Many adult handicapped individuals do not have children. This means that while children are available to help older individuals, many disabled people do not have this human resource. These individuals must rely on other groups to provide help.

Older disabled individuals need the assistance of rehabilitation services and mental health services. Unfortunately, these services are often not sought by this group. One study that investigated the utilization of mental health services by the elderly determined that if help for psychiatric problems was deemed necessary by older persons, they were more likely to seek such assistance from general physicians, not mental health professionals (Waxman et al. 1984).

Rehabilitation is also needed by many disabled, older persons. Unfortunately, rehabilitation agencies often have not provided appropriate services to this group because of the training of rehabilitation professionals and the emphasis on vocational closures (placing persons in jobs). The result has been that many disabled elderly individuals in need of vocational services or independent living services have been unserved. Myers (1983) suggests using the functional capacities of older persons as the criterion for determining what kinds of rehabilitation services are provided. "It may be expected that many young-old persons, those aged 60–74, will be potentially employable, while many old-old individuals, those aged 75+, will require independent living services" (Myers 1983, 51). At any rate, rehabilitation in the form of job training, part-time employment, full-time employment, or independent living training is appropriate and necessary for many disabled older individuals. Rehabilitation agencies should increase their efforts with this group.

Obviously, current knowledge of the elderly disabled is limited. Additional research is needed to better define the population, to determine the needs of the group, and to discover methods of providing necessary, appropriate services. Related to the limited use of mental health services, Waxman, Carner, and Klein (1914) suggest that future research determine the reasons behind the use of such services. As medical practices continue to expand the life expectancy of the population, it stands to reason that more and more mildly disabled adults will become elderly. Knowledge and services must be expanded to better meet the needs of this group.

SUMMARY

This chapter has focused on mildly handicapped adults, the problems they face, and the services available to facilitate their independence. The problems experienced by handicapped children do not end after the school years. Handicapped children grow up and often become handicapped adults. For disabled adults, some of the problems they experience are similar to those experienced during childhood, while other problems are new, created by the entrance into adulthood. Major problems of this group include social

HIGHLIGHT

Dyslexia Battle That Forged a Career

By Steven M. Schaefer

Just to be writing is sort of a thrill. It probably is for most writers, but in many ways it especially is to me. That is because there was a time when I might never be able to read, let alone write. But I've compensated for my problem—dyslexia. These days, I read and write for a living.

Early on, I understood that reading was important. Our home was filled with books, magazines and newspapers, and my parents and brothers spent much of their time reading. By the third grade all but a few of my classmates could read. But for me, trying to understand the symbols of our language led to confusion and often fury, which I took out on other students and my parents. Not surprisingly, I had grave doubts about myself, and serious problems with my behavior.

My parents, and a teacher named Helen Whittlesey, assured me that I was smart. They explained to me that I suffered from a learning disability called dyslexia. In the mid-1960's, few people could identify dyslexia. I was lucky. Mrs. Whittlesey was dyslexic herself and my parents both had doctorates in psychology. But despite being able to compensate for my disorder, it took me years to fully overcome feelings of inadequacy and rage that stem from my early troubles in school.

Dyslexia takes many forms. My main problem was with memory lapses in recalling numbers, letters, words and rules of grammar. I also had problems discriminating between sounds and between symbols. In particular, I had trouble with B's, D's, and P's, and could not distinguish among words such as bad, dad and pad. My mind simply did not process the complex symbols and structure of our language easily.

In many ways my biggest problems during my first years of school were behavioral. The least bit of teasing or ridicule enraged me, and starting fights was one method I used to make sure no one laughed at me. As a result, I spent a lot of time in the principal's office.

Despite all that, my parents encouraged me and loved me without question. They told me I was intelligent and convinced me that even if I could not read I was very good at some things, like drawing and sculpture. My father was particularly good at helping me develop interests, and then giving me tools to learn, which usually included books and magazines.

My mother first suspected I had a learning disability in 1964 when I was in the first grade and my performance was dramatically inferior to that of my older brothers. One had learned to read with little difficulty. Since I was talented in some areas, and generally seemed bright, my parents wondered why I was at such a complete loss with English.

After concluding that I had a learning disability, my parents met with the principal of my school, Horace Mann in Newtonville, Mass. He put me into a special reading class in the first grade. Mrs. Whittlesey got me the next year, and remained my primary reading teacher through second and third grade.

(continued)

New York Times, 15 April 1984.

Mrs. Whittlesey had an eclectic approach to teaching. She told my parents, "You try everything once, and whatever works you use." One thing that seemed to help me was repetition. Unlike many dyslexics, I had no coordination problems, and could print well. Mrs. Whittlesey used that to my advantage by having me copy simple sentences over and over. To help me read I was taught to sound out each letter in a word phonetically. With practice, these rote methods seemed to help.

Like my parents, Mrs. Whittlesey believed that keeping a troubled student's morale high was of the utmost importance. Not only did she encourage me when I answered correctly, but if I subtracted 14 from 26 and got 21 she would recognize that I had simply reversed the numbers. She would then use arrows to point out the reversal and draw a happy face on my paper to indicate I had done well.

After struggling all summer with a reading tutor, I entered the third grade prepared for defeat. I remember fighting with my mother, and telling her, "I don't want to learn to read. Reading is boring." My arguments against the written word were probably just a defense mechanism, in case I never did learn to read.

But sometime in the spring of that year, my reading ability began to improve. Although my teachers promoted me with reluctance, my school records show my reading ability dramatically improved in the fourth grade. After three years of work, I suddenly jumped from having reading test scores in the lowest 10 percent to the 50th percentile. My behavioral problems also subsided.

From about the sixth grade on reading took care of itself. The more I read the more enjoyable it became. Then came the next step, learning how to write. This took longer than learning to read, but it was less frustrating because I could see improvement. My aspiration to write well began in the ninth grade. I decided during my sophomore year of high school to join the school paper, in part because reading made me respect good writing. I participated in sports year round, and the local sports section was usually one of the first things I read, so I became a sports writer.

Every article I wrote was edited by one of my parents. My mother simply corrected my mistakes and encouraged me; my father was more critical, and his editing usually meant I had to re-type the piece. This annoyed me, but I realized at the same time that he was a good writing coach. Next year I became sports editor, although in retrospect my writing was poor.

I continued to work on writing, and during my junior year at the University of Wisconsin, because I didn't want to lose the knack, I decided to major in journalism. After school I worked part time in a sports department of a local daily newspaper. A week after graduation, in December 1981, I took over as sports editor of a small daily in south-central Wisconsin, covering area high-school sports, but also major college and professional sports, including the 1982 World Series. In July 1983 I got a job in Chicago with United Press International, and today I hear my work read over the air by radio and television broadcasters.

I seldom view my dyslexia as a hindrance anymore. In fact, I think the effort I put into learning how to read and write has strengthened me. My struggles have helped me learn the importance of perseverance, and enabled me to better handle pressure and frustration. Even as a writer and editor my learning disorder may have positive effects; sometimes I think my slower, more deliberate style of reading enables me to catch mistakes that other editors might slip right over.

adjustment, vocational opportunity and adjustment, and community acceptance. Other problems such as alcohol abuse, stress, poor memory, and improper use of leisure time were also presented. All of these problems are not experienced by all mildly handicapped adults; rather, many mildly handicapped adults experience some of these problems, but without assistance, their efforts to live independently will likely fail.

The services available for mildly handicapped adults are based on the philosophy of normalization and include post secondary education and training, vocational rehabilitation, housing assistance, and services related to recreation and leisure time. A final service was self-help groups. These groups allow disabled individuals to provide support and counseling for other similarly disabled individuals. Self-help groups frequently fill gaps left by services provided by state agencies, education agencies, and other formal groups. Without appropriate services, many mildly handicapped adults will not become as independent as possible, but will remain more dependent on society than necessary. While the provision of services does not guarantee total independence for disabled adults, it does facilitate their reaching a maximum level of independence. This serves two purposes. First, by encouraging independence, disabled individuals become contributors rather than simply consumers. And more importantly, as purported in the normalization philosophy, disabled adults have the right to be independent.

REFERENCES

Bellamy, G.T., P.E. Bourbeau, and J.A. Sowers, Work and work-related services: Postschool options. In *Systematic instruction of the moderately and severely handicapped*, edited by M.E. Snell. Columbus, Ohio: Charles E. Merrill, 1983.
Best, G.A. *Individuals with physical disabilities: An introduction for educators*. St. Louis: C.V. Mosby, 1978.
Blalock, J.W. Persistent auditory language deficits in adults with learning disabilities. *Journal of Learning Disabilities* 15 (1982):604–609.
Blalock, J.W. Residual learning disabilities in young adults: Implications for rehabilitation. *Journal of Applied Rehabilitation Counseling* 13, no. 2 (1982):9–13.
Brolin, D.E. *Vocational preparation of retarded citizens*. Columbus, Ohio: Charles E. Merrill, 1976.
Brolin, D.E., and C.J. Kokaska. *Career education for handicapped children and youth*. Columbus, Ohio: Charles E. Merrill, 1979.
Bruininks, R.H., M.J. Kudla, F.A. Hauber, B.K. Hill, and C.A. Wieck. Recent growth and status of community residential alternatives. In *Deinstitutionalization and community adjustment of mentally retarded people*, edited by R.H. Bruininks, C.E. Meyers, B.B. Sigford, and K.C. Lakin. Washington, D.C.: American Association on Mental Deficiency, 1981.
Chaffin, J., R. Davison, C. Regan, and C. Spellman. Two follow-up studies of former mentally retarded students from the Kansas work-study project. *Exceptional Children* 37 (1971):733–38.
Cordoni, B. A directory of college LD services. *Journal of Learning Disabilities* 15 (1982):529–34.
Crain, E.J. Socioeconomic status of educable mentally retarded graduates in special education. *Education and Training of the Mentally Retarded* 15 (1980):90–94.
D'Alonzo, B.J. *Educating adolescents with learning and behavior disorders*. Rockville, MD: Aspen Systems Corporation, 1983.
Delaney, A.M., and R.L. Nuttall. Assessing the needs of a blind client population. *Journal of Visual Impairment and Blindness* 72 (1978):46–54.
Disabled citizens in the community: Zoning obstacles and legal remedies. *AMICUS* 3 (1978):30–34.

Drew, C.J., D.R. Logan, and M.L. Hardman. *Mental retardation: A life cycle approach*. St. Louis: C.V. Mosby, 1984.

Edgerton, R.B. Crime, deviance, and normalization: Reconsidered. In *Deinstitutionalization and community adjustment of mentally retarded people*, edited by R.H. Bruininks, C.E. Meyers, B.B. Sigford, and K.C. Lakin. Washington, D.C.: American Association on Mental Deficiency, 1981.

Fafard, M.B., and P.A. Haubrich. Vocational and social adjustment of learning disabled young adults: A follow-up study. *Learning Disabilities Quarterly* 4 (1981):122–30.

Gearheart, B.R. *Special education for the 80s*. St. Louis: C.V. Mosby, 1980.

Geib, B.B., L.R. Guzzardi, and P.M. Genova. Intervention for adults with learning disabilities. *Academic Therapy* 16 (1981):317–25.

Greenan, J.P. Problems and issues in delivering vocational education instruction and support services to students with learning disabilities. *Journal of Learning Disabilities* 15 (1982):231–35.

Hallahan, D.P., and J.M. Kauffman. *Exceptional children: Introduction to special education*. Englewood Cliffs, N.J.: Prentice-Hall, 1982.

Hardman, M.L., C.J. Drew, and M.W. Egan. *Human exceptionality: Society, school, and family*. Boston: Allyn and Bacon, 1984.

Hasbrouck, J.M. Diagnosis of auditory perceptual disorders in previously undiagnosed adults. *Journal of Learning Disabilities* 16 (1983):206–208.

Hill, J.W., P. Wehman, and J. Pentecost. Developing job interview skills in mentally retarded adults. *Education and Training of the Mentally Retarded* 15 (1980):179–86.

Hoyer, W.J., C.L. Raskind, and J.P. Abrahams. Research practices in the psychology of aging: A survey of research published in the *Journal of Gerontology*, 1975-1982. *Journal of Gerontology* 39, no. 1 (1984):44–48.

Illinois is revamping its outdoor recreational resources. *AMICUS* 3 (1978):38–43.

Inana, M. Grocery shopping: Principles and techniques for the blind consumer. *Journal of Visual Impairment and Blindness* 74 (1980):329–32.

Intagliata, J., S. Kraus, and B. Willer. The impact of deinstitutionalization on a community based service system. *Mental Retardation* 18, no. 6 (1980):305–307.

Jackson, H.J., and P.J. Thorbecke. Treating obesity of mentally retarded adolescents and adults: An exploratory program. *American Journal of Mental Deficiency* 87 (1982):302–308.

Jacobson, J.W., and A.A. Schwartz. Personal and service characteristics affecting group home placement success: A prospective analysis. *Mental Retardation* 21 (1983):1–7.

Jaureguy, B.M., and R.L. Evans. Short term group counseling of visually impaired people by telephone. *Journal of Visual Impairment and Blindness* 77 (1983):150–52.

Johnson, C. LD Adults: The inside story. *Academic Therapy* 16, no. 4 (1981):435–42.

Jones, L.A., and R. Moe. College education for mentally retarded adults. *Mental Retardation* 18 (1980):59–62.

Juul, K. European approaches and innovations in serving the handicapped. *Exceptional Children* 44 (1978):322–30.

Kastner, L.S., N.D. Reppucci, and J.J. Pezzoli. Assessing community attitudes toward mentally retarded persons. *American Journal of Mental Deficiency* 84 (1979):137–44.

Kelley, J., and A. Simon. The mentally handicapped as workers: A survey of company experience. *Personnel* 46 (1969):58–64.

Kirchner, C., and R. Peterson. Worktime, occupational status, and annual earnings: An assessment of underemployment. *Journal of Visual Impairment and Blindness* 74 (1980):203–205.

Krishef, C.H., and D.M. DiNitto. Alcohol abuse among mentally retarded individuals. *Mental Retardation* 19 (1981):151–55.

Lakin, K.C., G.C. Krantz, R.H. Bruininks, J.L. Clumpner, and B.K. Hill. One hundred years of data on populations of public residential facilities for mentally retarded people. *American Journal of Mental Deficiency* 87 (1982):1–8.

Landesman-Dwyer, S. Living in the community. *American Journal of Mental Deficiency* 86 (1981):223–34.

Larson, R.W., and S.B. Johnson. Mobility techniques for blind workers in industry. *Journal of Visual Impairment and Blindness* 75 (1981):219–22.

McGee, D.W. Sharpen students' job seeking skills with employment applications and role played interviews. *Teaching Exceptional Children* 13 (1981):152–55.

Mandell, C.J., and E. Fiscus. *Understanding exceptional people.* St. Paul: West Publishing Company, 1981.

Margolis, J., and T. Charitonidis. Public reactions to housing for the mentally retarded. *Exceptional Children* 48 (1981):68–70.

Martin, V., R. Martin, and L. Hapeman. College preparatory program for visually impaired students: An evaluation. *Journal of Visual Impairment and Blindness* 72 (1978):55–58.

Matson, J.L. Depression in the mentally retarded: A review. *Education and Training of the Mentally Retarded* 17 (1982):159–63.

Megivern, K. Employment discrimination against blind and visually impaired persons in the United States: There ought to be a law! In *Blindness 1982-1983: American Association of Workers for the Blind (AAWB) Annual.* Washington, D.C.: AAWB, 1983.

Mesibov, G.B., B.S. Conover, and W.G. Saur. Limited guardianship laws and developmentally disabled adults: Needs and obstacles. *Mental Retardation* 18 (1980):221–26.

Mobilizing for a barrier-free zoo. *The Social and Rehabilitation Record* 1 (1974):22–23.

Moores, D.F. *Educating the deaf: Psychology, principles, and practices.* Boston: Houghton Mifflin, 1982.

Muraski, J.A. Designing career education programs that work. *Academic Therapy* 18, no. 2 (1982):65–71.

Murtaugh, M. The right to recreation: A review of legal action. *AMICUS* 3 (1978):46–48.

Myers, J.E. Rehabilitation counseling for older disabled persons: The state of the art. *Journal of Applied Counseling* 14, no. 3 (1983):48–53.

National Association for Superintendents of Public Residential Facilities for the Mentally Retarded. *Contemporary issues in residential programs.* Washington, D.C.: President's Committee on Mental Retardation, 1974.

Ochoa, V. Sections 503 and 504: New employment rights for individuals with handicaps. *AMICUS* 2 (1977):38–45.

Ohshansky, S. The disabled in the labor market. *Journal of Applied Rehabilitation Counseling* 4 (1973):164–70.

Ostertag, B.A., R.E. Baker, R.F. Howard, and L. Best. Learning disabled programs in California community colleges. *Journal of Learning Disabilities* 15 (1982):535–38.

Peterson, L., and L.L. Smith. A comparison of the post school adjustment of educable mentally retarded adults with that of adults of normal intelligence. *Exceptional Children* 26 (1960):404–408.

President's Committee on Mental Retardation (PCMR). President's committee on mental retardation Gallop poll shows attitude on mental retardation improving. In *President's Committee on Mental Retardation Message.* Washington, D.C.: PCMR, 1975.

Recreaction: The final dimension in equal opportunity for the handicapped. *AMICUS* 3 (1978):32–37.

Robinson, N.M., and H.B. Robinson. *The mentally retarded child: A psychological approach.* New York: McGraw-Hill, 1976.

Sandler, A., and R. Robinson. Public attitudes and community acceptance of mentally retarded persons: A review. *Education and Training of the Mentally Retarded* 16 (1981):97–103.

Schalock, R.L., R.S. Harper, and T. Genung. Community integration of mentally retarded adults: Community placement and program success. *American Journal of Mental Deficiency* 85 (1981):478–88.

Scheerenberger, R.C. Deinstitutionalization: Trends and difficulties. In *Deinstitutionalization and community adjustment of mentally retarded people*, edited by R.H. Bruininks, C.E. Meyers, B.B. Sigford, and K.C. Lakin. Washington, D.C.: American Association on Mental Deficiency, 1981.

Scheerenberger, R.C. Public residential services, 1981: Status and trends. *Mental Retardation* 20 (1982):210-215.

Schulman, E.D. *Focus on the retarded adult: Programs and services.* St. Louis: C.V. Mosby, 1980.

Seltzer, G.B. Community residential adjustment: The relationship among environment, performance, and satisfaction. *American Journal of Mental Deficiency* 85 (1981):624-30.

Seltzer, M.M., B. Seltzer, and C.C. Sherwood. Comparison of community adjustment of older vs. younger mentally retarded adults. *American Journal of Mental Deficiency* 87 (1982):9-13.

Siegel, E., and R. Gold. *Educating the learning disabled.* New York: Macmillan, 1982.

Sigelman, C.K. A Machiavelli for planners: Community attitudes and selection of a group home site. *Mental Retardation* 14 (1976):26-29.

Slaney, S.H. Adaption of a nature trail for use with visually handicapped students. *Journal of Visual Impairment and Blindness* 74 (1980):354-55.

Smith, C.R. Learning disabilities: *The interaction of learner, task, and setting.* Boston: Little, Brown & Co., 1983.

Smith, T.E.C. Employer concerns in hiring mentally retarded persons. *Rehabilitation Counseling Bulletin* 24 (1981):316-18.

Smith, T.E.C., J.S. Liska, and B.L. Smith. Housing discrimination toward blind persons. *Journal of Visual Impairment and Blindness* 74 (1980):75-79.

Snell, M.E. *Systematic instruction of the moderately and severely handicapped.* Columbus, Ohio: Charles E. Merrill, 1983.

Spreen, O. Neuropsychology of learning disorders: Post conference review. In *The neuropsychology of learning disorders: Theoretical approaches*, edited by R.M. Knights and D.J. Bakker. Baltimore: University Park Press, 1976.

Stewart, D.M. Survey of community employer attitudes toward hiring the handicapped. *Mental Retardation* 15 (1977):30-31.

Strickland, C.G. Employment of the mentally retarded. *Exceptional Children* 34 (1967):21-24.

Trippi, J., R. Michael, A. Colao, and A. Alvarez. Housing discrimination toward mentally retarded persons. *Exceptional Children* 44 (1978):430-33.

Vogel, S.A. On developing LD college programs. *Journal of Learning Disabilities* 15 (1982):518-27.

Waxman, H.M., E.A. Carner, and M. Klein. Underutilization of mental health professionals by community elderly. *The Gerontologist* 24, no. 1 (1984):23-29.

Wender, P.H. Hypothesis for possible biochemical basis of minimal brain dysfunction. In *The neuropsychology of learning disorders: Theoretical approaches*, edited by R.M. Knights and D.J. Bakker. Baltimore: University Park Press, 1976.

White, W.J., G.R. Alley, D.D. Deshler, J.B. Schumaker, M.M. Warner, and F.L. Clark. Are there learning disabilities after high school? *Exceptional Children* 49(1982):273-74.

Wiener, D., R.J. Anderson, and J. Nietupski. Impact of community-based residential facilities for mentally retarded adults on surrounding property values using analysis methods. *Education and Training of the Mentally Retarded* 17 (1982):97-103.

Wood, L.C., B.D. Meyer, and S.C. Grady. Exceptional adults learn in Broward community college's continuing education program. *Teaching Exceptional Children* 10 (1977):7-9.

Wordern, P.E., I. Malmgren, and P. Gabourie. Memory for stories in learning disabled adults. *Journal of Learning Disabilities* 15 (1982):145-51.

Chapter Ten

ATTITUDES AND THE MILDLY HANDICAPPED

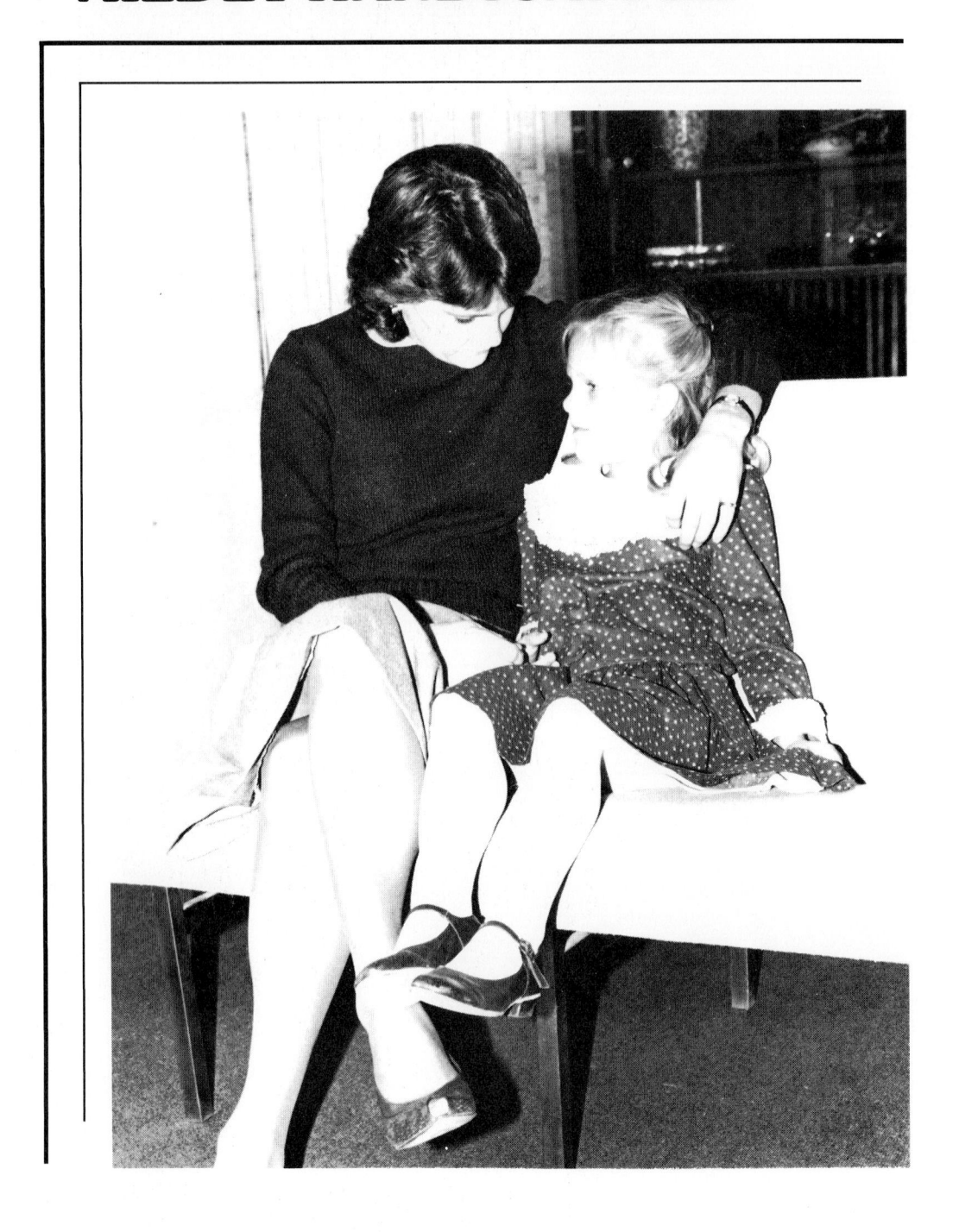

CHAPTER OUTLINE

INTRODUCTION
DEFINITION OF ATTITUDES
VARIABLES AFFECTING ATTITUDES
    Contact
    Knowledge
    Other Variables
    Labeling and Behavior
ROLE OF ATTITUDES IN THE EDUCATION AND TREATMENT OF MILDLY HANDICAPPED PERSONS
ATTITUDES OF KEY PERSONS
    Attitudes of Physicians
    Attitudes of Teachers
    Attitudes of School Administrators
    Attitudes of Parents
    Attitudes of Peers
    Attitudes of Employers
    Mildly Handicapped Self-Attitudes
CHANGING ATTITUDES
    Assessment of Attitudes
    Techniques to Change Attitudes
SUMMARY

CHAPTER OBJECTIVES

After reading this chapter, you should be able to:
- Define attitudes;
- State the relationship between attitudes and behavior;
- Describe the role of attitudes with the mildly handicapped;
- List and discuss variables affecting attitudes;
- Describe the importance of attitudes of teachers, administrators, parents, peers, and siblings; and
- List and discuss methods of changing attitudes toward mildly handicapped children and adults.

INTRODUCTION

The role of attitudes in special education has been discussed at length in the literature. Attitudes appear to affect behavior toward particular groups of individuals. As a result, the importance of attitudes held by various groups toward disabled persons cannot be overlooked. While attitudes toward the handicapped have long been considered important, in this era of integrating handicapped children into regular classrooms the criticality of attitudes held by teachers, administrators, peers, parents, and siblings becomes even more obvious. As handicapped children become adults, the attitudes toward them continue to be important. Disabled adults have to compete for jobs, for community acceptance, and for equal housing opportunities. The attitudes of key community members such as employers cannot be overestimated because they relate to the success of disabled adults.

During the entire development period, the attitudes of family members are important, including those of parents, peers, and siblings. Without positive attitudes and behavior from this traditional support group, handicapped persons face major barriers blocking their assimilation into school and the community. Opportunities for academic, vocational, and social success are limited without this support.

One way attitudes affect behavior is through expectations. If teachers have negative attitudes toward a particular group of children, they simply expect different levels of achievement and behavior from members of that group. Good (1982) suggests that lowered teacher expectations for low-achieving students can result in the following:

- Less time for low achievers to provide answers
- Giving low achievers the answer or calling on other students rather than giving assistance and clues
- Rewarding low achievers for inappropriate behavior and incorrect responses
- Criticizing low achievers for failure
- Providing less praise for low achievers for their success
- Interacting less often with low achievers
- Calling on low achievers less often
- Seating low achievers further from teachers
- Not giving the benefit of the doubt to low achievers, but doing so for high achievers
- Providing low achievers with less smiling and other nonverbal feedback
- Providing less overall feedback to low achievers
- Providing less direct instruction and more seatwork to low achievers
- Interrupting low achievers very quickly during errors in reading
- Giving longer assignments and more discussion time to high achievers
- Low achievers having difficulty understanding what they are to do
- Fostering a passive learning style among low achievers.

These are only some of the effects of low teacher expectations, negative attitudes, and preconceived notions about student abilities. Since attitudes may be directly related to expectations and behaviors, they must be a major consideration in the education of handicapped children. Regular classroom teachers, special education teachers, administrators, peers, and family members must have positive attitudes toward mildly handicapped children if the intent of legislation and litigation, which is to provide equal educational opportunities, is realized. Likewise, handicapped adults are not likely to lead normalized lives without significant persons in their lives displaying positive attitudes toward them. Federal and state laws have attempted to ensure that handicapped children and adults receive equal opportunities, but laws alone cannot guarantee the realization of the intent. Positive attitudes, however, can play a major role in this realization.

DEFINITION OF ATTITUDES

Although researched extensively, the term *attitude* is difficult to define. Lemon noted this difficulty by saying that "attitude is one of the most ubiquitous of all the terms used in social science" (Lemon 1973, 1). As expected with terms of this nature, there are many different definitions. One definition, similar to many, states that "an attitude is a relatively enduring organization of beliefs around an object or situation predisposing one to respond in some preferential manner" (Rokeach 1968, 112). In other words, attitudes affect behavior. Other concepts often associated with the term *attitude* include the following: attitudes are learned (Sherif and Sherif 1956; McGrath 1964; Osgood, Suci, and Tannenbaum 1957); they vary in intensity (Osgood et al. 1957); and they are relatively enduring (Sherif and Sherif 1956). Attitudes can therefore be described as *learned beliefs or predispositions that affect behavior toward groups, individuals, or institutions.* They affect the way people accept, behave toward, and feel about others.

VARIABLES AFFECTING ATTITUDES

Many different variables affect attitudes. As previously stated, attitudes are learned. Individuals are not born with a predetermined set of attitudes. They are not innate but develop over a period of time, and they can be changed. One only has to observe the way groups have changed their attitudes about certain things to realize how really changeable attitudes are. Not only do groups change their attitudes but so do individuals. Stop and think how you have changed your feelings about certain things, groups of people, or institutions during the past ten years. As a result of many Americans changing their attitudes toward certain minority cultural groups, individuals in these groups now have many more opportunities. Just how attitudes are developed is unclear; it is obvious, however, that attitude development is a complex process. Many studies have linked certain variables to attitude development.

Contact

One variable that many researchers have found to be related to attitudes is contact. For the most part, studies have supported the idea that the more contact one has with a group, the more positive the attitudes toward that group. In the area of handicapped children, studies have revealed that individuals who have had close contact with members of this group generally have more positive attitudes toward them than those with limited contact. For example, regular teachers who have had more direct experience with mentally retarded children have more favorable attitudes toward members of this group (Kennon and Sandoval 1978). Other studies have supported the contact relationship with attitudes toward handicapped children, including studies related to physically handicapped children (Higgs 1975), acceptance and attitudes toward severely handicapped children (Voeltz 1980), and attitudes toward the concept of mainstreaming (Schmelkin 1981).

While these studies appear to support the role of contact in attitude development, other studies have clouded the importance of the contact variable. In one such study,

> **HIGHLIGHT**
>
> ## Church Sets Quota on Retarded
>
> WICHITA, Kan. (AP)—A small Wichita church has adopted a policy that limits the number of mentally retarded adults who may attend Sunday worship services to 20 to 25.
>
> The church's board of directors says the retarded disrupt services. But Chet Jackson, who taught a Sunday school for retarded adults at the church for 20 years, says the policy is discriminatory and has resigned in protest.
>
> "It's an official position now for our church to be prejudiced, discriminatory and rejecting," says Jackson, 65. He says the discrimination is just as serious as excluding blacks or Mexican-Americans.
>
> Jackson became incensed two weeks ago when the board of St. Luke's United Methodist Church overwhelmingly adopted a committee recommendation to restrict the number of mentally handicapped adults attending worship services to about two dozen. Many of the retarded who come to the services live in area group care homes.
>
> The report said there were "indications of discontent within the congregation" because of "disruptions" the retarded adults caused during the service. Restricting the number would put the problem in a "manageable context," the report said.
>
> New Orleans Times—Picayne, 24 March 1980.

Reynolds, Martin-Reynolds, and Mark (1982) found that teachers who had prior teaching experience with educable mentally retarded children in regular classrooms did not have more positive attitudes toward mainstreaming these children than did teachers with limited contact. Other studies have indicated that contact can even have a negative effect on attitudes. After investigating the effects of social contact with handicapped adolescents on the attitudes of nonhandicapped adolescents, Strauch (1970) concluded that contact could actually change attitudes toward the negative.

Thus, contact *per se* may not positively affect attitudes toward the handicapped. But organized interaction between the disabled and nondisabled groups does appear to be more closely related to positive attitudes. Additional research into the relationship of contact and attitudes should be conducted. The only conclusion that can currently be drawn is that contact with handicapped persons may have a positive or negative effect on attitudes toward the handicapped.

Knowledge

One variable closely related to contact and attitudes is the knowledge possessed by individuals about certain groups. Obviously, the more contact individuals have with exceptional children and adults, the more knowledge they have about members of this group. Coursework and inservice training also increase knowledge. As knowledge gradually replaces misinformation, invalid stereotypes give way to a more realistic knowledge base.

Knowledge then does affect attitudes. Proctor (1967) investigated the relationship between knowledge and attitudes toward handicapped children. Results indicated that individuals who had extensive coursework in the area of special education had more realistic attitudes toward mainstreaming handicapped children than teachers who had limited coursework in this area. Another study that related knowledge to attitudes focused on administrators. After surveying administrative personnel in 100 school districts, Newman (1970) found a direct relationship between training in special education and the performance of administrative tasks related to special education.

Inservice training through workshops is also a method of increasing knowledge of exceptional children. Two studies investigated the effects of inservice training on the attitudes of teachers and administrators toward exceptional children. Lovitt (1974) studied the effects of a workshop on the acceptance of learning disabled students by regular primary teachers. It was concluded that the training had a significant positive effect on the attitudes of the treatment group. Another study evaluated the effects of a summer workshop on the attitudes of administrators and teachers toward handicapped children; its findings also revealed a positive effect from the experience (Brooks and Bransford 1971).

Although the above studies support the relationship between knowledge and attitudes, other studies have failed to find any relationship (Conine 1969; Reynolds et al. 1982). Knowledge then may or may not affect attitudes toward handicapped people; as with the contact variable, the type of knowledge and the manner in which it is acquired may also play a role in determining the effect of the information. Inaccurate knowledge, or knowledge emphasizing the negative aspects of disabilities, may have a negative impact. On the other hand, positive, accurate information may have a positive effect. While the literature does not suggest that increased knowledge automatically leads to improved attitudes, studies have suggested that knowledge is necessary in order to have positive attitudes (Siperstein and Bak 1980). The emphasis must be on the *type* of knowledge.

Other Variables

Several studies have investigated the role of variables other than contact and knowledge as they relate to attitudes toward the handicapped. The roles of these variables, however, remain equivocal. For example, Gottlieb and Corman (1975) found a relationship between age and attitudes toward the disabled, while Conine (1969) and Reynolds, Martin-Reynolds, and Mark (1982) did not find these two variables related. Other studies have found relationships between attitudes toward handicapped children and sex (Higgs 1975), ethnic background (Kennon and Sandoval 1978), and grade level of teachers (Reynolds et al. 1982; Kavale and Rossi 1980). These variables, however, do not always relate to attitudes.

Labeling and Behavior

A great deal of literature suggests that the labels attached to children are also related to behavior. Labeling children in special education is common. Indeed, to be eligible for services under P.L. 94-142, children must meet the criteria for one of the specific handicapping conditions defined by the act. Labeling has obvious advantages, which include increasing the visibility of a group that needs special services and considerations, and helping school personnel provide appropriate services for various types of children (Haring 1982). Several assumptions underly the labeling of handicapped children, but these

Table 10-1 **Assumptions Underlying Labeling**

Assumption	Validity
Disabilities are absolute and not simply a result of labels	Probably valid for severely handicapped children but not valid for mildly handicapped children. Many mildly handicapped children are not considered handicapped before or after school years.
Labeling helps to protect society and get benefits for persons with disabilities	Efficacy studies have found that the benefits received by handicapped individuals as a result of their being labeled are fewer than suspected.
Benefits from being labeled outweigh the disadvantages	Studies have found that labels often negatively affect teachers' expectations and the interactions between children and teachers, and distort teachers' observations.

Source: Smith et al. 1983.

assumptions may not always be valid. Table 10-1 describes three basic assumptions concerning labeling and the validity of these assumptions.

Labeling handicapped children does have its negative results. Of primary concern are the preconceived notions labels given by teachers and others who interact with labeled children. Several studies corroborating this concern have found that teachers and student teachers often react negatively to labeled children and hold lowered expectations for them (Schloss and Miller 1982; Foster, Ysseldyke, and Reese 1975; Ysseldyke and Foster 1978; Foster and Salvia 1977).

Obviously, many variables can affect the attitudes of individuals toward handicapped children and mainstreaming. The roles played by these variables, however, remain unclear. While many have the potential of positively affecting attitudes, positive change does not always result. In fact, variables can negatively affect some attitudes. What can be concluded then is that attitudes are complex, learned, and changeable. Their importance in the education and treatment of handicapped children and adults cannot be overlooked.

ROLE OF ATTITUDES IN THE EDUCATION AND TREATMENT OF MILDLY HANDICAPPED PERSONS

If persons with disabilities are to be given equal opportunities in education, jobs, and community living, society must have positive attitudes toward this group. People may say that they have positive attitudes toward the handicapped but at the same time may deny them the right to equal opportunities in education and employment. For example, if regular classroom teachers do not feel that handicapped children should be mainstreamed, the actions of those teachers toward mainstreamed handicapped children will likely be negative. Being successful in a regular classroom is difficult enough for mildly handicapped children when they are accepted; it is often impossible when they are rejected by teachers who have negative attitudes toward them.

Negative attitudes can result in many negative actions. Some of these include the following:

The attitude of the regular classroom teacher may affect the child's educational experience in the classroom.

- Unfair grading practices by regular classroom teachers
- Unfair assignments by regular classroom teachers
- Less than adequate funding for special programs by school administrators
- Lack of inservice training for teachers provided by school administrators
- Lack of concern for specialized teaching needs

These are but a few of the many manifestations from negative attitudes by teachers and administrators toward mildly handicapped children. In the community, negative attitudes toward handicapped adults can result in job discrimination, housing discrimination, legal discrimination, and personal rejection.

While negative attitudes toward handicapped persons can result in discriminatory practices, positive attitudes have the expected opposite effect. For example, regular classroom teachers who have positive attitudes toward mainstreamed mildly handicapped children may go to extremes to provide accommodative strategies that will maximize chances for academic and social success. Administrators who are supportive of special education programs are likely to provide the necessary funding to ensure successful programs as well as the necessary training for staff. Studies have shown that administrative support for special education programs has a positive effect on the quality of those programs (Smith, Flexer, and Sigelman 1979). Positive attitudes of special education teachers also affect program quality. A study by McGuire (1973) determined that the attitudes of special education teachers toward educable mentally retarded children were related to the quality of program provided for this group.

> **HIGHLIGHT**
>
> ## Court to Decide Rights of Retarded in Texas Case
>
> By PHILIP HAGER,
> Times Staff Writer
>
> WASHINGTON—In 1887, California became the first state to enact a law establishing institutions for the "imbecile or feeble-minded." Eventually, all states joined the trend toward segregating what an official report in Vermont described in 1916 as "this blight on mankind."
>
> Since then, widespread reform has dramatically reduced the forced isolation of the mentally retarded—people with learning disorders but not mental illnesses. However, there are still many legal restrictions in the United States that, critics say, unfairly deny the retarded the rights enjoyed by other citizens.
>
> One such restriction is under heavy attack before the U.S. Supreme Court in a case that could extend to the nation's 2 million mentally retarded people the same kinds of constitutional protections that the court has already given minorities and women.
>
> The justices will hear arguments on Tuesday over an attempt by the city of Cleburne, Tex., to use its zoning authority to exclude a home for the mentally retarded from a residential neighborhood. The court will decide the case this summer.
>
> The Cleburne ordinance freely allows apartment houses, fraternities, hospitals and homes for the elderly. But it bars facilities for "the insane or feeble-minded" without special permission—which it denied to a proposed home for 13 mildly and moderately retarded adults.
>
> The case has commanded extraordinary attention, with dozens of advocacy groups for the retarded, several civil liberties organizations and attorneys general from 11 states—including California—all opposing the city's action.
>
> Those attorneys say that a court decision striking down the ordinance might not only ease housing barriers to the retarded but could add impetus to efforts to remove other restrictions. Some states, they said, still authorize compulsory sterilization of the retarded or prohibit them from marrying, and dozens of states restrict the voting rights of the retarded.
>
> "It could have a major impact all over the country," said Paul Hoffman, legal director of the American Civil Liberties Union Foundation of Southern California. "It would enable lawyers to go into federal court to redress restrictions on the mentally retarded of all kinds."
>
> A favorable ruling, the lawyers said, could also carry vast symbolic importance. "This case can mean for retarded people what the (1954 school desegregation) decision meant for society with respect to black people," said Thomas K. Gilhool, chief counsel for the Public Interest Law Center of Philadelphia. "A signal from the court could serve to open many doors that have been closed to the retarded."
>
> On the other side, the city of Cleburne vigorously denies that it is trying to ban the retarded from the community. "That's a completely ridiculous, fabricated claim," said Earl Luna of Dallas, an attorney representing the city.
>
> *(continued)*
>
> *Los Angeles Times*, 18 April 1985.

The city says that it is only exercising its duty to regulate a business—in this case, the privately operated facility for the retarded. Another kind of facility in another area might well have been permitted, the city said, and the retarded, as individuals, are not restricted.

The proposed home, with four bedrooms and two baths, would have been too small for 13 men and women plus two adult supervisors, Luna said. "They all would be going off to jobs or training workshops at 8 o'clock every morning," he said. "Their choice would be to go without bathing or have 13 people trying to take baths in two bathrooms."

The city argues that the home would have been located across the street from a junior high school, increasing congestion in the area. It also points to objections raised by elderly residents and property owners in the neighborhood.

The city has picked up an ally of sorts in the Reagan Administration. Justice Department lawyers, while expressing doubt about the validity of the city's refusal to permit the home, have filed a friend of the court brief urging the justices not to grant the retarded the same kind of special protection the court has previously granted to blacks, women and some other groups.

The Justice Department argues that giving the retarded special protection would make it difficult to deny the same protection to the physically handicapped, the infirm or those suffering such diseases as alcoholism. It also would invite judges to overturn laws that aid particular groups—such as the aged or physically handicapped—if those laws do not make similar provisions for the retarded, the government says.

"In the best of all possible worlds, each of these worthy groups would be amply accommodated," the department's brief said. "But the (legislative) decision to accommodate some now and others later, some here and others there, cannot be allowed to become, as a regular matter, grist for the judicial mill."

Although ordinances such as Cleburne's remain on the books in many places, the retarded have made many gains in recent years. New federal and state laws provide them a wide variety of aid and protection. Discrimination against the handicapped, including the retarded, is barred in federally assisted programs. Numerous groups lobby for the rights of the retarded in Congress and elsewhere.

California, which in 1937 repealed its statute segregating the "feeble minded," is one of 31 states to forbid local zoning policies that could be used unfairly against homes for the retarded. Many states, including California, actively promote "deinstitutionalization"—the transfer of the retarded from remote, warehouse-style institutions to smaller group homes in communities. As a result, the number of retarded in public institutions through the nation declined from 213,000 in 1960 to 119,000 in 1982.

But discrimination against the retarded, based on discredited stereotypes, still exists, according to advocates for the retarded. In Texas alone, they said, 12 other cities still have ordinances similar to the one in Cleburne, and countless other communities in the country have resisted efforts to locate homes in their areas.

The case before the court (City of Cleburne vs. Cleburne Living Center, 84-468) arose in 1980 when a group that operates other homes for the retarded in Texas was denied permission to open a home in Cleburne, a city of about 29,000 near Fort Worth.

Last year, the U.S. 5th Circuit Court of Appeals in New Orleans struck down the ordinance, issuing a sweeping opinion that likened the historic discrimination and segregation of the retarded to that suffered by blacks.

(continued)

It held that the retarded constitute a "quasi-suspect" class—and thus any law that discriminates against them must be subject to heightened scrutiny. The city, the appeals court said, had failed to meet its burden of showing that the ordinance "substantially furthers a significant governmental interest."

Next week's argument will be the case's second before the Supreme Court. The case was first argued on March 18, but Justice Lewis F. Powell Jr. was absent, recovering from prostate surgery. The court, in a rare action, subsequently ordered another argument when Powell would be present, indicating that the eight other justices may be evenly divided on the case.

In the March arguments, Luna denied that Cleburne was discriminating against the retarded. Their needs and capacities differ from the rest of society, he said, and the ordinance was invoked for the well-being of both.

Luna cited concern over whether residents of the proposed home could adequately cope with fires or other emergencies that might arise. "We think the ordinance protected the mentally retarded," he said.

Renea Hicks of Austin, Tex., an attorney representing the operators of the proposed home, ridiculed the city's claim that it was protecting both the retarded and their neighbors.

"This is a classic example of government's historical justification for exclusion of mentally retarded people from many areas of American life," he said. As for the concern for the safety of the retarded in an emergency, they were "quite likely" to be better equipped than most other adults because group homes provide special training for such eventualities, Hicks said.

If the Supreme Court rules in favor of the home, even California—among the trend setters in reducing legal barriers to the retarded—could feel the impact, said Joseph Lawrence, legal director for the Western Law Center for the Handicapped in Los Angeles.

"There is still the notion here and in the rest of the nation that the mentally retarded are dangerous or in some fashion people who present serious problems to the community," he said, "This case could go a long way to reducing those fears."

The significance of attitudes toward handicapped persons cannot therefore be underestimated. When positive attitudes are present in the home, school, and community, equal opportunities for handicapped persons are evident; negative attitudes toward this group result in actions that limit opportunities for success.

ATTITUDES OF KEY PERSONS

While the attitudes of all segments of society toward handicapped individuals are important, the attitudes of members of several groups rank in the critical area. These include individuals who give advice to parents and families of handicapped children; persons who are responsible on a day-to-day basis for the treatment, education, and care of handicapped persons; individuals in charge of programs for the handicapped; the family of handicapped persons; peers; employers; and finally, handicapped persons themselves. The attitudes held by members of these groups are crucial because of the direct role they play in the lives of individuals with disabilities.

Attitudes of Physicians

Parents of preschool children often first seek advice from physicians concerning the atypical development of their children. Also, it is not uncommon for parents or teachers to seek medical advice and consultation when older children are either performing atypically in school or when they do not respond to typical educational interventions (Levine 1982). Frequently, they request the advice of family practice physicians or pediatricians. The attitudes of these physicians are so critical because they are often the first professionals to assist families in adjusting to the presence of a handicapped child and to give advice concerning the future of the child (Harth 1977). Beyond these initial roles, physicians later become involved in diagnosis and treatment of behavior and learning problems, which also require positive attitudes.

The current trend is for physicians to be involved with more than the traditional roles of diagnostic and medical intervention of handicapped children. New roles include (1) making referrals to early intervention programs, (2) assisting in the coordination of the child's programs, (3) parental counseling, (4) collaborating with early intervention programs, and (5) working with other community agencies (Howard 1982). As a result of these expanded roles, the attitudes of physicians toward handicapped children are more critical than ever. Unfortunately, their attitudes have not always been positive. Wolraich (1982) reviewed several studies that revealed negative attitudes of physicians, namely, pediatricians, toward handicapped children. These negative attitudes resulted in recommending institutionalization, when such a move was viewed by others as unnecessary. They also elected not to perform surgery on their own hypothetical child with Down's Syndrome to remove an intestinal blockage. A later study determined that these somewhat negative attitudes were changing positively (Wolraich 1980). In this study, a majority of pediatric practitioners reported that they would do cardiac surgery on children with Down's Syndrome, without any qualifications.

Attitudes may affect the way physicians deal with mildly handicapped children. Therefore, with parents placing so much trust in physicians for advice and diagnosis, physician attitudes must be positive. Otherwise, parents may find themselves following inappropriate advice that they will later regret.

Attitudes of Teachers

Teachers are another group of professionals whose attitudes toward handicapped children are important (McGuire 1973). Teachers are directly responsible for the education and training of school-aged handicapped children, so their attitudes toward these children are critical to the success of this group. Before the current trend of mainstreaming handicapped children into regular classrooms, the attitudes of special education teachers were the only ones meriting attention; regular classroom teachers had little contact with these children. But federal and state legislation placed the burden of educating these children on both regular and special education teachers, calling for a "shared responsibility." Now the attitudes of regular classroom teachers have also become important. In many respects the attitudes held by regular teachers are even more vital than attitudes of special education teachers. This is because special education teachers are involved with handicapped children by choice, whereas regular classroom teachers have become involved due to legal mandates. Many regular classroom teachers, however, resent the presence of handicapped children in their classes and the apparent increased workload caused by this arrangement. When regular classroom teachers have negative attitudes toward mainstreamed handicapped children, the effects of their placement in regular classes may be more detrimental than beneficial. Not only do negative teacher attitudes affect teacher behaviors, but they also affect the attitudes of nonhandicapped children, thereby influencing the acceptance of handicapped children by their nonhandicapped peers. "Teachers can help foster positive and accepting attitudes of nondisabled students toward their disabled peers" (Handlers and Austin 1980, 228). Or by consistently displaying negative attitudes toward handicapped children, teachers can act as negative role models for nonhandicapped students in the classroom (Siperstein and Bak 1980).

Several studies have examined the attitudes held by teachers toward handicapped children. Kennon and Sandoval (1978) studied the attitudes of regular classroom teachers and special education teachers toward educable mentally retarded children. Results indicated that the attitudes of both groups were similar, without major differences between the groups. Other studies have focused on the category of handicapped children that teachers prefer to teach. In most of these studies, when given an opportunity to choose which handicapping category they would most and least like to teach, teachers tended to prefer those with the least debilitating condition; they preferred the more severely disabled groups the least (Kingsley 1967).

Mainstreaming is the current educational practice with mildly handicapped children, so teacher attitudes toward mainstreaming are important. Reynolds, Martin-Reynolds, and Mark (1982) found that elementary teachers had positive attitudes toward mainstreaming mildly mentally retarded children. In another study, Schmelkin (1981) determined that regular classroom teachers and special education teachers possessed similar attitudes toward mainstreaming, without any indication as to the type of child being mainstreamed. T.E.C. Smith (1979) found that principals, regular classroom teachers, and special education teachers were in close agreement concerning which types of handicapped children should be integrated into regular classrooms; the major disagreement was dealing with the borderline and mildly mentally retarded students. Research seems to suggest, therefore, that attitudes toward mainstreaming are generally positive and are shared by regular classroom teachers and special education teachers.

For teachers to understand the importance of attitudes in educating handicapped children, they first need to determine what attitudes they hold toward this group of children. Kroth (1978) suggests three ways teachers can determine their attitudes toward the handicapped: (1) by engaging in values clarification activities, (2) by engaging in values assessment techniques, and (3) by developing their own values assessment techniques. Kroth considers it important for teachers to know their own values because it enables them to be more aware and understanding of parental attitudes, and therefore better able to deal with negative attitudes that parents may have toward their children or the education program. Also, if teachers are aware that they have negative attitudes toward handicapped children, they can more fairly deal with these children than if they deny their negative feelings.

Attitudes of School Administrators

School **administrators** are involved in all aspects of school programs, including the education of handicapped children. Prior to the current mainstreaming movement, however, administrators were not greatly involved in special education programs. With only a few special education teachers and handicapped children in public school programs, and with special education classrooms being isolated and self-contained, administrative tasks related to these programs were minimal. The expansion of programs for handicapped children in public schools, especially for mildly handicapped children, has greatly changed administrative roles as they relate to special education. No longer are there only fifteen mentally retarded students and one special education teacher in a self-contained classroom per school building. Now there may be several resource room teachers, each serving twenty-five to thirty students with one of several disabilities. What compounds the problem is that most of these mildly handicapped students are currently being integrated into regular classrooms, at least a portion of each school day. This means that the education of these children is shared by the entire school staff, so a great deal of cooperation, collaboration, and support is required. School administrators must deal with the inherent problems of these programs. Facilitating planning, cooperation, and the implementation of mandated requirements has become a major responsibility of administrative personnel.

An important element in the support of special education programs is the attitudes of administrators toward handicapped children. Administrators can be either supportive and facilitative or nonsupportive. Attitudes may be related to the directions these administrators take. For example, if school administrators have positive attitudes toward handicapped children and special education programs, these attitudes are conveyed either directly or indirectly to the school staff. If programs are supported by administrators, they are more likely to be supported by staff. On the other hand, if administrators have negative attitudes toward this group of children and programs that serve them, chances for program success are significantly lessened. School administrators convey their attitudes by the amount of support they provide (Powers 1983).

Administrators' actions reflect their attitudes and set the tone for school priorities. For example, a principal could make the following comments to teachers at the beginning of the year: "I am sorry to have to tell you that this year we will all have to be involved in teaching handicapped children. I know that most of you were trained to teach normal children; however, federal laws are now forcing us to place handicapped children in regular classes. Do your best; we must comply. We have no choice." A much more positive approach would be for the administrator to say: "This year we will be involved in providing appropriate educational programs for handicapped children. Some of these children will be in your classes; they should be accepted and you should do everything possible to provide them with appropriate instruction. You are not alone in this endeavor. Our special education staff is here to assist you in any way possible, and I will be fully supportive of your efforts. It must be a collaborative effort. Mainstreaming can work, and we will prove that it can be effective."

Administrators' attitudes are frequently modeled by school personnel (Licata 1975). If school staff perceive positive attitudes from administrators concerning special education programs, they are likely to display similarly positive attitudes. Studies have even shown positive relationships between principals' support for programs and the quality of those programs (Smith, Flexer, and Sigelman 1979; McGuire 1973).

Several studies have been conducted to determine the attitudes of school administrators toward handicapped children. Cline (1981) found that principals in a large metropolitan school district had more positive attitudes toward handicapped children than were previously suggested in other studies, indicating a possible trend toward more positive attitudes. In fact, the principals in Cline's study were more in favor of placing some categories of handicapped children closer to the mainstream than a group of experts in special education.

Another study compared the attitudes of principals toward mentally retarded, learning disabled, and normal children. This investigation revealed that principals have the most positive attitudes toward "normal" children, and the least positive toward mentally retarded children. Although viewed more positively than mentally retarded children, attitudes toward learning disabled children were closer to the mentally retarded group than to the normal group (Smith, Flexer, and Sigelman 1980).

Davis (1980) studied principals' attitudes toward mainstreaming various types of disabled children and found that principals were more in favor of integrating mildly handicapped children (e.g., mild learning disabled, mild speech impaired, mild sensorily impaired, and mild physically disabled) than children with more severe handicaps. However, it is interesting that Davis found principals to rank mainstreaming mildly mentally retarded children only twelfth out of twenty-one disability categories. This group is one of the largest currently being served in public schools, and also one of the largest groups of handicapped children being mainstreamed, so these findings should cause concern. Principals need to support mainstreaming this group if their integration is to be successful.

Attitudes of Parents

In most children's lives, parents are the most significant persons. Acceptance by parents is vitally important for children, including those who are mildly handicapped. Problems often arise because parents and potential parents want the "perfect" child, or at least a child that fits society's expectations of normalcy. Parental desires for this type of child only reflect the value our society places on physical and intellectual fitness (Cleland and Swartz 1982).

Parents often react with shock to the birth of a handicapped child or the awareness that a school-aged child is handicapped. Parental adjustment to this shock depends on several factors, including the severity of the handicap, marital status of the parents, religion of the parents, age of the parents, age of the child, and prognosis for the child (Cleland and Swartz 1982). Although there is a usual pattern of reaction, each family will react somewhat differently, depending on its unique characteristics. The important parental reaction for the handicapped child is final acceptance. Before children with disabilities can lead "normalized" lives, they must be accepted at home. For some parents, this is extremely difficult. Formerly athletic fathers who want their sons to follow them with athletic prowess may have an extremely hard time accepting a child with physical disabilities. For mothers who always had a dream of a child who would achieve high academic goals, the problems faced by children with academic deficits may be traumatic.

One variable affecting final acceptance is the parents' attitudes toward the disabled child. These attitudes are reflected in many areas and are extremely influential on the child. Harth (1977) cited several studies that indicated the magnitude of the importance of parental attitudes toward their mentally retarded children. Areas found to be related to parental attitudes include:

- speed of institutionalization,
- reading achievement level,
- child-rearing practices, and
- acceptance of the child.

The attitudes of parents of learning disabled children have also been shown to be related to parental behavior. In a study that compared the attitudes of parents of learning disabled children with parents of children without learning problems, Wetter (1972) found that the parents of learning disabled children had distinctive attitudes, which included (1) overindulgence, (2) rejection of their children, and (3) disagreement in the assessment of the child's overall adjustment. Another study that compared mothers of

Mildly handicapped children need support, acceptance, and encouragement from parents.

learning disabled and nondisabled children indicated that the mothers of the learning disabled group described their children as having "fewer academic strengths, exhibiting fewer behaviors likely to facilitate academic and perhaps social achievement, and being less skilled than classmates in both academic and behavioral domains" (Bryan et al. 1982, 157). In summing up the attitudes of parents toward their learning disabled children, Bryan and Bryan (1975) stated that parents often use such terms as obstinate, sassy, bossy, stubborn, and negativistic. These terms suggest negative attitudes.

When parents have these negative attitudes toward their disabled children, negative parental behavior is often manifested. Mildly handicapped children need support,

Table 10-2 **Negative Parental Attitudes and Consequences**

Negative Attitude	Results
Toward Learning	
Covert parental disregard for school authority	Parent blames school for child's learning problems
Denial of seriousness of the learning problem	Parent abdicates and leaves the child to drift
Toward the Child	
Believe child is intellectually limited	Parents' insistence despite proof to the contrary may create a block to adequate performances
Disinterest in child's achievement	Parents resist involvement in intervention program or parents are involved in treatment and fear improvement in child's problems will lead child away from needing the parents
Subculture does not expect academic success until puberty	This conflicts with majority culture that expects achievement throughout development
Subculture places extreme emphasis on academic success	Increased pressure on child could lead to rebellion

Source: Klein et al. 1981.

acceptance, and encouragement. Often, negative parental attitudes prohibit these actions.

Parental attitudes toward educational programs for their children are probably most important to educators. Several negative parental attitudes have been identified as they relate to learning and behavior problems in school. These problems fall into two categories: attitudes toward learning and attitudes toward the child. Table 10-2 describes these negative attitudes and their consequences.

As has been stated, the current educational trend for mildly handicapped children follows the normalization philosophy. Integrating handicapped children into regular classrooms is intended to create as normal a learning environment as the child can successfully tolerate. One study specifically assessed parental attitudes toward normalization activities. The sample of 250 parents of mentally retarded children were surveyed to determine their attitudes toward normalization in general, and specific normalization activities that affected their child. Results indicated that the parents had generally positive attitudes toward the normalization concept, but often opposed normalizing activities involving their own child. A conclusion drawn from the study was that "implementation of legislative and judicial policies mandating normalization will encounter resistance at the 'grass roots' level" and "although supportive of the construct, parents, particularly those most likely to be immediately affected, do not endorse its application to their child" (Ferrara 1979, 150). Another study investigating the acceptance of normalization found that parents of older mentally retarded children were least likely to accept the normalization concept (Suelzle and Keenan 1981). The main reason for rejecting normalization activities for their own child is probably overprotection. Parents are often concerned that normalizing activities leave their child open to abuse and ridicule. If parents are to support normalization activities such as mainstreaming, their attitudes must change. Otherwise, they may be barriers to the successful implementation of normalization activities.

The attitudes of parents of handicapped children must be considered when planning and implementing programs. This is a major reason why parents should be involved in individual educational program planning. Regardless of the legal mandate for parental involvement, knowing and understanding parental attitudes is a more important reason for involvement. If negative attitudes prevail, school personnel should attempt to change them because positive parental attitudes are important for the success of educational programs.

Attitudes of Peers

The attitudes of nonhandicapped peers is an important variable in the successful integration of mildly handicapped children into regular classes and mildly handicapped adults into communities. All children need to feel accepted, not only by adults but also by their peers. For some children, acceptance by peers is even more important than acceptance by adults. The significant amount of time that many mildly handicapped children spend in regular classrooms with nonhandicapped peers makes the attitudes of these peers more essential than ever. Simply integrating mildly handicapped children into regular classrooms does not ensure their acceptance by nonhandicapped students, however (Siperstein and Bak 1980). "Special educators must recognize the significance of earning the support and acceptance of these nonhandicapped students if placements in the least restrictive environment are to be successful" (Frith and Mitchell 1981, 82).

Unfortunately, much of the research on acceptance of handicapped students by their nonhandicapped peers is not encouraging. Corman and Gottlieb (1978) reviewed the literature on the perceptions of other students toward children classified as educable mentally retarded. They summarized their review by saying that (1) EMR students are less accepted than nonretarded students, and (2) EMR students integrated into regular classrooms are not accepted more than those segregated in self-contained rooms.

Another review of the literature on attitudes of nonhandicapped students toward the mentally retarded revealed the following:

- Younger mentally retarded students were more satisfied with placement in special education classes than were older students
- Interaction between nonhandicapped and mentally retarded students did not generally improve acceptance, and acceptance was improved with less contact
- Nonhandicapped females were more accepting of mentally retarded children than were nonhandicapped males (Frith and Mitchell 1981).

Studies investigating the attitudes of nonhandicapped children toward their learning disabled peers are similarly negative. Bryan (1974) used a sociometric scale with sixty-two nonhandicapped children in the third, fourth, and fifth grades. Results indicated that learning disabled children, when compared to nonhandicapped children matched by sex and race, were rejected significantly more often. Other research concurs with this finding (Bryan and Bryan 1978).

The attitudes of nonhandicapped students must be changed to maximize the assimilation of handicapped students into regular classrooms. Methods of changing student attitudes toward the handicapped will be presented in another section of this chapter.

Attitudes of Employers

While not as critical to school-aged handicapped children, the attitudes of employers are a major concern for handicapped adults. If individuals with mild handicaps are to be successful as adults, they must have equal employment opportunities. When employers have negative attitudes toward handicapped individuals, they limit the vocational opportunities for this group. Even though federal and state statutes prohibit discrimination of handicapped workers, negative employer attitudes can still prohibit vocational success of handicapped workers. It is very difficult to prove discrimination; therefore, employers with negative attitudes are still a concern, regardless of legislated anti-discrimination policies.

In a study by T.E.C. Smith (1981), potential employer concerns with hiring mentally retarded persons were determined through interviews and mail questionnaires. Results of this study indicated that while potential employers view many jobs as appropriate for mentally retarded individuals, certain prerequisite job-seeking skills must be present to acquire these jobs. One skill considered important was being able to complete a job application. The unfortunate conclusion that can be drawn is that the capability of mentally retarded individuals to perform a job might be overshadowed by their inability to do such a mundane task as completing a job application. This may reflect a bias of employers against handicapped employees and therefore result in unequal employment opportunities.

Mildly Handicapped Self-Attitudes

Up to this point, the discussion has focused on the attitudes of nonhandicapped persons toward the handicapped. Obviously, attitudes of several groups are important if handicapped individuals are to be assimilated into society and given an equal opportunity to be successful both during and after school years. In addition to the attitudes of others, the attitudes handicapped individuals hold toward *themselves* is critical. What individuals think about themselves will undoubtedly affect their success in school, employment, and life. The old adage, "If you do not think you can do it you probably cannot," is ever so true when considering **self-attitudes** of handicapped persons. Mildly handicapped people who have positive self-attitudes or self-concepts have a much better chance of achieving success than those with negative self-attitudes.

Not only is **self-concept** important in academic performance, but it is also related to socialization. Several behaviors are necessary in the socialization process, including the emergence of self-identity and self-concept (Fewell 1982). Inadequate self-concepts in handicapped children will hamper them in relationships with other people. Still another area affected by the self-concept of handicapped persons is employment. Poor self-concepts often become a personal barrier to obtaining jobs (Cleland and Swartz 1982). Handicapped persons' negative self-concepts, therefore, may be related to academic performance, socialization, and vocational success.

Many studies have found that the handicapped have lower self-concepts than the nonhandicapped. In the area of mental retardation, most studies, though inconclusive, suggest that mentally retarded individuals exhibit inferior self-concepts (Patton and Payne 1982). One such study examined the self-concepts of children with low, average, and high intelligence. Results revealed that children with low intelligence had the most negative self-concepts of the three groups (Ringness 1961).

Learning disabled children also appear to have poor self-concepts. Cullinan, Epstein, and Lloyd (1981) studied learning disabled and nondisabled students using teachers' ratings on the Behavior Problem Checklist. The findings indicated that one of the areas accounting for major social-emotional differences between the two groups was in the Personality Problem dimension, which includes self-consciousness, feelings of in-

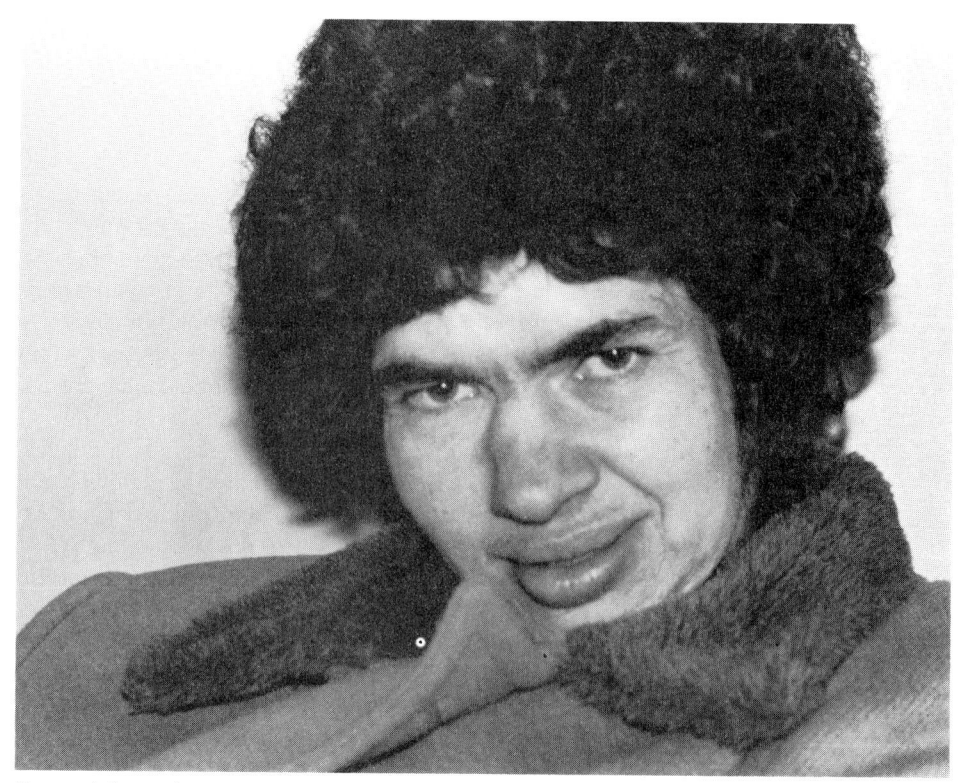

Research has indicated that handicapped individuals often have lower self esteem than nonhandicapped persons.

feriority, and lack of self-confidence. A conclusion drawn from the study was that intervention programs must deal with areas within the Personality Problem dimension, regardless of the cause of any behavior problem.

Other studies have examined the self-concepts of mildly handicapped students in various educational settings. Since mainstreaming these children into regular classrooms is the current educational focus, the hope is that the self-concepts of integrated handicapped children would be more positive than the self-concepts of those remaining in self-contained classrooms. Unfortunately, research suggests that integrated educational placements do not necessarily increase self-concepts among these children. In reviewing research on the topic, Gottlieb (1981) summarized that some studies have shown no differences in self-concepts of mainstreamed versus special class children. The only consistent finding reported by Gottlieb is that children who are mainstreamed and segregated only a portion of the school day have more positive self-concepts than those segregated all day.

CHANGING ATTITUDES

Attitudes toward handicapped children and adults are critical to the success of these individuals in schools and communities. Unfortunately, the attitudes of significant individuals—physicians, teachers, administrators, parents, peers, and employers—are not

Programs such as Special Olympics help the handicapped to improve their attitudes toward themselves.

always positive. The manifestation of these negative attitudes may lead to poor advice from physicians, unequal treatment from teachers and administrators, rejection from parents and peers, and discrimination by employers.

The attitudes of teachers and administrators toward handicapped children must be positive for integration to be successful. Prior to the current trend of mainstreaming, special education teacher attitudes were the most critical. As a result of mainstreaming, however, the need for positive attitudes toward this group of children and the mainstreaming concept is now shared among all school personnel. Regular classroom teachers must be provided with training opportunities for developing positive attitudes (Powers 1983). And, attitudinal change for school administrators must be a high priority because they often play the key role in successful mainstreaming. Attitudes are stable, but they are learned and can be changed. Change attempts must therefore be made when school personnel have negative attitudes toward handicapped children.

Assessment of Attitudes

Prior to changing attitudes, the attitudes currently held by various individuals and groups must be assessed. Without assessment, there is no way of determining which attitudes need to be changed and which ones strengthened. Knowing attitudes also helps in developing attitude-change programs. Attitude assessment is therefore a first step in initiating attitude change.

Anastasi (1969) pointed out several problems in assessing attitudes, including:

- the relationship between verbally expressed opinions and "real" attitudes;
- the relationship between observed behavior and attitudes;
- the similarity between publicly expressed and privately expressed attitudes;
- questions that avoid ambiguity, suggested responses, and other errors; and
- adequate sampling to ensure representativeness.

Although attitude assessment has many inherent problems, the number of attempts to determine attitudes has been endless. Two basic types of attitude scales are most often used: the Thurstone-type scale, which uses judges to predetermine the categorization of opinions on the ideas being investigated; and the Likert-type scales, which require subjects to indicate along a continuum their degree of agreement or disagreement with various statements (Anastasi 1969). In addition to these two major approaches, many researchers have used other means to determine attitudes, including semantic-differential scales, simulation, and observations.

Rather than looking at attitude assessment as a simple construct, Podemski and Marsh (1981) viewed the assessment of attitudes toward handicapped individuals from a systems approach. While their model was proposed to assess attitudes toward the learning disabled, its rationale also applies to assessing attitudes toward the broader mildly handicapped category.

A systems approach was suggested because of the complexities involved in assessing attitudes toward handicapped children, and the effects of attitudes on the education of these children. In order to comprehensively assess attitudes toward the handicapped, a three-level organization was provided. This organization addressed the attitudes of many more individuals than simply those who directly teach mildly handicapped children. Level I involves the total community, including the board of education. It is at this level that district policies and priorities are established. Without support at this level, more direct individual efforts may go unsupported and may even be thwarted. Level II focuses on the administrative levels within the school district, including central administration, building administration, and special education program administration. Finally, Level III deals with the student's immediate environment. This level includes handicapped and nonhandicapped peers, special education teachers, and regular classroom teachers. This is the level where actions most directly affect handicapped children. Table 10-3 depicts the relationships among the three levels, while table 10-4 describes the functions of each level and their implications.

Techniques to Change Attitudes

There have been many attempts to effect changes in attitudes of individuals toward handicapped children. Donaldson categorized the methods for changing attitudes into six major groups:

- Direct or indirect (media) contact with or without exposure to disabled persons
- Information about disabilities
- Persuasive messages
- Analysis of the dynamics of prejudice
- Disability simulation
- Group discussion (Donaldson 1980, 505)

The following describes attempts to change attitudes using some of these techniques.

Table 10-3

SPECIAL EDUCATION SYSTEMS FRAMEWORK

Level I System Goals

Parents 1.3 → Board of Education 1.1 ← Citizens 1.2

Parents of Handicapped Children 1.4

Level II Organizational Structure

Central Office Administrators 2.1

Special Education Administrators 2.3

Building Administrators 2.2

Level III Student Environment

Learning Disabled Students 3.1 ↔ Nonhandicapped Students 3.2

Learning Disability Specialists 3.4 ↔ Regular Ed. Teachers 3.3

3.0

2.0

1.0

Reprinted, by permission, from Podemski and Marsh, 1981, 219.

Contact. Esposito and Peach (1983) studied the effects of direct, structured contact with severely handicapped children on the attitudes of nonhandicapped preschool children. Following pretesting of attitudes, the handicapped and nonhandicapped children were integrated for one hour per week over a thirty-week period. Results indicated a significant positive change between pre-and post-testing. The conclusion drawn by the authors was that attitudes of young children toward handicapped persons can be changed positively "as a result of direct contact with peers having considerable and observable disabilities" (Esposito and Peach 1983, 362).

Another study investigated the effects of contact and discussion on the attitudes of nonhandicapped children toward handicapped individuals. In this study, seventy-four

Table 10-4 **Individual's Roles in a Systems Framework**

Level	Key Individuals	Role	Consequences
LEVEL I System Goals	Parents, citizens, and members of the board of education	Set policy, authorizes district special education plan; allocates finances; sets priorities.	Negative attitudes result in a nonprogressive plan that meets minimal requirements. Limited funds are authorized; special education program has low priority.
LEVEL II Organizational Structure	School administration, including central office administration, building administration, and special education program administration	Creates the environment for teaching and learning. Provides leadership for implementing district plan for special education. Distributes financial resources.	Negative attitudes can create morale problems, encourage negative teacher attitudes, limit necessary financial resources.
LEVEL III Student Environment	Handicapped and nonhandicapped peers, special education and regular classroom teachers	Most direct influence of attitudes on handicapped children. Affects student-teacher relationships, special education-regular education teacher collaboration, peer acceptance, and self-concepts.	Negative attitudes can result in poor self-concepts, peer and teacher rejections, special teacher and regular education teacher conflicts.

Source: Podemski and Marsh 1981.

nonhandicapped elementary school children participated in two, 2-1/2 hour sessions aimed at changing their attitudes toward handicapped persons. The sessions included activities that were designed to (1) enable the subjects to experience various handicaps, (2) provide opportunities for discussion following experiential activities, and (3) enable subjects to understand their perceptions of handicapped individuals. Results indicated that short-term treatment can have a positive effect on the attitudes of young nonhandicapped children toward handicapped persons (Jones et al. 1981).

Discussions. In addition to contact, discussions concerning handicapped students have been the focus of research into attitudinal changes among nonhandicapped children toward their handicapped peers. Gottlieb (1980) investigated the effects of a five- to ten-minute discussion on attitudes toward handicapped children following the viewing of a two-minute videotape of a mentally retarded boy. Results indicated that the discussion had a significantly positive impact on the children who had previously expressed negative attitudes toward the handicapped. Gottlieb viewed the results as important because they indicated that "it is possible to improve the attitudes of nonhandicapped children toward retarded children so as to put the former in a positive mind set prior to the introduction of retarded children into their classes" (Gottlieb 1980, 110). Therefore, discussion before the entry of handicapped children into regular classrooms could improve peer attitudes and possibly reduce peer rejection.

Combination of Techniques. Rather than using a single attitudinal change technique, some studies have investigated the effects of a combination of several change techniques

Group discussions can improve peer attitudes prior to the introduction of the handicapped child into the classroom.

on attitudes of nonhandicapped children toward their handicapped peers. One such study used five activities: (1) discussion of terminology, laws, and problems, (2) student research on disabilities, (3) discussion following a film about handicapped individuals, (4) simulation activities, and (5) direct contact with handicapped persons. Results indicated that 82 percent of the twenty secondary students in the study felt that their attitudes had changed toward the positive as a result of the activities (Handlers and Austin 1980).

While the above studies reveal positive effects from attitudinal change efforts, some studies have resulted in no change. No positive changes in attitudes of elementary nonhandicapped children occurred following a six-week course designed to change attitudes, which included lessons on the handicapped, fictional stories about handicapped children, and simulation activities (Miller, Armstrong, and Hagan 1981). Therefore, attempts to change the attitudes of nonhandicaped children toward their handicapped peers may or may not produce the desired results. The success that has been reported, however, provides evidence to support continued change efforts and research to determine the best way to effect attitude changes.

Changing Teachers' Attitudes. In addition to changing the attitudes of children toward their handicapped peers, other efforts have been made to change the attitudes of teachers. As previously stated, the attitudes of teachers and administrators are extremely important, and some studies have indicated that these two groups do not always have positive attitudes. Therefore, attempts to change attitudes need to focus on professionals as well as school-aged peers. Using methods similar to those used with attitudinal change efforts with children, studies have found that providing information through inservice training workshops (McDaniel 1982) and intensive training over a long period of time (Larrivee 1981) result in positive attitude change among teachers.

Since teacher attitudes toward handicapped children are so important, and since inservice training of teachers to improve attitudes is not available for all teachers, attempts at the preservice level to change attitudes of prospective teachers are needed. In order to focus on teachers at this level, teacher trainers must be the target of attitude change efforts. The Office of Special Education has supported these change attempts through funding Dean's Grants. These projects have attempted to revamp college training programs to better prepare teachers to deal with mainstreamed handicapped children. The Dean's Grant at West Virginia University included a focus on attitude change. Following treatment that included workshops on sensitivity, development of library materials, and technical assistance for course modifications, the attitudes of teacher trainers were significantly positively changed (Lombardi, Meadowcroft, and Strasburger 1982).

As a result of some research concluding that attitudes toward handicapped children can be changed, several schools have developed and implemented programs focusing on changing attitudes of school children toward the handicapped. These programs often include information, simulations, and direct contact experiences. In one such program, developed in the St. Charles public schools in Missouri, a committee composed of representatives from nine elementary schools in the district developed a child-awareness program. A manual was developed that included lists of guest speakers, lesson plans for activities, audiovisual materials, and suggested simulations (Dewar 1982). Popp (1983) described another program that included activities for children in grades K-12 as well as modifications to make these lessons appropriate for older children.

Activities focusing on changing attitudes of nonhandicapped children and teachers toward the handicapped do not have to be elaborate, expensive, or time-consuming. Research previously cited has indicated that attitudes can be changed. The major ingredients in developing an attitude-change program are the understanding of why attitudes need to be positive and the initiative to implement change strategies. Negative attitudes should not be considered a valid excuse for the failure of school programs for handicapped children. Negative attitudes only convey the need for change efforts.

SUMMARY

This chapter has focused on attitudes. The first part of the chapter attempted to define *attitudes*, even though the term is difficult to define. The majority of definitions seem to indicate that attitudes are feelings, beliefs, or predispositions that affect behavior. They are learned, relatively enduring, but can be changed. The attitudes individuals have toward the handicapped are very important because they affect behavior toward the handicapped.

Several variables are related to attitudes toward the handicapped. These include the amount of contact with handicapped persons, knowledge about the handicapped, age, sex, and ethnic background. While some studies suggest a relationship among these variables and attitudes toward the handicapped, other studies have found no relationship. This only adds to the confusion of what attitudes are and how they are developed.

Another major section of the chapter dealt with how attitudes affect handicapped people, and the attitudes certain groups have toward the handicapped. The effects of attitudes on handicapped children and adults cannot be underestimated. Mainstreaming handicapped children into the classroom of a teacher who has negative attitudes toward the handicapped may create serious problems for the child. Likewise, employers who have negative attitudes toward handicapped adults will likely discriminate against handicapped individuals who apply for jobs.

Attitudes of certain groups of individuals are critical. These include teachers—both special education teachers and regular classroom teachers—school administrators, physicians, peers, parents, employers, and handicapped persons themselves. Although the attitudes of all people are important, individuals in these professions and roles have direct contact with handicapped children and adults; their attitudes are very important.

The final section of the chapter focused on changing attitudes. Since the attitudes of certain people are so important, and since research has shown that often these individuals have negative attitudes toward the handicapped, change efforts must be made to produce positive attitudes. Some of the successful change efforts include providing information, facilitating contact between handicapped and nonhandicapped individuals, discussing handicapped people, simulations, and a combination of all these efforts. Although not always successful, these efforts have proven effective in some cases. As a result, continued efforts to change attitudes toward the positive must be made, and research must continue on attitude change to determine better methods of effecting positive attitudes toward persons with disabilities.

REFERENCES

Anastasi, A. *Psychological testing.* New York: Macmillan, 1969.
Brooks, B.L., and L.A. Bransford. Modifications of teachers' attitudes toward exceptional children. *Exceptional Children* 38 (1971):259–60.
Bryan, T. Peer popularity of learning disabled children. *Journal of Learning Disabilities* 7 (1974):261–68.
Bryan, T., and J. Bryan. *Understanding learning disabilities.* Port Washington, N.Y.: Alfred Publishing Company, 1975.
Bryan, T.H. and J.H. Bryan. *Understanding learning disabilities.* 2nd ed. Sherman Oaks, Calif.: Alfred Publishers, 1978.
Bryan, T., R. Pearl, D. Zimmerman, and F. Matthews. Mothers' evaluations of their learning disabled children. *The Journal of Special Education* 16, no. 2 (1982):149–59.
Cleland, C.C., and J.D. Swartz. *Exceptionalities through the lifespan.* New York: Macmillan, 1982.
Cline, R. Principals' attitudes and knowledge about handicapped children. *Exceptional Children* 48, no. 2 (1981):172–74.
Conine, T.A. Acceptance or rejection of disabled persons by teachers. *The Journal of School Health* 39 (1969):278–81.
Corman, L., and J. Gottlieb. Mainstreaming mentally retarded children: A review of research. In *International review of research in mental retardation*, edited by N. R. Ellis. New York: Academic Press, 1978.
Cullinan, D., M.H. Epstein, and J. Lloyd. School behavior problems of learning disabled and normal girls and boys. *Learning Disabilities Quarterly* 4, no. 2 (1981):163–69.
Davis, W.E. Public school principals' attitudes toward mainstreaming retarded pupils. *Education and Training of the Mentally Retarded* 15, no. 3 (1980):174–78.
Dewar, R.L. Peer acceptance of handicapped students. *Teaching Exceptional Children* 14, no. 5 (1982):188–93.
Donaldson, J. Changing attitudes toward handicapped persons: A review and analysis of research. *Exceptional Children* 46, no. 7 (1980):504–14.

Esposito, B.G., and W.J. Peach. Changing attitudes of preschool children toward handicapped persons. *Exceptional Children* 49, no. 4 (1983):361–63.

Ferrara, D.M. Attitudes of parents of mentally retarded children toward normalization activities. *American Journal of Mental Deficiency* 84, no. 2 (1979):145–51.

Fewell, R.R. The early years. In *Exceptional children and youth*, edited by N. G. Haring. Columbus, Ohio: Charles E. Merrill, 1982.

Foster, G.G., and J. Salvia. Teacher response to label of learning disabled as a function of demand characteristics. *Exceptional Children* 43, no. 8 (1977):533–34.

Foster, G. G., J. E., Ysseldyke, & J. H. Reese, I wouldn't have seen it if I hadn't believed it. *Exceptional Children* 47, no. 7 (1975):469–73.

Frith, G.H., and J.W. Mitchell. The attitudes of nonhandicapped students toward the mildly retarded: A consideration in placement decisions. *Education and Training of the Mentally Retarded* 16, no.1(1981):79–83.

Good, T.L. How teachers' expectations affect results. *American Education* (1982):25–32.

Gottlieb, J. Improving attitudes toward retarded children by using group discussion. *Exceptional Children* 47, no. 2 (1980):106–111.

———. Mainstreaming: Fulfilling the promise? *American Journal on Mental Deficiency* 86, no. 2 (1981):115–26.

Gottlieb, J., and L. Corman. Public attitudes toward mentally retarded children. *American Journal on Mental Deficiency* 80 (1975):72–80.

Handlers, A., and K. Austin. Improving attitudes of high school students toward their handicapped peers. *Exceptional Children* 47, no. 3 (1980):228–29.

Haring, N.G. Introduction. In *Exceptional children and youth*, edited by N.G. Haring. Columbus, Ohio: Charles E. Merrill, 1982.

Harth, R. Attitudes and mental retardation: Review of the literature. In *Mental retardation: Social and educational perspectives*, edited by C.J. Drew, M.L. Hardman, and H.P. Bluhm. St. Louis: C.V. Mosby, 1977.

Higgs, R.W. Attitude formation—Contact or information? *Exceptional Children* 41, no. 7 (1975): 496–97.

Howard, J. The role of the pediatrician with young exceptional children and their families. *Exceptional Children* 48, no. 4 (1982):316–22.

Jones, T.W., V.M. Sowell, J.K. Jones, and L.G. Butler. Changing children's perceptions of handicapped people. *Exceptional Children* 47, no. 5 (1981):365–68.

Kavale, K., and C. Rossi. Regular class teachers' attitudes and perceptions of the resource specialist program for educable mentally retarded pupils. *Education and Training of the Mentally Retarded* 15, no. 3 (1980):195–98.

Kennon, A.F., and J. Sandoval. Teacher attitudes toward the educable mentally retarded. *Education and Training of the Mentally Retarded* 13, no. 2 (1978):139–45.

Kingsley, R.F. Prevailing attitudes toward exceptional children. *Education* 87, (1967):426–30.

Klein, R.S., S.D. Altman, K. Dreizen, R. Friedman, and L. Powers. Restructuring dysfunctional parental attitudes toward childrens' learning and behavior in school: Family-oriented psychoeducational therapy; Part II. *Journal of Learning Disabilities* 14, no. 2 (1981): 99–101.

Kroth, R. Parents—Powerful and necessary allies. *Teaching Exceptional Children* 10, no. 3 (1978):88–90.

Larrivee, B. Effect of inservice training intensity on teachers' attitudes toward mainstreaming. *Exceptional Children* 48, no. 1 (1981):34–39.

Lemon, N. *Attitudes and their measurement*. London: B.T. Batsford, LTD, 1973.

Levine, M.D. The child with school problems: An analysis of physician participation. *Exceptional Children* 48, no. 4 (1982):296–304.

Licata, W.W. Is the principal an effective change agent? *National Association of Secondary School Principals Bulletin* 59 (1975):75–81.

Lombardi, T.P., P. Meadowcroft, and R. Strasburger. Modifying teacher trainers' attitudes toward mainstreaming. *Exceptional Children* 48, no. 6 (1982):544–45.

Lovitt, E.T. Teacher acceptance of classroom integration of children with learning disabilities. *Dissertation Abstracts* 34, no. 8A (1974):4930–31.

McDaniel, L. Changing vocational teachers' attitudes toward the handicapped. *Exceptional Children* 48, no. 4 (1982):377–78.

McGrath, J.E. *Social psychology: A brief introduction.* New York: Holt, 1964.

McGuire, D.J. An analytical survey of the attitudes of school administrators and teachers of educable mentally retarded children and the quality of education programs provided for educable mentally retarded children within selected school districts in New York State. *Dissertation Abstracts* 34, no. 5A (1973):2226–27.

Miller, M., S. Armstrong, and M. Hagan. Effects of teaching on elementary students' attitudes toward handicaps. *Education and Training of the Mentally Retarded* 16, no. 2 (1981):110–113.

Newman, K.S. Administrative tasks in special education. *Exceptional Children* 36 (1970):521–24.

Osgood, C.E., G.J. Suci, and P.H. Tannenbaum. *The measurement of meaning.* Urbana, Ill.: University of Illinois Press, 1957.

Patton, J.M., and J.S. Payne. Mild mental retardation. In *Exceptional children and youth*, edited by N.G. Haring. Columbus, Ohio: Charles E. Merrill, 1982.

Podemski, R.S., and G.E. Marsh II. A systems framework for assessing attitudes toward the learning disabled. *Learning Disabilities Quarterly* 4, no. 2 (1981):217–23.

Popp, R.A. Learning about disabilities. *Teaching Exceptional Children* 15, no. 2 (1983):78–81.

Powers, D.A. Mainstreaming and the inservice education of teachers. *Exceptional Children* 49, no. 5 (1983):432–39.

Proctor, D.I. An investigation of the relationship between knowledge of exceptional children, kind and amount of experience, and attitudes toward their classroom integration. *Dissertation Abstracts* 28 (1967):1721-A.

Reynolds, B.J., J. Martin–Reynolds, and F.D. Mark. Elementary teachers' attitudes toward mainstreaming educable mentally retarded students. *Education and Training of the Mentally Retarded* 17, no. 3 (1982):171–76.

Ringness, T.A. Self concept of children with low, average, and high intelligence. *American Journal of Mental Deficiency* 65 (1961):453–61.

Rokeach, M. *Beliefs, attitudes, and values.* San Francisco: Jossey–Bass, 1968.

Schloss, P., and S.R. Miller. Effects of the label "institutionalized" vs. "regular school student" on teacher expectations. *Exceptional Children* 48, no. 4 (1982):363–64.

Schmelkin, L.P. Teachers' and nonteachers' attitudes toward mainstreaming. *Exceptional Children* 48 (1981):42–47.

Sherif, M., and C.W. Sherif. *An outline of social psychology.* New York: Harper & Row, 1956.

Siperstein, G.N., and J.J. Bak. Students' and teachers' perceptions of the mentally retarded child. In *Educating mentally retarded persons in the mainstream*, edited by J. Gottlieb. Baltimore: University Park Press, 1980.

Smith, R.M., J.T. Neisworth, and F.M. Hunt. *The exceptional child: A functional approach.* New York: McGraw-Hill, 1983.

Smith, T.E.C. Attitudes of principals and teachers toward mainstreaming handicapped children. *The Journal for Special Educators* 16, no. 1 (1979):89–95.

———. Employer concerns in hiring mentally retarded persons. *Rehabilitation Counseling Bulletin* 24, no. 4 (1981):316–18.

Smith, T.E.C., R.W. Flexer, and C.K. Sigelman. The role of principals in work–study programs for the handicapped. *Education and Training of the Mentally Retarded* 14, no. 4 (1979):247–50.

———. Principals' attitudes toward the learning disabled, mentally retarded, and work–study programs. *Journal of Learning Disabilities* 13, no. 2 (1980):62–64.

Strauch, J.D. Social contact as a variable in the expressed attitudes of normal adolescents toward EMR pupils. *Exceptional Children* 36 (1970):495–500.

Suelzle, M., and V. Keenan. Changes in family support networks over the life cycle of mentally retarded persons. *American Journal of Mental Deficiency* 86, no. 3 (1981):267–74.

Voeltz, L.M. Children's attitudes toward handicapped peers. *American Journal of Mental Deficiency* 84, no. 5 (1980):455–64.

Wetter, J. Parent attitudes toward learning disability. *Exceptional Children* 38, no. 6 (1972): 490–91.

Wolraich, M.L. Pediatric practitioners' knowledge of developmental disabilities. *Journal of Developmental and Behavioral Pediatrics* 1 (1980):147–51.

———. Communication between physicians and parents of handicapped children. *Exceptional Children* 48, no. 4 (1982):324–29.

Ysseldyke, J.E., and G.G. Foster. Bias in teachers' observations of emotionally disturbed and learning disabled children. *Exceptional Children* 44, no. 8 (1978):613–15.

Chapter Eleven

THE FAMILY AND THE MILDLY HANDICAPPED STUDENT

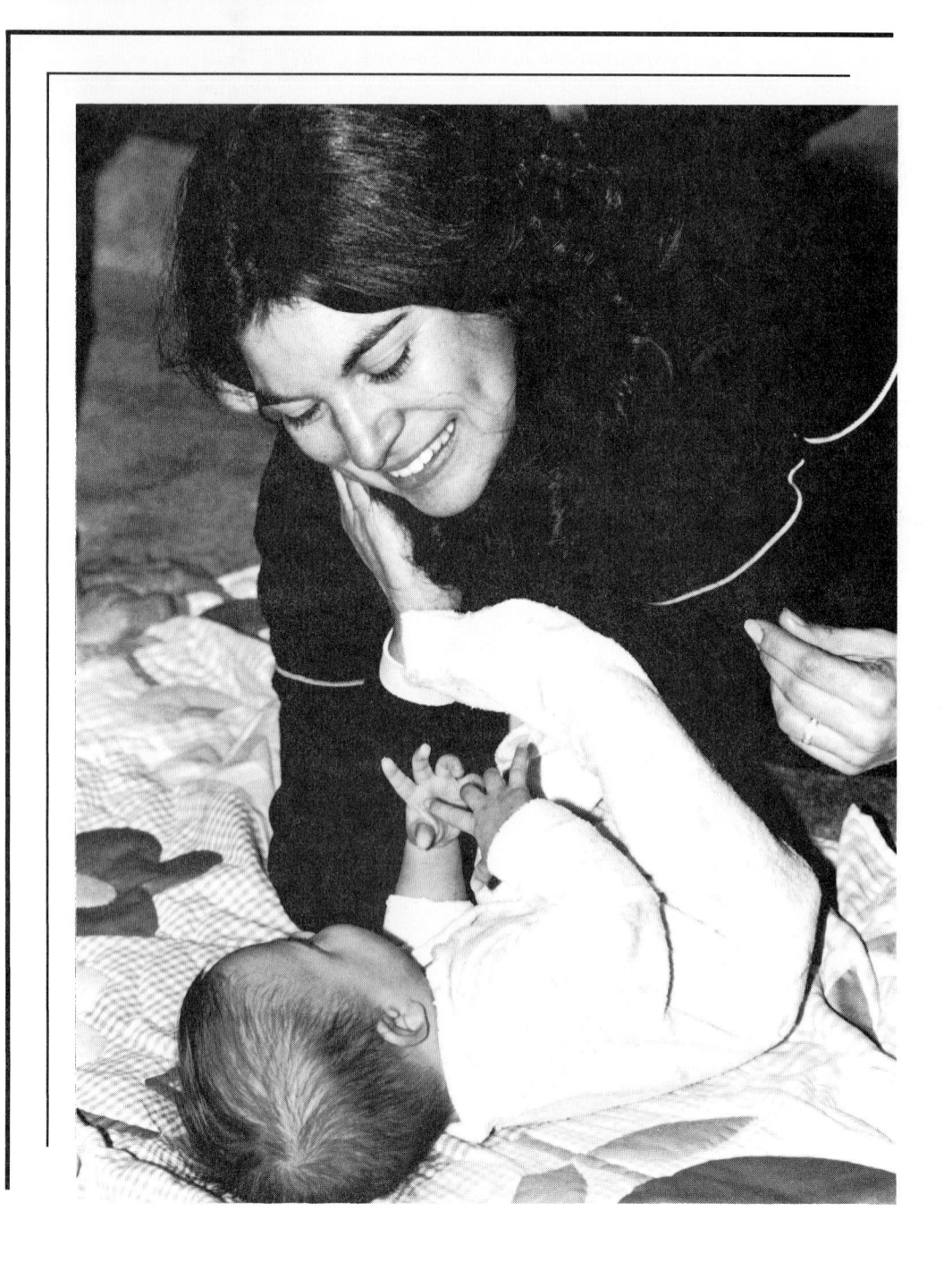

CHAPTER OUTLINE

INTRODUCTION
ORGANIZATIONAL PATTERNS OF FAMILIES
    Formation of Family: Its Life Cycle
PURPOSES OF THE FAMILY
    The Possible Effects of a Handicapped Child on Family Purposes
FAMILY REACTIONS
    Typical Reactions
SIBLINGS
RELATIONSHIP BETWEEN FAMILIES AND SCHOOL PERSONNEL
    Collaboration between Parents and School
    Primary Procedural Safeguards
    Role of School Personnel
SUMMARY

CHAPTER OBJECTIVES

After reading this chapter, you should be able to:
- Define family;
- Define extended family;
- Describe the life cycle of a family;
- List the purposes of the family;
- Discuss the effects of a handicapped child on the family;
- Describe the relationship between families of handicapped children and school personnel; and
- List the typical stages of parental reaction to a handicapped child.

INTRODUCTION

A family is "a natural social system, with properties all its own, one that has evolved a set of rules, roles, a power structure, forms of communication, and ways of negotiation and problem solving that allow various tasks to be performed effectively" (Goldenberg and Goldenberg 1980, 3). Chinn, Winn and Walters (1978) describe the family as a miniature society, complete with values and member expectations for performance, which also reflects the notion of the family as a system. This approach to understanding families requires knowing the definition of a system and the characteristics considered typical of a system.

A *system* is a group or set of things so related that they form a whole and are organized in such a manner as to preserve the whole and ensure its continued existence, a definition consistent with the nature and behavior of the family unit. The general characteristics of a system include the following:

1. *The functions of any system seem to be directed toward achieving the goals of the system.* Regardless of the vastness of the system, purpose and order direct the functioning of the unit. In some instances, the ultimate goals of the system may not be obvious or even acknowledged; in such instances, the objectives or intermediate steps and/or actions become the focus of the system.
2. *There is structure within the system.* Patterns of interdependencies among parts of the system and the roles performed by each during interactions represent the structure of the system. These patterns can be observed as family members interact, giving insight into the structure of the family.
3. *The system has rules to govern its members and functioning.* Family functioning is guided by a specific set of rules. The rules which are operating within the family system may be obvious to observers and yet obscure to family members. Regardless of family members' awareness of their existence, rules do exist and form the actions and behavior of individuals within the system and the system as a whole.
4. *Certain order or methods of functioning exist within the system.* The methods of functioning observed within the family give pattern to the activity and therefore provide the basis from which the rules of the system can be inferred. The observer notes how the family deals with internal and external events, looking for consistency and orderliness of pattern.
5. *Systems preserve and perpetuate themselves.* A balance must be achieved within the system in order for the system to survive. Balance must be achieved in order to allow the components of the system to function in harmony and to allow the overall system to function effectively. The balance grows as the system functions, making it more resistant to forces that might interfere or upset the balance and change the system. A healthy system must allow movement and change, yet keep the system intact. In a family, this balance between the functioning of individual members and the functioning of the family as a whole is critical (Chinn et al. 1978).

Figure 11-1 summarizes the general characteristics of a system.

One distinct intent of P.L. 94-142 was increased interaction between families of handicapped students and school personnel, resulting from the extension of the right and responsibility of parents to participate in educational decision making (*Federal Register*,

Figure 11-1: General Characteristics of a System

Characteristics of System	Manifestations in Family System
1. The functions of any system seem to be directed toward achieving the goals of the system.	Actions taken by family members are expected to be consistent with the needs of the family and to reflect the goals of the family. These goals may or may not be obvious; in those cases in which goals are obscure, intermediate steps are recognized and guide action.
2. There is structure within the system.	The structure found in families is seen in the interrelationships and interdependencies of its members.
3. The system has rules to govern its members and functioning.	Families may have rules dealing with daily activities, significant events, modes of behavior, and other important aspects of life. However, families may not be aware of all rules operating; in these cases, members infer appropriate behavior from other rules and/or actions of members.
4. Certain order or methods of functioning exist within the system.	Methods for operation can be observed in families in the ways internal and external events are handled.
5. Systems preserve and perpetuate themselves.	Families reorganize to compensate for additions or loss of members; this is an example of the system's ability to alter organizational patterns and characteristics in order for the system to survive.

Source: Chinn et al. 1978.

Vol. 42, no. 163, Tuesday, August 23, 1977, 42494-42495). The years since passage of the law have been characterized by a trend toward increased parental involvement in the education of handicapped students (MacMillan and Turnbull 1983). Therefore, any discussion of the education of mildly handicapped students must include an examination of types of family units, the roles played by families of handicapped students, the impact the handicapped student has on the family, including siblings, and the relationship between families and school personnel.

ORGANIZATIONAL PATTERNS OF FAMILIES

Currently there is no such thing as a typical American family (Goldenberg and Goldenberg 1978). The classic family type was composed of a housewife, working father, and children; however, this type is no longer the major family organizational pattern (Skolnick and Skolnick 1977; Wald 1981). Instead, several organizational patterns have become increasingly common. The future educator must become aware of the different types of family patterns presently found in America because of the high level of interaction with parents which can be anticipated. *Entering into such interactions without at least rudimentary knowledge of the variations in family organization and structure could put the educator at a distinct disadvantage and could lead to serious misunderstandings and miscommunications.* Understanding the familial organizational patterns of students is important for the following reasons:

1. Sending notices or forms home to be signed may become complex as a result of an organizational pattern other than the nuclear family
2. Being aware of the familial context in which students live can aid teachers in understanding student values and reactions to literature or course content
3. Recognition of a variety of family arrangements and the stresses and responsibilities associated with each organizational type can assist teachers in assessing the opportunity for parental involvement in homework and parent support activities
4. If a student lives within an organizational framework considered "unusual" within the school or community, the teacher may be able to provide support and aid in acceptance of the student
5. There may be legal constraints associated with a familial arrangement, such as visitation rights or rights to information, which could be violated by the teacher and/or the school.

There are several different organizational patterns of families that currently exist. These include the nuclear family, extended family, blended family, common law family, single-parent family, commune, serial family, composite family, and cohabitation. Table 11-1 summarizes these organizational structures.

Nuclear Family

The nuclear family, consisting of father, mother, and children, is the family that used to be pictured in basal reading series, on boxes of cereal, and in Norman Rockwell paintings. Dad was the breadwinner and mother was the full-time homemaker. However, today's nuclear family is changing. More mothers are working full-time to pursue professional careers that require a great deal of personal commitment. This can produce shifts in roles assumed by fathers, especially in the areas of child rearing and housekeeping. Changes in the nuclear family have produced an increased demand for child care outside the home, such as at day care centers and preschools.

Extended Family

The extended family includes father, mother, children, grandparents, and other family members. Historically, grandparents and, in some cases, aunts and uncles joined the nuclear family, with all living under the same roof. This extended family resulted from a number of factors, including economic difficulties, the need for child care in large families, and a cultural attitude that older family members should be taken in and provided care. During the Depression, extended families represented an important defense against hard times. Older family members gave additional help in the home where preparation of meals, making of clothing, and child care consumed huge amounts of time. Aunts, uncles, and cousins also helped with the field work and other responsibilities associated with survival during that period. These additional adults within the extended family also served as role models and examples of the strict role assignments typical of early agrarian America (Simpson 1982). The extended family model is often associated with families of European origin because of the custom of several generations sharing the same living quarters, and perhaps for the same reasons this model thrived in the earlier years of America.

Table 11-1 **Organizational Patterns of Families**

Type	Members	Description
Nuclear	Father, mother, children	
Extended	Father, mother, children, grandparents, uncles, aunts, cousins, etc.	
Blended	Father, mother, children	Children are from other marriages of father and/or mother
Common law	Man, woman, and children	All are living together as a family unit although adults have not been formally married
Single-parent	One parent and children	Man or woman functioning as the head of the house as a result of divorce, desertion, death, or having never been married
Commune	Men, women, and children	Members living as a family unit consisting of more than one male and female adult, typically sharing duties and rights and collectively engaging in family activities
Serial	Man or woman and children	There is a succession of marriages, consisting of one nuclear family at any one time
Composite	Man, two or more women, children; or woman, two or more men, children	A form of polygamous family living.
Cohabitation	Man and woman, perhaps children	Two unmarried persons of opposite sex living together in a nonlegal, nonbinding agreement

Source: Goldenberg and Goldenberg 1980.

The extended family model is less prevalent now because those conditions that nurtured the extended family model no longer prevail as widely (Simpson 1982). Grandparents are more often found living in their own homes, retirement villages, and nursing homes. Single aunts and uncles more typically live in their own apartments or homes.

Blended Family

Instances of divorce are more common now than at any other time in the history of our country. As a result, there are also more instances of divorced parents remarrying, producing the family organizational pattern identified as a *blended family*. The blended family consists of father, mother, and children from other marriages. It may also include those situations described as "yours, mine, and ours" in terms of the children in the marriage: one or both of the adults entering the marriage has children from a previous marriage and then perhaps they produce children from the new union.

Common Law Family

In this model the family is comprised of a man and a woman, and perhaps children, who are joined in a family unit by personal consent rather than through formal marriage vows.

Goldenberg and Goldenberg (1980) report pertinent information on this family type although they state that the occurrence of this model is not as easily documented as some other family patterns: therefore, it is difficult to assess the current status of the model. However, Goldenberg and Goldenberg submit that it is reasonable to recognize that this model does exist and could be a family pattern encountered by public school personnel. Logic would dictate that perhaps the prevalence of this model correlates with broader value systems and the degree of public tolerance for nontraditional living patterns (*Newsweek*, 17 January 1983).

Single-Parent Family

Single-parent families are those headed by a father or mother who has major responsibility for child rearing and economic support. An obvious result of the increased divorce rate in recent years has been a prevalence of this family model. There seems to be a growing number of these families in which the father is the single parent, although the typical parent in such a family structure is still the mother. Single-parent families also result from death of a partner, desertion, and increasingly, personal preference. In the last case, individuals elect to remain single yet raise a family. News items frequently describe instances of single persons who choose to adopt children or who give birth to a child with the plan of remaining single and supporting the child independently of the father. *Newsweek* (17 January 1983) reported that "between 1970 and 1982, the number of one-parent families headed by never-married women rose by a startling 367 percent."

Commune Family

The commune family consists of several men, women, and children living together in a communal relationship, sharing responsibilities, duties, and rights within the group. Income earning and other family responsibilities are shared among members; in many instances, property is even jointly owned by all commune members. Children within this setting are supervised and guided by all adults within the group or by certain members identified for that purpose, regardless of who are the natural parents.

Serial Family

Members of this organizational pattern include a man or woman or both who have been married at least twice before this marriage. In this pattern, the man and/or the woman *has had previous spouses* but only one at any given time. Thus the serial family is a pattern consisting of a series of nuclear families, actually a blended family, with children each time swept into a new, nuclear family. Divorced American adults tend to remarry; in fact, 75 percent of the women and 83 percent of the men remarry within three years of their divorces (Goldenberg and Goldenberg 1980). Therefore, serial families can be expected to become fairly common as a family organizational pattern.

Composite Family

The composite family consists of two or more nuclear families sharing a common wife or, more typically, husband. The prevalence of this pattern, a form of polygamous marriage, is extremely difficult to ascertain because of legal and cultural sanctions against it. Even in those religious sects that condone this family pattern, its existence is not often made public for obvious reasons.

Cohabitation

Cohabitation means that two adults of the opposite sex agree to form a unit and share familial responsibilities and rights without legally joining in marriage (Goldenberg and Goldenberg 1980). This model is distinguished from the common law family by the *absence* of the willingness to form a *formal family unit* (McGinnis and Finnegan 1976). It is more a sharing of habitat and duties. Its prevalence appears to have increased significantly during the last twenty years, making it a more common family pattern in some segments of our society. The acceptance received by this model varies, based upon the local cultural standards, religious beliefs, and values. However, it does seem to be a family with an organizational pattern common enough for the future educator to expect to encounter in dealing with patrons of public schools.

Formation of Family: Its Life Cycle

Understanding how a family is formed and its ensuing life cycle can be helpful when interacting with families of handicapped students. It provides a point of reference for interpreting the family's reactions to the handicapped student and the family's attitudes and approaches to dealing with the handicap and the resulting circumstances.

The life cycle of a family is just what the term implies; it is the successive patterns through which the family passes. The traditional concept of life cycle developed around studies of the nuclear family, the traditional middle-class familial arrangement. However, even though the nuclear family is changing and other patterns have become increasingly evident, the concept of a familial life cycle still appears relevant and useful when looking at family life (Duvall 1977).

The eight stages or sectors described by Duvall (see figure 11-2) are obviously based upon averages, not one particular family. The basic cycle was developed around the nuclear family, but certain aspects of it still hold true across organizational models. As general guides, these aspects provide insight for other experiences and developmental stages of family members.

The life cycle of families depicted in figure 11-2 shows that approximately half of the average family's life is spent without children, mainly in stages 6, 7, and 8. But the life cycle of a family with a handicapped child may be significantly different from the cycle depicted here, especially in these last three stages when typically only the husband and wife remain at home. Obviously, the severity of the child's handicapping condition may affect this particular phase. Those students with more severe handicaps are expected to continue in the period of parental dependency much longer than are mildly handicapped students. Even within the mildly handicapped group, however, parents may be directing the lives of the youngsters longer than normal. This would reduce the period of time in stages 7 and 8 when only husband and wife make up the family unit.

Examination of case studies of families with one or more handicapped children might also reveal a decrease in stages 1, 2, and 3 (see figure 11-2) because of the parent's reluctance to have another child or intense involvement with the handicapped child. In any event, the existence of a handicapped child could significantly affect these stages of the family's life cycle.

312 *Mildly Handicapped Children and Adults*

STAGES OF THE
FAMILY LIFE CYCLE

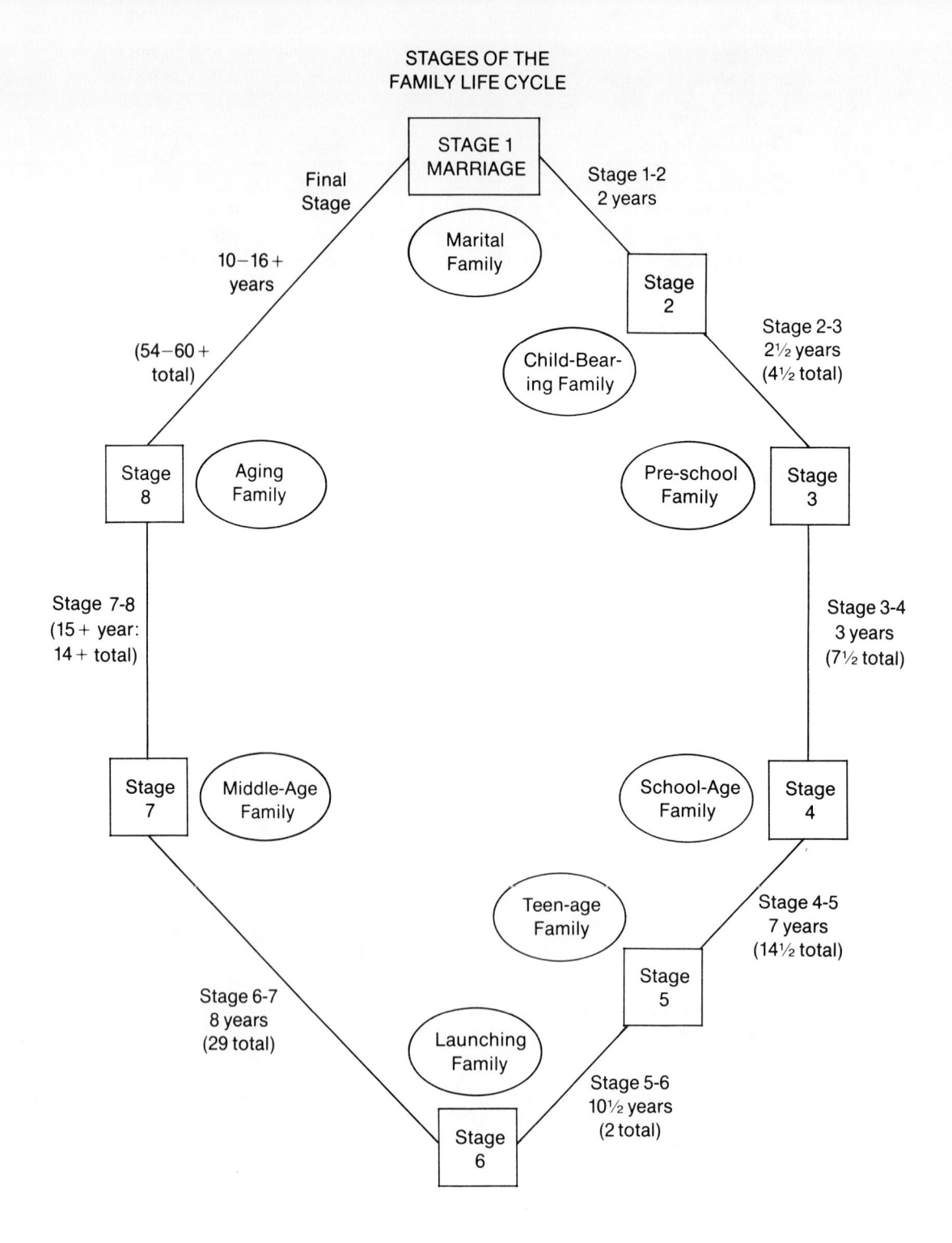

- STAGE 1 MARRIAGE
- Marital Family
- Stage 1-2: 2 years
- Stage 2
- Child-Bearing Family
- Stage 2-3: 2½ years (4½ total)
- Stage 3
- Pre-school Family
- Stage 3-4: 3 years (7½ total)
- Stage 4
- School-Age Family
- Stage 4-5: 7 years (14½ total)
- Stage 5
- Teen-age Family
- Stage 5-6: 10½ years (2 total)
- Stage 6
- Launching Family
- Stage 6-7: 8 years (29 total)
- Stage 7
- Middle-Age Family
- Stage 7-8 (15+ year: 14+ total)
- Stage 8
- Aging Family
- Final Stage: 10–16+ years (54–60+ total)

Figure 11-2   Stages of the Family Life Cycle from 0 to 60+ Years. E.M. Duvall. *Marriage and family development* (5th Ed.), Source: Duvall 1977.

Averages can be used to describe family cycles and inferences can be made concerning the impact of handicapped children on such cycles. Caution should be taken, however, in dealing with families that have a handicapped child. Each family unit is unique, reflecting varied backgrounds and the accomplishment of important development tasks as a couple (Minuchin 1974). Therefore, generalizations should be avoided, and each family viewed as objectively as possible.

PURPOSES OF THE FAMILY

The field of family studies is founded on a body of professional literature addressing a wide spectrum of issues, including the relationships among family members and the role the family plays in the lives of family members. These two aspects are related because the nature and intensity of the relationships among members of the family would obviously affect the role of the family and the family's ability to accomplish purposes. For example, a family formed as a result of two adults rushing to remarry following a divorce may be based primarily on a need for its members to remarry; therefore, once the new family unit is formed, its survival is dependent upon the two adults working out their relationship, based on some factor other than the need to remarry (Haley 1973).

The health of the family and its ability to function will largely be determined by its members' capacity to achieve strong, positive relationships. Therefore, in the following discussion, family role must be interpreted very generally because the purposes of the family and the degree of success to which a family fulfills those purposes are *specific to each set of individual relationships comprising the family*. Also, it should be reemphasized that families go through stages in a life cycle, reflecting changes in member relationships. The purposes of the family will also reflect these changes in its members.

Before it is possible to examine the purposes of the family of handicapped students, the general purposes which society seems to expect of all families should be examined. McGinnis and Finnegan identified six such generic purposes:

1. Procreation and rearing of children
2. Socialization of children
3. Fostering indepth personal relationships
4. Serving as primary reference group for context for development of individual members' identities
5. Serving as an economic unit
6. Caring for elderly parents (McGinnis and Finnegan 1976)

As the family progresses through the life cycle, the importance of each of these purposes will be affected. For example, as the family proceeds into the later stages of the life cycle, the first purpose—procreation—decreases significantly in importance and other purposes such as serving as an economic unit and providing care for older parents receive more attention from family members. These general purposes seem to apply to most families, despite such variables as economic status, educational level of members, and religious preference. Table 11-2 describes some of the family responsibilities associated with family efforts to serve the purposes of its members. These responsibilities would also be considered typical of the family with a handicapped child. However, this family may encounter much more pressure and difficulty in meeting these responsibilities because of the handicapped child (Halpern 1982).

Table 11-2 Purposes of the Family

*Purposes	Possible Family Responsibilities Associated with Purpose
1. Procreation and rearing of children	• Giving birth • Nurturing of infants • Providing for health care of children • Supporting intellectual development of children
2. Socialization of children	• Fostering self-esteem of children • Transmitting values
3. Fostering indepth personal relationships	• Providing secure context for personal interactions • Sharing intimate feelings and needs
4. Serving as primary reference group for context for development of individual members identities	• Accepting variance among family members • Serving as role models • Providing feedback on behavior and growth
5. Serving as an economic unit	• Providing for basic material needs of family members
6. Caring for elderly parents	• Securing appropriate health care • Providing for basic material needs • Nurturing personal interaction

*Purposes adapted from: McGinnis and Finnegan 1976.

The Possible Effects of a Handicapped Child on Family Purposes

It can be assumed that the purposes identified by McGinnis and Finnegan (1976) also apply to families of handicapped students because as Simpson points out, "It is logical that families with exceptional children would experience the same ecological changes as others and exist as heterogeneously as other parents and families" (Simpson 1982, 12). However, it can also be assumed that these purposes *may* be altered, extended, or in other ways affected by the presence of a handicapped child within the family. The precise manner in which the purposes might be affected cannot be predicted for obvious reasons; however, some general ways that having a handicapped child may affect the family's efforts to serve the anticipated purposes can be hypothesized.

Procreation and Rearing of Children. This purpose can become extremely complex for parents of handicapped students. In some instances, birth itself is difficult and fraught with problems. More typically, the major complexities of this purpose are encountered during the child-rearing process. Responsibilities such as *nurturing* can become extremely demanding for any parent, but if the child is handicapped, it can become even more so. Parents of children with severe handicaps may be faced with a wide range of difficulties related to caring for a handicapped child (Turnbull and Turnbull 1978), but parents of mildly handicapped students sometimes encounter difficulties as well. For example, some children within the group identified as mildly handicapped may achieve developmental benchmarks such as walking or talking later than other children, may have erratic sleep patterns, or may exhibit behavioral problems that make parenting extremely difficult.

Even in the area of health care and in interactions with medical personnel, families with handicapped children may encounter problems, especially during the pediatric care

The birth of a mildly handicapped child may elicit a variety of reactions in parents.

years. As Guralnick (1982) stated, historically pediatricians have tended to focus on a narrow diagnostic or medical management role, with pediatricians often found to be inadequately prepared to deal with the overall needs of handicapped children and their families (Dworkin et al. 1979; Roos 1978). Yet as Levine states, "When a child is underachieving or failing to adapt to school, it is not uncommon for a parent to consult a pediatrician or family physician" (Levine 1982, 296).

Supporting the intellectual development of a handicapped child, considered one of the possible family responsibilities, can also be complex. Support would logically include securing appropriate and adequate educational experiences for the child. Even with the advent of P.L. 94-142, which greatly aided in this endeavor, there may still be difficulties with this responsibility, and the family may have the sometimes burdensome task of negotiating educational arrangements for a handicapped child (Halpern 1982).

Socialization of Children. Parents have the responsibility of fostering the socialization of their children, and this typically includes a broad spectrum of social interactions, activities, and events. Typically parents engage in social interaction with the children, commensurate with the age of the child and the developmental level. In the case of handicapped students, however, these two levels may not be the same. Even in the case of mildly handicapped children, there may be some discrepancy between the chronological age of the child and the developmental stage which has been achieved, with delays in the latter possibly resulting from health problems, developmental difficulties, and a myriad of other possible causes. When such discrepancies do occur, it may complicate socialization

Parents have primary responsibility for the early socialization of their children.

efforts by the family and its members. For example, siblings who are younger or only slightly older than the mildly handicapped student may be given the same or similar privileges because of the handicapped child's limitations, real or perceived. Socialization may be further complicated by the family's tendency to protect the handicapped child; in some instances, the family becomes overprotective and so the child is not able to develop socially.

Although the category of mildly handicapped obviously does not include extremely handicapped individuals, sometimes the mild handicap has physical manifestations that are obvious to observers and may even appear somewhat severe to onlookers. Examples might include those children in wheelchairs or braces, those with behavioral characteristics considered atypical, or those with speech impairments. In such cases, the handicapped youngster may be subjected to curious stares or overly attentive behavior when out in public with the family. As Schulz (1978) relates, parents must learn to deal with such reactions and must also help the handicapped child cope.

Mildly handicapped students are often extremely aware of the reactions of others, both to the handicap and to the assigned label. As a resource room teacher, one of the authors was confronted with evidence of this awareness. Claudia was identified as mildly handicapped at the end of the first grade and placed in special education. When school began in the fall, Claudia reported to the special classroom, eager and quite happy. Following morning recess, however, she returned to the special classroom in tears and demanded to be taken home. "No one will play with me. All of my old friends from kindergarten and first grade told me to go away. They said I am not smart enough to play with them," Claudia exclaimed with heartbroken sobs. As the tale unfolded, it became apparent that Claudia had been rejected by her peers based solely on the fact that she had been assigned to a special education class. The tragedy of it all was underscored when she said, "I wish I was more dumb; then I would not know that they didn't like me." Families of handicapped students must attempt to foster the self-esteem of the child and transmit strong values in the face of circumstances that do not reinforce their feelings of self-worth or model their values.

Fostering Indepth Personal Relationships. Possible family responsibilities associated with this purpose might include providing a secure and consistent context for the development of personal interactions, and establishing an emotional climate that fosters, or at least allows, intimate feelings and needs to be shared openly. These and other responsibilities related to this purpose could be significantly affected by having a mildly handicapped child in the family. For example, the child's own erratic and rather unpredictable behavior could present extreme challenges to the parents' ability to react consistently and to establish a reliable and secure atmosphere. Also, the mildly handicapped child may not be able to relate personal feelings adequately and may have difficulty handling such interactions with other family members. It is possible that parents would have to devote more intense effort to foster such interactions when the family includes a child who is mildly handicapped.

Serving as Primary Reference Group for Context for Development of Individual Members' Identities. This particular family purpose might include responsibilities such as accepting variance among family members and serving as role models. These two tasks take on increased importance in the family with a mildly handicapped child. For example, accepting variance among family members may require accepting wide discrepancies between chronological age and motor performance, typical of certain mildly handicapped subgroups. This may mean that an eight-year-old child cannot be expected to meet the typical expectations for that age. In addition, comparison among siblings may increase the need for acceptance by all family members. For example, if the older of the two siblings is mildly handicapped with academic problems, it is conceivable that the younger may be "in the same reading book at school," a common complaint that can create extreme stress for the family. Thus, serving as a role model requires that the parents exhibit the type of acceptance and understanding of differences that taxes even adult emotions.

Serving as An Economic Unit. Providing for basic material needs of family members might be considered one of the major purposes of the family unit. Obviously, this is important for the survival of any family unit. In the case of the family with a mildly handicapped child, financial responsibilities may be increased because of the need for medication, special educational considerations not met by P.L. 94-142, or unique complications within the home, such as baby sitting.

Caring for Elderly Parents. Securing appropriate health care and providing for the basic material needs of elderly parents may not be directly affected by the presence of a mildly handicapped child. But the addition of these responsibilities to those most immediately related to rearing a mildly handicapped child might prove to be extremely demanding. Nurturing interpersonal relationships can also become an important aspect of caring for an elderly parent. In fact, sometimes this responsibility may be the most time-consuming for a family. However, as in all purposes of the family, the degree to which having a mildly handicapped child is a compounding variable will vary significantly with each family.

FAMILY REACTIONS

The manner in which a family integrates a mildly handicapped child into the family system and deals with the ensuing responsibilities can only be described in very general terms, for each family is unique. Also, various handicaps may elicit different responses and produce significantly variant responsibilities for the family and its members. In the case of the birth of a child with a serious developmental disability, the parents must *immediately* acquire a new identity and deal with a rush of stresses (Waisbren 1980). In the case of mildly handicapped children, the confirmation of the existence of a handicapping condition may not occur until the child is enrolled in school. Therefore, the initial reaction to a mild handicap may not be quite as strong as the reaction to an extremely severe handicap. Of course, the inclusion of certain medical conditions under the rubric of mildly handicapped may produce situations in which parents are aware of the condition prior to school. In any event, parental reaction should be expected (Keesler 1966; Miller and Janosik 1980).

It is unrealistic to expect that all parents will react in the same way, and it is also illogical to expect their reactions to conform to some theoretically stated timetable and description of stages (Fallen and McGovern 1978). However, some general responses have been observed and the professional literature has attempted to describe these general responses (Gardner 1973; Baroff 1974; Fallen and McGovern 1978; McWhirter 1977).

Typical Reactions

Parental reactions to having a handicapped child have been examined from a number of dimensions (Tulloch 1983; Diamond 1981). These and other investigations have produced several lists of typical parental reactions, including the following:

- Acute initial reactions, chronic adaptive reactions, and mature adaptations (summarized in Fallen and McGovern 1978, 306-307)
- Loss of self-esteem, shame, ambivalence, depression, self-sacrifice, and defensiveness (Roos 1963)
- Shock, refusal, guilt, bitterness, envy, rejection, and readjustment (Love 1973)

In addition to these, Roos (1978), as a parent of a child with a handicap *and* a professional special educator, suggests that the birth or awareness of a child with a handicap may reactivate previously critical areas of conflict in parents. Such rekindled conflicts within the individual and the marriage may include disillusionment, aloneness, vulnerability, inequity, insignificance, past orientation, and loss of immortality (Roos 1978). The authors can subscribe to the contention that having a mildly handicapped child, even one whose primary cause for concern is the inability to perform adequately in school, may elicit a variety of reactions from parents. These reactions can take numerous forms and stem from a wide range of factors.

When dealing with parents, educators should not infer parental feelings or attitudes or interact with them according to a predetermined set of expectations about how the parents will react. Instead, educators should approach interactions with parents of mildly handicapped students with full awareness that the child's situation cannot be addressed in isolation of the parents' reactions. It would probably also be wise to anticipate that eventually parents will adapt and learn the skills needed to guide their child's future (Spodek, Saracho, and Lee 1984).

SIBLINGS

The family of a mildly handicapped child must be examined in terms of the siblings as well as the parents. Special educators and others involved with providing services to handicapped children have long acknowledged that the existence of an exceptional child affects nonhandicapped siblings (Garwood 1983). However, there has not been as much agreement about the exact nature or degree of the effect.

Evidence may suggest that having a handicapped sibling can have a negative impact on nonhandicapped children (Garwood 1983; Simpson 1982). Nonhandicapped siblings may be confronted with a wide variety of pressures stemming from the problems of the handicapped child, including the following:

1. Increased parental expectations for achievement.
   Parents may transfer all of their expectations and hopes to the nonhandicapped child or children in an effort to compensate for the disappointment associated with the potential and/or performance of the handicapped child (Garwood 1983).
2. Increased feelings of responsibility.
   Nonhandicapped siblings may feel responsible for the handicapped family member (Farber 1959).
3. Resentment.
   Unimpaired siblings may resent the handicapped child because of the increased demands placed upon the family in terms of parental time and family resources (Grossman 1972).
4. Increased demands for caretaking.
   Sometimes nonhandicapped siblings, especially females, are required or feel required to assume inordinate caretaking tasks, resulting in some youngsters feeling pressured into sharing the parental role (Love 1973).
5. Feelings of being responsible for education of sibling.
   Michaelis (1980) reports that many aspects of educating the mildly handicapped child, especially in terms of daily routine, may fall to nonhandicapped siblings.

The relationship with siblings is important in the personal adjustment of a handicapped child.

Some evidence seems to contradict the expectation that the only possible effects a handicapped child can have on siblings are negative ones (Simpson 1982; Grossman 1972; Garwood 1983). Possible *positive* effects reported by siblings include the following:

1. Awareness of intolerance and prejudice.
   Siblings may have had to deal with intolerance and prejudice very early in their lives as a result of seeing their handicapped sibling as the victim of such attitudes. Therefore, these siblings appeared to demonstrate greater compassion and understanding (Grossman 1972).
2. Heightened sense of pride in sibling's accomplishments.
   S. Miller (1974) reported that normal siblings frequently reported extreme pride and sense of involvement associated with the handicapped child's progress.
3. Increased sense of love.
   Some siblings reported a greater awareness of the lessons associated with having a handicapped sibling, including an appreciation for and understanding of love (Turnbull and Turnbull 1978).
4. Greater awareness of parental responsibilities.
   Normal siblings are often quoted as recognizing the extra responsibilities required of their parents and admiring them for their ability to cope (Garwood 1983).

As Featherstone stated, detailed discussions of the possible problems encountered by normal siblings of handicapped youngsters "may suggest that for the brothers and sisters of the disabled the developmental path is strewn with frightful hazards, that all but the most skillful parents can expect to see their 'normal' children bruised irreparably by the experience of family living. The truth is quite otherwise" (Featherstone 1980, 163). What makes the difference includes parental skill and understanding. These are both rather nebulous concepts, making it difficult to describe what factors might contribute to observed differences among families. However, a few mediating factors have been identified in the professional literature. These include the following:

1. Extent to which siblings are held accountable for child care of the handicapped child (Garwood 1983)
2. Family size (Grossman 1972)
3. Sex of nonhandicapped sibling as females tended to be under more pressure to provide care (Garwood 1983)
4. Socioeconomic status of family (Garwood 1983)
5. Nature and degree of handicap (Miller and Janosik 1980)

RELATIONSHIP BETWEEN FAMILIES AND SCHOOL PERSONNEL

The role of parents in education has been accepted for many years. As early as 1899, parental communications were cited in the Harper Report as being important in problems such as dropping-out (Paul 1981). The importance of parental communications and involvement in education is heightened when the child is handicapped, a notion supported by major elements in P.L. 94-142. Family involvement in the education of mildly handicapped children is a logical necessity (Bricker and Casuso 1979) and should be considered an essential link between home and school (Spodek et al. 1984). The advent of P.L. 94-142 makes it a mandate.

Collaboration between Parents and School

Public law 94-142 very specifically states that parents, parental surrogates, or guardians are invited to participate in the decision-making processes associated with educating handicapped students. Parents or those fulfilling that role for the child must be involved in the major stages of the special education process: (1) initial stages, which include child-find, referral, and referral conference; (2) intermediate stages, which include evaluation, evaluation conference, IEP conference, selection of least restrictive setting; and (3) final stages, which include implementation of the IEP and evaluation of the program received by the child. While the opportunity for parental involvement is mandated and sought at each stage in the process of serving mildly handicapped students, the precise nature of the parental involvement required may vary among stages. A brief summary of the stages and the possible types of parental input involved have been adapted from Marsh, Price, and Smith (1983) and are shown in table 11-3.

The law also requires not only the opportunity for parental participation but also the documentation of this opportunity. Specific requirements for documentation resulted from concerns that parental and child rights might be violated; therefore, schools must provide proof that parents or some advocate or representative for the child did, in fact,

Table 11-3 Parental Input

Event	Parental Activities
Referral/Diagnosis	• Provide information on how the child behaves at home and/or in family situations • Cooperate with school personnel in their efforts to get accurate information about the child • Participate in conferences • Share pertinent information gained from other evaluations
Provision of Services	• Recognize goals and share concerns and feelings about appropriateness • Actively participate in selection of services • Attend all conferences • Communicate with school personnel • Read relevant literature • Join parent organizations • Support the educational program being conducted by the school
Program Evaluation	• Communicate with school personnel, providing feedback on program's effectiveness • Observe the child and inform the school of impressions • Participate in parent groups

Source: Marsh et al. 1983.

participate in the decision-making process. Written documentation must include parental notification of the following:

- initiation of the referral process
- scheduled time of referral conference
- outcome of referral conference
- initiation of evaluation process
- need for informed consent form, releasing student records and giving permission to evaluate student
- scheduled time for evaluation conference
- participation in evaluation conference
- outcome and decisions made by evaluation committee
- release form for initiation of services
- participation in development of the IEP
- participation in evaluation and review of the IEP

Obviously, these requirements can only be as effective as the individuals involved wish them to be. If schools comply in only the most cursory manner, the full intent of the requirements has been lost. The same is true if parents only "go through the motions" of becoming involved. Signing a form does not document involvement, but it can provide "intent" or open the door to parental communications. Therefore, all parties—parents and school personnel alike—are encouraged to view parental involvement in terms of its

Table 11-4 Procedural Safeguards

Safeguard	Description
Prior Notice	• Parents must be notified in writing before any change of status, evaluation or placement • Notification must be received within a reasonable period of time before such changes are made • Parents must be notified in writing of any school refusal of parental requests
Parental Consent	• Consent must be obtained from parents before a child may be placed or services initiated
Examination of Records	• Parents specifically have the right to examine all records on the child which are maintained by the school • Requests for interpretation of the data must be honored by the school • Parents may request that the files be altered if they suspect that they contain inaccurate or inappropriate data • If schools do not comply with requests concerning records, due process procedures can be initiated by parents
Independent Evaluation	• Parents may request that the child be evaluated by professionals outside the schools

own potential for merit and benefit for the child rather than as compliance with federal law.

Primary Procedural Safeguards

As Marsh, Price, and Smith state, "regardless of the motivation, parental involvement is required and must be handled in accordance with the regulations of P.L. 94-142" (Marsh et al. 1983, 110). To assure the rights of students and their parents, some major procedural safeguards have been established. These safeguards, summarized in table 11-4, are intended to guard against the exclusion of parents and to protect schools from charges of such exclusion. These safeguards should be viewed as a protection for all participants, especially the child.

Role of School Personnel

School personnel have contact with parents of mildly handicapped students in all of the traditional ways that they have contact with parents of nonhandicapped students, such as at school visits, school functions, grading conferences, and Halloween carnivals. Expectations about contact with parents of special students should be couched in the context of what is typical for that school district, building, and/or teacher. While the law does (as indicated above) specify certain types of interactions, much of the role of school personnel is consistent with the role played in the education of all children.

Parent groups can provide needed support to the parents of handicapped chiildren.

Some types of contact, however, may take on increased importance, such as *parent conferences*, because of the previous and possibly negative experiences that parents of mildly handicapped students have had. The parent conference is the major type of parent contact and is the primary method for communicating with parents. While many of the conferences are held to meet legal requirements, the conference can produce beneficial outcomes for parents, teachers, and children. For parents, its outcomes can include clarification of what happens to the child on a daily basis and greater understanding of progress.

Parent counseling and *parent support groups* have become more prevalent in recent years as parental rights and responsibilities have increasingly come into play in educating mildly handicapped students (Spodek et al. 1984). The precise nature of parent counseling and support activities varies greatly among groups. However, Lillie (1976) has identified four aspects of parent programs which could seem appropriate as general descriptors for such programs: providing social and emotional support, allowing for the exchange of information, providing assistance in improving parent-child interactions, and fostering parental participation in school programs.

Regardless of the means through which the school-parent relationship is accomplished, importance of parental support cannot be overstated. As Spodek and colleagues state, "The [child's educational] program's effects are likely to be severely limited without it [parental support]" (Spodek et al. 1984, 159). Therefore, school personnel should aggressively seek a strong relationship, built upon mutual trust and efforts toward a mutual goal: the best possible education for the child. The law does require certain types of communications and, thereby, does dictate a specific kind of relationship between schools and parents, but this should not overshadow the dedicated efforts of the individual educators and parents involved.

SUMMARY

The focus of this chapter is the family; it is described as a system, with specific characteristics and functions. Particular attention is given to the growing options found in this country in terms of family organizational patterns. Information is provided on blended families, single-parent families, and other patterns, in addition to the traditional nuclear family. From this general overview of the family unit, the possible impact on the family of having a mildly handicapped child is considered.

Parental reaction to having a mildly handicapped child is described, both from the viewpoint of professionals involved with parents, and perhaps more importantly, from the viewpoint of parents who have had the experience. Siblings are included in the discussion, including their feelings about the handicapped child in the family.

Attention is given to the purposes of the family and ways in which fulfilling these purposes might be affected by the family trying to deal with a mildly handicapped child. Inferences are couched in terms of the mildly handicapped student and the potential complications for public school programming. Parental involvement with school personnel and the child's program is specifically reviewed. Primary procedural safeguards from P.L. 94-142 are included as well as a discussion of general types of parental involvement that school personnel might expect.

REFERENCES

Baroff, G. *Mental retardation: Nature, causes and management.* Washington, D.C.: Hemisphere Publishing Corporation, 1974.

Bricker, D. and V. Casuso. Family involvement: A critical component of early intervention. *Exceptional Children* 46, no. 2 (1979):108–115.

Chinn, P.C., J. Winn, and R.H. Walters. *Two-way talking with parents of special children: A process of positive communication.* St. Louis: C.V. Mosby, 1978.

Diamond, S. Growing up with parents of a handicapped child: A handicapped person's perspective. In *Understanding and working with parents of children with special needs. See* Paul 1981.

Duvall, E.M. *Marriage and family development.* 5th ed. New York: Lippincott, 1977.

Dworkin, P.H., J.P. Shonkoff, A. Leviton, and M.D. Levine. Training in developmental pediatrics. *American Journal of Diseases of Children* 133, (1979):709–712.

Fallen, N.H., and J.E. McGovern. *Young children with special needs.* Columbus, Ohio: Charles E. Merrill, 1978.

Farber, B. Effect of a severely retarded child on family integration. *Monograph of the Society for Research in Child Development* 24 (1959).

Featherstone, H. *A difference in the family.* New York: Basic Books, 1980.

Gardner, R. *MBD: The family book about minimal brain dysfunction.* New York: Jason Arason, 1973.

Garwood, S.G. *Educating young handicapped children: A developmental approach.* 2d ed. Rockville, Md.: Aspen Publications, 1983.

Goldenberg, I., and H. Goldenberg. *Family therapy: An overview.* Monterey, Calif.: Brooks/Cole Publishing Co., 1980.

Grossman, F.K. *Brothers and sisters of retarded children.* Syracuse: Syracuse University Press, 1972.

Guralnick, M.J. Pediatrics, special education, and handicapped children: New relationships. *Exceptional Children* 48, no. 4 (1982):294–95.

Haley, J. *Uncommon therapy: The psychiatric techniques of Milton H. Erickson, M.D.* New York: Norton, 1973.

Halpern, R. Impact of P.L. 94-142 on the Handicapped Child and Family: Institutional Responses. *Exceptional Children* 49, no. 3 (1982):270–73.

Keesler, J. *Psychopathology of childhood*. Englewood Cliffs, N.J.: Prentice-Hall, 1966.

Levine, M.D. The child with school problems: An analysis of physician participation. *Exceptional Children* 48, no. 4 (1982):294–95.

Lillie, D.L. An overview of parent programs. In *Teaching parents to teach*, edited by D.L. Lillie and P.L. Trohanis. New York: Walker and Company, 1976.

Love, H.D. *The mentally retarded child and his family*. Springfield, Ill.: Thomas, 1973.

McGinnis, T.C., and D.G. Finnegan. *Open family and marriage: A guide to personal growth.* St. Louis: C.V. Mosby Co., 1976.

MacMillan, D.L., and A.P. Turnbull. Parent involvement with special education: Respecting individual differences. *Education and Training of the Mentally Retarded* 18, no. 1 (February 1983):4–9.

McWhirter, J.J. *The learning disabled child: A school and family concern*. Champaign, Ill.: Research Press, 1977.

Marsh, G.E., II, B.J. Price, and T.E.C. Smith. *Teaching mildly handicapped children: Methods and materials*. St. Louis: C.V. Mosby Co., 1983.

Michaelis, C.T. *Home and school partnerships in exceptional children*. Rockville, Md.: Aspen Publishing Co., 1980.

Miller, J.R., and E.H. Janosik. *Family-Focused Care*. New York: McGraw-Hill, 1980.

Miller, S. *Exploration study of sibling relationships in families with retarded children*. Doctoral Dissertation, New York: Columbia University, 1974.

Minuchin, S. *Families and family therapy*. Cambridge, Mass.: Harvard University Press, 1974.

Morton, K. Identifying the enemy—A parent's complaint. In *Parents speak out: Views from the other side of the two-way mirror*. See Turnbull and Turnbull 1978.

Newsweek, 17 January 1983.

Paul, J.L. *Understanding and working with parents of children with special needs*. New York: Holt, Rinehart, and Winston, 1981.

Roos, P. Psychological counseling with parents of retarded children. *Mental Retardation* (1963):345–50.

———. Parents of Mentally Retarded Children—Misunderstood and mistreated. *Parents speak out: Views from the other side of the two-way mirror.* See Turnbull and Turnbull 1978.

Schultz, J. The parent-professional conflict. In *Parents speak out: Views from the other side of the two-way mirror.* See Turnbull and Turnbull 1978.

Simpson, R. *Conferencing parents of exceptional children*. Rockville, Md.: Aspen Systems Corporation, 1982.

Skolnick, A.S., and J.H. Skolnick. Introduction: Family in transition. In *Family in transition: Rethinking marriage, sexuality, child rearing, and family organization*, 2d ed., edited by A.S. Skolnick and J.H. Skolnick. Boston: Little, Brown & Co., 1977.

Spodek, B., O.N. Saracho, and R.C. Lee. *Mainstreaming young children*. Belmont, Calif.: Wadsworth Publishing Co., 1984.

Tulloch, D. Why me? Parental reactions to the birth of an exceptional child. *Journal of the Division for Early Childhood* 7 (1983):54–60.

Turnbull, A.P., and H.R. Turnbull. *Parents speak out: Views from the other side of the two way mirror*. Columbus, Ohio: Charles E. Merrill, 1978.

Waisbren, S.E. Parents' reactions after the birth of a developmentally disabled child. *American Journal of Mental Deficiency* 84, no. 4 (1980):345–51.

Wald, E. *The remarried family: Challenge and promise*. New York: Family Service Association of America, 1981.

Chapter Twelve

CAREER AND VOCATIONAL EDUCATION

CHAPTER OUTLINE

INTRODUCTION
Career Education
    Objectives of Career Education
    Components of a Career Education Program
    Need for Career Education in Special Education
    Objectives of Career Education for Handicapped Students
    Developing Career Education Programs
    Career Education for Elementary Handicapped Students
    Career Education in Secondary Schools
    Role of Special Education Teacher
VOCATIONAL EDUCATION
    Developing Vocational Education Programs
    Goals and Objectives for Programs
    Problems in Delivering Vocational Education to the Handicapped
    Vocational Evaluation
    Service Delivery
    Role of Personnel in Vocational Education
SUMMARY

CHAPTER OBJECTIVES

After reading this chapter, you should be able to:
- Describe vocational problems experienced by mildly handicapped adults;
- Define career education;
- List and discuss the goals and objectives of career education for mildly handicapped students;
- Describe the components of career education;
- Discuss the need for career education for mildly handicapped students;
- Describe career education programs for elementary-aged students;
- Define vocational education;
- Discuss the relationship between career education and vocational education;
- List problems in delivering vocational education programs to mildly handicapped students;
- Discuss methods of accommodating handicapped students in regular vocational education classes; and
- List and discuss various vocational programs for mildly handicapped students.

INTRODUCTION

Mildly handicapped adults often experience significant difficulties with being assimilated into communities. One reason is their lack of vocational success. Unemployment, underemployment, and misemployment appear to be a characteristic of many mildly handicapped adults (Siegel and Gold 1982; Fafard and Haubrich 1981; Kirchner and Peterson 1980).

The vocational problems of mildly handicapped adults have many reasons, including:

- not knowing what jobs are available and not having ample information to develop an interest in particular jobs (Tyler 1982);
- lack of career counseling, training, and career information (Fafard and Haubrich 1981);
- lack of interview skills (Hill and Algozzine 1982);
- inability to complete job applications (T.E.C. Smith 1981); and
- difficulties in work interest, habits, motivation, and understanding job requirements (Stodden et al. 1979).

Many of these vocational-related problems can be corrected with proper educational and training experiences. For example, Hill, Wehman, and Pentecost (1980) found that many mentally retarded persons did not possess adequate interview skills but could develop competency in this area with proper training. The underlying problem, in this situation and many others, is that adequate, appropriate training is not always provided by school programs.

Career and vocational education programs for mildly handicapped students are often nonexistent (Fafard and Haubrich 1981; C.R. Smith 1983; D'Alonzo 1983). Reasons for a dearth of programs include difficulties with interagency agreements, attitudes, and personnel preparation (Greenan 1982), inappropriate curricula (C.R. Smith 1983), and simply a misunderstanding of the needs and rights of handicapped children. Regardless of the reasons, solutions must be achieved because "effective participation in career and vocational education programs is a critical factor for helping exceptional individuals secure employment" (Phelps 1983, 286). Without employment, mildly handicapped individuals will not only fail to achieve at their maximum level, but they may also become chronic burdens to society, existing on welfare and other social programs that would not be necessary if appropriate vocational programming were available.

Unfortunately, career and vocational programs have not received much emphasis in the past. While special education programming priorities have traditionally been at the elementary level, secondary students have often found themselves in educational programs that have very little to do with their actual needs, especially in the area of career and vocational education.

CAREER EDUCATION

Career education is a concept, or a philosophy, that is designed to modify existing curricula at both the elementary and secondary level (Marsh and Price 1980). Career education does not require extra teachers, additional courses, expensive materials, or sophisticated equipment. Career education, as a concept, can be infused into the existing curricula.

Many mildly handicapped adults are underemployed.

Many professionals have defined career education. While not all definitions concur on every aspect, most are similar to the one suggested by Mangum, Becker, Coombs, and Marshall:

> Career education is the total effort of public education and the community to help all individuals become familiar with the values of a work-oriented society, to integrate these values into their personal value systems, and to implement these values into their lives in such a way that work becomes possible, meaningful, and satisfying to each individual (Mangum et al. 1975, 8).

The concept of career education, therefore, can be accomplished within current educational activities. Ideally it begins early in the elementary school and continues throughout the public school experience (Cullinan, Epstein, and Lloyd 1983).

Career education was formally introduced by former U.S. Commissioner of Education Sidney Marland in 1971. Since that time, it has been completely accepted by many, rejected by others, and received by some with a "wait and see" attitude (Brolin and D'Alonzo 1979). As a result, career education has been implemented in many different ways by different groups, creating a hodge-podge of career education programs.

There still appears to be a great deal of confusion concerning career education. The following is presented in an attempt to capsulize some of the concepts included in career education (Mangum et al. 1975):

- Goals and objects of career education do not conflict with those of academic classes
- Career education is not a separate class
- Career education is incorporated into each academic discipline

- Career education is not a narrow concept, antihumanistic, antiliberal, or anti-intellectual
- Career education includes a focus on values, attitudes, knowledge, and skills related to lifelong careers
- Everything required for successful careers is included in career education including communication skills, good physical and mental health, human relations skills, motivation to achieve in work, and knowledge of the economy
- Career education is not limited to school years, but is lifelong
- Persons other than school personnel, such as family members, are involved in career education

Career education, therefore, is not a simplistic, one shot, one course approach that is intent on preparing a student for a particular job. It is broad, complex, and lifelong. When properly implemented, career education should greatly facilitate vocational adaptability for the mildly handicapped.

Objectives of Career Education

Career education has been shown to be a very broad concept that can be applied to American education. While an overall goal of career education would be to better enable individuals to experience successful employment, there are many other objectives. In 1972, shortly after the concept was introduced at the federal level by Marland, Duane Mattheis (then Deputy Commissioner for School Systems in the Office of Education) suggested the following objectives for career education:

1. To provide students with a more unified curriculum with career relevance
2. To provide students beginning in elementary school with knowledge concerning career options
3. To provide students with nonacademic career options without the traditional stigma attached to such options
4. To provide comprehensive, flexible career preparation programs
5. To provide opportunities for greater involvement by employers in school programs
6. To provide students with career counseling that emphasizes realistic career options
7. To provide opportunities for reentry into the system for those who have left the system
8. To provide graduating students with necessary skills either to enter into a vocation or additional training
9. To train students to be critics of the vocational system
10. To provide opportunities for students to have input into the career education system
11. To equalize credits provided for college preparatory and vocational courses (Marland 1974).

Components of a Career Education Program

These objectives could not be reached with a simplistic approach to career education. One course on careers, a vocational education program with only two or three options, or a work-study program alone would not achieve these objectives. A comprehensive career education program begins in the elementary grades and continues beyond high school. Phelps and Lutz (1978) describe such a comprehensive program as consisting

Table 12-1 Components of Career Exploration

Component	Activities
1. Career education-educational system relationship	• Development in academic areas, such as language and communication, math, and science
2. Prevocational	• Industrial arts, home economics, general business, fine arts
3. Vocational education and community relationship	• Work experiences, such as Junior Achievement, simulated work experiences, observation of various workers
4. Career education and community relationship	• Community youth activities, such as scouting, church groups, part-time employment

Source: Phelps and Lutz 1977.

of three phases: (1) career awareness, (2) career exploration, and (3) career preparation.

Phase I, career awareness, attempts to make students aware of the many vocational opportunities available and should begin in the elementary grades. A logical place to begin such a program is with the careers of parents of students. Following an example of parents' careers, Gillet (1980) suggests an exploration of workers who come into the home such as plumbers, workers in the school environment, such as teachers and cafeteria workers, and finally workers in the immediate community and beyond. Stories, pictures, role playing, and field trips are just a few of the many ways career awareness can occur.

Career exploration, Phase II, usually occurs in junior high or middle school and enables students to explore various vocations with hands-on experiences. There are several programs that have been developed to provide career exploration opportunities. These include American Industry, The World of Manufacturing, The World of Construction, Partnership in Vocational Education, Richmond Plan, and Project Feast (Phelps and Lutz 1978). While these programs have been used extensively, teachers can develop their own career exploration programs that might have more local relevance, depending on the type of industry and other vocational opportunities available in the community. The career exploration phase of the curriculum includes four basic components. Table 12-1 describes these components and the activities of each.

Phase III, the final phase of a comprehensive career education program, is career preparation. The final phase may occur in a post secondary education setting, an industry, a vocational-technical school, high school, or the military, to name a few. The type of career preparation activity is directly related to the target career. For example, if an individual wants to become a physician, extensive formal academic training beyond high school would be required. On the other hand, if a specific factory job were the career target, two weeks of training provided by the company might be the only post high school career preparation required. The career preparation phase, therefore, is designed to provide the necessary training, formal and/or informal, vocational and/or academic, extensive and/or minimal, required to prepare an individual to perform a specific job.

Too often public school vocational programs only focus on career preparation. High school students may find that at the tenth grade level they have to decide (1) whether to go into the vocational tract or academic tract and (2) which specific area of vocational training they wish. Options available for students are extremely limited. Limited vocational training options, coupled with a lack of career awareness and career exploration, often lead to adults who are not vocationally satisfied and who are working at their jobs because it was the best job available at the time. Comprehensive career education programs can alleviate much of this discontent.

Need for Career Education in Special Education

One of the major problems facing mildly handicapped adults is adequate employment. Often, mildly handicapped adults are at a loss in finding and maintaining appropriate jobs. Brolin and D'Alonzo (1979) reviewed several studies in determining the need for career education for handicapped individuals. Their findings included the following:

- Many mentally retarded students had difficulty after leaving school
- Students who had received vocationally oriented training were better adjusted than those not receiving such training
- Personal and social skills and daily living skills were related to vocational success
- Significantly fewer handicapped adults are working than are capable
- An extremely small percentage of handicapped students are served by vocational education

These findings led Brolin and D'Alonzo to state that "there obviously is a need to go beyond the academic and work-study approach that has characterized the 1960s and 1970s" (Brolin and D'Alonzo 1979, 247). They see career education programs as providing services that previously were missing in the educational experiences of handicapped students. Brolin adds that career education is "possibly the most significant development toward improving educational services to retarded students" (Brolin 1976, 38).

In addition to mentally retarded students being able to benefit from career education, other categories of mildly disabled students could also benefit. For example, Cullinan, Epstein, and Lloyd (1983) indicate the potential of career education for behaviorally disordered students. For learning disabled students, career education needs to be made an integral part of the curriculum to eliminate much of the unemployment, underemployment, and misemployment of this group (Siegel and Gold 1982; Mercer 1983). Therefore, while career education is beneficial for all students, it appears to hold some special significance for students with disabilities. Comprehensive career education programs increase the likelihood of handicapped persons finding appropriate, gainful employment and performing well on the job.

Objectives of Career Education for Handicapped Students

The objectives of career education for handicapped students are the same as those for nonhandicapped students. However, career education for students with disabilities also includes other objectives:

- To provide career guidance, counseling, and placement services for handicapped students
- To make available the necessary physical, psychological, and financial accommodations required to serve handicapped students
- To infuse career education in the existing curricula for exceptional children, from kindergarten through high school

Career education projects in the elementary school familiarize children with the world of work.

- To enable disabled students to develop an awareness concerning many careers
- To provide career exploration activities for handicapped students
- To provide job training activities over a broad range of opportunities
- To work with community groups to ensure adequate job adjustment (Brolin and Kokaska 1979)

These objectives specifically apply to handicapped students. If they are met in career education programs, along with the general objectives previously presented, disabled students would receive a well-rounded, comprehensive career education program and be better prepared for adulthood.

Developing Career Education Programs

Unfortunately, not all schools have comprehensive career education programs. Although some schools and districts have energetically initiated programs, others have adopted a wait-and-see attitude or have totally rejected the concept. For schools that have not developed such programs and have decided that such programming should be made available for handicapped and nonhandicapped students, several steps should be taken:

1. Step I—Survey resources. Find out what the district is currently doing in the area of career education. Various teachers may be doing their own activities. If this is the case, some coordination should take place to develop a truly comprehensive, sequential program.
2. Step II—Define community resources. Survey the community to determine what agencies and groups provide services to handicapped students. For example, CETA is an agency that facilitates the employment of these students. For CETA, and other agencies, develop a listing that includes services, entrance or eligibility requirements, and contact persons.
3. Step III—Modify an existing program for career exploration or preparation. If there are no existing programs available, then new programs must be developed (Muraski 1982).

The successful development of career education is dependent on school administrators. Without the support of the school administration, it is unlikely that the program will achieve optimal success. Innovators must therefore recognize the important role played by administrators and capitalize on their positions. Also, if an existing career education program is adapted or modified for handicapped students, diplomacy is important. The career education program may be someone's special project, and trying to modify such a program for handicapped students without working within the system may prove disastrous (Muraski 1982).

Career Education for Elementary Handicapped Students

Career education programs should begin early in the school years, preferably at the elementary school. Career education for handicapped children should begin early for the following reasons:

1. Special education students often exit the school without necessary academic skills for survival in society
2. There is often a perceived difficulty in relating what is learned with real life needs
3. Many poor habits related to work adjustment are begun during elementary years
4. Deciding on an appropriate occupation is a long-term process
5. Since children often develop vocational concepts at an early age, there needs to be structure to the process to facilitate later concepts
6. Value systems begin to develop during the elementary years (Gillet 1980)

With a comprehensive career education program, many of these problem areas can be dealt with early enough to eliminate their later effects on career decisions.

Career education in the elementary school is not deciding on a career nor does it attempt to address career decision making in any way. The goal of career education at the elementary level is career awareness (Marland 1974) not career preparation. Within this overall goal are many subgoals for the elementary career education program:

1. Becoming aware of the many career possibilities and seeing themselves in different roles
2. Understanding that participation in work is a productive way of life that has many benefits
3. Being exposed to the wide range of jobs through field trips, resource people, classroom discussion, games, audiovisual materials, and simulated experiences
4. Understanding the consequences of behavior as it relates to effective social, personal, and occupational interactions and accepting responsibility for this behavior
5. Developing maximum capabilities in the basic tool subjects and using communication skills and numerical concepts to solve problems encountered in every day living situations
6. Understanding that work is a part of daily activities
7. Verbalizing necessary work habits and attitudes
8. Learning about the community and its resources, which can be used for wholesome leisure activities
9. Focusing on the person in the job rather than on the career itself
10. Understanding that there are many jobs in the world, some they are capable of, and others they won't be able to do
11. Understanding that it takes many jobs to make a functioning family and community
12. Being exposed to general work habits necessary to all jobs through class assignments and simulated experiences
13. Understanding the difference between work and play
14. Being aware that men and women can do the same kinds of work (Gillet 1980, 18)

Career education at the elementary level can be infused into most of the existing curricula. Since reading is a major emphasis area in elementary classrooms, it would be an easy task to include readings on various careers. For students with reading problems, materials need to be geared to lower reading levels or presented on tapes or through class discussions. In math, careers that utilize math could be discussed and be the subjects of story problems and math application.

One method frequently used in career awareness activities is occupational clusters, or careers that are related. The U.S. Office of Education designated fifteen clusters that can be used in career awareness programs:

- Agri-business and natural resources
- Business and office
- Communication and media
- Consumer and homemaking education
- Construction
- Environment
- Fine arts and humanities
- Health
- Hospitality and recreation
- Manufacturing
- Marine Science
- Marketing and distribution
- Personal services
- Public services
- Transportation occupations (Phelps and Lutz 1978)

Teachers might develop units based on various career clusters, using reading programs that are categorized by career clusters, or utilize the clusters in many other modes of instruction. The concept, regardless of how it is implemented, is to make young students understand the relationships among various vocations as well as learn about specific careers.

In addition to infusing career concepts into an existing curriculum and using career clusters, teachers can also develop career awareness by (1) using jobs within the classroom, (2) using school jobs such as administrative messenger, or (3) establishing a business for the classroom (Gillet 1980). These methods can be used in conjunction with other career education approaches or in isolation. Career clusters infused in the curriculum, special activities to help students understand career groups, and school jobs and businesses can be used simultaneously. With such a broad coverage, students can be expected to develop a good understanding concerning various careers.

Career Education in Secondary Schools

Career education at the secondary level should be a continuation of the program initiated in the elementary school. As previously stated, comprehensive career education programs have three phases: career awareness, career exploration, and career preparation. Career exploration and career preparation are the two activities that occur at the secondary level. Career exploration begins after career awareness. This phase is usually found in the junior high or middle school and leads directly into the career preparation phase of career education. Brolin (1976) describes a career education program for secondary educable mentally retarded students that could easily be modified for other types of disabled students. The curriculum proposed by Brolin consists of three areas: daily living skills, occupational guidance and preparation, and personal-social skills. Academic skills is a fourth area that should be supportive of the other three areas. As with career awareness, career exploration and preparation includes many elements in addition to job selection and training. This emphasizes the fact that career education is designed to develop the total person and takes into consideration that to be successful on the job requires more than simple vocational preparation activities.

Figure 12-1 depicts the secondary career education model proposed by Brolin (1976) and shows the relationship among the four areas. Since the model is competency-based, several specific competencies are specified for each curriculum area. Table 12-2 lists the competency topics related to each curriculum area.

In addition to Brolin's model for secondary career education programs for handicapped children, several other models have also been used (D'Alonzo 1983). Clark (1979) developed a model career education program called "School-Based Career Education Model for the Handicapped." The program is based on four content area components: (1) Values, Attitudes, and Habits; (2) Human Relationhips; (3) Occupational Information; and (4) Acquisition of Job and Daily Living Skills. Another model, developed by D'Alonzo (1983), is called "Career Educational Model." This approach, which assumes that children advance through the school curriculum in a sequential manner, contains seven basic environments. The first two environments focus on personnel training, environments three through six include training opportunities for students, and the final environment includes post school opportunities.

```
┌──────────────┐    ┌──────────────────┐    ┌──────────────────┐
│ Daily Living │    │ Occupational     │    │ Personal-Social  │
│   Skills     │    │ Guidance and     │    │    Skills        │
│              │    │  Preparation     │    │                  │
└──────┬───────┘    └────────┬─────────┘    └────────┬─────────┘
       │                     │                       │
       └─────────────────────┼───────────────────────┘
                             │
                     ┌───────┴──────┐
                     │   Academic   │
                     │    Skills    │
                     └──────────────┘
```

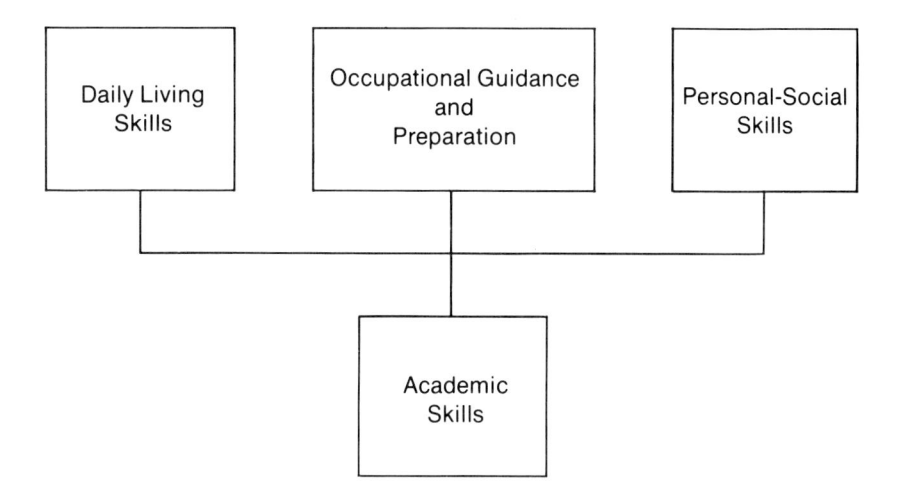

Figure 12-1   Curriculum Areas of a Career Education Program for EMR Students. Source: Reprinted, by permission, from Brolin, 1976, 194.

Table 12-2   Competencies Related to Curriculum Areas

Curriculum Area	Competency Topics
Daily Living Skills	1. Family finances
	2. Home furnishings and equipment
	3. Personal needs
	4. Children and family living
	5. Food
	6. Clothing
	7. Civic activities
	8. Recreation and leisure time
	9. Mobility
Personal-Social Skills	10. Self awareness and appraisal
	11. Self-confidence and self-concept
	12. Socially responsive behavior
	13. Appropriate interpersonal relationships
	14. Indepedent functioning
	15. Problem solving
	16. Communication with others
Occupational Guidance and Preparation	17. Occupational awareness and exploration
	18. Job selection
	19. Appropriate work habits
	20. Necessary skills
	21. Entry level skills
	22. Vocational adjustment

Source: Brolin 1976, 194–200.

Role of Special Education Teacher

Implementation of career education programs requires a change in the traditional role performed by special education teachers. At the elementary level, special education teachers would assist in the infusion of career education elements in the existing curriculum, as well as develop career education units to be used in the resource room. Self-contained special education teachers would develop career education units and would be the primary individuals integrating career education concepts in the curriculum.

The role of the secondary special education teacher also changes with career education. In schools implementing career education programs, special education teachers:

- become more like coordinators or advisors to teachers,
- integrate the resources of the school, community, and home in developing relevant career education options,
- advise other school personnel on methods of working with individual students, and
- take the responsibility to determine if the required competencies for graduation have been met by individual students (Brolin 1976).

VOCATIONAL EDUCATION

Vocational education has been a component in public schools for many years. Since around World War I, various aspects of vocational education have been in some schools (D'Alonzo 1983). During the past two decades, vocational education has grown significantly. Marsh and Price (1980) suggest that two of the major reasons for the recent growth in vocational education programs have been the shifting of the economy from an agrarian to an industrialized base and the population shift from rural to urban. Prior to these actions, a large percentage of students lived in rural areas and followed their families into the farming business. Schools were not required to provide specific **vocational training** because students did not enter jobs requiring specific skills. As a result of the economy shifting to its current industrialized base, however, the need for schools to prepare individuals for specific vocations increased. Not only are schools expected to train students in specific skill areas, but they are severely criticized when students graduate from high school without specific, saleable skills.

Vocational education in American schools is widespread. The focus of vocational education programs varies greatly and is directly related to the occupational composition of the community (Phelps 1983; Marsh and Price 1980). For example, rural school districts may still emphasize agricultural education while larger districts in urban areas would provide education in a broad range of skills such as metal working, carpentry, and cosmetology.

Vocational education has obviously been defined by many different groups and individuals in many ways. The definition used by the federal government states that vocational education.

> means organized education programs which are directly related to the preparation of individuals for paid or unpaid employment, or for additional preparation for a career requiring other than a baccalaureate or advanced degree; and, for purposes of this paragraph, the term "organized education program" means only, (a) instruction related to the occupation or occupations for which the students are in training, and (b) the acquisition, maintenance, and

repair of instructional supplies, teaching aids and equipment, and the term "vocational education" does not mean the construction, acquisition, or initial equipment of buildings, or the acquisition or rental of land. (Title 45, *U. S. Code of Federal Regulations*, 1979, p. 166)

Basically, the definition means training directly related to the preparation of students for employment or other training related to employment. This distinction is made between preparation for occupations that do not require a university degree and those that do.

The relationship between career and vocational education has been confusing to many people. Vocational education is a part of career education. Career education is the more encompassing and more general, while vocational education is more specific. A basic difference between the two is that vocational education occurs at the secondary or post secondary level, while career education can be implemented at any level and is considered lifelong (Phelps 1983). In addition to differences, there are similarities. Both focus on the employment of individuals, both occur in school and in the community, and both are major components in many school districts. Figure 12-2 illustrates the relationship between career and vocational education.

Vocational education is a critical need for many mildly handicapped individuals. Career education may help alleviate vocational problems experienced by handicapped adults; however, career education must include the vocational education component for specific job training and experiences. Vocational education can benefit many different types of handicapped children, including the typically identified mildly handicapped groups of educable mentally retarded and learning disabled (Mann et al. 1978), as well as others such as emotionally disturbed children (Cullinan et al. 1983). Without vocational training for handicapped students, the current problems faced by disabled adults will continue to plague these individuals.

Not only is vocational education needed by handicapped children, it is also mandated by law that it be provided to this population. Public Law 94-142, which requires a free appropriate public education for all handicapped children, includes vocational education as being an integral component of appropriate educational services for some handicapped children. The key element is the determination of what is appropriate for a particular handicapped child. This decision is reached after assessment information is presented to a committee of teachers, administrators, and parents. If it is determined that the child in question needs vocational education in order to be afforded a free appropriate public education, then the school is legally obligated to provide such a program.

```
SCHOOL              :              COMMUNITY
_____:_____
                    :
          CAREER  EDUCATION
                    :
             Vocational Education
                    :
```

Figure 12-2   Source: Phelps 1983.

Developing Vocational Education Programs

There is a need for comprehensive vocational education programs for handicapped children. Schools often have some vocational training programs, but these may be limited. Other schools may have ample vocational education programs for nonhandicapped children, but offer few of these services to the handicapped. Regardless of the reason for a lack of vocational options for handicapped children, school personnel must develop these programs for this group. In developing such programs, certain objectives should be considered. The Council for Exceptional Children has suggested several objectives for planning vocational education programs (Davis and Ward, n.d.). Figure 12-3 includes these suggestions.

Planning vocational educational programs requires a great deal of collaboration among several individuals and groups. Davis and Ward (n.d.) suggest that a vocational planning team conduct planning activities, and that this team include representatives from education, vocational rehabilitation, parents, and various community groups. Disabled students should also be included on the team in order to provide input from actual consumers of vocational programs. By involving several groups in the planning process, schools gain the perspective of persons both within and outside of the school that are

---

- Vocational education shall be available as a discrete element on a continuum of career education experiences provided for handicapped students to enable them to learn about and prepare for work.
- Appropriate prevocational experiences shall be provided to prepare each handicapped student for placement in vocational education.
- Every handicapped student shall have the opportunity to participate in a regular or special vocational education program in order to develop job-specific skills.
- Vocational assessment shall be provided to determine the student's interests and vocational aptitudes in order to develop an appropriate individualized education program.
- Supportive (related) services shall be provided as needed to maximize a handicapped student's potential for success in a regular or specially designed vocational education program.
- Work experience options shall be available to help handicapped students bridge the gap between the school program and the world of work.
- Vocational counseling and job placement and follow-up services shall be provided to assist handicapped students in securing and maintaining jobs suitable to their abilities and interests.
- Appropriate work activities or sheltered employment training programs shall be provided to develop work skills for those students whose handicapping conditions are so severe as to prevent their immediate inclusion in occupational skill preparation programs.

Figure 12-3 *Objectives for Planning Vocational Education Programs. Source: Davis and Ward, n.d., 2.*

crucial for the success of the program. For example, it makes sense to include business leaders in planning vocational programs since these are the individuals with whom schools must cooperate for on-the-job placements. Also business leaders can make suggestions for the training program that will train students for jobs that are available in the community, and thus enhance the likelihood that graduates will be employable upon completion of the training program. Comprehensive planning for vocational programs for the handicapped will increase the chances that handicapped students will receive appropriate vocational training that can lead to actual employment opportunities.

Goals and Objectives for Programs

The overall goal of vocational education for handicapped students should be to prepare students for jobs or additional training. Other goals would include meeting society's need for trained personnel; increasing the vocational options of students; providing students with information related to the relevance of work (Phelps 1983); increasing personal abilities, self-image, and emotional control; developing an awareness of interpersonal skills; and securing employment (Marsh and Price 1980). The goals listed are general. More specific goals must be developed for student IEPs so programming can be individualized and meet the unique needs of individual students.

Problems in Delivering Vocational Education to the Handicapped

Although the need for vocational education for disabled students is obvious and federal legislation mandates its provision, there are many problems in delivering these services, including negative attitudes, inadequate personnel preparation, low funding, and lack of interagency cooperation and agreements (Greenan 1982). Special education teachers must have a positive attitude concerning vocational education and attempt to learn more about vocational training programs. If special education teachers believe that vocational education programs are inappropriate for disabled students and that vocational education teachers are insensitive, then the likelihood that their students will benefit from vocational education is lessened. Similarly, if vocational education teachers do not want special education students in their classes, the chances of success are also diminished.

One variable that often affects attitudes is knowledge. Special education teachers need some training in vocational education, and vocational education teachers need some training in special education. Personnel preparation programs for these two disciplines should therefore be modified.

One potential problem that often surfaces in the area of vocational education for handicapped students is whether or not the program should be separate or integrated. In other words, should handicapped students be mainstreamed into regular vocational education programs or should separate vocational education programs be developed for this group of students? Public Law 94-142 requires that handicapped students be educated with nonhandicapped students when possible. Therefore, the legal mandate would appear to require that vocational education be provided for handicapped students in mainstreamed vocational classes. Several problems exist in providing services in this manner: untrained vocational education teachers, necessary modifications of training materials and equipment, and negative attitudes. Regardless of these potential problems, efforts should be made to include handicapped students in regular vocational education

Vocational success can have a direct effect on the individual's feelings of self worth.

programs. D'Alonzo suggests that in order to accommodate handicapped students in regular vocational classes, the following be considered:

- inservice education for all personnel involved with the students
- individualization of instruction
- flexibility in scheduling
- additional time for the students to complete assignments and develop vocational skills
- follow-along personnel to tutor and help the students adjust
- special education consultants to the vocational educator
- orientation periods during the academic year and special summer programs so the students can get a feel for vocational education and the vocational educator for them
- modification of textbooks, technical manual content, instruction, machinery, equipment, or methods
- peer tutoring, buddy systems, programmed learning, minicourses, instructional packages
- extended school day and year programs, evening and weekend courses
- extensive use of audiovisual equipment and materials, e.g., movies, overhead projectors, filmstrips, cassette slide projectors, videotaping, television, radio, record players, cassette tape recorders, opaque projectors, tutorgram
- alternate grading and testing procedures (D'Alonzo 1983, 443–44)

Modifications necessary to accommodate mildly handicapped students in regular vocational education programs will vary according to the type of disability served and the type of vocational training provided. For example, visually impaired students would require significantly different modifications than learning disabled students, hearing impaired students, and mentally retarded students. The types and extent of modifications will differ from student to student and must be a part of the individualizing of educational programs.

In some situations, schools may develop specialized vocational training programs for handicapped children. These programs have disadvantages in that they are isolated from the regular vocational programs and therefore minimize contact among handicapped and nonhandicapped children. Some advantages exist, however, in grouping handicapped children together in vocational classes: instructors can better prepare for the special needs of the group; program modifications may be similar for many members of the group; and special education teachers can spend entire periods of the day working with the vocational educator in the specialized class. The major problem in vocational education for handicapped children in special classes is that even though many of the modifications made for these children will be similar, different handicapping conditions require different accommodations (Mann et al. 1978). Consideration must therefore be made for the specific needs of each individual student, regardless of the classification or type of handicap. Generic vocational education whether provided in regular vocational education classes or in separate programs must take into consideration individual needs.

Vocational Evaluation

In order for vocational education programs to meet the needs of individual handicapped students, a comprehensive evaluation must be conducted. "Educational planning teams are looking for concrete, specific data to assist them in determining appropriate vocational objectives . . . that can be translated into individualized education programs (IEPs)" (Richter-Stein and Stodden 1981, 117). Without adequate assessment data to determine objectives and teaching strategies, the vocational programs designed for handicapped students may be inappropriate. Vocational evaluation should be a part of the overall assessment of handicapped students prior to developing the vocational portion of their IEP.

Many formal instruments have been developed to assess vocational interests and skills. Users of these tests must take into account several considerations:

- Student's probable motivation and ability to achieve on the particular test
- Relevance of the task to actual employment situations
- Likelihood of obtaining reliable meaurements from a single performance
- Usefulness of comparison of scores with general population norms
- Adaptability for use with handicapped students
- Validity for students with particular handicapping conditions
- Value of criterion-referenced rather than norm-referenced instruments (Davis and Ward, n.d., 28).

Many of the vocational assessment instruments do not meet the needs of handicapped individuals. They often present only forced choice response options, are biased against various groups, and have inappropriate reading levels (Stodden et al. 1979). Despite these criticisms of some tests, there are available tests that can be very useful. Individuals conducting vocational evaluations need to be aware of the various instruments and select those that are technically sound.

In addition to using standardized assessment instruments, other modes of assessing vocational skills can be used. Richter-Stein and Stodden suggest the use of simulated job samples to assess vocational aptitude. The advantage of such an approach is that examiners gather information "through a student-centered process, rather than through teacher/evaluator-directed, content-based data collection" (Richter-Stein and Stodden 1981, 117). The results should be more accurate and valid and have some relevance to programming decisions. Scores obtained on standardized tests do not always provide such useful information.

Brolin (1976) suggests that vocational evaluation must be comprehensive if it is to be of maximum benefit. He suggests that four components be included in the evaluation: (1) clinical assessment, (2) work evaluation, (3) work adjustment, and (4) on-the-job tryouts. The point made by Brolin is that many variables influence the success of individuals in a vocational setting. Merely assessing vocational skills such as manual dexterity will not provide ample information to determine the types and nature of needed vocational training. Vocational evaluation requires a great deal of time and planning and utilizes information gained from a variety of processes.

Service Delivery

Schools have several options to choose from in providing vocational education to handicapped children. These include (1) programs provided through the school, (2) agreements with other districts, (3) agreements with private agencies or schools, (4) collaborative arrangements with public agencies other than schools, and (5) collaboration with local employers (Davis and Ward, n.d.) The mode utilized by schools will probably depend on several variables including the size of the school, wealth of the school, geographic location of the school (rural or urban), composition of industry and businesses in the area, philosophy of the school, and location of regional programs such as a vocational-technical school. The important thing is that the school take the responsibility to provide appropriate programs to the children in the district.

Types of Vocational Programs. There are several different vocational options that should be available in a comprehensive vocational program. These program options can be divided into prevocational programs and vocational programs. Gearheart (1980) categorizes vocational programs as low-cost skill training programs and high-cost skill training. Table 12-3 lists the various program options subsumed under these categories.

Prevocational programs. While the literature does not often focus on prevocational skills, many skills are prerequisites to obtaining and maintaining employment. Although studies have shown that handicapped individuals are capable of employment, many are unemployed or underemployed due to their lack of prevocational skills. A study by Smith (1981) determined that employers often view skills such as being able to complete a job application and conduct job interviews as important. Smith concluded that handicapped individuals may not get the opportunity to prove their vocational worth without such prerequisite skills.

Other skills that are included in the prevocational realm include knowing how to find jobs, communication skills, interpersonal skills, behavior on the job, and realistic job aspirations. Several studies have investigated the skill levels of handicapped individuals in these areas, as well as programs designed to remove deficiencies. One such program de-

Table 12-3 **Major Vocational Training Programs**

Low-Cost Skill Training	High-Cost Skill Training
• Work Experience • Work-Study • On-the-Job Training • Off-Campus Work Stations • Cooperative Programs	• Skill Training in Very Specific Skills Areas

Source: Gearheart 1980.

scribed by Hill, Wehman, and Pentecost (1980) was aimed at developing job interview skills in mentally retarded adults. While the results indicated that mentally retarded subjects lacked certain prosocial behaviors, such as orienting to the interviewer, appropriate verbal responses, and other behaviors that lead to a good impression during interviews, it was also determined that such behaviors can be learned. Another study demonstrated that interview behavior of retarded individuals can be improved with minimal training (Elias-Burger et al. 1981).

McGee (1981) described a program designed to improve the job seeking skills of learning disabled students where students reviewed different application forms, practiced surveying classified advertisements for available jobs, and role played job interviews. Following participation in the program, approximately 70 percent of the students were functioning in jobs they had independently secured. A program to improve job-seeking skills of visually impaired persons was described by Robinson (1983). This program, implemented at the Lighthouse of Houston, includes self-awareness, interpersonal communication, and specific skills associated with finding jobs.

One area that should be dealt with in prevocational programs is vocational vocabulary. Schilit and Caldwell (1980) used the Delphi Technique to determine the primary 100 words needed by individuals seeking employment. One hundred professionals involved in career and vocational education were participants. The 100 words identified are listed in Table 12-4. Vocational education programs should ensure that students are cognizant of this word list prior to searching for employment.

Role playing is probably the best method for teaching appropriate on-the-job behavior. Punctuality, getting along with fellow workers, getting along with superiors, and job interviews, can all be included in role playing situations. Many commercial materials can be obtained that focus on these types of topics.

Low-Cost Skill Training Programs. Gearheart (1980) described five programs considered low-cost skill training: work experience, work-study, on-the-job training, off-campus work stations, and cooperative programs. **Work experience programs** are described as being slightly more advanced than prevocational programs; students are guided through simulated work experiences by instructors. This allows students to gain some experience related to an actual employment situation. Work experience programs are considered a part of some prevocational programs.

Work Study Programs. **Work-study programs** are found more often in public schools than work experience programs. These programs have become more prevalent, especially for mentally retarded students, during the past few years. Work-study programs are based on the concept that there should be a close relationship between academic training and vocational education. Although programs vary somewhat, the basic format is for stu-

Table 12-4 100 Most Essential Career/Vocational Words

1. rules	26. supervisor	51. entrance	76. withholding
2. boss	27. vacation	52. responsible	77. vote
3. emergency	28. apply	53. hospital	78. break
4. danger	29. fulltime	54. hourly rate	79. cooperation
5. job	30. income	55. schedule	80. dependable
6. social security	31. quit	56. instructions	81. money
7. first-aid	32. check	57. save	82. physical
8. help wanted	33. careful	58. union	83. hazardous
9. safety	34. dangerous	59. credit	84. net income
10. warning	35. employee	60. elevator	85. strike
11. signature	36. layoff	61. punctuality	86. owner
12. time	37. take-home-pay	62. rights	87. repair
13. attendance	38. unemployed	63. hours	88. alarm
14. absent	39. cost	64. payroll	89. gross income
15. telephone	40. deduction	65. attitude	90. manager
16. bill	41. fired	66. reliable	91. reference
17. hired	42. closed	67. work	92. uniform
18. overtime	43. parttime	68. caution	93. hard-hat
19. punch in	44. correct	69. license	94. authority
20. directions	45. foreman	70. poison	95. training
21. paycheck	46. time-and-a-half	71. office	96. holiday
22. wages	47. worker	72. power	97. late
23. appointment	48. buy	73. qualifications	98. personal
24. income tax	49. raise	74. earn	99. tools
25. interview	50. on-the-job	75. transportation	100. area

Source: Reprinted, by permission from Schilit and Caldwell 1980, 115.

dents to be in academic classes part of the school day and on a job away from the school the remainder of the day. The academic portion of the program is geared to provide necessary skills for vocational success (Hallahan and Kauffman 1982). All work-study programs attempt to facilitate the student's bridging the gap between the school world and the vocational world (D'Alonzo and Mauser 1973). They also serve to prepare the student for future employment (Kalwara and Kokaska 1969); assist in emotional, social, and occupational adjustment (Carroll 1967); motivate the student to apply basic skills he has learned; promote the development of a positive self-concept (D'Alonzo and Mauser 1973); provide foundations in practical academic knowledge and skills (Walthall and Love 1974); and produce graduates who receive better pay and work more hours per week than handicapped students who do not participate in programs (Chaffin et al. 1971; Brolin et al. 1975).

The other three types of low-cost skill training are more often used with severely handicapped individuals. Table 12-5 briefly describes these options.

High-Cost Skill Training Programs. High-cost training programs are designed to train students for specific vocations. Programs typically found in some schools include those that focus on secretarial skills, auto engine mechanics, construction, plumbing, cosmetology, welding, horticulture, auto body mechanics, graphic arts and drafting, and appliance repair. The variety of programs offered at any one school will vary considerably. As new careers emerge, such as data processing, schools are expected to include them in their vocational program options. High-cost skill training can occur in a regular vocational

Table 12-5 **Low-Cost Skill Training for More Severely Handicapped Students**

Training Program	Description
• On-the-Job Training	Training essential skills for a particular job either at the job site or with work samples at school
• Off-Campus Work Station	An intermediate step between sheltered and competitive employment. Disabled individual works in a factory, business, or other job on the premises under supervision from school.
• Cooperative Programs	Agreement between an institution and local school or vocational-technical school to provide training for residents

Source: Gearheart 1980.

education program or in a separate program specifically designed for children who are disabled.

When separated for handicapped children, vocational skill training can take on many designs. The arrangements vary from the very simple to the complex. An example of a simple approach to providing separate vocational training for handicapped students would be a program at Rindge and Latin High School in Cambridge, Massachusetts. This program turned a Xerox room into a copy center operated by handicapped students. Students learned such skills as using the photocopy machine, sorting, delivery, and consulting with customers (teachers). The goal of the program is to expand into a mail/central supply center (Copy center is a classroom, 1982).

Adams (1981) described a program for emotionally disturbed children established in the Salem County (New Jersey) Vocational Technical School District. This program combined the services of special education teachers and vocational educators. During the first phase of the program, students were placed in a regular shop setting for emotionally disturbed children. Following success in the segregated setting, students were moved into a transitional program designed to facilitate their participation in the regular vocational program. The team approach and transitional program have increased the number of emotionally disturbed children mainstreamed into regular vocational classes by 500 percent (Adams 1981). Another vocational training program for emotionally disturbed children was described by Webster (1981). This program, called the Alternative Vocational School (AVS), served secondary emotionally disturbed children from fourteen different school districts. Four components are included in the program: vocational-technical training component, clinical services component, learning disabilities component, and job preparation and placement component. Figure 12-4 details the subcomponents of each area.

Role of Personnel in Vocational Education

Vocational Education Teachers. Prior to the mainstreaming movement, vocational education teachers rarely came into contact with handicapped students. As a result of current practices, however, vocational education teachers must play a major role in the

```
┌──────────────┐                              ┌──────────────┐
│Job Preparation│                              │ Vocational-  │
│     and      │                              │  Technical   │
│  Placement   │                              │   Training   │
└──────┬───────┘                              └──────┬───────┘
       \                                             /
        \                                           /
         \         ┌──────────────┐                /
          _____│Administration│_____/
          /        └──────────────┘               \
         /                                          \
        /                                            \
┌──────┴───────┐                              ┌──────┴───────┐
│   Clinical   │                              │   Learning   │
│   Services   │                              │ Disabilities │
└──────────────┘                              └──────────────┘
```

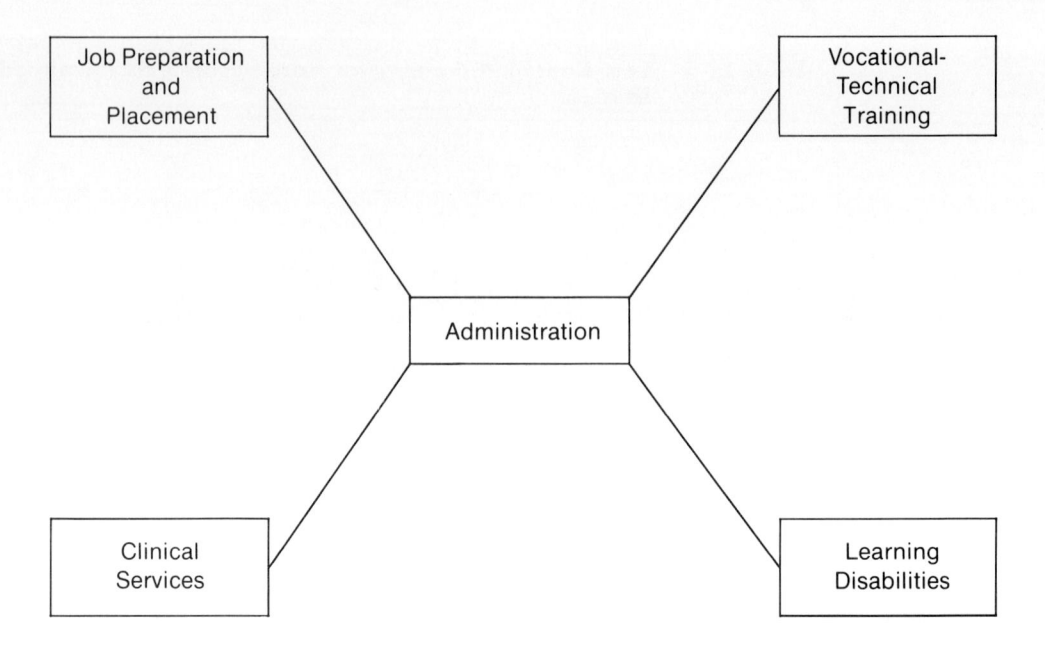

Figure 12-4   Organization of the Alternative Vocational School, East Hartford, Connecticut. Source: R.E. Webster, Vocational-technical training for emotionally disturbed adolescents. *Teaching Exceptional Children*, 1981, *14*(2), 75–59.

vocational preparation of handicapped children. Often vocational teachers are the primary instructors of mainstreamed handicapped children. Even though special education resource teachers are available for consultation, the burden of education is placed on the regular vocational staff. This means that vocational teachers need to be competent in teaching techniques for special children. Methods of accommodating children with below average cognitive abilities, limited reading skills, sensory impairments, and mobility handicaps need to be understood and practiced. This requires inservice training, one-on-one consultation with special education personnel, and above all, a positive attitude on the part of vocational educators.

Special Education Teachers. Special education teachers need to become more involved with vocational education than they have been in the past. If vocational education teachers are having to assume a major role in the education of handicapped children, special education teachers should be available to provide support services such as suggestions for teaching strategies, materials modification, equipment modification, and behavior control. Close collaboration must occur beginning with the referral process and continuing through IEP development and program implementation and ending with the annual review of progress. Special education teachers should assume a role of consultant to the vocational education specialist.

Other School Personnel. In addition to the vocational education teacher and the special education teacher, other school personnel must be involved in the vocational education program if it is to meet the needs of handicapped children. Administrators are needed to

With proper training many mildly handicapped adults become successful workers.

provide leadership and administrative support; counselors must be available for necessary assessment information, counseling, and assistance in scheduling. Other regular classroom teachers who come into contact with handicapped children should also be involved in providing appropriate services. The bottom line is that the education of handicapped children, including vocational education, must be a team effort. Collaboration and team work must prevail if appropriate educational services are provided to this segment of the school population.

SUMMARY

This chapter focused on career and vocational education for mildly handicapped children. It was emphasized that many mildly handicapped adults have difficulty in obtaining and maintaining jobs because of their poor vocational preparation. Career education, a concept that developed in the early 1970s, was defined and suggestions were provided for developing career education programs for handicapped children. This approach requires limited resources; there is no need for additional teachers, materials, or space. The entire program can be implemented into the existing program. It includes a broad range of areas beginning with career awareness and culminating with successful employment. Since it is intended to be a comprehensive approach to lifelong employment, most professionals agree that it should begin in the elementary school. Although career education can be beneficial to all children, it has a particular place in the education of handicapped children.

The second major section of this chapter presented information related to vocational education. Vocational education, which is a part of career education, primarily occurs at the secondary and post-secondary levels. It trains individuals in particular job skills. Not only is vocational education needed by handicapped children, but federal law also requires that it be made available to handicapped children when considered appropriate.

Methods for implementing vocational education programs were presented, along with the various options for providing such programs. It was pointed out that there is some controversy concerning whether or not vocational education programs for handicapped children should be provided in regular vocational education classes or segregated classes for special education. Although there are advantages and disadvantages for both options, most professionals agree that vocational education for handicapped children should be provided in regular vocational classes alongside nonhandicapped children. Not only does this option meet the least-restrictive-setting mandate of P.L. 94–142, it also provides handicapped children with the opportunity to interact with their nonhandicapped peers.

The point made during the entire chapter was that many mildly handicapped adults who experience vocational problems might be better vocationally adjusted if they had been exposed to comprehensive career and vocational programming during their public school program. Although not a panacea to many problems of the adult handicapped, career and vocational education can do much to eliminate the vocational problems of this group.

References

Adams, W.H. Vocational training that works for the emotionally disturbed. *Phi Delta Kappan* 63, no. 1 (1981):64.

Brolin, D.E. *Vocational preparation of retarded citizens*. Columbus, Ohio: Charles E. Merrill, 1976.

Brolin, D., R. Durand, K. Kromer, and P. Muller. Post-school adjustment of educable retarded students. *Education and Training of the Mentally Retarded*, 10 (1975):144–49.

Brolin, D.E., and B.J. D'Alonzo. Critical issues in career education for handicapped students. *Exceptional Children* 45, no. 4 (1979):246–53.

Brolin, D.E., and C.J. Kokaska. *Career education for handicapped children and youth*. Columbus, Ohio: Charles E. Merrill, 1979.

Carroll, H.L. Work-study programs—A positive approach for slow learners. *Digest of the Mentally Retarded* 4 (1967):13–17.

Chaffin, J.D., C.R. Spellman, C.E. Regan, and R. Davison. Two follow-up studies of former educable mentally retarded students from the Kansas work-study project. *Exceptional Children* 37 (1971):733–38.

Clark, G.M. *Career education for the handicapped child in the elementary classroom.* Denver: Love Publishing Company, 1979.

Copy center is a classroom for special education. *American School and University* 54 no. 11 (1982):10–11.

Cullinan, D., M.H. Epstein, and J.W. Lloyd. *Behavior disorders of children and adolescents.* Englewood Cliffs, N. J.: Prentice–Hall, 1983.

D'Alonzo, B.J. *Educating adolescents with learning and behavior problems.* Rockville, Md.: Aspen Systems Corp., 1983.

D'Alonzo, B.J., and A.J. Mauser. Programming for the high school age educable mentally retarded: An emerging model. *Contemporary Education* 44 (1973):275–80.

Davis, S., and M. Ward. *Vocational education of handicapped students.* Reston, Va.: Council for Exceptional Children, n.d.

Elias-Burger, S.F., C.K. Sigelman, W.E. Danley, and D.L. Burger. Teaching interview skills to mentally retarded persons. *American Journal of Mental Deficiency* 85, no. 6 (1981):655–57.

Fafard, M.R., and P.A. Haubrich. Vocational and social adjustment of learning disabled young adults: A followup study. *Learning Disabilities Quarterly* 4, no. 2 (1981):122–30.

Gearheart, B.R. *Special education for the 80s.* St. Louis: C.V. Mosby, 1980.

Gillet, P. Career education in the special elementary education program. *Teaching Exceptional Children* 13, no. 1 (1980):17–21.

Greenan, J.P. Problems and issues in delivering vocational education instruction and support services to students with learning disabilities. *Journal of Learning Disabilities*, 15, no. 4 (1982):231–35.

Hallahan, D.P., and J.M. Kauffman. *Exceptional children: Introduction to special education.* Englewood Cliffs, N.J.: Prentice-Hall, 1982.

Hill, C., and R. Algozzine. An analysis of employment decision making with implications for training the mentally retarded. *Education and Training of the Mentally Retarded* 17, no. 4 (1982):299–304.

Hill, J.W., P. Wehman, and J. Pentecost. Developing job interview skills in mentally retarded adults. *Education and Training of the Mentally Retarded* 15, no. 3 (1980):179–86.

Kalwara, S., and J. Kokaska. Preparing the retarded for semi-skilled and skilled occupations. *Education and Training of the Mentally Retarded* 4 (1969):71–74.

Kirchner, C., and R. Peterson. Worktime, occupational status, and annual earnings: An assessment of underemployment. *Journal of Visual Impairment and Blindness* 74, no. 5 (1980):203–205.

McGee, D.W. Sharpen students' job seeking skills with employment applications and role played interviews. *Teaching Exceptional Children* 13, no. 4 (1981):152–55.

Mangum, G.L., J.W. Becker, G. Coombs, and P. Marshall. Introduction to career education in the academic classroom. In *Career education in the academic classroom* edited by G.L. Mangum, J.W. Becker, G. Coombs, and P. Marshall. Salt Lake City, Utah: Olympic Publishing Company, 1975.

Mann, L., L. Goodman, and J.L. Wiederholt. *Teaching the learning-disabled adolescent.* Boston: Houghton Mifflin, 1978.

Marland, S.P., Jr. *Career education: A proposal for reform.* New York: McGraw-Hill, 1974.

Marsh, G.E., II, and B.J. Price. *Methods for teaching the mildly handicapped adolescent.* St. Louis: C.V. Mosby, 1980.

Mercer, C.D. *Students with learning disabilities.* Columbus, Ohio: Charles E. Merrill, 1983.

Muraski, J.A. Designing career education programs that work. *Academic Therapy* 18, no. 1 (1982):65–71.

Phelps, L.A. Vocational and career education. In *The exceptional child: A functional approach*, edited by R.M. Smith, J.T. Neisworth, and F.M. Hunt. New York: McGraw-Hill, 1983.

Phelps, L.A., and R.J. Lutz. *Career exploration and preparation for the special needs learner.* Boston: Allyn and Bacon, 1977.

Richter-Stein, C., and R.A. Stodden. Simulated job samples: A student-centered approach to vocational exploration and evaluation. *Teaching Exceptional Children*, 14, no. 3 (1981):116–119.

Robinson, K. Employment skills development. In *Blindness: 1982-1983 AAWB annual*, edited by G.G. Mallinson. Alexandria, Va.: American Association of Workers for the Blind, 1983.

Schilit, J., and M.L. Caldwell. A word list of essential career/vocational words for mentally retarded students. *Education and Training of the Mentally Retarded*, 15, no. 2 (1980):113–117.

Siegel, J., and R. Gold. *Educating the learning disabled.* New York: Macmillan, 1982.

Smith, C.R. *Learning disabilities: The interaction of learner, task, and setting.* Boston: Little, Brown and Co. 1983.

Smith, T.E.C. Employer concerns in hiring mentally retarded persons. *Rehabilitation Counseling Bulletin*, 24, no. 4 (1981):316–318.

Stodden, R.A., R.M. Inanacone, and A.L. Lazar. Occupational interests and mentally retarded people: Review and recommendations. *Mental Retardation*, 17, no. 6 (1979):294–98.

Tyler, G.T. Vocational information seminar. *Journal of Visual Impairment and Blindness*, 76, no. 10 (1982):419–420.

U.S. Government. State vocational education programs. *Title 45 a.s. Code of Federal Regulations 1361.* Washington, D.C.: U.S. Government Printing Office, 1 October 1979.

Walthall, J.E., and H.D. Love. *Habilitation of the mentally retarded.* Springfield, Ill.: Charles C. Thomas, 1974.

Webster, R.E. Vocational-technical training for emotionally disturbed adolescents. *Teaching Exceptional Children*, 14, no. 2 (1981):75–79.

Wurster, M.V. Career education for visually impaired students: Where we've been and where we are. *Education of the Visually Handicapped*, 14, no. 4 (1983):99–104.

Zucker, S.H., and R. Altman. An on-the-job vocational training program for adolescent trainable retardates. *The Training School Bulletin*, 70 (1973):106–109.

Chapter Thirteen

THE FUTURE

CHAPTER OUTLINE

INTRODUCTION
CURRENT AND FUTURE TRENDS
    Reduced Federal Role
    Parent Advocacy
    Special Education and Professional Standards
    Technology and Special Education
    Deinstitutionalization
    The Reform Movement
CONCLUSIONS
SUMMARY

CHAPTER OBJECTIVES

After reading this chapter, you should be able to:
- Discuss difficulties in predicting the future of special education and services for mildly handicapped children and adults;
- List and discuss various predictions of future trends in special education;
- Describe the reduced federal involvement in special education and its impact on programs;
- Identify ways parents will influence services for mildly handicapped children in the future;
- Discuss the future role of technology in services to the mildly handicapped;
- List new technological aids for the handicapped;
- Describe medical advances and their role with mildly handicapped persons;
- Define deinstitutionalization; and
- Identify the role of the new right in special education.

INTRODUCTION

The future of special education for mildly handicapped children and adults is unclear. As a result of legislation and litigation in the 1970s and early 1980s, services for mildly handicapped children and adults have reached a new dimension. Children are guaranteed a free appropriate education at public expense in the least restrictive setting; handicapped adults are protected by law from discrimination in employment, housing, and other areas. Whether these gains will be maintained, expanded, or reversed remains to be seen.

If the future is not anticipated, educators and other service providers may lack adequate preparation. But by projecting the future, professionals are better able to plan appropriate services for handicapped children and adults, as well as to develop contingency plans to counter any predicted negative effects on services, such as reduced funding, reversals of litigation, and the introduction of legislation to counter previous legislative gains. To be prepared for the future, "educators need to search for, become aware of, and prepare for alternative futures" (Schipper and Kenowitz 1976, 401).

Although it is not possible to predict the future with any degree of certainty, some trends in special education and other services will likely continue during the next decade (Podemski et al. 1984). In 1983, a study was conducted to predict future trends in special education. It surveyed administrators, teachers, and advocacy group members in three states. Some of the predictions for future trends include the following:

1. Parents will be involved in programs aimed at teaching techniques for supporting learning in the home
2. Parents will insist on cost effectiveness
3. Computers will be used in IEP development
4. Inadequate preparation for post–high school success will be addressed
5. Placement committees will be required to visit special schools and classrooms prior to decision making
6. Graduating special education students will provide input for program evaluation
7. Federal regulations under P.L. 94-142 will be eliminated with states filling the void
8. "At risk" children will be identified and provided early intervention programs
9. Minimum wage laws will be changed to allow handicapped workers to be paid based on production rates
10. Improved methods will be used for selecting students to be mainstreamed
11. Group homes and sheltered workshops will be emphasized for disabled adults
12. Preservice instruction for regular educators will be a focus
13. Classroom teachers will be utilized for inservice training over university and administrative personnel
14. Individuals will be required to demonstrate teaching skills (O'Shea and Gajar 1983).

These conclusions were drawn using the Delphi technique, a method that utilizes the expectations of knowledgeable persons to make projections for the future (Schipper and Kenowitz 1976). While not comprehensive, it does provide a data base for predicting future trends in special education.

Another study predicted events that would occur in special education from 1976 through 2000. The participants in this study were 121 special education administrators. Results, also obtained with the Delphi technique, were divided into four categories. Table 13-1 describes some of the trends projected.

Table 13-1 **Special Education Trends: 1976–2000**

Trend	Target Date
Highly Valued Events	
Due process procedures guaranteed to all exceptional students	1980
All exceptional children will be receiving services	1990
Uniformity of opportunities will transcend state and district boundaries	1995
Somewhat Valued Events	
Mainstreaming is a reality in most public schools	1985
Residential institutions provide services for only severe and profound persons	1989
Programs for profoundly retarded students are part of public school programs	1990
Local, state, and federal governments share in planning, managing, and funding programs	1990
National parent groups form a coalition	1990
Neutrally Valued Events	
Bureau of Education for the Handicapped is decentralized	1985
Block grants replace categorical funding	1985
Negatively Valued Events	
Supreme Court rules compulsory school	2000
Teacher unions dictate decisions concerning special education	1990

Source: Schipper and Kenowitz 1976.

Although some of these projections may not become reality, planning for them precludes educators from being surprised by new developments. Of course, not all trends can be predicted, but attempts to predict and plan accordingly can only add to the quality of services provided to disabled individuals.

The future of special education and other services for handicapped individuals will definitely hinge on several factors. These include the role of the federal government, strength of current reform movements, financial resources, direction of the courts in litigation, the technological explosion, and results from research investigating topics such as the efficacy of serving mildly handicapped children in resource rooms.

Some interesting developments in education are likely to have implications for the handicapped and nonhandicapped. An example is the notion that a highly intelligent person is able to retain more information and to access it more quickly than a person with less intelligence. Obviously, this is an oversimplification, but it is a popular characterization of "smart people." Computers are far superior to any individual in the ability to organize, store, manipulate, and retrieve information. In fact, many of the characteristics that have been prized among children and adults, the lack of which characterizes many mildly handicapped persons, are trivialized by the computer.

Ordinary people are now gaining access to machines and data bases that will give them power over information. As a result, some of the distinctions among people will be altered. And what about the effects of this development on individuals classified as mildly handicapped who have difficulties with gaining access to information "locked up" in written words? This too will become less of a problem, as will spelling and a host of other skill areas that today define and torment many students. In any event, for many students and adults, the computer will open vistas of learning while reducing or eliminating many of the previously noted distinctions among people.

Students who learn to use technology and compensate for deficiencies in acquiring information will cause schools to deal with learning and evaluation much differently. Printers and word processors will alleviate deficiencies of written communication; data bases and talking computers will circumvent textbooks; and the individual will be allowed to think and deal with information rather than be deprived of information due to "input" deficits. The use of the computer with mildly handicapped individuals could therefore greatly alter the future of special education.

CURRENT AND FUTURE TRENDS

Many variables will affect the future of special education and other services for mildly handicapped persons. These include litigation, funding, research findings, activism of advocacy groups, role of the federal government, technology, the reform movement, and actions within professions serving this population. Other less well defined variables will also affect the future. Many of these factors are very unpredictable. For example, the philosophy of the United States Supreme Court changes as new justices are appointed. What may be the legal interpretation underlying one decision may change over a one to two year period with a change in the Court.

Questions that must be answered to more accurately predict the future include the following: Will the current reform movements in education which emphasize back-to-basics and educating academically gifted students have a negative effect on disabled students? Will the reduced role in education played by the federal government drastically reduce the availability of funds and regulatory power and therefore force a reduction in programs? Will the movement to require all students to pass competency tests before graduation cause handicapped students to lose out on their recently won right to an equal opportunity in education? These are the types of questions that have relevance for the future of special education and other services for the mildly handicapped, but there are no easy answers. The remainder of the chapter will discuss some current practices that could affect the future.

Reduced Federal Role

The current movement to reduce the role of the federal government in the education of handicapped children began with the Reagan administration in 1980. Two major principles of the Reagan administration appear to be the main rationale for the reduced role: (1) to reduce federal spending to attack inflation and (2) to transfer programs funded by the federal government to state and local governments (McConville and Ritter 1981). Attempts were made in 1980 to reduce the federal financial contribution to special education. An example of the budget reduction can be seen in the president's budget request for special education in fiscal year 1981. The request was approximately 25 percent lower than the amount requested by the Carter budget, from $1.27 billion to $0.96 billion. While the Congress did not accept this reduced request, the ultimate amount allocated for special education was approximately 7 percent lower than the Carter budget request (McConville and Ritter 1981). When P.L. 94-142 was passed in 1975, the bill authorized up to $2.1 billion for educating handicapped children. In 1984, the amount authorized was barely over $1 billion. A major reduction in the federal role, therefore, has been in the amount of funds appropriated for special education programs. Should this trend continue, states and local governments will have to assume a greater financial role, or services may have to be reduced substantially.

Besides attacking inflation and attempting to transfer programs to state and local governments, which reflected the Reagan policy of New Federalism, the reduced role resulted in the belief that education was not the responsibility of the federal government. Bakalis (1983) points out that for the first time there is scarcity in America: enrollments have declined; local tax bases have eroded; the state and federal governments face large deficits; and education is no longer a "growth" industry. The nation and its schools must now adjust to this scarcity. As Bakalis notes, "We are facing a shift in purpose from asking who will go to school to asking what should happen in school" (Bakalis 1983, 12). With fewer resources, decisions must be made concerning how the available funds should be spent.

With fewer federal dollars in special education programs, schools may have to prioritize their available resources, and the current trend to fund programs for gifted students may mean a reduction in funds available for special education programs for the mildly handicapped. Therefore, while the reduced federal role in funding special education programs would not in itself reduce special education services, the limited funds available to schools could. Schools could be in the position to decide whether to fund programs for the majority of students or for those with disabilities.

While the Reagan administration would like to reduce the role of the federal government by reducing financing and transferring programs to states, the trend can be reversed. Congress has rejected administration requests in the past and is apparently responsive to advocacy lobbying efforts.

Parent Advocacy

Parents have long played a major role in the changes in services to handicapped children. Parents organized in the early 1950s and began questioning some of the services not available to their handicapped children. Parents were involved in the first landmark right-to-education litigation, *PARC v. Pennsylvania* in 1971, which resulted in the state and local district agreement to provide services to mentally retarded children. Parents were also strongly involved in the drafting and passage of P.L. 94-142, the Education for All Handicapped Children Act.

No longer do parents simply accept what the schools say without question. They are more sophisticated about educational issues and have demanded that schools accept children previously denied educational programs and improve the achievement levels of mislabeled children. These attitudes should continue in the future (Jones 1978). The active involvement of parents and parent groups should continue to be a major factor in future services to handicapped children.

Special Education and Professional Standards

The Council for Exceptional Children (CEC), the major professional organization for special educators, recently adopted a Code of Ethics, Standards for Professional Practice, and Standards for the Preparation of Special Education Personnel. The documents, adopted in April 1983, reflect a growing trend to make special education a responsible profession that provides appropriate services to children with disabilities. The adoption of

The adoption of standards for the preparation of special education teahers will have a direct impact upon preservice training.

such documents, notes Heller (1983), marks the willingness of a profession to abide by a code of ethics and standards.

Heller suggests that the Code of Ethics is the major of the three documents passed because this document "forms the basis for the standards of practice and personnel preparation" (Heller 1983, 199). While the code forms the basis, the standards adopted enable objective evaluations of current practices and programs serving handicapped children, as well as programs that prepare individuals to be special education teachers. Without such evaluation criteria, the field of special education will continue to provide services haphazardly, with little semblance of continuity or consensus. Standards enable a profession to move forward as a profession, not as a disjointed group of individuals who profess to have the same aims.

Although the adoption of these standards and the code will not automatically lead to changes in the profession, it is a beginning. The actions tend to support the current efforts to raise the quality of all education. While the reform movement is attempting to upgrade the entire educational system in this country, the actions by CEC contribute to the search for excellence in the small but important realm of special education. As the Code of Ethics and Standards is implemented, the movement toward professionalism and accountability will move forward. This is a trend in special education that has not occurred too soon; its outcome should be improved quality services for all disabled children in special education programs.

Table 13-2 **Current Applications of Technology**

Application	Description
Information Processing and Interactive Learning	• Computer is most commonly used technology in special education • Well designed software provides individual attention, feedback, and is based on positive reinforcement. • Computer is interactive
Instructional Planning	• IEPs can be maintained and updated • Enhances decision making • Permits criterion-referenced testing
Communication	• Information is received and expressed using computers and software • Student's strong modalities can be used
Problem Solving	• Permits students to problem solve • Learned concepts can be applied • Learning simulations can occur with computers and interactive video
Prosthetic Devices	• Permits deaf and hard-of-hearing to communicate with Super Phone • Braille keyboards and printers • Voice synthesizers

Source: Cain 1984.

Technology and Special Education

Certainly, technology has recently begun to impact special education and other services to handicapped children and adults. But its future impact is difficult to predict. One fact is clear, however: "The field of special education must begin to address the issues raised by the challenge of technology" (Cain 1984, 239). If technology is not used in special education, mildly handicapped students will not receive the most quality education available. They will leave the educational system without the necessary knowledge to use the technology to increase the quality of their lives.

Technology in special education and rehabilitation currently falls into five applications: (1) communication, (2) problem solving, (3) vocational preparation, (4) recreation, and (5) prosthetic devices (Cain 1984). See table 13-2.

Computers and the Mildly Handicapped. The use of computers in education has increased dramatically with the mass infusion of *microcomputers* into our society. No longer are computers large, expensive machines that can only be operated by sophisticated, highly trained persons. They are currently compact, inexpensive, and relatively easy to use. As a result, some school districts have mandated that all students become computer literate (Davis 1984), and many others have introduced computer courses into their curricula and have made computers available for student use.

Until recently, the uses of computers in special education have focused on hardware adaptions, courseware selection, and in-service training for teachers (Chiang et al. 1984). The primary direct use with mildly handicapped students has been in *computer assisted instruction* (CAI). CAI has captured the imagination of many educators but has had little effect on the delivery of instruction. The advantages of CAI include individual pacing,

Microcomputers are increasingly augmenting instruction for special students.

immediate feedback, drill, and overlearning. CAI has been successful in settings that include the presence of an innovative teacher to direct the curricula. It utilizes a "drill-and-practice or question-and-answer system" (Turkel and Podell 1984, 259).

Besides these advantages, CAI also has some disadvantages:

- It is directly related to the teacher's ability to structure the course and to impose order on the content
- It is used principally as a supplement to traditional classroom instruction
- Content is commonly single-concept material
- Elements of human interaction are missing
- It has no direct bearing on the curriculum.

HIGHLIGHT

Blind Boy Learning to 'See' With Help of Sonic Glasses

By Katie Thomas
Tribune Correspondent

PANGUITCH—"As I look up or down, I can 'hear' the ceiling or the floor," said Peter Frandsen, a junior at Panguitch High School who has been blind since birth.

Frandsen demonstrated his new "sonic glasses," or more correctly Sonic Guides, to a group of Lions Club members in Panguich whose generosity helped purchase the device for him.

Shortly before Christmas, donations gathered through the local chapter of the Veterans of Foreign Wars were matched by the Lions Club to make more than $3,200. The money was used to purchase the glasses for Peter to "see with sound."

Frandsen spend two months at the Ogden School for the Blind, where full-time training helped him learn to use the special sonic device.

He explained that the sonic guide, which looks like an ordinary pair of sunglasses, is fitted with three small round projections, one centered over the other two in a diamond or pyramid shape, over the nose piece of the glasses. The units are called transducers and are only about one-half inch in diameter.

The units are connected to two plastic tubes that are connected to ear plugs that carry sounds to the ears.

"When the power is turned on," Frandsen said, "the center unit sends out a pulsing beam that bounces off the object I'm 'looking at' and returns to hit the two units underneath. The bounce back registers in different tones. I'm learning to distinguish between them."

The bouncing tones tell him the difference between flesh, wood, brick, glass and other substances responding to the surface contacted. He said the device is so sensitive that he can tell if a curtain is over a window.

The unit's maximum effective distance is about 20 feet. Frandsen said proper maintenance is critical in its functioning and he cannot touch the transducers because oil from the skin can cause the unit to malfunction.

Salt Lake Tribune, 22 March 1985, Vol. 230 No. 183

Although CAI has been shown to be effective with handicapped students (Davis 1984), if CAI is the predominant approach used with computers in special education, the full potential of the technology will not be achieved. Other, more innovative uses include computer assisted learning (CAL) (Turkell and Podell 1984) and using the computer in teaching strategies and classroom management (Chiang et al. 1984).

CAL requires problem solving and decision making by students. Rather than having to work with restricted existing programs, students are able to develop their own programs and commands, and then test the programs (Turkell and Podell 1984). They are more involved in the learning process. Mildly handicapped students are capable of learning and performing the higher level skills required in CAL. The LOGO system, which is considered a user-friendly graphics language, requires students to find their own solutions to problems. In a study that examined the best methods to teach LOGO to mildly handicapped students, Chiang, Thorpe, and Lubke concluded that "both LD and non-LD children made substantial progress in learning the concepts and processes presented and did so at about the same levels when IQ differences were taken into consideration" (Chiang et al. 1984, 303).

The computer will have the greatest impact on education when it can be integrated with existing printed matter and audiovisual materials, including videotapes, to serve as the primary instructional conveyance. And the computer must be decentralized. Presently, many schools centralize the microcomputers and use them to augment instruction through drill and practice, basically with CAI. The emerging technology can be expected to grow rapidly as schools seek ways to assure that students will be able to acquire skills in areas of the curriculum where teachers are few (Price and Marsh 1983). Aside from theoretical concerns and projections, some facts about computer usage should be considered:

- Students can learn effectively with computers
- Students are interested in working with the computer; this may serve as a motivating factor for some students
- Students generally have a positive attitude about working with computers
- Computers can be used as a tutor, exploratory learning environment, diagnostician, and provider of information.

One problem faced by schools in developing computer programs in special education is the selection of appropriate software—"the heart of a computer assisted learning system" (Shanahan and Ryan 1984, 242). One solution to this problem was used by the Huntington-Commack Software Evaluation Project in New York. This project used teachers to evaluate educational software and to develop a teacher's guide for specific software (Shanahan and Ryan 1984). Another method of determining the usefulness of computer software is through reviewing reference materials. These include periodicals, books, organizations, resource groups, networks, and projects. Bailey and Raimondi (1984) compiled a listing of such references that could provide important information for schools. In the future, as more schools use computers, such reference information will become increasingly important because although the shortage of software available for educational purposes was once severe, a deluge of software is becoming available from many different sources. Selecting appropriate, cost-efficient materials will be an increasingly difficult job.

New Technological Aids. In addition to the expanding use of computers in special education, other technological developments have also been made that will assist handicapped students and adults. These include electronic devices to assist visually impaired individuals with travel, communication devices for individuals with hearing problems, and advance prosthetic devices for physically disabled persons. Table 13-3 describes some of these technological advances for various types of disabilities.

Medical Advances. As in all fields, medical advances have greatly benefited handicapped persons and will continue to have an impact on the education provided handicapped children and on other services available to handicapped adults. One area where the impact of medical technology has been increasing is the prenatal detection of disabilities. Various methods now exist to detect disabilities prenatally, enabling parents to opt to terminate the pregnancy and thus prevent a disabled child from being born.

Table 13-3 **Technological Advances**

Disability	Advances
Cognitive Deficits	Computer Assisted Instruction
	Computer programs for drill and practice
Visual Problems	Paperless Braille recorders
	Talking calculators
	Reading machines
	Mobility aids—Sonicguide, Sonic Glasses, Laser Cane
Hearing Problems	Television captioning
	Telephone adaptions—Teletypewriter (TTY) and Superphone
	Hearing Aids
	Electronic device that converts speech into print
Physical Disabilities	Modified, more usable Wheelchairs
	Robot arms attached to workplaces
	Environmental control systems
	Devices to electrically stimulate muscles
	Communication boards

Source: Kneedler 1984.

Amniocentesis. Amniocentesis, the medical procedure of withdrawing amniotic fluid from the uterus, has increased dramatically during the past few years. The process enables the detection of several disorders, including Down's Syndrome, spina bifida, and Tay Sach's disease. The sex of the child can also be established using the procedure. In cases where there is a history of sex-related disabilities in families, such as hemophilia or muscular dystrophy, parents may choose to abort a male fetus (Batshaw and Perret 1981).

Other Prenatal Detection Methods. In addition to amniocentesis, other medical methods of detecting disabilities prenatally are being developed and used. These include fetoscopy, which enables physicians to see parts of the fetus to determine any maldevelopment; amniography, where dye is injected into the amniotic sac enabling x-rays to depict the gastrointestinal tract of the fetus; and sonography, or ultrasound, which provides a "sound" picture of the fetus (Batshaw and Perret 1981). These types of medical advances will continue to provide parents with the opportunity to detect disabilities in their child prenatally, and enable them to choose to abort the child should major disabilities be present.

Genetic Counseling. Another improvement during the past few years is genetic counseling. While genetic counseling includes informing parents of the results of amniocentesis, fetoscopy, and amniography, it also includes determining *before* conception the chances of having a child with various disabilities. Parents can decide whether or not to have children based on the probability that a genetic anomaly will occur (Hardman et al. 1984). The impact of genetic counseling should increase in the future as new techniques are developed to ascertain risk factors for certain disabilities.

Once prenatal detection methods have determined that a child *in utero* is disabled, parents are faced with a major decision: Should the fetus be aborted? This is obviously a moral or value question, one that each set of parents will have to deal with in their own way. While medical technology can advance to the point of determining whether or not a

> **HIGHLIGHT**
>
> ## Alternative to Amniocentesis?
>
> As more women delay child-bearing, a prenatal test for genetic defects is becoming almost as much a part of pregnancy as morning sickness or Lamaze class.
>
> Yet sticking a needle through the abdomen to take a small sample of amniotic fluid surrounding the fetus—to isolate a few cells of its tissue—is neither painless nor risk free. Nor is the chief alternative, a newer procedure called chorionic villi biopsy, in which the doctor snips off a small piece of the placenta.
>
> Michigan State researchers think they've found a better way. Early in pregnancy, certain fetal cells called trophoblasts appear to cross the placental barrier and circulate in the mother's blood stream. Although these cells never number more than about one in 4.5 million maternal red cells, microbiologists Harold Miller and Harold Sadoff are able to separate and culture as many as 10,000 of them from a single ten-milliliter sample of a pregnant woman's blood by using a special antibody that cleaves to the trophoblasts. Says Miller, "We can take a blood sample not long after the first time a woman comes in after missing her period, and usually have results within a week."
>
> This alternative method should be able to pick up the same genetic defects (Down syndrome and spina bifida, for example) as amniocentesis, as well as determine the fetus's sex much earlier in pregnancy (amniocentesis usually isn't performed before the 16th week). But although the procedure looks promising, only two women who have undergone the test have given birth (the test predicted the sex correctly both times). Admits Miller, "There's a lot to be done to convince the scientific community that this is for real."
>
> Discover May 1985 Vol 6 No. 5

fetus is apparently healthy or disabled, it is the decision of the parents to abort or to carry the fetus to term and delivery. These are issues for which medical technology cannot provide the answers.

Better Life-Saving Techniques. Methods to keep previously hopeless babies alive have also been developed. Premature babies that could not have been saved ten years ago are now surviving the perils that accompany prematurity. But by saving more premature children, the number of potentially disabled children is increased because premature children have a higher risk than full-term children of developing biochemical and physical disturbances, growth deficiencies, and other problems (Batshaw and Perret 1981). These advances are thus enabling physicians to prevent many problems such as "an increase in the number of people who have severe or profound disabilities" (Kneedler 1984, 26).

Deinstitutionalization

Deinstitutionalization is the process of (1) removing individuals from institutions and placing them in community programs, and (2) preventing initial admission into institutions. It has been a major trend in this country since 1972 (Scheerenberger 1981). Spurred on by litigation and advocacy groups, the movement of individuals into community programs has resulted in a major shift of services from institutional-based to community-based. The philosophy underlying deinstitutionalization is *normalization*, which, simply defined, calls for facilitating as normal a life as possible for disabled individuals.

As a result of deinstitutionalization, community residential programs have grown dramatically since the early 1970s. For example, the number of such residences doubled between 1973 and 1977 (Bruininks et al. 1981), and the growth since 1977 has not slowed. Although the movement to place handicapped persons into the community has been a major success, the process has some barriers. These include the availability of community programs, funding community programs, and the quality of community support services (Scheerenberger 1981). Zoning laws in local communities have also been a barrier. These laws, which were originally established for the health and safety of the communities, have been circumvented through litigation and the passage of state legislation. As of 1978, eleven states had passed legislation facilitating the development of community residential programs, and another eight states were considering such legislation (Disabled Citizens, 1978).

But the trend to develop community residential programs has continued, despite the barriers presented. Deinstitutionalization, although criticized by some proponents of large, residential institutions, has continued to be a major trend. In 1984, Senate Bill 2053 was written to tie federal funds to states' efforts to further deinstitutionalize large institutional populations. The bill, sponsored by Senator Chaffee and labeled the Chaffee Bill, was not passed, but it did signify the continuing trend to move handicapped persons from large institutions to smaller, community-based programs. If this trend continues, states will have to develop more community programs, refocus state dollars, and develop more extensive community support services.

The Reform Movement

The future of special education will be greatly determined by what happens to education in general. Schools are currently the subject of a great deal of attention in the United States, and much of this recent attention is negative, focusing on the poor quality of our educational system. In 1983, a task force organized by the secretary of the Department of Education released its report entitled "A Nation at Risk: The Imperative for Educational Reform." Some of the report's findings were the following:

- The quality of teaching in public schools is inadequate
- Secondary schools offer too many electives that are not part of the traditional academic curricula
- Seventy percent of high schools require only one year of math and science
- Colleges and universities are becoming less selective, often focusing more on enrollment than quality students
- United States students do not match up to students from other industrialized nations

Over the last decade, credibility, prestige, and even public confidence in our educational system have been lost—facts rarely disputed (Weiler 1982). In general, many school practices are being challenged as inappropriate (Campbell 1983).

The result has been a call for reform. "Nation at Risk" called for compulsory instruction in basic subjects, higher college admission requirements, extended school hours and additional school days per year, and higher standards for teachers. Many states have

The effects of the trend toward competency testing is uncertain with regard to handicapped children.

gun to institute some of these reforms. In Texas, reforms already passed include longer school days, stiffer attendance requirements, and specific graduation requirements. Florida now requires competency testing as a requirement for passing the third, fifth, eighth, and eleventh grades. Standards and graduation requirements have been raised in Oregon, Virginia, Georgia, Utah, Michigan, Washington, Delaware, Illinois, and New York (Michaels 1984). In a special session of the Arkansas legislature, comprehensive education reforms were passed in 1983, including a controversial provision for teacher competency testing.

Reforms, therefore, are being initiated. Unfortunately, the reform movement has not taken the time to scientifically determine what needs to be changed and how the changes should ccur. While the reformers have focused on simplistic types of change, such as lengthening school days, they have made the assumption that schools are bad because of internal problems. At the same time, others have underlined the fact that the problems of public education are a reflection of a lack of confidence in public authorities and institutions in general (Weiler 1982). "Changes needed in public education are both internal to the schools and external to the larger society" (Campbell 1983, 5).

Regardless of this broader view, the reforms being implemented are basic and simplistic: they test students more, add school time, and require more basic courses. Some of these steps could have a devastating effect on the education of the mildly handicapped. Gains made during the 1970s that attempted to individualize educational programs for handicapped students could be threatened. Two areas that could affect mildly handicapped students in particular are competency testing and tracking.

Competency Testing. The competency testing movement has been spreading throughout the United States during the past decade. A majority of states have now passed legislation concerning testing. As far back as 1980, seventeen states required the passage of minimum competency tests for graduation from high school (McCarthy 1980). The movement has picked up a great deal of support as a result of the recent reform movement that has demanded more accountability from schools (Podemski et al. 1984). Critics who have charged that students are graduating from high schools without the necessary skills for functioning in the adult world have adopted the minimum competency test as a means of ensuring that high school graduates have acceptable skills.

In general, a minimum competency test assesses the practical application of survival skills in the areas of reading and math (Amos 1980). Its primary function, from the school's perspective, is accountability. From the special education advocate's perspective, the problem is whether such tests can be administered to disabled students in a nondiscriminatory fashion.

One of the basic assumptions underlying the right to education for handicapped students is that they will be provided the opportunity to attend school, graduate, and receive a diploma (Ross and Weintraub 1980). If minimum competency tests are required for graduation, and they are applied to handicapped students without modification, this assumption may be undermined. Obviously, children with basic disabilities that affect academic skills development will be at a severe disadvantage on minimum competency tests without adaptions.

Most states that require competency tests do require that modifications be provided for handicapped students. For example, in North Carolina handicapped students who are in special education programs may have the following modifications:

- braille or large-print editions
- audiocassette editions
- extended time limits
- permission to write in the test booklet
- instructions in sign language
- recording of answers by proctors (McKinney 1983)

These are the types of modifications that must be provided for handicapped students in order to minimize the effects of disabilities on test performance. If not, then the competency testing movement could have detrimental effects on the education of handicapped children. "In any event, there can be little doubt that the competency testing

While the future of special education is optimistic, the nature of programs is still unknown.

movement will have serious implications for the handicapped" (Podemski et al. 1984, 318).

Tracking. Another piece of the reform package that could negatively affect special education students is tracking. Rigid tracking is currently being proposed in some states as a means of improving the quality of education. The conflict over mainstreaming and the least restrictive environment will be renewed in the event of the implementation of widespread tracking. If handicapped students are prevented as a group from attending classes with their age peers, a constitutional issue will be raised. Litigation and legislation have consistently mandated that disabled children receive at least a portion of their education with nonhandicapped peers. Schools that totally rely on tracking students based on their academic abilities would negate this mandated right.

CONCLUSIONS

So what is the future of special education and services to handicapped children and adults? First, as a result of past litigation and legislation, and the actions of advocacy groups, attention to the needs of disabled persons will continue. It would be very difficult to conceive of society once again turning its back on atypical individuals and their needs. While legislation and litigation make this unlikely, the major force to prevent this is advocacy groups. Since the 1950s, parents, professionals, and disabled individuals have learned how to use their collective power. The utilization of this influence will not wane. Parents in particular should remain a strong force in the future (Jones 1978).

Special education will continue, though its exact nature, organization, and service delivery approaches cannot be predicted with a great deal of accuracy. Certainly, changes and trends in general education, as a result of the reform movement, will affect special education. Probably the major force in future educational changes will be technology. The expanding use of computers and continued development of software will have a major impact on educational practices. All signals also indicate that the deinstitutionalization movement will continue. More community-based programs will be developed, and the rights of individuals in communities will be expanded. So, the future for mildly handicapped children and adults should be bright; the gains that have been made should continue. However, advocates and professionals should be aware that there are forces, such as certain reform movements and the declining federal role in services, that could impact negatively. By planning for such possibilities, their effects should be minimized.

SUMMARY

This chapter has attempted to present information related to the future of services for handicapped children and adults, including the future of special education. It was pointed out that predicting the future of services is extremely difficult because of the ever-changing variables that affect such services. If professionals are not cognizant of what could occur in the future, however, they will not be prepared to take advantage of new developments or be ready to deal with potentially adverse changes that could negatively affect handicapped persons.

Although it is difficult to predict the future with any degree of certainty, some trends are currently affecting special education and other services that will likely continue to have an impact. These include the reduced federal role in special education, reduced federal funding, current reform movements, including competency testing and tracking, the technological explosion, parent advocacy, deinstitutionalization, and the growing professionalism in special education. While each of these factors will affect the future of services for handicapped persons, technology probably will have the most significant impact.

The future of services, despite certain negative forces, appears to be very favorable. Gains made during the 1970s and 1980s are unlikely to be reversed. Equal opportunities for handicapped adults and a free appropriate education for handicapped children should continue. Although the forecast is positive, professionals and advocates must be aware of the factors that could negatively affect services and be prepared to counter them.

REFERENCES

A nation at risk: The imperative for educational reform. The National Commission on Excellence in Education. U.S. Department of Education, 1983.

Amos, K.M. Competency testing: Will the LD student be included? *Exceptional Children* 47, no. 3 (1980):194–97.

Bailey, M.N., and S.L. Raimondi. Technology and special education: A resource guide. *Teaching Exceptional Children* 16, no. 4 (1984):273–77.

Bakalis, M.J. Power and purpose in American education. *Phi Delta Kappan* 65, no. 1 (1983):7–13.

Batshaw, M.L., and Y.M. Perret. *Children with handicaps: A Medical Primer.* Baltimore: Brookes Publishing Company, 1981.

Bruininks, R.H., M.J. Kudla, F.A. Hauber, B.K. Hill, and C.A. Wieck. Recent growth and status of community-based residential alternatives. In *Deinstitutionalization and community adjustment of mentally retarded people,* edited by R.H. Bruininks, C.E. Meyers, B.B. Sigford, and K.C. Lakin. Washington, D.C.: American Association on Mental Deficiency, 1981.

Cain, E.J., Jr. The challenge of technology: Educating the exceptional child for the world of tommorow. *Teaching Exceptional Children* 16, no. 4 (1984):239–41.

Campbell, R.F. Time for vigorous leadership in the public schools. In *Bad times, good schools,* edited by J. Frymier. West Lafayette, Indiana: Kappa Delta Pi, 1983.

Chiang, B., H.W. Thorpe, and M. Lubke. LD students tackle the LOGO language: Strategies and implications. *Journal of Learning Disabilities* 17, no. 5 (1984):303–304.

Davis, N.C. Computer literacy for the special student: A personal experience. *Teaching Exceptional Children* 16, no. 4 (1984):263–65.

Disabled citizens in the community: Zoning obstacles and legal remedies. *AMICUS* 3, no. 2 (1978):30–34.

Hardman, M.L., C.J. Drew, and M.W. Egan. *Human exceptionality: Society, school and family.* Boston: Allyn and Bacon, 1984.

Heller, H.W. Special education professional standards: Need, value, and use. *Exceptional Children* 50, no. 3 (1983):199–204.

Jones, R.L. Special education and the future: Some questions to be answered and answers to be questioned. In *Futures of education for exceptional students: Emerging structures* edited by M.C. Reynolds. Reston, Va. Council for Exceptional Children, 1978.

Kneedler, R.D. *Special education for today.* Englewood Cliffs, N.J.: Prentice-Hall, 1984.

McCarthy, M.M. Minimum competency testing and handicapped students. *Exceptional Children* 47, no. 3 (1980):166–72.

McConville, L.S., and R.J. Ritter. Recession and consolidation: New directions for the federal role in the education of handicapped children. *Education and Training of the Mentally Retarded* 16, no. 4 (1981):284–87.

McKinney, J.D. Performance of handicapped students on the North Carolina minimum competency test. *Exceptional Children* 49, no. 6 (1983):547–50.

Michaels, M. The good news about out public schools. *Parade,* 1 January 1984, 4–6.

Nation at risk: The imperative for educational reform.

O'Shea, L.J., and A. Gajar. Comparing predictions of future trends in special education. *Exceptional Children* 50, no. 2 (1983):177–79.

Podemski, R.S., B.J. Price, T.E.C. Smith, and G.E. Marsh. *Comprehensive special education administration.* Rockville, Md.: Aspen Systems, 1984.

Price, B.J., and G.E. Marsh. Interactive learning and the dreaded change in education. *T.H.E. Journal,* May 1983, 42–47.

Ross, J.W., and F.J. Weintraub. Policy approaches regarding the impact of graduation requirements on handicapped students. *Exceptional Children* 47, no. 3 (1980):200–203.

Scheerenberger, R.C. Deinstitutionalization: Trends and difficulties. In *Deinstitutionalization and community adjustment of mentally retarded people. See* Bruininks et al. 1981.

Schipper, W.V., and L.A. Kenowitz. Special education futures—A forecast of events affecting the education of exceptional children: 1976–2000. *Journal of Special Education* 10 (1976):401–413.

Shanahan, D., and A.W. Ryan. A tool for evaluating educational software. *Teaching Exceptional Children* 16, no. 4 (1984):242–47.

Turkel, S.B., and D.M. Podell. Computer assisted learning for mildly handicapped students. *Teaching Exceptional Children* 16, no. 4 (1984):258–62.

Weiler, H.N. Education, public confidence, and the legitimacy of the modern state: Do we have a crisis? *Phi Delta Kappan* 64, no. 1 (1982):9–14.

Glossary

aberration A deviation from what is normal

accommodation Steps taken to adapt schools and classrooms for handicapped children

ACLD Association for Children with Learning Disabilities, a parent/professional advocacy group

adaptive behavior ability to adapt to the environment through levels of independence and responsibility

administrative support support received from school administrators

administrator an individual who oversees school activities, such as a superintendent, principal, or supervisor

adolescence period between childhood and adulthood. Commonly thought of as the teen-aged years. Can be defined as beginning with puberty and ending with economic independence

adult A level of development, commonly thought of as beginning at the chronological age of twenty-one, or when adolescence ends

advocacy the act of defending a particular cause, such as rights of mildly handicapped children

annual goals goals established for each handicapped child and described on an individual education program (IEP)

anoxia a lack of oxygen

assessment the process of determining strengths and weaknesses of individuals

attitudes predispositions to behavior

audiogram graphic representation of the results from an audiometric exam. Indicates decibel loss

audiometer electronic equipment that measures hearing acuity in terms of decibels (dB) and frequencies or cycles per second indicated by Hertz (Hz) units

behavior disordered classification for children whose behavior deviates to such a degree that academic and social problems develop

behavior objective statement indicating what students are projected to do; stated in terms that are measurable

behaviorism theory related to learning and management, based on operant conditioning

biophysical theory related to disabilities, based on organic disease or dysfunction

blind severely visually impaired. Legally, someone with visual acuity of 20/200 or less in the better eye with best correction or with a field of vision of 20 degrees or less

braille a system of reading used by blind individuals where raised dots are "read" rather than visual symbols

brain damage injury to the brain

brain dysfunction a suspected injury to the brain

brain injury injury to the neurological tissue

career education a lifelong process beginning in the elementary school and continuing through adulthood. Includes learning about jobs, job preparation, and job satisfaction

categorical classification categorizing children and adults with specific labels, such as mental retardation and learning disability, rather than with generic labels such as mildly handicapped

CEC Council for Exceptional Children, the primary professional group for special education professionals

child abuse physical, sexual, or emotional abuse to a child

child-find program mandated by federal legislation to locate handicapped children and bring them to the attention of public school authorities

chromosomal disorder a problem with chromosomes in the body; either too many, too few, or defective

chromosome normal human bodies have twenty-three pairs of chromosomes which carry genes for genetic transmission

classification grouping for type or severity level of handicapped person

cognitive related to learning

computer assisted instruction (CAI) the use of computers to provide instruction. Drill and evaluation are the two main components of CAI

conduct disorder a type of behavior disorder primarily characterized by acting out behavior

congenital present at birth

consultant model a method of providing services to handicapped children through consultants that travel from school to school

continuum of services a group of sequential services available for handicapped children. Range from services for severely handicapped children to services for mildly handicapped children

criterion-referenced tests tests that compare students with their own mastery level

curriculum totality of experiences provided by schools, including academic, social, and physical

deaf category of people with severe hearing deficits. Individuals with a ninety or greater decibel loss

decibel unit of loudness of sound

deinstitutionalization the movement to place handicapped persons in settings as near normal as possible. Includes taking individuals out of institutions and preventing the placement of some individuals in institutions

Deno's cascade of services a model depicting a continuum of services for handicapped children

developmental disability a condition developed before twenty-one years of age that results in a chronic disability and impedes functional independence

developmental period a period from birth through eighteen years

disability an organic impairment or malfunction

Down's syndrome a chromosomal disorder resulting from one too many chromosomes in the twenty-first pair

due process basic rights of children and parents

dysgraphia disability in writing

dyslexia disability in reading

early childhood education educational programs for preschool handicapped children

educable mental retardation (EMR) category of mental retardation designated by an IQ range of approximately fifty-five to seventy-five

efficacy studies research comparing the performance of educable mentally retarded children in self-contained classrooms and regular classrooms

elderly mildly handicapped individuals in their later years who experience mild handicapping conditions

emotionally disturbed a category of handicapped children where the following characteristics are exhibited over an extended period of time and affect educational achievement: an inability to learn which cannot be explained by intellectual, sensory, or health factors; an inability to build or maintain satisfactory interpersonal relationships; inappropriate types of behavior or feelings under normal circumstances; a general pervasive mood of unhappiness or depression; or a tendency to develop physical symptoms or fears

environmentally based causes causes of disabilities that are found in the environment, such as poverty, abuse, and malnutrition

etiology cause of disability

evaluation assessment of handicapped children

exceptional children children who deviate from the norm, either positively or negatively

free appropriate public education the goal of P.L. 94-142. All handicapped must be provided a free appropriate public education, one that meets their needs and is free of charge

generic classification classifying handicapped children based on functional abilities rather than cause, using the mildly handicapped label rather than educable mental retardation or learning disability

group home semi-independent living arrangement in communities for handicapped persons. Usually houses no more than ten to twelve individuals

handicap reaction to a disability or impairment. Functional result of a disability or impairment

hard-of-hearing classification for individuals with a hearing loss but not serious enough to be considered deaf; some residual hearing

hearing impaired individuals with hearing problems, including deaf and hard-of-hearing persons

hyperactive a characteristic of many handicapped children. Behavior is at abnormally increased levels

hypoactive opposite of hyperactive. Behavior is at abnormally decreased levels

impairment a physical problem of the body that results in a handicap

impulsivity acting without thinking of consequences

independent living the status of handicapped persons living without support services

individual educational program (IEP) written educational plan for handicapped children. Mandated by P.L. 94-142, includes annual goals for the child, as well as services to be provided

informal assessment measurement conducted by teachers, parents, and others without formal testing instruments. Includes observation and anecdotal information

interdisciplinary team team of professionals from various backgrounds, such as teachers, psychologists, health professionals, and administrators

intervention actions taken by schools to provide appropriate educational services for handicapped children

itinerant services services provided to handicapped children by professionals who travel from school to school

labeling the process of formally placing children into a deviant category

learning centers physical locations where children go to receive instruction on certain topics

learning disability (LD) a disability experienced by children that results in academic deficiencies that are not the result of mental retardation, emotional disturbance, sensory deficits, or environmental conditions. Makes up one of the largest special education categories

least restrictive setting the place where handicapped children must receive their education. Whenever possible it should be with nonhandicapped children in regular classrooms

legal blindness visual acuity of 20/200 or less in the better eye with best correction or a field of vision of twenty degrees or less

legislation laws enacted by state legislators and the United States Congress

litigation state and federal court cases

low incidence handicaps handicapping conditions that affect relatively low numbers of people; examples include visual impairment, hearing impairment, and other health impairments

mainstream regular educational program

mainstreaming the process of integrating handicapped children into regular educational programs, implementing the least restrictive environment concept

mental retardation (MR) the handicapping category defined as individuals with deficits in intellectual functioning, an IQ of approximately seventy or below, and with concurrent deficits in adaptive behavior. The condition must occur before the eighteenth birthday

microcomputers a class of computers that are portable and relatively inexpensive

mildly handicapped a generic category for individuals whose handicaps are disabling, but not to the extent of those classified as severely and profoundly handicapped. The group is composed of previously identified educable mentally retarded, learning disabled, and emotionally disturbed persons. Also, many individuals with visual and hearing disabilities are considered mildly handicapped

minimal brain dysfunction damage to the brain that is minimal and results in minimal disability

modeling learning from observing others

mosaicism a type of Down's syndrome where the individual has some aberrant cells with forty-seven chromosomes and some normal cells with forty-six chromosomes

National Association for Retarded Citizens (NARC) the largest parent/advocacy group for mentally retarded persons

noncategorical classifying handicapped individuals based on functional disability, not cause

nondiscriminatory assessment assessment of handicapped persons that is not biased by racial, cultural, or socioeconomic factors

nondysjunction the cause of approximately ninety percent of the cases of Down's syndrome. The number twenty-one chromosome pair does not split during meiosis

normalization the philosophical base for mainstreaming and deinstitutionalization. The basic premise is to allow handicapped persons to live as normal a life as possible

norm-referenced test tests that enable users to compare scores with a normative sample

normative sample group of individuals that make up the norm reference group for comparison purposes on norm-referenced tests

observation collection of assessment data through observing individuals in their normal environments

on-the-job training type of training program where individuals receive job training on the job rather than in a classroom setting

organically based causes causes of disabilities that affect the physical aspects of the body

orthopedically impaired the classification used to group children with disabilities caused by congenital anomaly, disease, and other causes that result in physical problems

other health impaired a handicapped category included in P.L. 94-142 that includes children who have a disability such as autism, cardiac problems, diabetes, epilepsy, asthma, and hemophilia

paraprofessionals individuals who work with handicapped persons who do not have professional degrees, such as teacher aides

parent groups groups of parents established to advocate services for their handicapped children

partially sighted a category for individuals with visual problems but who have some functional, residual vision. Legally, individuals with a visual acuity of 20/70 to 20/200 in the better eye with best correction

perinatal during birth

phenylketonuria (PKU) a condition resulting from an inability to metabolize an amino acid, phenylaline. Can result in mental retardation; can be prevented with specific diet

physically handicapped a category for individuals who have a disability directly related to a physical anomoly, such as amputation, cerebral palsy, or spina bifida

postnatal after birth

prenatal before birth

prenatal diagnosis diagnosis of a handicap before birth

preschool programs educational programs for children who are below minimal school age

prevalence incidence or rate of disabilities

programmed instruction teaching method that uses materials developed to allow self-paced progress and evaluation

Public Law 94-142 federal legislation passed in 1975 and implemented in 1978. Called the Education for All Handicapped Children Act, P.L. 94-142 mandated that states and local school districts provide a free appropriate public education for all handicapped children

punishment application of a negative stimulus following a specific behavior

regular classroom the classroom where nonhandicapped children receive the majority of their educational program. Usually organized on a graded system

regular classroom teacher teachers who teach predominantly in regular classrooms with nonhandicapped children

rehabilitation services provided to handicapped persons to regain skills lost as a result of a disability

rehabilitation counselor individual responsible for carrying out a rehabilitation plan

reinforcer an event that follows a behavior that makes the behavior more or less likely to recur

reinforcement the practice of providing reinforcers to individuals following particular behaviors

related services services that enable handicapped children to benefit from special education. Examples: physical therapy, speech therapy, counseling, and transportation

reliability a characteristic of a test if scores earned on that test are stable over time

residential school school where students live in addition to receiving academic and/or vocational training

resource room room where mildly handicapped children go to receive special education and related services

resource room model service delivery model where mildly handicapped children spend part of their class time in regular classrooms with nonhandicapped children, and receive special education and related services in the resource room.

resource room teacher special education teacher who teaches in the resource room

respite care short-term care for handicapped persons

rubella German measles. If contracted during the first trimester of pregnancy, it can lead to many disabling conditions

screening the process of determining which individuals require in-depth assessment

self-attitudes attitudes held by individuals about themselves

self-concept the way individuals feel about themselves

self-contained classroom special education classroom where students spend the entire day

self-contained special education teacher special education teacher who teaches the same group of children all subjects every day

severe discrepancy gap between potential to achieve and actual achievement. Usually considered 1½ to 2 years below expected achievement level

severely handicapped individuals whose handicap is so severe that they cannot benefit from education in regular educational settings

sheltered workshops a location where handicapped individuals are employed in a noncompetitive environment. Training is provided as well as employment opportunities

Snellen chart chart used for visual screening where individuals must read letters of various sizes at a distance of 20 feet

special class self-contained classroom

special day school school apart from the regular public school where more severely handicapped children attend school all day

special education as defined by P.L. 94-142: specially designed instruction, at no cost to the parent, to meet the unique needs of the handicapped child, including classroom instruction, instruction in physical education, home instruction, and instruction in hospitals and institutions

special education teacher a teacher who has been trained and certified in providing special education to handicapped children

special olympics athletic events organized and designed for handicapped children to compete at the local, regional, and national levels

Strauss syndrome a group of characteristics used to describe children who are distractible, hyperactive, inattentive, and uncoordinated. Originally associated with brain damage

technology new techniques used to educate handicapped children. Microcomputers are currently the major technological advance in special education

translocation the cause of Down's syndrome where the number 21 chromosome attaches itself to another chromosome before meiosis. Accounts for fewer than 10 percent of the cases

validity a characteristic of tests that indicates that what is purported to be measured is actually measured

visual acuity how well one sees

visual impairment a disability resulting from an inability to see normally. Includes blind and partially sighted or low-vision persons

vocational education education directed at preparing students for specific careers

vocational training teaching of vocational skills. Includes vocational education for school-aged individuals, as well as vocational training for adults

work experience school program where actual work samples are used to teach students about particular jobs

work-study programs programs in secondary schools where students spend part of the school day in classes and part on jobs

written expression skills included in the ability to express oneself in writing.

Resources

Federal Government

Office of Special Education and Rehabilitation
  Services
Department of Education
400 Maryland Avenue, S.W.
Washington, D.C. 20202
(202) 245-8492

Office of Special Education and Rehabilitation
  Services
Division of Assistance to States
Department of Education
400 Maryland Avenue, S.W.
Washington, D.C. 20202
(202) 245-9722

The Division of Policy Analysis and Planning
  Office of Special Education and
  Rehabilitation Services
Department of Education
400 Maryland Avenue, S.W.
Washington, D.C. 20202
(202) 472-1747

National Library Service for the Blind and
  Physically Handicapped
The Library of Congress
1291 Taylor Street, N.W.
Washington, D.C. 20542
(202) 287-5000

National Organizations— Learning Disabilities

Association for Children and Adults with
  Learning Disabilities
4156 Library Road
Pittsburgh, PA 15234
(412) 341-8077

Council of Learning Disabilities
University of Louisville
Department of Special Education
Louisville, KY 40292
(405) 325-4842

Foundation for Children with Learning Disabilities
99 Park Avenue
New York, NY 10016
(212) 687-7211

The Orton Society
8415 Bellona Lane
Towson, MD 21204
(301) 296-0232

National Organizations— Mental Retardation

National Association for Retarded Citizens
PO Box 6109
Arlington, TX 76011
(817) 640-0204

Joseph P. Kennedy, Jr. Foundation
719 13th Street, N.W. Suite 510
Washington, D.C. 20005
(202) 331-1731

American Association on Mental Deficiency
5101 Wisconsin Avenue
Washington, D.C. 20016
(202) 686-5400

President's Committee on Mental Retardation
Regional Office Building #3
7th and D Streets, S.W.
Washington, D.C. 20201
(202) 245-7634

National Organizations— Behavior Disorder

National Society for Autistic Children
1234 Massachusetts Avenue, N.W.
Suite 1017
Washington, D.C. 20005
(202) 783-0125

National Organizations— Hearing Impaired

Alexander Graham Bell Association for the Deaf
3417 Volta Place, N.W.
Washington, D.C. 20007
(202) 337-5220

National Association of the Deaf
814 Thayer Avenue
Silver Spring, MD 20910
(301) 587-1788

International Association of Parents of the Deaf
814 Thayer Avenue
Silver Spring, MD 20910
(301) 585-5400

National Organizations—Visually Impaired

American Foundation for the Blind
15 West 16th Street
New York, NY 10011
(212) 629-2000

National Association for Visually Handicapped
305 E. 24th Street, Room 17-c
New York, NY 10011
(212) 889-3141

American Association of Workers for the Blind/Association for the Education of the Visually Impaired Alliance
206 N. Washington Street
Suite 320
Alexandria, VA 22314
(703) 548-1884

National Society for the Prevention of Blindness
79 Madison Avenue
New York, NY 10016
(212) 684-3505

National Federation for the Blind
1629 K Street, N.W., Suite 701
Washington, D.C. 20006
(202) 785-2974

National Organizations—Physically Handicapped

The National Easter Seal Society for Crippled Children and Adults
2023 W. Ogden Avenue
Chicago, IL 60612
(312) 243-8400

United Cerebral Palsy Foundation
66 E. 34th Street
New York, NY 10016
(212) 481-6300

Muscular Dystrophy Association
810 Seventh Avenue
New York, NY 10019
(212) 586-0808

March of Dimes
1275 Mamaroneck Avenue
White Plains, NY 10605
(914) 428-7100

Spina Bifida Association of America
343 South Dearborn Street
Room 317
Chicago, IL 60604
(312) 663-1562

National Multiple Sclerosis Society
205 E. 42nd Street
New York, NY 10017
(212) 986-3240

National Organizations—Other

Epilepsy Foundation of America
4351 Garden City Drive
Landover, MD 20785
(301) 459-3700

Cystic Fibrosis Foundation
3379 Peachtree Road, N.E.
Atlanta, GA 30326
(404) 233-2195

American Speech and Hearing Association
10901 Rockville Pike
Rockville, MD 20852
(301) 897-5700

Council for Exceptional Children
1920 Association Drive
Reston, VA 22091
(703) 620-3660

Closer Look
National Information Center for the Handicapped
1201 16th Street, N.W.
Washington, D.C. 20037
(202) 822-7900

President's Committee on Employment of the Handicapped
1111 20th Street, N.W., Room 600
Washington, D.C. 20036
(202) 653-5010

National Information Center for Handicapped Children and Youth
PO Box 1492
Washington, D.C. 20013
(703) 528-8480

National Rehabilitation Information Center
4407 Eighth Street, N.E.
The Catholic University of America
Washington, D.C. 20017
(202) 635-5822

National Association of State Directors of
  Special Education
1201 16th Street, N.W., Suite 610E
Washington, D.C. 20036
(202) 822-7933

State Government

Special Education Section
State Department of Education
State Capitol

State Associations

Most national associations have state affiliates.

Local Government

Superintendent
Local Public School District

AUTHOR AND PERSONAL NAME INDEX

Abeson, A., 122
Adams, W. H., 349
Adamson, G., 139
Adleman, P., 234
Affleck, G. 58
Ahm, J., 11
Algozzine, B., 2, 34, 35, 36, 51, 100, 111
Algozzine, R., 330
Allen, D., 58
Alley, G., 218
Aloia, G. F., 35, 36
Alvarez, A., 248
Amos, K. M., 371
Anastasi, A., 295
Anastasiow, N. J., 177, 178, 212, 225, 226
Anderson, M. A., 206
Anspaugh, D. J., 166
Anspaugh, S. J., 166
Armbruster, M. A., 158, 165, 168, 169, 172
Armstrong, S., 298
Austin, K., 286, 298
Axline, V., 40

Bachman, J., 221
Bailey, D. B., 97, 98
Bailey, M. N., 366
Bak, J. J., 279, 286, 291
Bakalis, M. J., 361

Barbaro, F., 234
Barber, L., 135
Barber, P., 2
Baroff, G., 318
Baroff, G. S., 76
Batshaw, M. L., 75, 367, 368
Becker, J. W., 331
Belch, P. J., 52
Bender, M., 159
Bennett, R. E., 99
Berenbeim, P., 186
Berry, K., 139
Bersoff, D. N., 148
Best, G. A., 240
Bierman, M. S., 228
Binet, A., 4
Birch, H. G., 75
Birch, J. W., 25, 38
Blalock, J. W., 265
Blatt, B., 11
Bloom, B. S., 219
Bloomgarden, K., 199
Bost, J. M., 199
Boyer, C., 44
Bransford, L. A., 279
Breitenbucher, M., 77
Bricker, D. D., 159
Bricker, W. A., 159
Brolin, D. E., 242, 256, 257, 331, 334, 335, 337, 338, 346, 348
Bronfenbrenner, U., 223

Brooks, B. L., 279
Brown, V., 141
Brownlee, J., 218
Brownlee, J. R., 83
Bruininks, R. H., 260, 369
Bryan, J. H., 289, 291
Bryan, T., 219
Bryan, T. H., 289, 291
Burdg, N. B., 35, 36

Cain, E. J., Jr., 363
Caldwell, B. M., 158
Caldwell, M. L., 347
Cambron, N. H., 12
Campbell, N. J., 199
Carner, E. A., 266
Carroll, H. L., 348
Cass, C., 202
Cegelka, P. T., 136, 139
Chaffin, J., 242
Chaffin, J. D., 348
Chalfant, J., 134, 135
Chalfant, J. C., 37, 63
Chandler, H. N., 6, 46, 48
Chaney, R. H., 58, 68
Charitonidis, T., 248
Chiang, B., 363, 365, 366
Chinn, P. C., 306
Christopolos, F., 11
Clark, G. M., 338
Cleland, C. C., 288, 292

385

Cline, R., 287
Cohn, A. H., 77
Colao, A., 248
Coleman, J. M., 206
Coleman, J. S., 218
Coles, G. S., 38
Conine, T. A., 279
Cook, L., 152
Cook, R. E., 158, 165, 168, 169, 172
Coombs, G., 331
Cooper, J. M., 192
Cordoni, B., 253, 263, 264
Cordoni, B. K., 234
Corman, L., 279, 291
Countermine, T., 35
Crain, E. J., 242
Cremins, J. J., 14, 23, 36, 44, 49
Cremins, J. P., 14
Cross, L., 165, 168
Cruickshank, W., 6
Crump, W. D., 188
Cullinan, D., 2, 46, 47, 67, 74, 77, 80, 81, 83, 185, 292, 331, 334, 340

D'Alonzo, B. J., 255, 330, 331, 334, 338, 339, 344, 348
Dardig, J. C., 175
Darlington, R., 158
Davis, C., 44
Davis, E. E., 51
Davis, N. C., 363, 365
Davis, S., 341, 342, 345, 346
Davis, W. E., 190, 288
Deno, E., 138-139
Deno, S. L., 93
Deshler, D., 218
Deshler, D. D., 220
Dewar, R. L., 299
Dexter, B. L., 232
Diamond, S., 318
Disabled citizens in the community, 261, 262
Dobbing, J., 218
Dobson, J. E., 199
Donaldson, J., 295
Draper, D. A., 179
Drew, C. J., 184, 185, 188, 206, 265
Duffey, J. B., 97, 98
Duffy, F., 65, 67
Dunn, L. M., 5, 9, 11
Duvall, E. M., 311
Dworkin, P. H., 315

Early, G. H., 202
Edgerton, R. B., 241

Egan, J., 40
Egeland, B., 77
Ehrlich, E., 25
Elias, M. J., 188, 206
Elias-Burger, S. F., 347
Ellis, N. E., 165, 168
Epstein, M. H., 2, 46, 47, 67, 77, 83, 185, 292, 331, 334
Erikson, E. H., 212
Esposito, B. G., 296
Evans, R. L., 264
Eyman, R. K., 58, 68

Fafard, M., 221, 232
Fafard, M. B., 241, 244
Fafard, M. R., 330
Fallen, N. H., 171, 173, 318
Farber, B., 319
Featherstone, H., 321
Feingold, B. F., 78-79
Fenton, K. S., 153
Ferrara, D. M., 290
Fewell, R. R., 292
Fielder, V., 38
Finnegan, D. G., 311, 313, 314
Fiscus, E., 34, 35, 63, 80, 177, 250
Fiscus, E. D., 105, 106, 116
Fish, B., 40
Fisher, H. K., 11, 12
Fisher, J., 135
Flexer, R. W., 281, 287, 288
Foster, C. D., 195
Foster, G. G., 280
Freeman, J. M., 71
Freud, S., 216
Friend, M., 196
Frisch, L. E., 77
Frith, G. H., 291
Frodi, A. M., 77

Gajar, A., 34, 47, 48, 185
Galaburda, A., 65
Galfo, A., 13
Gallatin, J. E., 212
Galton, F., 4
Gardner, R., 318
Gardner, W., 221
Garrett, M. K., 188
Garwood, S. G., 319, 320, 321
Gearheart, B. R., 3, 90, 143, 152, 251, 252, 253, 254, 255, 346, 347
Geib, B. B., 263
Geschwind, N., 66-67
Giannettino, E., 197
Gillespie, P., 38
Gillet, P., 333, 336, 337

Gilliland, M., 166
Gold, R., 37, 109, 110, 124, 142, 244, 330, 334
Gold, R. F., 68, 69, 70, 71, 74
Goldenberg, H., 306, 307, 310, 311
Goldenberg, I., 306, 307, 310, 311
Goldhammer, K., 195
Good, T. L., 276
Gottlieb, J., 279, 291, 293, 297
Graham, S., 35, 36
Greenan, J. P., 330, 342
Greer, J. G., 45, 46, 48, 49, 185
Grossman, F. K., 319, 320, 321
Grossman, H. J., 36, 58, 69, 70, 80, 83, 110
Guerin, G. R., 115
Guralnick, M. J., 315

Haas, T., 197
Hagan, M., 298
Haley, J., 313
Hall, G. S., 217
Hallahan, D. P., 2, 23, 45, 47, 48, 64, 67, 80, 83, 185, 218, 219, 242, 244, 245, 348
Halpern, R., 106, 313, 315
Hammill, D. D., 141, 142
Handlers, A., 286, 298
Haperman, L., 254
Harbin, G. L., 97, 98
Hardman, M. L., 77, 184, 265, 367
Haring, N. G., 279
Harmon, S., 234
Hart, C., 260
Harth, R., 285, 288
Haubrich, P. A., 232, 241, 244, 330
Haubrick, P. A., 221
Havighurst, R. J., 212, 215
Heaney, 15
Heller, H. W., 362
Hertzig, M. E., 75
Heward, W. L., 175
Hewett, F. M., 3
Higgins, J., 58
Higgs, R. W., 277, 279
Hiles, P., 227
Hill, C., 330
Hill, J. W., 247, 330, 347
Homan, S. P., 200
Horwitz, A. L., 71
Houck, C. K., 64
Howard, J., 171, 172, 285
Howe, C., 127, 148
Hoyer, W. J., 265

Hresko, W. P., 63, 68, 74, 75, 80, 83, 137, 139, 141
Huffman, E., 202

Intagliata, J., 259
Irvine, J., 75–76

Jacobson, J. W., 260
Jani, L. A., 75, 76
Jani, S. N., 75, 76
Janosik, E. H., 318, 321
Jansen, M., 11
Jarolimek, J., 195
Jarrow, J. E., 233
Jaureguy, B. M., 264
Jensen, P. E., 11
Johnson, C., 263, 264
Johnson, G. O., 11, 37
Johnson, J. L., 8
Johnson, S. B., 244
Jones, K., 6, 46, 48
Jones, L. A. 251, 254
Jones, R. L., 361, 373
Jones, T. W., 297
Juul, K., 250
Juul, K. D., 7

Kahn, M. S., 232
Kalwara, S., 348
Karnes, M. B., 174, 175, 176, 178
Kastner, L. S., 248
Kauffman, J. M., 2, 23, 39, 41, 45, 47, 48, 64, 67, 80, 83, 185, 218, 219, 242, 244, 245, 348
Kaufman, M., 134
Kavale, J., 279
Keeffe, S. D., 165
Keenan, V., 290
Keesler, J., 318
Kelley, J., 242
Kemper, T., 65
Kennon, A. F., 277, 279, 286
Kenowitz, L. A., 358
Keogh, B. K., 34, 44
Kephart, N. C., 6
Kett, J. F., 218
Kingsley, R. F., 286
Kirchner, C., 243, 244, 256, 330
Kirk, S. A., 6, 63, 37, 39, 158, 159
Kleber, D. J., 202
Klein, M., 266
Klesius, J. P., 200
Kneedler, R. D., 368
Knoff, H. M., 106, 92
Kokaska, C. J., 242, 335
Kokaska, J., 348

Kolstoe, O. P., 2, 4, 11, 12
Konopka, G., 212, 221, 226
Kraus, S., 259
Krieger, I., 58
Kronick, D., 218, 219
Kroth, R., 286
Kulin, H. E., 218

Lakin, K. C., 259
Landesman-Dwyer, S., 248
Langdon, H. W., 98
Larrivee, B., 152, 299
Larson, C. E., 202
Larson, R. W., 244
Laski, F., 13
Lazar, I., 158
Leary, W. E., 71
Lee, R. C., 319
Leerskov, A., 11
Lehtinen, L. E., 5, 63
Lemon, N., 277
Lerner, J., 184, 185, 188, 199, 200, 202, 204, 205, 206
Lessen, E. I., 166, 179
Levine, M. D., 285, 315
Lewis, R. B., 89, 98, 99, 102, 103, 109
Licata, W. W., 287
Lillie, D. L., 159, 324
Lilly, M. S., 52
Lilly, S., 4, 5, 23
Liska, J. S., 248
Lloyd, J., 292
Lloyd, J. W., 67, 77, 83, 331, 334
Logan, D. R., 184
Lombardi, T. P., 299
Lorterman, A. S., 232
Love, H. D., 318, 319, 348
Lovitt, E. T., 279
Lutz, R. J., 332, 333, 337

MacMillan, D. L., 35, 36, 139, 307
Maher, C. A., 188, 206
Maier, A. S., 115
Mancuso, E., 14
Mandell, C. J., 34, 36, 63, 80, 105, 106, 116, 177, 250
Mangum, G. L., 331
Mann, L., 44, 340, 345
Mansergh, G. P., 177, 178
Margolis, J., 248
Mark, F. D., 278, 279, 286
Marland, S., 331
Marland, S. P., Jr., 332, 336
Marsh, G. E., 14, 23, 49, 80, 115, 122, 124, 127, 141, 142, 143, 152, 153, 159, 168, 169, 195, 196, 201, 202, 204, 213, 218, 219, 221, 222, 223, 225, 226, 231, 295, 321, 323, 330, 331, 339, 342, 366
Martin, R., 14, 95, 254
Martin, V., 254
Martin-Reynolds, J., 278, 279, 286
Marvell, T., 13
Mattheis, D., 332
Mauser, A. J., 348
Mayron, L. W., 70, 74, 78, 79, 83
McCarthy, M. M., 12, 13, 15, 371
McConville, L. S., 360
McDaniel, L., 299
McFadden, A. C., 224
McGee, D. W., 244, 247, 347
McGinnis, T. C., 311, 313, 314
McGovern, J. E., 171, 173, 179, 318
McGrade, B. J., 58
McGrath, J. E., 277
McGuire, D. J., 281, 285, 287
McKinney, J. D., 371
McKinnon, A., 138, 139
McLoughlin, J. A., 89, 98, 99, 102, 103, 109
McNutt, G., 24, 196
McQueeney, M., 58
McWhirter, J. J., 318
Meadowcroft, P., 299
Megivern, K., 246
Mercer, C. D., 35, 64, 67, 77, 203, 204, 334
Merulla, E., 138, 139
Metz, C., 44
Meyen, E. L., 13, 73
Michael, R., 248
Michaelis, C. T., 319
Michaels, M., 370
Miller, J. R., 318, 321
Miller, M., 280, 298
Miller, S., 320
Miller, T., 38
Miller, T. L., 51
Millman, R. B., 223
Minuchin, S., 313
Mitchell, J. W., 291
Moe, R., 251, 254
Money, J., 76–77
Montgomery, M. D., 143
Moore, K., 225
Moores, D. F., 243, 41
Mori, A. A., 158
Morse, W. C., 40
Moses, C. Warren, 197, 198
Muraski, J. A., 247, 335
Murtaugh, M., 249, 250

Myers, J. E., 266

Neisworth, J. T., 23, 45, 46, 48, 49, 70, 71, 73
Nelson, D. A., 202
Nesbitt, J., 262
Nesbitt, J. A., 198
Newman, K. S., 279
Nirje, 7

Ochoa, V., 240
Ohlson, E. L., 64, 83
Ohshansky, S., 243
Ojemann, G., 66
Olive, J. E., 158
Olivier, J., 233
Orlansky, M. D., 175
Osgood, C. E., 277
Ostertag, B. A., 253
Ostrow, L. S., 69
Ott, J. N., 83

Pasanella, A. L., 142
Patton, J. M., 292
Paul, J. L., 321
Payne, J. S., 201, 292
Payne, R. A., 201
Peach, W. J., 296
Pentecost, J., 247, 330, 347
Perkins, S. A., 75, 76
Perret, Y. M., 75, 367, 368
Peterson, L., 241
Peterson, R. L., 138, 139
Peterson, R., 243, 244, 256, 330
Pezzoli, J. J., 248
Phelps, L. A., 330, 332, 333, 337, 339, 340, 342
Piaget, J., 178
Podell, D. M., 364, 365
Podemski, R., 123, 138, 142, 143, 152, 232
Podemski, R. S., 14, 16, 19, 295, 358, 371, 372
Polloway, E. A., 201
Popp, R. A., 299
Postlewaite, J., 13
Powers, D. A., 287, 294
Prehm, H. J., 136, 139
President's Committee on Mental Retardation, 248
Price, B. J., 14, 23, 49, 80, 115, 122, 141, 153, 159, 168, 169, 195, 213, 218, 219, 221, 222, 223, 225, 226, 231, 321, 323, 330, 339, 342, 366
Proctor, D. I., 279
Pysh, M., 135

Quay, H. C., 39

Rader, B. T., 195
Ragan, W. B., 190
Raimondi, S. L., 366
Ramey, C. T., 83
Redl, F., 40
Reese, J. H., 280
Reid, D. K., 63, 68, 74, 75, 80, 83, 137, 139, 141
Renz, P., 11
Reppucci, N. D., 248
Reuschlein, P., 195
Reynolds, B. J., 278, 279, 286
Reynolds, G., 198
Reynolds, M. C., 25, 38, 136, 139, 143
Rhoads, F. A., 77
Richardson, S. A., 75
Richardson, S. O., 141, 142
Richey, L., 51
Richter-Stein, C., 345, 346
Ringness, T. A., 292
Ritter, R. J., 360
Robertson, B., 234
Robinson, H. B., 69, 70, 73, 242
Robinson, K., 347
Robinson, N. M., 69, 70, 73, 242
Robinson, R., 248
Robson, D. L., 152
Rockwell, J., 13
Rokeach, M., 277
Roos, P., 315, 318, 319
Rose, E., 77
Rose, T. L., 166, 179
Rosegrant, T., 204
Rosenberg, D., 77
Rosett, A., 175
Ross, A. O., 40
Ross, J. W., 371
Rossi, C., 279
Ryan, A. W., 366
Ryan, K., 192
Ryckman, D. B., 188

Saffort, P. L., 159
Salend, S. J., 199
Salvia, J., 88, 89, 98, 99, 100, 101, 102, 107, 109, 110, 280
Sandler, A., 248
Sandoval, J., 77–78, 277, 279, 286
Saracho, O. N., 319
Schalock, R. L., 261
Scheerenberger, R. C., 258, 368, 369
Schilit, J., 347
Schindler, W. J., 152
Schipper, W. V., 358
Schloss, P., 280

Schmelkin, L. P., 277, 286
Schmickel, R., 58
Schulman, E. D., 241, 242, 265
Schultz, J., 160, 317
Schultz, L. R., 199
Schultz, J. B., 150
Schumaker, J. B., 219, 220, 221
Schwartz, A. A., 260
Schwartz, L. L., 17
Scranton, T. R., 188
Seltzer, G. B., 261
Sermier, E., 136
Shanahan, D., 366
Shearer, D. E., 174
Shearer, M. S., 174
Sheldon-Wildgen, J., 219
Shepherd, G. D., 190
Sherif, C. W., 277
Sherif, M., 277
Sherman, J. A., 219
Siegel, E., 37, 68, 69, 70, 71, 74, 109, 110, 124, 142, 244
Siegel, J., 330, 334
Sigelman, C. K., 248, 281, 287, 288
Silver, L. B., 78, 79
Simon, A., 242
Simpson, R., 308, 309, 314, 319, 320
Siperstein, G. N., 279, 286, 291
Skolnick, A. S., 307
Skolnick, J. H., 307
Skrtic, T., 219
Slaney, S. H., 262
Slate, N. M., 98
Smart, J., 218
Smith, B. L., 248
Smith, C. R., 64, 73, 184, 185, 200, 330
Smith, J. E., 201
Smith, J. E., Jr., 152
Smith, L. L., 241
Smith, R. M., 70, 71, 73, 91
Smith, S., 66
Smith, T. E. C., 14, 21, 23, 49, 115, 122, 159, 168, 169, 195, 244, 248, 261, 281, 286, 287, 288, 292, 321, 323, 330, 346
Snell, M. E., 256, 257
Sparks, R., 141, 142
Spaulding, R. L., 166
Spence, E. S., 24
Spodek, B., 319, 324
Spreen, O., 241
Spring, C., 77–78
Stevens, G. D., 32
Stewart, D. M., 244

Stodden, R. A., 330, 345, 346
Stotland, J. F., 14
Strasburger, R., 299
Strauch, J. C., 278
Strauss, A. A., 5, 63
Strickland, C. G., 242
Suci, G. J., 277
Suelzle, M., 290
Swanson, H. L., 103, 94
Swartz, J. D., 288, 292
Swisher, J. D., 223

Tannenbaum, P. H., 277
Taylor, R. L., 89, 90, 91, 97, 101, 102, 104, 105, 107, 109, 110, 111
Terman, L., 4
Teska, R. R., 174, 178
Thoene, J., 58
Thompson, S. A., 40
Treegoob, M., 202
Trippi, J., 248, 261
Tulloch, D., 318
Turkel, S. B., 364, 365
Turnbull, A. P., 13, 21, 136, 150, 160, 307, 314, 320
Turnbull, H. R., 2, 13, 21, 136, 160, 314, 320

Tyler, G. T., 330
Tymitz, B. L., 152

Umbreit, J., 69
Unger, R. A., 224

Vacca, R. S., 179
Valletutti, P. T., 159
Van Etten, G., 139
Van Riper, C., 43
Voeltz, L. M., 277
Vogel, S. A., 253
Volkmor, C. B., 142

Waisbren, S. E., 318
Wald, E., 307
Walden, E. L., 40
Walker, J., 103
Walters, R. H., 306
Walthall, J. E., 348
Ward, M., 341, 342, 345, 346
Warner, R. W., 223
Watson, B. L., 103
Watson, J., 94
Waxman, H. M., 265, 266
Webb, G., 233
Webster, R. E., 349
Wechsler, D., 36

Wehman, P., 247, 330, 347
Weiler, H. N., 369, 371
Weintraub, F., 122
Weintraub, F. J., 20, 371
Weishahn, M. W., 143
Weiss, L., 58
Wender, P. H., 241
Wetter, J., 288
White, B., 158
White, W. J., 240, 241, 244
Wiederholdt, J. L., 142
Wiederholt, J. L., 25, 141
Wiener, D., 249
Willer, B., 259
Wilton, K. M., 75–76
Winn, J., 306
Wolford, B., 44
Wolman, B. B., 40
Wolraich, M. L., 285
Wood, L. C., 254

Yoshida, J. E., 9, 12
Ysseldyke, J. E., 2, 34, 51, 88, 89, 98, 99, 100, 101, 102, 107, 109, 110, 111, 280

Zehrbach, R. R., 174, 175

SUBJECT INDEX

AAMD. *See* American Association on Mental Deficiency
Academic characteristics:
    of elementary mildly handicapped children, 184–185, 187
Academic Therapy, 37
Accommodative strategies:
    for mainstreaming, 200
    in postsecondary education, 252
Accommodation:
    definition of, 141
Achievement levels:
    of mildly handicapped, 46–47
Achievement tests, 109
    characteristics of, 112–113
    listing of, 111
Adaptive behavior, 110–111
Administrators. *See* School administrators
Adolescence:
    definition of, 212
    problems of, 223–226
    theories of, 212–213, 215–218
        biological, 217–218
        developmental, 215
        evolutionary, 217
        psychoanalytic, 216–217
Adolescent developmental tasks, 212
    effect of handicap on, 214

Adolescent subculture, 218–223
    influence of, 219–220
Adolescents:
    mildly handicapped, 210–237. *See also* Mildly handicapped adadolescents
Adults:
    Mildly handicapped, 210–237. *See also* Mildly handicapped adults
Advance notice:
    right of, 148
Affirmative action for handicapped, 240
Alcohol:
    and mildly handicapped etiology, 69–70
Alcoholism:
    in mildly handicapped adolescents, 224
Aldelphi University, 233–234
Aldern-Boil Development Profile, 167
Allergies:
    and mildly handicapped etiology, 78–79
Alternative Vocational School (E. Hartford, Conn.), 349, 350
American Association on Mental Deficiency (AAMD), 36, 58, 110
    mental retardation etiological

system, 60–63
American Camping Association, 199
American Psychological Association:
    Standards for Educational and Psychological Tests, 99
Amniocentesis, 367
    alternatives to [highlight], 368
    definition of, 171
Anoxia, 70
Anxiety:
    and mildly handicapped etiology, 82–83
Arithmetic achievement tests:
    characteristics of, 113
    listing of, 111
Arithmetical concepts:
    and Piagetian theory, by age, 205
Arkansas:
    handicapped programs in, 44
Armstrong v. Kline, 14
Assessment of mildly handicapped, 87–118. *See also* Evaluation
    definition of, 88, 132
    discriminatory, reduction of, 97
    informal, 115
    instruments for, 106–111
    legal considerations in, 94–98

392 Subject Index

Assessment of mildly (continued)
  of preschool handicapped, 168–169
  personnel for, 104–106
  policymaking in, 101–103
  purposes of, 89–94
  relation of stages to programming, 98
  relative importance of data in, 93
  requirements for adequate, 99–101
  sources of information for, 88
Assessment domains, 103–104
Assessment process, 98–99
  parental involvement in, 96
  regulatory safeguards on, 95–96
Assessment tools, 99–100. *See also* Testing
Association for Children with Learning Disabilities, 37
Attitudes:
  and the mildly handicapped, 275–303
  assessment of, 294–295
  definition of, 277
  of employers, 291–292
  of parents, 288–291
  of peers, 291
  of physicians, 285
  of school administrators, 286–288
  of self in mildly handicapped, 292–293
  of teachers, 285–286
  and mainstreaming, 195
  techniques to change, 295–299
  variables affecting, 277–280
Audiometer, 42

Barat College, 234
Bayley Scales of Infant Development, 170
Behavior:
  labels and, 279–280
  of mildly handicapped, 46
Behavior disordered:
  career education for, 334
Behavior disorders, 6, 39–41
  definition of, 39
Behavior rating tests:
  listing of, 111
Behavioral model:
  for preschool curricula, 177–178
Behaviorism:
  and emotional disturbances, 41

Bias in testing, 94
Biological theory of adolescence, 217–218
Biomedical disorders:
  and mildly handicapped etiology, 70–71
Black children. *See also* Minority children
  in special education classes, 14
Blended family, 309
Blind. *See also* Visually impaired
  sonic guide for [highlight], 365
Board of Education v. Rowley, 14–15
"Borderline" children, 134
Boyd Developmental Progress Scales, 167
Brain:
  damage to, and learning disabilities, 63–64
  development of, and nutrition, 75
  injury diagnosis, and perceptual-motor tests, 109
  newborn disorders of [highlight], 71
  oxygen deprivation of, 70
Brain disease, and mental retardation etiology, 60
Brain studies, and learning disabilities [highlight], 65–67
Brigance Diagnostic Inventory Early, 167
Broward Community College, 254
Brown v. Board of Education, 12, 17
Buckley Amendment, 95
Building-level support teams, 135

CAI (Computer assisted instruction), 363–365
CAL (Computer assisted learning), 365–366
CEC. *See* Council for Exceptional Children (CEC)
Camps, day [highlight], 197–199
Career awareness:
  as component of career education program, 333
  in elementary grades, 336
Career decisions:
  for mildly handicapped adolescents, 232, 235
Career education, 330–338
  components of program, 332–334
  concepts included in, 331–332

  definition of, 331
  for elementary handicapped, 335–337
  in secondary schools, 337–338
  need for, in special education, 334
  objectives of, 332
    for handicapped, 334–335
  program development, 335
  vs vocational education, 340
"Career Educational Model", 338
Career exploration:
  as component of career education program, 333
  in secondary schools, 337
Career preparation:
  as component of career education program, 333
Cascade of Services Model, 138–139
Categorical approach to disabled services, 2
  classifying children in, 92
  in education, 8
  criticism of, 23
  problems with, 46
Cattell Infant Intelligence Scale, 170
Center-based models:
  following home-based service models, 175
  for preschoolers, 176–177
Certification in special education, 52
Chaffee Bill, 369
Chapel Hill Project (North Carolina), 176
Child abuse and neglect:
  and mildly handicapped etiology, 76–77
Child find, in IEP process, 124, 125
  activities for preschool, 158–159
  examples of activities for, 125
  factors influencing, 125
Child-Find Project:
  for preschoolers, 166
Child rearing:
  and mildly handicapped etiology, 80, 81
  impact of handicapped on family, 314–315
Chromosomal abnormalities:
  and mental retardation etiology, 60, 62
  and mildly handicapped etiology, 72–73

Subject Index   393

Civil rights:
  of handicapped, 240
  of special education students, 13
Civil Rights Act of 1964, 14, 246
Civil Service Act:
  1948 Amendment, 245
Classification:
  as part of assessment program, 91–92
Classroom environment, 195–196
Classroom teachers, 193–196.
  See also Teachers
  attitudes of, 285–286
  in mainstreaming process, 151
  role of, 195
  skills for teaching handicapped, 195, 199
Classrooms:
  regular, 192–196
    mildly handicapped in, 196, 199–206
Cleburne (City) v. Cleburne Living Center [highlight], 282–284
Closer Look, 234
Cognitive developmental model:
  for preschool curricula, 178
Cohabitation, 311
College of the Ozarks, 234
College. See Postsecondary education
Common law family, 309–310
Commune family, 310
Communication:
  between parents and school personnel, 321–325
Communication disorders:
  definition of, 43
Community acceptance:
  of mildly handicapped adults, 248–250
Community residential facilities:
  placement in, 260–261
  trends, 369
Compensatory service model:
  in secondary education, 231
Competency testing, 370
  impact on mildly handicapped, 371–372
Composite family, 310–311
Computer assisted instruction (CAI), 363–365
Computer assisted learning (CAL), 365–366
Computer software evaluation, 366
Computers:
  and mildly handicapped, 363–366

implications for handicapped and nonhandicapped, 359–360
Conduct disorders, 39
Conference of Executives of American Schools for the Deaf, 41
Contact with handicapped:
  and attitude change, 277–278, 296
Cooperative group tasks:
  to deal with social problems, 206
Council for Exceptional Children (CEC), 186, 341
  Code of Ethics and Standards, 361–362
Counseling:
  of parents, 324
Courts. See Litigation
Crime:
  and mildly mentally retarded adults, 241–242
Criterion-referenced tests:
  definition of, 102–103
  for preschool assessment, 168
Curriculum:
  definition of, 177
Curry College [highlight], 233
Cursive writing:
  vs printing, 202

DASI (Developmental Activities Screening Inventory), 167
DIAL (Developmental Indicators for the Assessment of Learning), 167
Dating:
  in adolescent subculture, 220
Day camps [highlight], 197–199
Deaf person:
  definition of, 41
Deinstitutionalization, 8, 9, 257–259
  trends in, 368–369
Delphi technique, 350
Deno's Cascade of Services, 138–139
Denver Developmental Screening Test, 167
Departmentalization:
  implications for special education, 192
  in elementary schools, 190
Depression:
  and mildly handicapped etiology, 82–83

Development Test of Visual Motor Integrations, 170
Development Test of Visual Perception, 170
Development stages (Piaget), 178
Developmental Activities Screening Inventory (DASI), 167
Developmental Indicators for the Assessment of Learning (DIAL), 167
Developmental Screening Inventory, 167
Developmental Test of Visual Perception, 101
Developmental theory of adolescence, 215
Developmentally Disabled Assistance Bill of 1974, 245
Diagnosis:
  definition of, 89
  of preschool handicapped, 168
Diagnostic achievement tests, 109
Diana v. State Board of Education, 95
Diet. See Nutrition
Disability:
  definition of, 32
Disabled. See Handicapped
Discipline:
  and school policies for mildly handicapped, 191
Discrimination in handicapped evaluation, 21
  reduction of, 97
Divorce:
  blended family as a result of, 309
Documentation:
  of parental involvement, 321–322
Down's Syndrome, 72–73
Dress codes:
  of adolescents, 219–220
Drug abuse:
  by mildly handicapped adolescents, 223–224
  definition of, 223
Drug therapy:
  for emotionally disturbed, 40–41
Drugs:
  and mental retardation etiology, 60
  and mildly handicapped etiology, 69–70
Due process procedures:
  for handicapped children, 21, 22

Subject Index

Due process procedures: (continued)
  in Individualized Education Program, 148–150
Durrell Analysis of Reading Difficulty, 101
Dyslexia [highlight], 267–268

Early intervention, 158
  assumptions of, 158–159
  funding for, 179
  [highlight], 162–164
Economic unit:
  family as, 318
Education. See also Postsecondary education
  classification by needs for, 48
  impact of standards on mildly handicapped adolescents, 230
  reform of, and special education, 369–372
  trends in, and mildly handicapped adolescents, 229–230
Education for All Handicapped Children Act (P.L. 94-192), 5, 14–15, 16–17, 19–22, 37, 245
  and assessment, 91
  and assessment personnel, 99
  and Individualized Education Program, 93, 122
  and legal aspects of assessment, 95
  and learning disabled, 38
  due process rights, 21, 22
Efficacy studies, 9, 12
Elderly mildly handicapped, 264–266
Elderly parents:
  care of, impacted by mildly handicapped, 318
Electromagnetic radiation:
  and mildly handicapped etiology, 70, 79
Elementary schools:
  and the mildly handicapped, 188–196
  curriculum, 192, 193
  impact of policies on special education students, 191, 193
  organizational arrangement of, 190, 191–192
Elementary-aged mildly handicapped children, 182–208
  career education for, 335–337
  characteristics and needs of, 184–185, 187–188
  early educational experiences of, 184

Emotional characteristics:
  of mildly handicapped children, 188
Emotional disturbances, 39–41
  categories of, 39–40
  drug therapy for, 40–41
  etiology of, 64, 67–68
Emotional skills:
  teaching strategies for, 205–206
Emotionally disturbed, 6
  access to public education, 13
  vocational education program for, 349
Employers:
  attitudes of, 291–292
Employment of handicapped: 242–248
  and self-concept, 292
  federal legislation relating to, 245
  state legislation on, 246–247
Endogenous mental retardation, 6
Environment:
  and learning disabilities, 64
  and mental retardation etiology, 63
  and mildly handicapped etiology, 74–83
  and preschool handicapped, 173
Environmental pollution, and mildly handicapped etiology, 70
Equal employment opportunity, 245
Etiology,
  definition of, 58
  for mildly handicapped, 46, 68–83
  of emotional disturbances, 64, 67–68
  of learning disabilities, 63–64
  of mental retardation, 60–63
  organization of systems of, 59
  reasons for determining, 58
Evaluation, 132, 136. See also Assessment
  as part of IEP process, 133
  definition of, 89, 132
Evaluation of Individualized Education Program, 148
Evaluation team:
  potential members of, 132
Evolutionary theory of adolescence, 217
Exceptional children:
  definition of, 23
Exogenous mental retardation, 6
Extended family, 308–309

Family:
  and mildly handicapped etiology, 80
  and the mildly handicapped, 305–326
  definition of, 306
  life cycle of, 311–313
  organizational patterns of, 307–311
  purposes of, 313–318
    effect of handicapped child on, 314–318
  reactions to mildly handicapped, 318–319
Federal Register, 132
Federal government:
  and trends in special education, 360–361
Feingold diet, 78–79
Fetal alcohol syndrome, 69
Formative period:
  adolescence as, 215
Full-Range Picture Vocabulary Test, 101
Full-time special classes, 139–140
Funding:
  for preschool services, 179
  for special education, 360–361

Gallaudet College, 254
Gates-McKillop Reading Diagnostic Tests, 101
Generic special education. See Noncategorical approach to special education
Genetic counseling, 367–368
Genotypic classification, 45
German measles:
  and mildly handicapped etiology, 68
Gessell Development Test, 170
Gestational disorders:
  and mildly handicapped etiology, 74
Gilmore Oral Reading Test, 101
Graded schools:
  implications for special education, 191
Gray Oral Reading Test, 101
Group homes, 248–249
  for mildly handicapped, 259
Group tests, 101–102
  achievement, 109
  intelligence, 107

Handicap:
  definition of, 32

Handicapped:
  civil rights act for, 22
  classification systems for, 44
  financial aspects [highlight], 10
  identification of, 13–14
  legislation relating to
    employment of, 245
  nondiscriminatory assessment
    of, 21
  preschool programs for, 158
  specialized vocational education
    for, 345
Handwriting:
  teaching strategies for, 201
Hard-of-hearing person:
  definition of, 41
Head Start, 158
Health impairments, 43
Hearing (proceedings):
  right to, as part of due process,
    148
Hearing impaired, 41–42
  employment prospects of, 243,
    244–245
  postsecondary education for,
    254
  problems of, 251
  rights of, 14–15
  segregation of, in school, 41
  social adjustment of, 242
  technological aids for, 367
Hearing loss:
  testing for, 42
Heredity:
  and mildly handicapped
    etiology, 73
Herpes:
  and mildly handicapped
    etiology, 69
Home and center-based service
  delivery models:
  for preschool services, 175
Home-based service delivery
  models:
  followed by center-based
    models, 175
  for preschoolers, 174–175
Horizontal organization:
  of elementary schools, 190
Housing:
  equal opportunity, 248
  for handicapped adults,
    257–262
  for mentally handicapped
    [highlight], 260
Houston Test of Language, 170
Huntington-Commack Software
  Evaluation Project, 366

Hypoglycemia, 71

IEP. See Individualized Education
  Program.
IQ. See Intelligence quotients.
ITPA. See Illinois Test of
  Psycholinguistic Abilities.
Identification:
  as part of assessment program,
    90
  negative aspects of, 90
  of children for special education,
    124, 125
  of preschool handicapped, 158
    process for, 165–169
    problems in, 159–161,
      164–165
    professionals in, 169–173
Illinois Test of Psycholinguistic
  Abilities (ITPA), 101, 114
Impairment, 32
Individual tests, 101–102
  achievement, 109
  intelligence, 107–108
Individualized Education Program
  (IEP), 20–21, 120–155
  and mainstreaming, 151–152
  as process, 123–133, 136
  conference for, 145
  definition of, 122
  development of, and
    assessment, 93–94
  evaluation and monitoring, 145,
    148, 149
  misconceptions about, 153
  placement selection, 143–144
  referral form in, 126–130
  relation to daily instruction, 145
  vocational education and, 342
  writing, 144–145
Individualized Education Program
  (IEP) form, 144–145
  sample, 146–147
Infections:
  and mental retardation etiology,
    60
  and mildly handicapped
    etiology, 68–69
Informal assessment techniques:
  for preschoolers, 168
Inservice training:
  for teachers and administrators,
    279
Institute for Behavioral Genetics,
  66
Institutionalization, 9
Institutionalized mental patients:
  rights of, 14

Instruction methods:
  and labels, 49–50
  for mildly handicapped, 48–50
Instructional objectives:
  in IEP, 145
Integration:
  as goal of special education
    services, 140
Intelligence:
  definition of, 107
Intelligence quotients:
  as means of classifying
    handicapped, 47
  of mentally handicapped, 36,
    37
Intelligence testing, 4, 5
  to identify mentally
    handicapped, 13–14
Intelligence tests, 107
  characteristics of, 112
  listing of, 111
Intervention strategies:
  for emotional disturbances,
    40–41
Interviews:
  in assessment process, 115
Itinerant teacher model, 142–143

Job application:
  as obstacle to employment for
    mildly handicapped, 244
Job interview skills, 347
Journal of Learning Disabilities, 37

Kaiser-Permanente (K-P) Diet,
  78–79
KeyMath Diagnostic Arithmetic
  Test, 113
Knowledge:
  affect on attitudes of
    handicapped, 278–279

Labels for handicapped, 32–36
  advantages and disadvantages
    of, 34–36
  assumptions of, 280
  and behavior, 279–280
  and instruction methods, 49–50
  and least restrictive setting, 137
  and special education, 33–36
  and traditional service patterns,
    136
  for preschool child, 165
  necessity of, 44
  sociological aspects, 32–33
Landmark College [highlight], 233
Language Achievement tests, 114
Language disorders, 43

396 Subject Index

Larry P. v. Riles, 13–14, 95
Learning Accomplishment Profile, 167
Learning disabilities, 6, 37–39
  and heredity, 74
  brain studies and [highlight], 65–67
  definition of, 38
  early identification [highlight], 162–164
  etiology of, 63–64
Learning disabled,
  adjustment as adults, 240
  and perceptual-motor tests, 109
  career education for, 334
  children as [highlight], 18–19, 24–25
    programs for [highlight], 134–136
  employment prospects of, 244
  [highlight], 227–229
  job seeking skills of, 347
  lists of college programs for, 253
  parents' attitudes toward, 288–289
  peer attitudes toward, 219, 291
  postsecondary education for, 253
    [highlight], 233–234
  problems of, as adults, 251
  self-concepts of, 292
  self-help groups for, 263–264
  social acceptance as adults, 241
Least restrictive environment, 17, 19, 136–144. *See also* Mainstreaming
  definition of, 137
  service models for, 137–143
Legal blindness, 42
Legislation. *See also* Education for All Handicapped Children Act
  P.L. 19-8, 16
  federal, 16
  relating to handicapped employment, 245
  state, on employment of handicapped, 246–247
Likert-type scale, 295
Litigation, 12–15
  mentally handicapped housing, 258
LOGO, 365–366

Mainstreaming, 8, 11–12, 17, 44, 150–153
  accommodative strategies for, 200
  administrators' attitudes toward, 288
  and classroom teacher attitudes, 193–194, 286
  and school environment, 81
  definition of, 150
  [highlight], 24–25, 227–229
  impact on role of administrators, 286–287
  in vocational education, 342–345
  misconceptions about, 150
  parental attitudes toward, 290
  requirements for success of, 151, 199
  self-concepts and, 293
Malnutrition. *See* Nutrition
Massachusetts:
  education for handicapped in, 44, 49
  handicapped programs in, 44
Maternal malnutrition:
  effect on fetus, 75
Mathematics:
  skills by grade levels, 204–205
  teaching strategies for, 204–205
Mattie T. v. Holladay, 13
McCarthy Scales of Children's Abilities, 170
Medical model:
  for early intervention, 159
Medical personnel:
  in identification of preschool handicapped, 170–171
Medical trends benefiting handicapped, 366–368
Medication. *See* Drug therapy
Mental retardation:
  as label, 32
  classifications of, 6, 37
  definition of, 36–37
  etiology of, 60–63
Mentally handicapped:
  access to public education, 13
  church restrictions on [highlight], 278
  contact with, and attitudes, 277
  discrimination in housing for, 248
  peer attitudes toward, 291
  problems of, as adults, 251
  self-concepts of, 292
Mentally retarded:
  career education for, 334
  career education model for, 337–338
  civil rights of [highlight], 282–284

Metabolism:
  and mental retardation etiology, 60
  and mildly handicapped etiology, 70–71
Michigan Genetic Screening Program, 58
Microcomputers. *See also* Computers
  to teach written expression, 204
Mildly handicapped, 2, 45–52
  achievement levels of, 46–47
  and computers, 363–366
  behavioral characteristics of, 46
  definition of, 50–51
  environmental factors and, 74–83
  etiology of, 46, 57–85
  family and, 305–326
  future for, 358–374
  impact on family life cycle, 311
  instruction methods for, 48–50
  obstacles to category of, 51–52
  personality problems of, 48
  postsecondary education for, 232, 251–255
  prevalence of, 51
  reasons for category of, 45–50
  reasons for vocational problems of, 330
  self-attitudes, 292–293
  social characteristics of, 46
Mildly handicapped adolescents, 210–237
  educational needs of, 229–232
  peer acceptance of, 219
  peer membership and, 220–223
Mildly handicapped adults, 50–51, 238–272
  needs and characteristics of, 241–250
  obstacles to employment, 243–244
  problems of, 251
  recreational activities for, 249–250
  services for, 250–264
  social adjustment of, 241
Mildly handicapped children. *See also* Elementary-aged mildly handicapped children; Preschool mildly handicapped children
  educational needs of, 20
  and noncategorical special education, 23
  treatment in public schools, 5
Mildly handicapped elderly, 264–266

Subject Index

characteristics of, 265–266
needs of, 266
Mills v. Board of Education, Washington, D.C., 13
Minimal brain damage, 64
Minimal brain dysfunction, 64
Ministers:
  in identification of preschool handicapped, 173
Minnesota Child Developmental Inventory, 167
Minority children,
  and assessment of adaptive behavior, 110
  and norm-referenced tests, 101
  and testing in assessment, 95
Mongolism, 72–73

NARC. *See* National Association for Retarded Citizens
Nation at Risk: The Imperative for Educational Reform, 229, 369
National Association for Retarded Children, 5
National Association for Retarded Citizens (NARC), 5
National Association of State Directors of Special Education, 103
National Commission on Excellence in Education, 229
National Association of Superintendents of Public Residential Facilities for the Mentally Retarded, 258
Nature-nurture controversy, 73
Newborns:
  brain disorders of [highlight], 71
Noncategorical approach to special education, 2, 23–26, 45
  classifying children in, 92
  teacher training and, 52
Nondiscriminatory assessment, 97
Nongraded schools:
  implications for special education, 191
Nonverbal children, 43
Norm-referenced tests, 101
  administration of, 114
  definition of, 102
  types of, 106
Normal development model:
  for preschool curricula, 177
Normalization, 7–8, 12
  definition of, 250
  for handicapped adults, 250–251
  for handicapped children. *See* Mainstreaming.

Norms, 33–34
Nuclear family, 308
  life cycle of, 311
Nurses:
  in identification of preschool handicapped, 172
Nutrition:
  and mental retardation etiology, 60
  and mildly handicapped etiology, 74–76, 77–79

Observation forms, 116, 117
Observation methods:
  direct and indirect, 115
Obstetrician:
  in identification of preschool handicapped, 171
Occupational clusters, 336–337
Oxygen supply, to brain, 70

PEECH (Precise Early Education of Children with Handicaps), 176
PEEP (Preschool and Early Education Project), 176
PIAT (Peabody Individual Achievement Test), 109, 113
PKU (Phenylketonuria), 70–71
Parent conferences, 324
Parental consent, 136
  written, 149–150
Parental involvement:
  aspects of, 148
  in assessment process, 96, 106
  in IEP, 148–150
Parents:
  and preschool referrals, 160
  as source of referral, 125
  attitudes of, 288–291
  communication with school personnel, 321–325
  counseling for, 324
  socioeconomic status of, and access to preschool services, 179
  support groups for, 324
  trends in advocacy by, 361
Part-time special classes, 140–142
Peabody Individual Achievement Test (PIAT), 109, 113
Pediatrician:
  in identification of preschool handicapped, 171–172
Peer groups in adolescence. *See* Adolescent subculture.
Peers:
  attitudes of, 291
  discussions to change, 297
  rejection by, 188

relations with, 317
Pennsylvania Association for Retarded Citizens (PARC) v. Pennsylvania, 13
Perceptual-motor tests, 109–110
  listing of, 111
Performance standards:
  and identification of preschool handicapped, 158
Personality problems:
  of mildly handicapped, 48
Personnel:
  for assessment, 99, 104–106
  in vocational education, 349–351
Phenotypic classification, 45
Phenylketonuria (PKU), 70–71
Physical agent:
  and mental retardation etiology, 60
Physical injury:
  and mildly handicapped etiology, 70
Physically disabled, 43
  access to public education, 13
  employment prospects of, 245
  technological aids for, 367
Physicians:
  attitudes of, 285
  role of, in treating handicapped, 285
Piagetian theory:
  and arithmetical concepts, by age, 205
Picture Story Language Test, 113
Placement process, 92, 137
Poisons:
  and mildly handicapped etiology, 69–70
Polygamy, 310–311
Portage Guide to Early Education, 167
Portage Project (Wisconsin), for preschoolers, 174
Postsecondary education:
  for learning disabled [highlight], 233–234
  for mildly handicapped, 232, 251–255
  preparation of handicapped for, 254–255
Poverty:
  and mildly handicapped etiology, 76
Pre-school Language Scale, 170
Precise Early Education of Children with Handicaps (PEECH), 176

Subject Index

Pregnancy:
  in mildly handicapped adolescents, 225–226
Prenatal detection of disabilities, 367
Prenatal influences, and mental retardation etiology, 60
Preschool and Early Education Project (PEEP), 176
Preschool mildly handicapped children, 156–181
  curricular approaches for, 177–178
  diagnosis of, 165
  referrals of, 159–161
Preschool services. See also Early intervention
  barriers to, 178–179
  importance of, 158
  state laws prohibiting, 179
Prevocational programs, 346–347
Primary reference group:
  family as, 317
Principals. See School administrators
  role in special education, 190
Professionals:
  as service providers to handicapped students, 152
  for preschool handicapped, 164
  in preschool identification, 169–173
Project Casa (San Antonio, Texas), for preschoolers, 174
Project Read, 135–136
Psychiatric disorders:
  and mental retardation etiology, 63
Psychoanalytic theory of adolescence, 216–217
Psychological factors:
  and mildly handicapped etiology, 80

Radiation:
  and mildly handicapped etiology, 70, 79
Randolph Sheppard Act Amendments of 1974, 245
Reading:
  behavior of children with problems in, 201
  teaching strategies for, 199–201, 202
Reading achievement tests:
  characteristics of, 113
  listing of, 111

Records:
  in assessment process, 116
  parents' access to, 95
Recreational activities:
  for mildly handicapped adults, 249–250, 262
Recreational facilities, public, accessibility goals, 262
Referral:
  of preschoolers, 159–161
  purpose of, 124
Referral conference, 127, 131–132
Referral form, 126–130
Referral team, 131–132
Regular classrooms, 192–196
  mildly handicapped in, 196, 199–206. See also Mainstreaming
Rehabilitation:
  as need of elderly mildly handicapped, 266
Rehabilitation Act of 1973, 14, 240, 245, 253
  Section 504, 22–23
Rehabilitation workshops, 257
Related services (P.L. 94-192):
  for handicapped children, 21–22
Reliability of tests:
  definition of, 100
Remedial service model:
  in secondary education, 231
Resource room model, 140–142
  advantages and disadvantages, 143
  for mildly-handicapped elementary children, 196, 199
  requirements for success of, 199
Resource rooms:
  heterogeneous groups in, 23
  survey of use, 196
  types of, 141
"Right to education case," 13
"Right to treatment case," 14
Role failure:
  measurement standards for, 33–34
Role modeling, 80
Rubella:
  and mildly handicapped etiology, 68
Runaways:
  mildly handicapped adolescents as, 224

Scandinavia, 7
School administrators:

and vocational education for handicapped, 350–351
  attitudes of, 286–288
  communication with parents, 321–325
  in elementary schools, 189–190
  special education training, and attitudes, 279
"School-Based Career Education Model for the Handicapped," 338
School year:
  extended, 14
Schools. See also Elementary schools
  and mildly handicapped etiology, 80–81
Screening:
  as part of assessment program, 90
  for preschoolers, 165, 166
Screening achievement tests, 109
Screening instruments:
  for preschool children, 167
Secondary schools:
  career education in, 337–338
Segregation:
  of handicapped students, 9
Self-concept:
  and mildly handicapped etiology, 81
  of mildly handicapped, 292–293
Self-contained classes, 8, 139–140
  advantages and disadvantages, 140
  implications for special education, 192
  in elementary schools, 190
  limitations of, 139–140
Self-help groups, 263–264
Serial family, 310
Service delivery:
  for preschoolers, 173–177
Service delivery models:
  definition of, 173
  in secondary education, 231–232
Severely handicapped:
  definition of, 50
Sexual behavior:
  in adolescent subculture, 220
Shared responsibility, 151–152
Sheltered workshops, 256–257
Shoplifting:
  by mildly handicapped adolescents, 224–225
Siblings:
  and learning disabilities, 163

Subject Index

of mildly handicapped, 319–321
Single-parent family, 310
Skill training programs:
  high cost, 348–349
  low-cost, 347–348, 349
Slang:
  in adolescent subculture, 220
Slosson Intelligence Test, 112
Smoking:
  and mildly handicapped etiology, 70
Social adjustment:
  of mildly handicapped adolescents, 220–223
  of mildly handicapped adults, 241–242
Social characteristics:
  of mildly handicapped, 46
  of mildly handicapped children, 188
Social classes:
  and learning disabilities, 38
Social competence:
  definition of, 241
Social integration of handicapped, 19
Social problems of disabled children:
  characteristics of, 206
Social service workers:
  and preschool referrals, 161
  in identification of preschool handicapped, 173
Social skills, 188
  teaching strategies for, 205–206
Social-cognitive problem solving approach, 206
Socialization of handicapped:
  as family responsibility, 315–317
Socially handicapped children:
  access to public education, 13
Soldier's Rehabilitation Act of 1918, 255
Sonic guide, for the blind [highlight], 365
Spache Diagnostic Reading Scales, 113
Special education:
  alternatives to, 134–136
  and educational reform, 369–372
  and intelligence testing, 107
  and professional standards, 361–362
  and technology, 363–368
  categorical groupings in, 36–43
  criticism of, 9, 11

evaluation of, 90–91
federal funding for, 360–361
history, 3–4
implications of graded and nongraded schools for, 191
influences on, 8
need for career education in, 334
principals' role in, 190
support for, 11
trends, 358–359
Special education supervisor:
  role in referral process, 127
Special education teachers. See also Teachers
  and vocational education, 342, 350
  role in career education, 338
Specific Learning Disabilities Act of 1969 (P.L. 91-230), 37
Speech disorders, 43
Spelling:
  teaching strategies for, 201, 202–204
Standards:
  for preschool handicapped, 165
Stanford-Binet Intelligence Scale, 101, 112, 170
Stealing:
  by mildly handicapped adolescents, 224–225
Stress:
  and mildly handicapped etiology, 82–83
Student-support teams, 135
Suicide:
  by mildly handicapped adolescents, 226
Supportive services model, 142–143
Syphilis, congenital:
  and mildly handicapped etiology, 69
System of Multicultural Pluralistic Assessment, 101
System:
  definition and characteristics of, 306, 307
Systems approach:
  to attitude assessment, 295, 296, 297

Teacher-assistance teams, 135
Teacher-directed teaching strategy, 178
Teacher rejection, of mildly handicapped, 188

Teacher support services, as special education alternative, 143
Teacher training:
  and special education categories, 51–52
  for mainstreaming, 151
Teachers. See also Classroom teachers; Special education Teachers
  and mildly handicapped etiology, 80–81
  as source of referral, 124
  attitudes of, 285–286
    and education of mildly handicapped, 280–281
    efforts to change, 298–299
    and college training, 299
  expectations of mildly handicapped, 276
  and labels, 35
  in identification of preschool handicapped, 172
  in resource room settings, 141
  interaction of classroom and special education [highlight], 24–25
  mainstreaming attitudes and knowledge of handicapped, 279
  need for understanding of family patterns, 308
  reasons for referral by, 124
  role in assessment, 105, 111–112, 114–116
Teaching program evaluation:
  as part of assessment program, 90–91
Teaching strategies, 199–206
  for math, 204–205
  for reading, 199–201, 202
  for social/emotional skills, 205–206
  for written expression, 201–204
  in elementary schools, 195
Technology:
  and special education, 363–368
Test administrators:
  and labels, 36
Testing, 88
  as component of assessment, 88–89
  criterion- vs norm-referenced, 102–103
  criticisms of, 94
  environment for, 103
  group vs individual, 101–102
  regulatory safeguards on, 95

Testing (continued)
　selection and use in assessment, 99–100
Thurstone-type scale, 295
Tracking:
　impact on mildly handicapped, 372
Trauma:
　and mental retardation etiology, 60
Treatment of handicapped:
　eras of, 4
　history, 3–23
Trends:
　in special education, 358–359

U.S. Office of Education
　occupational clusters, 336–337
Utah Test of Language Development, 170

Validity of tests:
　definition of, 100
Vertical organization:
　of elementary schools, 190
Very Special Arts Festivals [highlight], 186–187
Vietnam Era Veteran's Readjustment Act of 1974, 245
Visually impaired, 42–43
　discrimination in housing for, 248
　employment prospects of, 243, 244
　job seeking skills of, 347
　problems of, 251
　recreational services for, 262
　self-help groups for, 264
　technological aids for, 367
Vitamin deficiencies:
　and mildly handicapped etiology, 77–78
Vocabulary needs of job seekers, 347, 348
Vocational assessment instruments, 345–346
Vocational assistance:
　for mildly handicapped adults, 255–257
Vocational education, 255, 339–351
　definition of, 339–340
Vocational education programs for handicapped,
　development of, 341–342
　goals and objectives of, 342
　problems in service delivery, 342–345
　service delivery, 346–349
Vocational education teachers:
　and handicapped, 349–350
Vocational evaluation, 345–346
　components of, 346
Vocational opportunity, for mildly handicapped adults, 242–248
Vocational programs. See also Prevocational programs.
　types, 346, 347
Vocational rehabilitation, 255–256
Vocational rehabilitation counselors, 256
Vocational service model, in secondary education, 231
Vocational services, for mildly handicapped elderly, 266
Vocational vocabulary, 347, 348

WPPSI. See Wechsler Pre-school and Primary Scale of Intelligence.
WRAT See Wide Range Achievement Test
Wagner-O'Day Act, 245
Wechsler Intelligence Scale for Children—Revised, 112
Wechsler Pre-school and Primary Scale of Intelligence (WPPSI), 170
Wide Range Achievement Test (WRAP), 109
Wide Range Achievement Test (WRAT), 112
Woodcock Reading Mastery Tests, 113
Work experience programs, 347
Work setting, organized, 256–257
Work-activity centers, 257
Work-study programs, 347–348
Written expression tests, 113
Written expression, teaching strategies for, 201–204
Wyatt v. Stickney (1972), 14, 258

Zoning laws, 261–262
　by state, 261